praise FOR *Intim*

"Intimate Politics is breathtakingly important. In this stunningly written memoir, Bettina Aptheker affirms the old adage: The truth shall set you free. Her daring act of speaking truth to power not only liberates Bettina Aptheker, it offers each of us the promise of personal peace and political integrity if we can find a way to truthfully tell our own stories."

—Dr. Johnnetta Cole, past president of Spellman College and author of *All American Women: Lines the Divide, Ties that Bind* and *Dream the Boldest Dreams*

"I could not put this book down. What a story! It is enlightening and enriching."

—Tom Hayden, author of *The Lost Gospel of the Earth,*
The Port Huron Statement, and *Street Wars*

"A brave and passionately written memoir that reveals intricate connections between personal experience and political action. Bettina Aptheker provides an inside account of social movements and events that helped shape the latter half of twentieth-century U.S. history. She also conveys the emotional turmoil—and epiphanies—of her own changing beliefs and consciousness. A compelling read."

—Barrie Thorne, professor of sociology and women's studies,
University of California, Berkeley

"This book is riveting, a unique and compelling memoir that seamlessly weaves the personal and political life of a major figure in the Free Speech, civil rights, antiwar, and lesbian feminist movements. Aptheker rereads the history of the Left through the lens of gender, bravely exploring a childhood marked by the secrecy of sexual abuse as well as the repression of Communism. *Intimate Politics* offers both a powerful story of engaged activism and a poignant account of healing and forgiveness."

—Estelle B. Freedman, Edgar E. Robinson professor of U.S. history,
Stanford University, and author of *Feminism, Sexuality, and Politics*

Intimate Politics

HOW I GREW UP RED, FOUGHT FOR FREE SPEECH, AND BECAME A FEMINIST REBEL

BETTINA F. APTHEKER

SEAL PRESS

Intimate Politics
How I Grew Up Red, Fought for Free Speech, and Became a Feminist Rebel

Published by
Seal Press
An Imprint of Avalon Publishing Group, Incorporated

AVALON
publishing group incorporated

1400 65th Street, Suite 250
Emeryville, CA 94608

ISBN-13: 978-1-58005-160-6
ISBN-10: 1-58005-160-X

9 8 7 6 5 4 3 2 1
Library of Congress Cataloging-in-Publication Data

Aptheker, Bettina.
Intimate politics : how I grew up Red, fought for free speech, and became a feminist rebel / Bettina F. Aptheker.
p. cm.
ISBN-13: 978-1-58005-160-6
ISBN-10: 1-58005-160-X
1. Aptheker, Bettina. 2. Incest victims-United States-Biography. 3. Political activists-United States-Biography. 4. Feminists-United States-Biography. I. Title.

HV6570.7.A67 2006
305.42092-dc22
[B]
2006012047

Cover design by Kimberly Glyder
Interior design by Megan Cooney
Printed in the United States of America by Worzalla
Distributed by Publishers Group West

The author has changed some names, places, and identifying details in this book to protect the privacy of individuals.

For Kate

In the clearing, where the mind flowers
and the world sprouts up at every side,
listen
for the sound in the bushes
behind the grass.

—Marcia Falk

table of contents

prologue

BEARING WITNESS

THE POET MURIEL RUKEYSER once asked, "What would happen if one woman told the whole truth about her life?" And answered, "The world would split open." This question and her response troubled my sense of self and purpose for many years, and became a kind of koan for writing this memoir. The poet Adrienne Rich, moving along a similar path, wrote in the poem "Transcendental Etude": "The longer I live the more I mistrust / theatricality, the false glamour cast / by performance, the more I know its poverty beside / the truths we are salvaging from / the splitting-open of our lives." As I began thinking about writing a memoir, I was asked to contribute to the anthology *Red Diapers: Growing Up in the Communist Left.* I began writing, and what emerged first were these lines I had read years before in a lesbian anthology called *Nice Jewish Girls:* "Of the Jewish daughter it has been written: To inherit a father's dreams makes you the eldest son. To further his ambitions makes you heir to the throne."

My father, Herbert Aptheker, was both an historian of African American history and a well-known member of the U.S. Communist

Party. He began publishing in the 1930s, in the *Communist*, under the pseudonym H. Beal. Later, in the 1950s, *The New York Times* would describe him as the Communist Party's "leading theoretician." As a child I stood in awe of him, of his intellectual prowess, physical stamina, his orations. My mother, Fay P. Aptheker, organized our family life; she also held steady employment, and her salary supported us for most of my childhood. She was my father's emotional bedrock—and his first cousin.

While reading an interview with the Israeli novelist David Grossman, I came upon a description of childhood that stunned me with its emotional accuracy. He said that childhood is a very lonely time, that it is "the most complicated and sometimes even tragic period in our lives. . . . It's difficult for a child to decode and adjust to the hidden intentions of adults. . . . You don't know that every little thing is not the end of the world, that things are going to change."

As I began writing, sifting through my childhood memories, they erupted in ways I would never have predicted. A story emerged. A fault line opened, and my world underwent a seismic shift. I continued writing in the hope that my story might be of use to any who have struggled to come into their own sense of being, their own sense of life purpose and meaning. I also wrote in the hope that others might know that healing is possible. From reactions to my story I realized that I had made a hard journey, but most of the time, when I was just living my life day to day, I didn't think about it being hard or not hard. I just lived it and did what I had to do, or what I thought I should do. My parents gave me a rich cultural heritage; I had extraordinary opportunities for scholarship and travel. Encouraging me from the very young age of six to carry placards and sign petitions at political rallies in the tumultuous period of the McCarthy hearings and Communist witch hunts, my parents taught me that it was possible—and necessary—to be part of a movement to effect change in the world. But these gifts came to me at a terrible cost.

In the 1950s, when I was growing up, issues such as rape, sexual harassment (for which there was no language), sexual abuse of children, domestic violence, reproductive rights (referred to only as abortion), childbirth (assumed to be best left in the hands of the doctor), childcare (needed only by women who were derelict in their maternal duties), and sexuality (even between men and women) were spoken of in the hushed tones of shame and guilt. All were considered personal issues having absolutely nothing to do with politics. These issues became political as a result of the women's movement of the 1970s and 1980s. Rising from the cauldron of the most terrible personal pain, women of all hues, cultures, classes, and geographical sites broke their long-held silences. As a result, we came to understand that the personal is political—or, more precisely, that the personal reveals the political.

In one sense, politics is about the distribution of land and water, wealth and resources. In another, related sense, politics is about relations of power, whether these are economic, racial, cultural, social, or religious. Equality, whether it is racial or gender equality, or economic equality, or all of these together, is about establishing a politics of access and opportunity, citizenship and respect, and dignity.

However, for women and for children, especially girls, relations of power are often enacted in moments of intimacy, when we are the most vulnerable, in our families, with our parents or lovers, when we should experience the greatest sense of safety. Relations of power between women and men are likewise enacted in public places, when we are at work, or walking the streets, or riding public transportation. These instances also can take on an intimate quality because we experience them as a violation of personal space, or violence against our own person. What I am describing are widely shared experiences affecting the lives of millions of women virtually everywhere in the world, such as marital rape, domestic violence, and the sexual abuse of children. Taken together, in a feminist context, these experiences can be recognized and named as a politics of trauma. Healing is both individual and collective.

Part of my purpose in writing this book was to contribute to a collective healing process. While I came from an intensely political family and co-led widely recognized movements for peace and social justice, I was, at the same time, experiencing very serious personal trauma, reliving the fear and shame of being molested by my father from early childhood until age thirteen. It was only when I gained a feminist consciousness that I was able to make political sense out of what had happened to me, and to see it in a wider political landscape. What seemed almost impossible to talk about because it was so personal and so painful became possible precisely when set to a feminist purpose and employed as an act of political resistance. I did this in the belief that no truly progressive or revolutionary or spiritual vision can come if systems of abuse and domination are left hidden and unchallenged. And what I have found throughout my years as an activist and in my early years as a Communist, when I had no lens with which to understand what was taking place, is that political beliefs can be very different from personal actions. Indeed, my father and other Communist men passionately believed in social justice and racial and class equality. But in their homes it could be a very different story. Sexism, racism, and often even abuse were alive and well. Certainly this isn't confined to men on one end of the political spectrum or the other. But this chasm between political acts and personal beliefs must be acknowledged. Those who have committed acts of violence or abuse should not be excused or protected no matter who they are, no matter how famous or how important. I believe they should be held accountable. In a feminist context this becomes a politics of healing and a revolutionary practice, precisely because all forms of violence are interconnected; separately and together they hold multiple systems of domination in place.

Healing begins when we shine some light, however initially feeble, upon that which has been hidden and silenced. With disclosure, cycles of violence may be stopped. When we, as individuals, are less fractured and fearful, angry and possessive, we can participate in movements for peace and social justice in more wholesome and fruitful ways. Otherwise, I have learned, these movements simply replicate the very systems of domination they are seeking to overcome. I think this is the fuller meaning of Muriel Rukeyser's challenge, and it is the reason "the world would split open."

More deeply, though, also in response to Rukeyser's question, we have to ask, what is the *whole* truth? And how can any of us know what that wholeness is? The answer, of course, is that we cannot know the whole truth because none of us can see widely enough. In writing this memoir I did decide upon three things. First, I believed I was a "reliable witness" to my own life. I borrowed this idea of a "reliable witness" from an essay by the feminist social critic and novelist Jane Lazarre. She was also a "red diaper baby," a child of the 1950s, a radical of the '60s, and one whose writings spoke deeply to my experiences. Second, I made the decision that I would write about particular individuals only from my own direct experience with them, so that I would not engage in rumor or hearsay. Finally,

I decided to tell only my own story, and not those of others whose lives overlapped mine, unless I had their permission. Even with permission, this is a difficult and complex border to maintain. In some cases I changed people's names in order to preserve their privacy, or to protect the innocent in their families.

Even with all of these provisions, memoir writing is a tricky business, particularly for women, who are already subordinate in society and stereotyped, for example, as overly emotional and subjective, self-serving, unreliable, and vindictive. I bristled at the idea that I would be seen in this way; nor did I want readers to think that I was confessing. When I found a book titled *Bearing Witness* by the Zen teacher Bernard Glassman, I felt that I had found the words to describe what I was doing. As Glassman explains, bearing witness is a political and spiritual practice in which the participants go to a place of great suffering and publicly acknowledge its existence. They shine a light all over it so that those who have suffered are no longer alone, or forgotten, or ashamed, and so that no one can claim that they didn't know what was happening.

As witness and participant I describe movements for peace and social justice beginning in the 1950s, including my nineteen-year membership in the U.S. Communist Party, the civil rights and black power movements, the free speech movement at the University of California, Berkeley, the trial of Angela Davis, whom I had known since childhood, the struggle to end the war in Vietnam. Likewise, I bear witness to the struggles for gay and lesbian rights, for a progressive Jewish politics and identity, and the effort to create women's studies and a feminist scholarship. In each instance, I also describe my personal and psychological state and the ways in which the political and the personal intertwine. Today, I remain both activist and witness.

Ultimately, I think, it has been the unconditional love of my life partner, Kate Miller, and my commitment to a meditation practice in the Buddhist tradition that have made it possible for me to heal as much as I have. I did not inherit my father's dream, and I gave up the drive to further his ambition. But I did not give up my father, or my mother. I sought a middle ground between the grief of an irreconcilable break and the long shadow of denial.

I am filled with gratitude.

introduction

BEGINNINGS

My last name has always attracted a lot of attention. Nobody ever knows how to spell it or how to pronounce it. It is derived from "apteka" in Russian, meaning druggist. The English equivalent is "apothecary." Our spelling, with an "h" after the "t," is also unusual, except in India, where Aptheker is apparently a more common name. I think about all the Russian Jews fleeing pogroms in Czarist Russia, and how some must have gone to India. In correspondence with Indian scholars I am even sometimes mistaken for an Indian, or thought to have married one.

My mother's last name didn't change when she married my father because they were first cousins. That is, their fathers were brothers. My mother's father, Philip, my maternal grandfather, was the oldest. My mother tells me he was a revolutionary with a flair for acting. He fled Czarist Russia, came to America, married, was poor, and died before my mother was born. My father's father was Benjamin, my other grandfather. He also fled Czarist Russia, came to America poor, married, and made a fortune manufacturing ladies' undergarments.

He died of a heart attack trying to put out a minor fire in his factory, not waiting for the fire engines that were on the way. This happened long before I was born. I was told about my lineage from when I was very little, because it was so unusual and made me so special. "An Aptheker thoroughbred," my mother used to say.

My father first met my mother when he was eight years old, at his family's home in Brooklyn. He saw her occasionally afterward, as he was growing up, at family gatherings. His story about falling in love with my mother was one he told often. He said he ran out of paper one Sunday while working at the Brooklyn Public Library, where he frequently went to study, and remembered that she lived not too far away. At the time he was twenty. He walked to her apartment building, knocked on her door, and asked for paper. His account always ended there, and we never found out whether or not she gave him any paper.

One thing was clear: My parents adored each other, were devoted to each other, waited years to marry each other over the objections of his family. They lived together for seven years as an unmarried couple, which was very unusual in those days. My mother, an orphan, had been raised in poverty on the Lower East Side. My father's family objected to their marriage because she was poor, ten years older than my father, and they were first cousins. Finally, they married in 1942, unable to wait any longer because my father had enlisted in the Army. They believed an overseas assignment was only a matter of time. They saw their marriage as a perfect union.

Two years later, on a small card with a pink bow provided by the U.S. Army hospital in Fort Bragg, North Carolina, where my father was stationed during World War II, came the printed announcement: "Born to Captain and Mrs. Herbert Aptheker, a daughter, Bettina." "You were so funny looking," my father always said, remembering the moment of my birth, his first sight of me, "with black hair and enormous feet, and breathing, breathing, like this." He illustrated, pursing his lips together like a fish, taking in great gulps of air. My mother didn't appreciate his humor. For her I was to be the perfect daughter: immaculate, feminine, exquisitely cultured. And ultimately for my father, too, I was to be perfect: a communist essence, like a perfume, pure in my revolutionary devotion.

My mother had me when she was just shy of her fortieth birthday. Back then, it was almost unheard of for a woman to have her first child at such an advanced age. Before my parents married, my mother was a secretary in a social work agency and also trained as a professional dancer with modern dance pioneer Doris Humphries. All of her life, well into her late eighties, my mother loved to dance and carried herself with remarkable spirit and grace. Mom used to say that she "worked in a social work agency" because she was embarrassed that she was "only" a secretary. She was also a fine pianist, a lover of classical music and of the theater. She sang in the Jewish People's Philharmonic Chorus, which gave concerts at Town Hall and Carnegie Hall.

I can remember sitting next to my father in the orchestra section of Carnegie in the mid-1950s, long before the hall was renovated. We sat in maroon-colored seats with a rough-textured fabric. I loved the music and was so proud of my mother onstage. She wore a white silk blouse with ruffles down its center and a long black skirt that draped in pleats to her ankles. I could always pick out her voice, a pure soprano soaring above the chorus for my ears alone.

My mother was a beautiful woman. Every morning she came from her bath in a thin, flowered dressing gown, smelling of soap and talcum powder. Her dark brown hair, almost black in its lushness, extended below her hips. I watched her stand before the half-mirror above the vanity as she braided her hair in one long strand, which she then wrapped around her head in a shining crown—her daily coronation. She wore smart, tailored blouses and skirts, suits and dresses, picked with exquisite care from the racks of Lord & Taylor or Abraham & Strauss. She was stunning in these clothes. She applied makeup with discretion: lipstick, powder, a bit of rouge, then maybe a dash of perfume, a light, flowery scent. I remember the smell of her freshness, the breadth of her smile, the expanse of her laughter, the optimism of her energetic thrust out into the world. These are my earliest memories of her, and they are filled with the sensual pleasure of an innocent and still-carefree happiness.

When I was six, Mom returned to work full-time, this time as a travel agent. She did this for twelve years, during the late 1950s and early 1960s, when travel to Eastern Europe and the Soviet Union opened up. She knew all of the best places to stay because of her Communist Party connections and her travels with my father. She led tours all through Europe; travel was a great passion in her life. When she conducted a tour, usually for two or three weeks at a time, she left my father and me to fend for ourselves, which meant we ate hot dogs and hot pastrami sandwiches and ice cream sundaes at Howard Johnson because my father had no cooking skills to speak of. "Did you spoil her?" Mom always asked my father upon her return, with a certain Yiddish-sounding sarcasm that meant the question was purely rhetorical. Her salary and commissions supported our family. My father never had regular employment because he was blacklisted. He worked as a writer and editor for the Communist Party for a small and often sporadic salary. Though of course I enjoyed all of the treats at Howard Johnson, I didn't like being alone with my father at home, at night. I was so on edge when Mom was away that my grades in school plummeted.

Even when I was very young, I was acutely aware of my father's standing in New York's close-knit Communist community. My father always told us that he was blacklisted in 1938, although in actuality it was 1940 when the Rapp-Coudert Hearings were convened by the the New York State legislature, purging alleged Communists from the faculty of the City College of New York. These hearings had begun in 1931 and continued through 1942. Though he was not teaching at City College, he was friends with many who were, and got caught in the cross fire of the general attack. He was outraged, not because he was named—he was a Communist and proud of it—but because they got the year wrong (he had joined the party in 1939). Although my father had studied Marxism at Columbia, it was my mother who introduced him to the party. He got his PhD from Columbia, whose press published the original edition of his dissertation, "American Negro Slave Revolts," but he could not get a job there because of his affiliation with the party. My mother had joined the Communist Party in 1929, only eight years after it was founded. Having been raised in poverty, and having gone to work in a garment factory when she was fifteen, my mother had an acute class consciousness. Later, when she worked as a secretary, she helped to organize a union. This was when she first met members of the Communist Party, including Clara, who Mom used to say was the best organizer. Clara became one of my mother's best friends and recruited her into the party.

For my father especially, the party was everything: glorious, true, righteous, the marrow out of which black liberation and socialism would finally come. The truth was in absolutes. Loyalty, loyalty to this movement, above all else. "Arise ye prisoners of starvation," my mother sang in a piercing, haunting rendition of "The Internationale." "Avante, Popular!" my father called, chanting the song of the Italian Popular Front against fascism, without melody and with resolute confidence. It was his version of "Avanti Popolo" with a New Yorker's inflection.

Every morning, I watched my father shave. He stood bare chested in front of the sink, looking into the mirror on the medicine cabinet. He ran the hot water only, and built a thick lather in his hands using a bar of soap. He then smeared the lather onto his face, careful to get it between his lips and nose and down under his chin. Then he moved the razor in firm parallel strokes down his face and under his nose and along his chin. Once finished, he rinsed off his face and dried it with a towel, inspecting the results in the mirror. Then he opened the medicine cabinet, took out the roll-on deodorant—"my anti-stinko," he called it. For years I believed this was what everyone called it. I was fascinated by his shaving and practiced it on myself after school, imitating each of his actions; however, I was careful not to use a razor blade in the heavy silver-handled holder.

I remember my father in his thirties, with a broad chest and defined waist, the body of an athlete. He had very short, curly, almost black hair, hazel eyes, and a large nose. By his forties his stomach and hips had filled out, making for a straight line, shoulders to thighs, and he wore reading glasses with thick black rims. His hair seemed to turn white all at once the summer of my fourteenth birthday as he turned forty-five. I remember seeing my mother walking up the path toward me at summer camp, and wondering who the man was next to her until I saw it was my father, newly shorn and white haired. On closer inspection I saw a small trace of black curls at the back of his neck that would remain for years.

As a historian my father was always reading or writing, settled at the vast mahogany desk inherited from his mother with the lion heads at each of its four corners. He wrote by hand on a yellow pad with large, broad, confident strokes of the pen. Each letter was definitively shaped, every word plainly legible. Occasionally he worked at his typewriter, set on a rickety metal table next to the desk. It was a very old model Royal with keys that seemed to stick up on springs. He pecked away at it with the index finger of each hand.

My father's study of African American history is at the center of my earliest memories. Magically, this history came alive when many of the people he wrote about attended my parents' parties. My parents were part of a large intellectual and artistic community of Communists and progressives in 1950s New York. At its center were African American writers, artists, and activists: W. E. B. Du Bois, Paul Robeson, William L. Patterson, Alphaeus Hunton, Louis Burnham, John O. Killens, Charles White, Doxey Wilkerson. There were women also: Shirley Graham Du Bois, Eslanda Robeson, Dorothy Hunton, Alice Childress, Beah Richards, Louise Thompson Patterson, Dorothy Burnham, Elizabeth Catlett, Yolanda Wilkerson. I came to feel, however, that the men were the history. The conversation that seemed to count flowed from and around their ideas, their experiences. The women seemed to me to be on the periphery, circulating, listening, commenting.

My mother loved to entertain on these occasions. Chicken, bread, and an assortment of salads and desserts arrived from the kitchen in individual baskets when dinner was served. My mother always made sure that everyone had plenty to eat. Bottles of scotch and rye, wines and liqueurs, ginger ale and club soda, along with a silver ice bucket, covered what normally served as my father's desk. The bartender early in the evening, my dad stood near the desk mixing drinks. Later, people just helped themselves. My mother would make introductions, circulate, orchestrate the evening. Ultimately, my father would find a chair, sit down, come in and out of conversations as people moved around him.

My father's first book was called *American Negro Slave Revolts.* It was published in 1943, a year before I was born. I remember as a child hearing many visitors say how important this book was to them, "to know our own history." Then, in 1948, when I was four years old, my father published another book, called *To Be Free,* which included stories about African Americans fighting for their own freedom during the Civil War and working against tremendous obstacles during Reconstruction to start schools, farm their own land, and build free communities. At a few of these parties I heard Dr. Du Bois talk about the term "color line," and I remember thinking as a child that even though we were white, we seemed to be on the right side of this line. This was a good thing, and it was a relief for me to know this. Years later, my father told me that *To Be Free* was his favorite book of all that he had written. He lived for this history, and I grew to love the men and women who came to our home, their stories, their robust laughter, the warmth that enveloped our living room with such good times.

The Sunday mornings after these get-togethers the house was littered with clear plastic cups, half-filled drinks, Mother's china cups and saucers, cigarette butts overflowing from ashtrays, and napkin-festooned baskets piled with chicken bones. Dishes and silverware were stacked in the kitchen sink. The smell of cigarette smoke and alcohol permeated the house. Mom flung open the windows, even in the coldest weather. My parents sat together at the kitchen table drinking coffee, talking over the success of the evening. Although my father never secured regular university employment, my mother adopted the role of the traditional faculty wife, organizing his social life and keeping up his status within the party. Of course, I didn't know this until I was older. I think it was my mother's way of asserting my father's rightful place in an educational world from which he was barred.

By age eight, I was attending my father's lectures, first at the Jefferson School, run by the Communist Party, until it was shut down by the government in 1956, and its doors literally padlocked. A couple of years later the Party reopened a school and called it The New York School for Marxist Studies. I continued attending my father's lectures at the new location in an office building on Broadway near 14th Street. I can still recall how I felt in the lecture hall, seated in one of those straight-backed, red-cushioned chairs and smelling the wet, dirty, grimy odor of an old Manhattan building. I was breathless for an hour in anticipation of my father's thundering indignation at the oppression of black people, hailing the abolitionist movement, John Brown, the slave revolts, Reconstruction, Du Bois, the struggle against lynching, the fight for education and suffrage. He was passionate and utterly committed. In his mind and many others', the struggle for black liberation was central to world history. He asserted this again and again, tying together the struggles in the United States and the national liberation movements in Africa.

Though my father was passionate and articulate on behalf of causes he believed in, particularly Communism, this fire could also quickly turn to unrestrained anger. Of the dozens of stories from his time in the army during World War II, a few were very funny; most were harrowing. Once, he held a gun to the head of the mayor of a small village in Germany. He demanded milk for the children in a refugee center. The mayor said he didn't know where to get the milk. My father cocked the gun and told him to find the milk or "I'd blow his goddamned head off." The milk arrived, but my father still regretted not shooting "the son of a bitch anyway." Most of his war stories were filled with nostalgia, a longing for something in some way unfulfilled. These were the stories of his attachment to the men he commanded, and of the love he had for his lieutenant. Over and over again, he would describe the stormy night in which the two of them—my father and his lieutenant—were wrapped in each other's arms in the back of a truck, "for warmth," he would say. "We would have died for each other," he said. Listening to these stories when I was older, I heard the pathos in them that I had missed as a child. The only time my father allowed himself to express his love for men was in the extremity of war, when rules were suspended. For him, in his tellings, the war took on a dreamlike quality. The stench of battle was erased. His responsibility for the killing of hundreds if not thousands of people, from the artillery whose fire he directed, was only an emotional blip on the radar of his experience. He defended "just" wars with a self-righteousness that allowed no exceptions—or differing opinions.

When I was four or five, my father took me out to the great green expanse of Prospect Park and began to teach me how to play baseball. As a student he had pitched for Columbia, and for a brief time he'd actually gone into the pros, pitching in the minor leagues. That day in the park he was teaching me how to bat. We were using a Spaulding, a very light pink rubber ball. I hit it. It sailed out of the park and bounced off a policeman's head. I can still see my father off in the distance retrieving the ball, explaining to the policeman, waving his arm in my direction. I stood still, raising the bat high above my head in confirmation.

My father and I played other games too, besides baseball. I was three or four years old when we began playing "choo-choo train."

We were in the living room in the apartment on Washington Avenue, crawling around on the Persian rug my mother treasured. Many years afterward, this memory came to me: My father was behind me, and then the train arrived "at the station," and we had to wait for the "passengers" to get off and on. Our train rocked back and forth, back and forth, and my father had his right arm tightly around me. He was the "locomotive" even though he was behind me. Our train shuddered just before it was supposed to leave "the station," except it didn't leave. I was wet and sticky and I remember my father was crying, and I was sitting on the floor next to him and he had put a towel down so we wouldn't dirty the rug. I remember stroking his hair and saying, "It's okay, Daddy. It's okay." And then he stood me up and we went into the bathroom and he washed me off, very gently. It didn't hurt. He never hurt me. And I knew not to tell. As I grew bigger we played different games, but they always had the shudder. Older still, I knew it was not a game. I still knew not to tell because he told me "terrible things will happen." My father stopped molesting me when I was thirteen and we moved to a new house.

I did not remember these games until I began writing about my early life and reconstructing the details of childhood for the first time. The beginning of memory had the force of a tornado. It ripped through me. I loved my father in those childhood years. I felt him to be my emotional bedrock. He was steady and sure of himself, of me and of my mother, of our world.

When I was eight years old, my father was called to Washington, D.C., to testify before the McCarthy Senate committee investigating the "Communist threat" to the "American way of life." Of course I was too young to understand what all of this meant, but my father was very proud of the fact that *The New York Times* referred to him as "the Communist Party's leading theoretician." I had no idea what a "theoretician" was but it sounded important. The McCarthy hearings were televised, and when my dad was called to testify I was at a friend's house. The TV was on, and all of a sudden I saw him on television. It was all very surreal. I remember feeling very proud and shouting, "Look! My daddy's on television!" There was a terrible silence in the house, and my friend's parents turned off the TV. Nobody said anything, and then I went home. It was May 6, 1953. I was not invited to my friend's house again.

After that I just played baseball with the boys on our block, in the empty lot near where the subway tracks surfaced for the Franklin Avenue shuttle. I climbed the fence and retrieved our ball when it went into the tracks, picking my way carefully over the "live" third rail. This was the unspoken rule I had to follow in order to play. It was a few years later, when I was in high school, before I understood that televising the McCarthy Senate hearings had been a way to further intimidate people. Once before the committee, any witness who did not "cooperate" by naming more Communists was presumed guilty of sympathy with the Communists. Many of these people had been fired from their jobs and forced to move from their homes. The children of some of them were subjected to unceasing hostility in school and sometimes even physically attacked by other kids.

I remembered the McCarthy hearings and my father on television because he was a hero to so many people for the way he stood up to the committee. In a prepared statement, he denounced Senator McCarthy, defended the right of the Communist Party to exist, explained Marxism, and challenged the constitutional authority of the committee to hold such hearings. Looking back now, I know I couldn't have allowed for any memory of my father's "games" with me if I was going to survive the fear that he would be taken away and the terror that surrounded those times. Julius and Ethel Rosenberg were executed as Communist spies only six weeks after my father's testimony before the McCarthy committee. In those months and long afterward, I could hear my father shouting and screaming in the middle of the night as he awakened from nightmares; then I would hear my mother's gentle, urgent whispers calming him down. And then there were those times when he came to me in the middle of the night.

The Rosenberg case marked the political nightmare of my childhood. The trial and subsequent execution of Julius and Ethel Rosenberg, for allegedly conspiring to give the Soviet Union the secret of the atomic bomb, was a pivotal event in my childhood. Saving them came to mean everything to my parents and to all of their friends. My cousin Phyllis, the daughter of one of Mother's sisters, was fifteen years older than I and worked in a childcare center the Rosenberg children attended before and after the arrests. Julius and Ethel's faces, pinched, taut, in dozens of different newspaper photos, all with the same frozen, grief-stricken expression, haunted my mind. My father and mother had no doubt of their innocence. They ranted and wept over their impending executions, and protested— with petitions, demonstrations, speeches, articles, pamphlets. There was a march on Washington, and picketing of the Eisenhower White House. I went too, and insisted on carrying my own sign. "Save the Rosenbergs," it said.

Thousands of people filled Union Square on the afternoon of their execution, Friday, June 19, 1953. It was Julius and Ethel's fourteenth wedding anniversary. News of their electrocution swept through the crowd. Convulsive waves of grief passed through the square; the keening surged and fell like the tide. Holding my father's hand, I looked up into his face. Tears rolled down his cheeks. With his other arm he held my mother. She was dry eyed and grim, her face drained of color. "They rushed to be done with it," my father hissed, "so it would be done before the Sabbath." It was a Friday night just before sunset. And so I registered for the first time that Julius and Ethel were *Jewish*. "Oh," I whispered, holding my breath. "Oh."

In December 1953, six months after Julius and Ethel Rosenberg were executed, W. E. B. and Shirley Graham Du Bois held a Christmas party for the Rosenberg children at their Brooklyn home. Its purpose was to raise money for a trust fund that had been established for them. The Du Boises' living room was festooned with decorations, and a huge tree glittering with tinsel stood by the windows fronting the street. Its starred tip touched the ceiling, and presents spilled from under its canopy of branches. A shiny black Steinway grand piano stretched toward the center of the room from the opposite corner. A woman played it with a grand flourish of arpeggios and chords. We all sang Christmas carols. There was eggnog and lots of other drinks and food. I saw Robby and Ray and thought about what they were seeing and feeling. I was nine, Ray was ten, and Robby was six.

After the execution, my mother pulled me onto her lap one evening when she got home from work. We were in the big green leather chair in the living room. She said, "I have something very important to tell you." Her voice was soft, almost without inflection. I could feel her breath on my cheek. "Your daddy and I are Communists. You must never, ever tell anyone. Do you understand?" I remember nodding my head. I already knew my parents were Communists. After all, I had seen my father on TV. But now Mom had made it a secret, and it was one that I would soon betray by mistake.

A year after the Rosenbergs' execution I was in the bunkhouse at Camp Wyandot, where so many of us children of Communist and progressive parents spent our summers. "Progressive" meant people who were not actually members of the Communist Party, but who had political ideas very close to those of the party. I was ten. We were all in our beds comparing parental status, seeing who outranked whom. "My parents are Communists," someone said. "Mine aren't," someone countered, challenging the virtue of still being a member of something as stupid as the Communist Party. I piped up. "My parents are Communists too," I said. Then I froze. I had betrayed the secret. I was terrified. FBI agents were lurking outside our bunkhouse. They would have heard me. They would arrest my parents. . . . I fell into an exhausted, terror-filled sleep, the image of my parents dead, executed like the Rosenbergs, filling my dreams for weeks afterward. Irrational fear gripped me. I had betrayed the secret, a secret that was not a secret, but that my mother had said was a secret. I prayed to be forgiven by a God I knew my parents did not believe existed. I was not sure. I thought maybe He would help.

In fact, my parents were never arrested. My father never went underground, as happened to so many of the fathers of the children I knew. My father did go to Mexico, however, to find the comrade in the Mexican Communist Party who had betrayed Gus Hall, a party leader who had fled the country after being convicted, under the Smith Act, of "conspiring to advocate the overthrow of the government by force and violence." Gus had been sentenced to eight years in a federal prison. He was brought back into the United States without even the pretense of an extradition hearing. My father found the informer, but I never learned what happened to him.

Everywhere in my life there were secrets. There were those I was told to keep, and others about myself that I chose to keep. One of my biggest secrets was that I loved women. I fell in love with my first woman when I was five: Dorothy Hunton, the wife of my father's colleague, Alphaeus. I thought she was the most beautiful woman I had ever seen. Then I fell in love with Martha Schlamme, a Jewish folksinger who fled Vienna before the war, then with my third grade teacher, then with my best friend's mother, then with my high school English teacher.

I knew to hide these feelings, just as I had to hide what my father did. I knew I was twisted, deformed in some terrible way. I hid the blemishes upon the perfection I was supposed to be. I was consumed with fear and guilt.

At thirteen I wrote a short story for our high school magazine. It was called "A Knight in a Brooklyn Morning." It was about a black boy and a white girl. They met at the polar bear's cage in the zoo at Prospect Park. The little girl lost her red balloon. It drifted over the big iron spikes toward the bear. The little boy climbed the fence, reached up and over. He saved the balloon.

Of course I saw in writing this account of the story that I was the black boy, a fictional hero providing for my ultimate redemption. He was the perfection I thought my father desired and which I strove to become.

Thirteen was also the dividing line, the demarcation, because it was the year my father stopped molesting me. As I was finishing my last year in elementary school, we moved into our new house on Ludlam Place. It was 1957.

In winter there were often big snowstorms in Brooklyn. I'd wake up early in the morning, look out the window of our apartment, and see Washington Avenue and the botanical garden beyond, all white and pristine. Cars, buses, and trucks would be at a standstill. Even the subway was delayed because miles of tracks lay aboveground. Orange trucks with huge plows cleared the streets. As it was plowed, the snow became muddied with the soot and grime of the city. The plows would bank the snow up against the curb. Some cars, which had been left on the street and were parked illegally, were ticketed by the police. The trucks plowed around the cars, burying them in the snow for a week or more. After the plowing, traffic resumed and the remaining snow was churned into blackened slush.

Walking to school in my snowsuit and boots, a wool hat pulled down over my ears, I stomped through the snowbanks. The snow came up to my hips, even my waist, and it crunched under my boots. The crunching felt good; it sounded like bones cracking. Each step was harder to take, and my breath came in short spurts, the puffs of steam condensing into balls of mist.

When I was about ten years old I went to a ski resort in Vermont with friends of my parents. My parents did not ski and had not wanted to go. The friends showed me the rudiments of skiing. On the lift I swung my skis back and forth in the air. Then I skied down a long pass. The wind seared my cheeks, and my eyes teared. I felt exhilarated in the cold. The friends had forgotten to show me how to slow down and how to stop. I gathered speed, faster and faster. Then I lost a ski; I slid on my butt to a stop in a snowbank at the foot of a slope. I was laughing. A small crowd of onlookers laughed with me and cheered as I stood up, unhurt.

Vermont in winter seemed to me a fairytale, a never-never land. When it began to snow I went out from our hotel and stood in the forest. I stood very still like the trees. Snowflakes glistened on my jacket, forming small mounds on my shoulders. This was when I first noticed how quiet a forest is; the snow fell with only a whisper of sound. It blanketed everything. Cedar, evergreen, and pine were ornamented in crystal, while maple, elm, and oak stood at attention like whitened sentinels.

In winter, the young saplings in mountain forests are completely covered, smothered in snow. Only the heartiest survive and make it to the spring thaw.

I was the young sapling, in emotional hibernation, spaced out, waiting for a spring thaw I did not know would come.

One of my earliest childhood memories is sitting on the couch in the living room of our apartment on Washington Avenue during one of my parents' parties. I am scrunched into the corner, my hands folded in my lap and my short legs straight out in front of me. I can see the white socks and black patent leather shoes with little straps. I am wearing a starched white party dress with blue polka dots, and the linen fabric of the couch is scratching my bare thighs. I am watching the crowd of people in front of me, undulating like the long stalks of kelp in the big tank at the aquarium. They are holding cocktail glasses and smoking, talking, and eating. Every so often one of the women guests sits down next to me or peers down at me, smiling, making funny little sounds in her throat, and tells me what a good girl I am. I look back on the scene and think about the intended kindness of the women, the smallness of the child, and the way goodness and silence were so deeply intertwined.

Despite my nearly constant anxiety as a child, I always had every-thing I needed or wanted. Toys. Clothes. Books. A bicycle. I had no chores other than to keep my room neat. My parents took me on trips with them, they took me to museums and the public library. They took me to concerts. They bought me ice cream sundaes. From the outside it all looked normal, and even idyllic. I would have thrived had it not been for my father's abuse and the silence to which I was condemned at all costs. After all, I had been instructed by him to not tell or "terrible things would happen." I internalized his warning to the point that for many years I wouldn't even remember it myself; it was simply too scary and threatening to contemplate. I tucked it deep inside myself, though the feelings around it seeped out in the form of anxiety, fear, self-inflicted wounds, and an almost constant sense of dread. Before I recalled specific memories of the abuse, I felt for so many years a strong sense of dread and guilt, especially around anything having to do with my parents. It was a terrible irony that my parents faced the terror of the McCarthy era with so much courage, and yet lined my heart with so much fear.

A few months after I started writing the story of my life, I took my parents out for lunch. It was 1995. I was fifty, Mom was ninety, and Dad had just turned eighty. By then they had been living in San Jose, California, for many years. I took them to The Fountain, the coffee shop at the Fairmont Hotel, because it was one of Mother's favorite places, the tables set with linen cloths. All through lunch my father sniped at me. I tuned out his mean-spirited jibes about my appearance, my work, my lack of productivity, my children, my political view, as quickly as he made them. The only reason I remember them now is because it was so bad that our waitress, with whom my father had been "joking" in a series of thinly disguised sexual innuendos, intervened.

My father had wanted to order dessert. The waitress said, "I'll bring you dessert if you stop being so nasty to your daughter!" I was startled from my reverie. I had been "gone" from the table, "checked out," as I so often was when in the company of my parents, this pattern of dissociation long in place as a way to deal with the untenable. I thought, *Has he been nasty to me?* With friends present, my father always extolled my virtues, praised me, seemed proud that I was a professor. *And now, in private?* His words came roaring back into sound. I had erased the memory of his conversations almost instantaneously, a habit of fifty years. I was so grateful to that waitress. This was how it was in my childhood; what was untenable was erased. As a result, I was almost completely without access to my emotions. As I write this I have had to go back into the experience, relive it as it was happening, have the re-memory of sexual violence, and recover the feelings as they finally erupt. But the eruption is now, not then, not in childhood. Then I was silent, and almost completely absent from myself.

Sometimes when I hear a piece of classical music, for example a Brahms concerto I particularly like, I feel a swell in my throat for the beauty of the music. And I feel so much for the child, the small child who escaped into the concertos and symphonies, who vanished from her seat and soared over audiences and orchestras, blissed out in the sounds of heaven, whose heart broke open in the weeping of the cello.

Incest survivors know despair. It is not your ordinary, run-of-the-mill despair. It is not depression. It's a different feeling. All through childhood, all through my twenties, I had this feeling. It was bottomless, endless, bone deep, down to the marrow. I choked on it, fell prostrate with it. It was connected to a self-loathing so deep, so limitless, so without end that suicide seemed the only possible relief. Short of suicide there was self-mutilation. That could work, at least for a while.

I knew the feeling without knowing its cause. I knew it was connected to my parents, but I didn't know how. By every outward measure they were paragons of virtue, self-sacrificing pillars of the revolutionary movement.

By my late twenties, the feelings of despair came less frequently and were of shorter duration. I was immersed in the party, in my marriage, in the social movements of the time. When I fell in love with Kate, my life partner, in 1979, I didn't tell her about the despair because I couldn't explain it and I had learned to function with it, though not always well. But she knew I was wounded. She nurtured and supported me so that the despair became like a distant fog, the way fog hovers on the ocean at the horizon. You know it's going to come in again, but not yet, not today.

When I started writing this memoir the despair crept back into my life. One morning as I was preparing breakfast for my family, I had a strong sense of needing to get out of the kitchen. I've never been claustrophobic, but at that moment I wanted everyone to leave me alone and yelled at my family to get away from me. Then I became sullen and angry. I felt suicidal—the first time I had felt that way in many years—and told Kate. We speculated about the causes, and she stayed close by me. After about two weeks the despair receded.

Then I went to see a movie that I was eager to see, *Sense and Sensibility*, based on Jane Austen's novel, which I had read and loved. Kate and I had even read it aloud. I thought it would be a great way to spend my evening. But that's not how it turned out. It was about five weeks after the incident in the kitchen, and Kate was away, visiting her daughter in Norway. I had been with them, but had returned home early because my classes were beginning at the university.

Near the end of the film there is a scene on a meadow overlooking the sea in a hard rain. Marianne, the sister whose lover has married another woman, walks out onto that meadow, heedless of the storm, consumed with grief and despair. She has no life left in her. As I watched, my throat tightened and I began to cry. Despair engulfed me, and suddenly, I had a hard time breathing. The movie ended, but as I left the theater I still felt like I was inside Marianne's despair. I got into my car and began to sob, great, cracked, heaving sobs. I drove toward the beach at Rio Del Mar, just south of our home, where Kate and I frequently walked. It was after nine in the evening and I knew the beach would be deserted. I intended to walk into the ocean and into my death.

A voice, very adult, very calm, broke through the hysteria. It ordered me home, where I could go to the calm space of the meditation room and the familiarity and peace of comfortable surroundings. I exited the freeway, circled back toward the house. I could not stop sobbing. I got back on the freeway heading toward the ocean. The voice returned. I exited the freeway, circled back toward the house, got back on the freeway, headed toward the ocean. I had no direction, and no sense of what to do next. I had no content, I didn't know what was wrong, and I was frightened and struggling for a control I could not summon. Tears blinded me so much that I thought it was raining. I slowed down, exited the freeway, went home, made it into the house. No lights. I couldn't bear the thought of light.

I fell in front of our altar with its beautiful golden statue of Tara, the Tibetan goddess of compassion, called "the Mother of all the Buddhas."

I could not stop crying.

I didn't know what was happening to me.

I had no content.

I wanted to mutilate myself, went for the knives in the kitchen. I hadn't done anything like that in thirty years.

I had no content.

The voice of reason came through again, clear and calm.

"Call for help."

We had no telephone in our cottage. We had wanted to preserve our privacy.

I stumbled back to the car, drove two miles to a service station, dialed. Wrong number. Dialed again. My dear friend answered on the first ring. Where was I? I couldn't remember the names of the streets. All I could say was, "Near the house." She said, "Go home. Get into bed. I'll come and get you."

I went home. I couldn't bear to be inside, so I lay on the ground outside. We lived in the countryside, in the hills as they begin their ascent into the Santa Cruz mountains. A horse stirred, walked to the fence where I lay, whinnied softly. A resident cat came and walked over my body, meowing and clawing gently. Our cat, black as the night, stood at my head talking to me urgently, the way he did when he wanted to be fed.

A thought came: *I shouldn't be on the ground when my friend comes. It will frighten her.*

I got up. I went back into the house. No lights.

I still had no content.

I jammed my left arm into the door of our meditation room, slammed against it again and again. I knew I was externalizing the pain I felt inside, the pain I had been feeling for years.

The first flash of memory came.

"Oh . . . my . . . God!" I said in a hoarse whisper.

It wasn't a memory really. It was a knowing, a certainty.

"My father!" I whispered again.

I heard the gate click open on the walkway outside our cottage.

"Thank God," I breathed.

My friend came into the house. She didn't turn the lights on. She stood in the dark in the middle of the room and called my name. I went to her, fell into her arms. In a clear, solid voice, holding me in a firm grip, she said: "Whatever it is, it isn't happening now."

one

A CHILDHOOD IN TWO WORLDS

WHEN I WAS a little girl I wanted to be just like my father. Whatever he did, I did, or tried to do. He had been a baseball pitcher so I became one too. I remember afternoons in Prospect Park, where he tried to impart his wisdom about the perfect curveball, or how to throw a screwball. To be like him, I pretended to read voraciously and, at the precociously young age of six, to take notes on yellow legal pads. I sat at my desk with my feet just like his, toes pressed to the ground, heels up, one foot on each side of the chair. My father was a creature of habit, so once I had him down, I had him.

I read the Sunday *New York Times* like he did (although I couldn't understand much of it), carried a pen in my shirt pocket (if I had a pocket), ate the bagel and lox that he did, and feared my mother as he did. Together, we obeyed her. My father was charismatic, and a forceful personality given to fierce outbursts of righteous anger against injustice and betrayal of the Communist cause. He was known in the U.S. Communist Party for his brilliant theorizing, and for his explosiveness, but his anger was never directed at me. It was my mother whose anger was closest to the surface, at least at home, and often directed at me. "Can't you do anything right?" my mother would shout at me. "Stand up straight! Stop crying!" I tried so hard to be good, to remember all of the things I was not to do, to do all of the things I was supposed to do. She had a lot of rules. One of her rules was that once I went to bed I was not to get up again or ask for anything. Another was that I finish the food on my plate. But because of my fear of my parents, I had trouble eating. My mother became furious if I didn't finish my food, but fear of her anger made me too nervous to eat.

Occasionally she lashed out at me physically. Once, when I was about eight, I was fussing as she brushed knots out of my hair, and she got so angry that she hit me on the forehead with the brush. I remember a small trickle of blood ran down over my nose. She blotted up the blood with a wet washcloth and continued brushing my hair. She didn't say anything and I didn't dare move or speak.

I learned early on that what went on in private was not to be discussed outside our house. I was the keeper of family secrets. And we were a very special family in my mother's vision of the world. As an only child, I was like a third adult in the family, an extension of my parents. I was rarely with kids my own age, except when I played baseball with the boys on our block. Secrets kept me isolated, especially from other children, and instilled in me the belief that what went on at home had nothing to do with my parents' political beliefs—those of socialism, peace, social justice, racial equality, and civil rights. Of course, I didn't see the contradiction between the way they lived and what they believed until much later, when I realized that I had to live what I believed if I was going to overcome my past and thrive as an authentic person.

To avoid my mother's anger, I made the practice of goodness and compliance an art form. Looking back, I think I was also trying to live a life of perfect goodness to protect my father. I lived in fear that my mother would catch my father being sexual with me, and that I would disappear along with my world.

Despite their outbursts, my mother and father had great affection for each other. When my father came home from work he would kiss Mom noisily on the mouth and say in Yiddish, *"Du bist azoy geshmak!"* (Literally translated it means, "You are so tasty.") In stories about his boyhood, my father told us that this was what his father said to his mother every morning when he first woke up. My father was in charge of making breakfast, brewing coffee, and setting the table. The love my parents had for each other was palpable.

Still, their rage terrified me, intensifying my feeling that I had no place of refuge, and no safety from unpredictable eruption.

The double life I lived caused me a great deal of anxiety, whether I was actually home or not. And sometimes it came out in terrible dreams. One night when I was about five or six I had a nightmare. I don't remember the dream, but I remember screaming, crying out in terror. My mother called out from the living room, where my parents slept, that she was coming. But when I heard her voice I remembered that I was not supposed to wake her in the middle of the night. So I muffled my sobs, the terror of my nightmare overcome by my fear of Mom's retribution. To reach my room she had to pass the grandfather clock in the hallway. As she rounded the corner and approached the clock, I screamed in renewed terror to warn her of the tiger. I was sure it would leap out of the clock and attack her, but she passed unharmed. I don't remember what she said when she reached me, but I know she comforted me. Later, as an adult, I remembered that ather who would come past the clock and into my room. doors reflected the light from the kitchen windows and hadows in the night. When he came into my bedroom to do wrong things to me, he came out of the shadows of the clock. My father was the tiger.

The life I lived at home, in private, was confusing and often lonely. Outside, though, my parents presented us as the perfect family, and I always did my best to show this to be true. Nowhere was this more apparent than when I accompanied my father to work during school vacations or the occasional day off from school.

Besides lecturing on behalf of the Communist Party, my father worked as a writer and editor at New Century Publishers, the party's publishing operation. In the 1950s, when I was growing up, he was a contributing editor to the party's two official magazines, *Masses & Mainstream* and *Political Affairs*. His coworkers included V. J. Jerome, the Polish-born Jewish writer who was imprisoned for three years during the McCarthy era and later returned to Poland, and Elizabeth Gurley Flynn, the iconic union organizer and leader of the Industrial Workers of the World (IWW). When I met Elizabeth she was in her early sixties, a very large, heavy woman with short gray hair, blue eyes, pastel pink cheeks, and rimless glasses. A hushed scurrying affected everyone during her visits. I remember her as being friendly, always taking an interest in whatever writing or reading project I busied myself with while my father worked. I was an avid reader of Nancy Drew mysteries and I imagine that more than once I must have regaled her with plot details. She laughed a lot and encouraged me. As a young child, once I felt comfortable with someone, I was an energetic talker, and Elizabeth was a truly attentive listener. I remember her as one of the very few adults who related to me as an individual, rather than as an extension of my father. When I was eleven, her autobiography, *I Speak My Own Piece*, was published and she signed a copy for me: "To Bettina, with love." I still have her book.

I arrived at the New Century offices holding my father's hand, dressed in a green plaid coat with a corduroy collar, a red and green plaid wool skirt, a white cotton blouse with a Peter Pan collar, and two pigtails neatly braided and tied with white or green ribbons. I carried a brown leather satchel brought to my father from a visiting comrade from Europe. I had commandeered it and used it all through elementary school. I'm sure we looked like the perfect father-and-daughter set; we were always greeted with smiles. My father was at ease in his office. He loved his work. Sitting at his desk, typing away furiously, he was in his element. I typically spent the day at one or another temporarily vacated desk, with paper and pencil, writing, just as my father did. Sometimes I might even have access to an old Royal typewriter, and I would peck away at it with two fingers, a pencil stuck behind my ear. At lunch, we left the office holding hands as we walked down Broadway toward one of the delis we frequented. I remember feeling proud and happy.

In addition to his work at New Century, my father was an ardent polemicist, a revolutionary muckraker who wrote scathing denunciations of U.S. foreign policy, and equally laudatory accounts of Soviet life. As editor of *Political Affairs* from the mid-1950s to the early 1960s, his editorials and articles provided the ideological bellwether of Communist thought. These editorials and articles were then published in books my father edited. For example, *Laureates of Imperialism* (1954) and *American Foreign Policy and the Cold War* (1962) contain one article after another of denunciation of and outrage at U.S. foreign policy. A very typical example is his article "Imperialism and the [Atomic] Bomb," in which he gave what he described as the real but hidden reason for the bombing of Hiroshima and Nagasaki at the end of World War II.

Citing relevant statements by the secretary of war and the secretary of the Navy, and articles in *U.S. News and World Report*, he wrote that the real object of the atomic bombing of Japan had been to intimidate the Soviet Union and give the United States unchallenged claims in the Pacific by the war's end. "Professor P. M. S. Blackette," Dad wrote, "the distinguished British scientist, concluded that the atomic bombing of Hiroshima marked the opening salvo in the Cold War."

My father's forte lay in building a careful documentation from the non-Communist press—*The New York Times, The Wall Street Journal, Foreign Affairs,* the *Progressive,* the *Nation,* the *New Republic,* and the *Christian Century* are the publications I most vividly recall stacked on the radiator shelf in the kitchen—to substantiate the reality of U.S. imperialist intrigues, interventions, assassinations, and economic policies. He wrote about the U.S.-backed interventions in Nicaragua and Guatemala in the mid-1950s, decried the UN-deployed Korean conflict in the same period as a U.S.-engineered war (principally against the Chinese Communists), and wrote extensive histories of U.S. policies in Western Europe before, during, and after World War II. He defended the Soviet invasion of Hungary in 1956, the erection of the Berlin Wall in 1961, and denounced the Bay of Pigs invasion against Cuba in 1961. He explained and supported Soviet policy toward its Jewish people, which he did not view as anti-Semitic because Jews were recognized as a national group rather than a religious one, and as such had their own republic like other nationalities. He wrote extensively on Vietnam, beginning in the early 1960s, and visited Hanoi with antiwar activists Staughton Lynd and Tom Hayden in 1965.

Upon his return from North Vietnam, my father worked at his usual fever pitch to publish a book based upon his experiences and observations. *Mission to Hanoi*, a 128-page account, complete with photos, was rushed into print by International Publishers in 1966, a few months after his return, the hardcover edition selling for only $3.75. Tom Hayden and Staughton Lynd each wrote a preface. The first chapter was called "There Are So Many Children . . ." and Dad's first lines capture how he felt at that moment and exactly represent his rhetorical style:

It is the Christmas season back home, where responsible statesmen are considering the bombing of this city of Hanoi. I walk the tree-lined streets; about me are hundreds of people. . . . There are many little children and many, many women.

It is absolutely fantastic. A short time ago at home on my TV, a Senator was explaining how necessary it was that we bomb Hanoi.

He thought—it was Sen. John Tower (Republican, Texas)—that not many civilians would be killed, but without bombing Hanoi the vital interests of the United States would be threatened. . . .

Is it possible that any government—the American government—is seriously considering whether or not to destroy this city, 13,000 miles away from Washington?

In Hanoi live one million men, women and children.

Not one has harmed an American, and most have never seen an American. No one here threatens Los Angeles or Detroit or Brooklyn. Everyone here wants desperately to live in peace—finally—after 25 years of war. Yet back home crackpot "realists" insist the city threatens U.S. interests.

My father's membership in the Communist Party permeated every part of my life. All of my parents' friends were either in the party or were sympathetic to its cause. I went to a Communist-run summer camp, attended rallies and meetings from the time I could walk, and heard my parents talk about the party and its various activities until I went away to college. Though my parents were open about their affiliation with the party, they instilled in me at a young age an awareness of FBI surveillance. I knew our phone was tapped. I was just a child during the McCarthy hearings, but I understood that my father's prominence in the Communist Party made us different.

This was the case in June 1959, near the end of the worst of the anti-Communist purges, when I was fifteen. A man who identified himself as U.S. Marshal Charles Haggerty began calling at our house looking for my father, to serve him a subpoena to appear before the House Committee on Un-American Activities (popularly known as HUAC). For three weeks Marshal Haggerty preoccupied my thoughts, as I was sure he was going to show up any minute and arrest me for preventing his access to my father.

Sidney Finkelstein, a fellow Communist and friend of my father's, had alerted us to the subpoena. As was the custom with party members, Sidney called my father to warn him a subpoena could be coming; he had received one himself. Whenever the FBI, police, or U.S. marshals visited one party member, they would likely make the rounds. This was the routine. Once alerted, my parents instructed me to answer the telephone and the doorbell. If anyone whom I did not personally know asked for my father, I was to say that he was not at home, that I did not know when he would be home, and that I did not know where he was.

A few days after Sidney's call, when Charles Haggerty telephoned, I told him my father wasn't home and I didn't know where he was, although, in fact, Dad was at home. A few days later when Marshal Haggerty came to the house, I answered the door. Although my parents were upstairs, I stood in the doorway, trying to look as big as possible, and told him no one was home, repeating myself more forcefully when he showed me his identification. I summoned the courage to defy Marshal Haggerty because I was protecting my father. He telephoned again a few days later, and so it went. I became adept at saying my father wasn't home, and he was just as adept at repeating himself.

Meanwhile, my father went to work every day. He changed his routine, coming and going at different times, but he was still at New Century—where apparently Marshal Haggerty never thought to look.

Though Marshal Haggerty's subpoena in itself was routine, I was often afraid for my parents, although my father never gave the appearance of being intimidated. He had, in fact, testified before dozens of committees and at the trials of many Communists all over the country.

The subpoena being served by Marshal Haggerty, then, was more of an inconvenience than anything else, as it interfered with our planned trip to Europe, during which my father was to meet with a number of Communist Party leaders and heads of state in socialist countries. He was certain the reason for the subpoena was to prevent our travel overseas. Though we rearranged our travel plans to avoid any additional attempts to subpoena my father, our trip was still a go. The day of our departure my father and I headed to the airport for an afternoon flight on Air France, and my mother went to work as usual. She would fly out later that week. I remember sitting in an airport lounge area for hours before check-in, lest we run into Mr. Haggerty. I paced around nervously while my father sat calmly reading. About an hour before our flight, I went alone to the Air France desk to check our baggage. If the clerk thought it strange that a fifteen-year-old girl appeared to check enough luggage for two, he didn't say anything. My heart was pounding, my throat was parched, and my hands were shaking: I expected Marshal Haggerty to materialize at any moment, handcuff me, and demand to know my father's whereabouts.

Instead, nothing happened. The agent gave me our boarding passes and wished me a nice trip. I returned to the lounge and to my father, lost in his reading, but I was still scared that we would be stopped at the last minute. I remembered reading somewhere that once we were a certain number of miles out of New York on Air France we were considered to be on French soil, but I couldn't recall if it was three miles or twelve. When I asked my father as we prepared to board the plane, he said he thought it applied only to ships. Only after we were airborne did I finally breathe a sigh of relief.

Our first meeting in Paris was with Jacques Duclos, who had been vice president of France after World War II and then, in 1959, was head of the French Communist Party. I remember being surprised when my father told me that there were a half-million members of the party in France, with the party's newspaper, L'Humanité, available at any newsstand. It was the first time I realized that Communism as a political party could be legitimate, acceptable, and out in the open, a marked contrast to the secretive, persecuted Communism I was used to at home and the painstaking, hand-to-hand distribution of the Worker.

Communist Party headquarters in Paris was then in a multi-storied, old, reddish gray building. The front door was of reinforced steel, a tiny barred window near the top. Two fully uniformed French soldiers armed with bayonets stood at attention outside. Several more armed soldiers stood in the entrance hallway, and in adjoining rooms. Shocked by the level of security, given how open and legal the party was, I was told by my father that the increased security measures were due to France's war in Algiers. At the time a national liberation movement was fighting to free Algeria from French colonial rule, leading to considerable violence. This explanation puzzled me because I knew the party would have supported the Algerians in their struggle, but I made no further inquiries.

Duclos was a rotund, balding man with a round face, round dark-rimmed glasses, and a very forceful presence. His office was spartan: no rug, no curtains on the windows, no plants. Two giant portraits hung on the wall behind his desk, one of Marx and the other of Lenin. He spoke to my father in French. Dad understood French but he answered Duclos in English, and in this way they understood each other. I sat very quietly, watching, unable to follow the *ping* of French to English. Sometime near the end of this conversation on party affairs, Duclos picked up his office phone. A few minutes later a young man appeared. A member of the Young Communist League, he had been assigned to take me on an afternoon excursion through Paris. As we left, Duclos called after him in French the equivalent of "And no hanky-panky with her," my father later recalled, highly amused. I didn't think it was funny.

Though he was frequently traveling, lecturing, and writing on behalf of the party during my childhood, it wasn't always work with my father. Sometimes we went on fun excursions on Sundays—to Coney Island, the Brooklyn Botanic Garden, Prospect Park, the Brooklyn Zoo, or the library. I cherished these times.

Coney Island was a mass of rides and thrills along the boardwalk fronting the Atlantic Ocean, the tangle of wires, pillars, wheels, and colors reminding me of a giant erector set. In spring and summer, the beaches were packed with bathers. In winter and fall, when we went most often, only a few older women and men sat on the benches along the boardwalk, or on folding chairs on the beach, talking and sunning themselves. They all seemed to me to be Jewish, noticeable either by their still-evident European manner or the Yiddish flowing between them, one conversation fading into another as we passed by.

In winter, most of the rides were shut down. But my favorite, the carousel, was always open. I always wanted the same horse, the one on the outer circle that moved up and down. As we circled round and round, the circus music playing, I would reach for the metal rings protruding from a long bar mounted on the side of the building. If a gold ring came up and you caught it, you got a free ride. No matter how far I stretched I could never manage even to touch the rings. My father rode the carousel too. He easily reached the rings, but he never caught a gold one.

After the carousel, we would take a long walk along the boardwalk, the ocean breeze wetting our faces and the salt air filling our lungs. I felt uplifted, lighthearted, as though I could simply float off the ground and fly. After our walk we would stop at Nathan's for hot dogs and orange sodas. We ate our hot dogs standing on the sidewalk, balancing our drinks in one hand, the hot dogs in the other, trying not to let the mustard and sauerkraut drip all over us.

Our most frequent outings on Sunday afternoons, however, were to the Brooklyn Botanic Garden or Prospect Park, as both were within walking distance of our house. If it was warm enough we brought our baseball and mitts, and maybe a bat, if one of us was willing to carry it. In Prospect Park we might also visit the zoo. I remember the monkeys and polar bears, a lion and sea lions, and several elephants. I loved the elephants the best. They had soft brown eyes, and would extend their trunks over the fence and into my raised hands filled with peanuts. Very gently they vacuumed the food from my hands.

These times with my father were some of the best of my childhood, but they were also confusing. As a child, I didn't know how to reconcile this gentle, kind side of my father with the raging, judgmental, and irrational side that I saw more frequently.

In contrast to the carefree Sundays with my father that I looked forward to all week, I dreaded the occasional Saturdays with my mother when we went shopping for clothes. These shopping trips started when I was eight or nine years old. I loathed my body in very contradictory ways, especially as I reached adolescence. My skinny, boyish figure was all sinewy and taut. I had tiny breasts and no hips. I seemed to be caught somewhere between the growing, muscular strength of the boys I knew and the budding breasts and feminine curves of the girls. I always felt most comfortable in jeans, T-shirts, and flannel shirts. I liked sneakers and baseball caps. Such things, of course, could not be worn to school. My mother, herself a fashion plate, would never have permitted it, even if the school dress codes of the 1950s hadn't been strictly enforced. Her style ran more to tailored shirtwaists and well-cut skirts with matching sweaters. Those Saturdays with my mother exacerbated my feelings about my body, and I withdrew into myself even further. I never argued with her; I was silent and compliant.

We shopped at the large department stores in downtown Brooklyn, like Abraham & Strauss, or the more elaborate ones in midtown Manhattan, like Macy's and Gimbel's. We would go to the children's and later the "Junior Misses" departments, where my mother, having already determined what I needed, installed me in a dressing room and went off in search of these things. She would return periodically, clothes draped over her arms. I would dutifully (and pathetically, I felt) try on one dress or skirt and blouse after another. Soon I would be anxious and sweaty from the close confines of the dressing room, and my mother would become increasingly annoyed at what seemed like the utter futility of ever finding anything that might fit me. According to her, I was too thin, too small on top, too short in the waist, too narrow in the hips. It went on for what seemed to me like hours, my stomach knotted in tension as Mother's irritation finally grew into rage and she shouted things like, "Nothing ever fits you," and "We'll never find anything for you." From the dressing room I would at last emerge, having survived another shopping trip, Mom settling on perhaps one or two items that would do. She always asked me if I liked whatever skirts or blouses she picked out, as if it mattered. But of course I did, if for no other reason than that they got me out of there.

I've often looked back on those times, wondering why these shopping trips affected me so viscerally. Of course, I was already anxious in my mother's presence, always waiting for the inevitable explosion. But it was something more, too. I've come to believe that my mother's obsession with fashion and outfitting my body in what she considered the proper way reinforced the shame I felt from the incest at the hands of my father, however repressed my memory of it was at the time. I truly loathed my body and did not want to draw attention to it in any way. Although I had no words for it at the time, I've recognized a similar feeling in the body anxiety expressed in contemporary memoirs of transgendered writers.

It was on one of these shopping trips, when I was about ten years old, that I learned that my mother had been married to someone else before my father, a shocking revelation for me. We were leaving one of the department stores when a woman called out to my mother in greeting, "Fay! Fay Steiner!" They hadn't seen each other in years, and there were several moments of animated conversation, but Mom didn't introduce me. When we were alone together again, I asked Mom, "Why did she call you Fay Steiner?"

"Oh," Mom said casually, "I was married once before."

Choking on this news, the whole structure of my world disintegrating, I asked, "Is Daddy my real father?"

"Of course," Mother said with an irritable laugh. "Of course he is." I fell silent. Now I knew that Mother and Father had lied to me my whole life about something that felt very important to me. What else had I not been told? What else had I been told that wasn't true? Later, when I was older, I saw my birth certificate and confirmed that Herbert Aptheker was, indeed, my father. Lying was a new idea to me. At ten, I didn't know that people lied. I was devastated to think that my parents would lie to me.

Despite her rage and lying, my mother did give me some wonderful gifts. She introduced me to classical music. From a young age, I accompanied my parents to the symphony, the ballet, and numerous music festivals. The layers of sound, the crescendos, the players, and the drama of it all captivated me. Sol Hurok, a well-known producer of the 1950s, opened up cultural exchanges with the Soviet Union at a time when the McCarthy era was waning but the Cold War was in full tilt. Mom and I attended virtually every performance, from pianist Emil Gilels to the Bolshoi Ballet and the Moiseyev Dancers, who performed traditional dances from a variety of republics in the Soviet Union and were renowned for their authentic costuming and technically brilliant choreography. While I liked the ballet, I was enthralled by the male dancers in the Moiseyev troupe; the enormity of their grace and strength literally took my breath away. My mother also took me to hear pianist Rudolf

Serkin, violinist Isaac Stern, and the New York Philharmonic under
Leonard Bernstein. Some summers, we went to the Marlboro Music
Festival in Vermont, where Serkin and Stern and violinist Alexander
Schneider collaborated. In the afternoons we would sit quietly in or
just outside the barnlike theater and listen to their rehearsals. I was
fascinated by how the music suddenly stopped, then started again as
a passage would be replayed. My young and untrained ears couldn't
discern any noticeable difference of course, but I liked the rhythm
of the musicians stopping, stopping, then moving on once they were
satisfied. One such summer the famed cellist Pablo Casals performed
at the Marlboro Festival after many years of boycotting the United
States to protest the U.S. colonization of Puerto Rico, where he lived
in exile from Franco's regime in his Spanish homeland. He was then
in his eighties. I remember his bald head bent over the instrument,
his rigorous motion, his intense focus and occasional audible moans
as he swept bow across strings.

In addition to these cultural excursions and the Sundays with my
father, I spent my summers at camp. These were wonderful times
for me. From age six through my teen years I attended three summer
camps: Wyandot and Kinderland, both of which were in the Catskills,
and Higley Hill in Vermont. Of these I loved Higley Hill the best and
went there the longest. All were run and staffed by people in or close
to the Communist Party and largely attended by sons and daughters
of party members. Even at the young age of six I was overjoyed to
get on the train at Grand Central and begin a fun-filled and carefree
summer away from the tension of home. Unlike most six-year-olds, I
had no fears about being away from home. Camp was refuge.

At camp I could be a kid. Although most children and staff
at Higley Hill were white, African American children attended as

well, and racial equality and civil rights were emphasized in our everyday activities, in the songs we sang and in the stories we were told. For example, we often sang freedom songs and spirituals, and were taught their meaning embedded in the history of slavery. Not surprisingly, we sang many peace songs. Folksinger Pete Seeger made frequent appearances at camp. Tall, lanky, with a receding hairline and reddish nose, a banjo slung across his shoulders, seemingly ageless, head thrown back, Adam's apple bobbing, he led us in songs like "Study War No More," "If I Had a Hammer," "This Land Is Your Land," "Last Night I Had the Strangest Dream," "Oh, Freedom!" "I Dreamed I Saw Joe Hill Last Night"—all emphasizing themes of peace and social justice. Film nights introduced us to Charlie Chaplin and to working-class and antifascist films like *How Green Was My Valley, The Grapes of Wrath,* and *Open City.* These films had a huge emotional impact on me, and we often talked about them, whispering to each other from our bunk beds late into the night.

My favorite camp game was called "Capture the White Flag," a war game. We played it on a huge field surrounded by woods. The area of fair play extended into the woods, which was very important to the game's purpose and outcome. Halfway down the field was a line, and each team occupied the territory extending from that line back to the team's goal post. Upon each post was mounted a white flag, and behind the flag was the "prisoner's pen." The object of the game was to capture the opposing team's flag and carry it safely back into your own team's territory. If you were tagged while in the opposing team's territory, you became a "prisoner." You could be "freed" if a member of your team managed to run or sneak into the prisoner's pen. Any number of people could play, of any age, as long as you were more or less equally divided. It was ironic that we played a war game at a camp so strongly devoted to peace, but ours was not a pacifist world; it was a fiercely partisan one.

In my imagination I was always an antifascist or guerrilla fighter in these games, and I spent my time crawling through and hiding in the woods, trying to get all the way to our "prisoners" and the flag. Once I was "captured" by Bobby Starobin. He was in his late teens or early twenties, with a mass of black curly hair and a marvelous dimpled grin. He was the son of Joe Starobin, a revered member of the Communist Party, a journalist and correspondent for the *Worker* who wrote books such as *Eyewitness in Indo-China* and *Paris to Peking.* We all loved Bobby, and I didn't mind being "captured" by him at all. We were both laughing so hard after he found me that we sat on the ground holding our sides. I think I was about twelve. Bobby ended up in Berkeley in the 1960s as a graduate student of history, and he was a leader of the Graduate Students Association during the Free Speech Movement. We saw each other a lot then. His book, *Industrial Slavery in the Old South,* launched his academic career. Then I heard that Bobby had committed suicide in 1971, a year after it was published. When I heard the news the image that came to my mind was Bobby smiling at me in that forest fifteen years earlier.

I also spent a number of summers and holidays at Lake Hopatcong, a New Jersey village where my Aunt Leona and Uncle George—Father's older sister and her husband—owned a house and guest cabins. Leona was my favorite aunt. She was short, fat, and blond with a mouth that hooked out to one side, blue, blue eyes, and a heart the size of the sun. She had a raspy voice with a thick Brooklyn accent, with which she told countless hilarious stories about her adventures in the world.

Aunt Leona was devoted to my father. We were always welcomed into her home with wonderful food, miraculous treats, and seemingly boundless love. "I don't know from politics," she used to say to me, "but I know a good heart when I see one. Your father has a good heart." Every year Aunt Leona took me to the Ringling Bros. and Barnum & Bailey Circus at Madison Square Garden. We laughed at the clowns, gasped at the trapeze artists, and loved the animals, especially the bears riding bicycles. We ate pink cotton candy and ice cream and waved our sparklers together in the darkened arena. We held hands the whole time.

At the circus they sold live green turtles. They were very little, with pretty green shells and tiny clawed feet and beautiful yellow designs on their undersides. Every year Aunt Leona bought me a turtle. They gave me a little box in which to carry it, like the take-out containers from Chinese restaurants. The turtle crawled around inside the box and I could hear its feet scratching the surface. Once home I placed the turtle in a small terrarium. It had glass sides with black rims, and a fake shell turned upside down to serve as a rock. I put some water in it so the turtle could swim around, but left it shallow enough so it could climb up onto its shell. I fed it special turtle food. Sometimes I felt like the turtle, all closed in, inside glass walls. I loved my turtles, but they died after a few months and Mom flushed them down the toilet.

Most years, in mid-August after my six-week stay at camp, my parents would drive to camp in my father's Plymouth and pick me up. For the remaining weeks of the summer the three of us would drive across the United States or into Canada. One year we drove through Nova Scotia and the Gaspé Peninsula, and another we traveled over the Great Smoky Mountains and into the South. Still another time our destination was Pikes Peak in Colorado. Mom mapped the routes; my father drove. We drove all day, and spent each night in a motel. While on the road I especially loved to eat at Howard Johnson because of their ice cream sundaes. However, when my parents learned of their segregated lunch counters in the South, we stopped going there. This was in the late 1950s, after the Montgomery Bus Boycott but before the lunch counter sit-ins. Although I enjoyed these travels and saw a huge portion of the United States, I much preferred to be at camp, where I was free to be myself, away from my parents and their unpredictable tempers.

My mother sometimes took pictures with her small camera on our summer travels. The photos were in black and white, vintage 1950s. When I think back now to this time, I have only these photographic impressions, a momentary freeze with no real memory of the place. In one picture I look to be about eleven years old. My father is sitting on a stone embankment. He is facing the camera, his head tilted slightly, a half smile on his lips. I am in his lap, resting back on him, legs straight out, my arms draped over his legs. I too am looking at the camera, my head tilted the same way, a half smile on my lips. I look formless, like a Raggedy Ann doll flung over a chair. I have no memory of where we were or the picture being taken. I think sometimes when I was in close proximity to my father, especially if he had recently molested me, I checked out, unaware of my surroundings or even what I was doing. It would have been too scary to do otherwise.

When I was growing up, my father's fury was most often directed against those in the party he perceived as "renegades," or those public intellectuals—professors and writers—whom he perceived as "pundits" and "apologists" for the ruling class. To my father, these

men were "bastards" and "sons of bitches," "maniacs" and "liars."
He snarled these epithets, dumping these men onto the garbage
heap of history. If challenged at lectures or forums, Daddy became
enraged, his voice rising. I was filled with anxiety that he would
lose control, and that people would see that he was crazy, because
this was how he felt to me in his rages at home and when he cried
after we "played." Usually, in public, Mother caught his eye, and he
regained control of himself. Later, she might tell him that he'd gotten
"too excited." He would look at her and say, very mildly, "Really?"
or "You think so?"

A frequent witness to these tirades, I developed a tremendous
fear of being associated with any of these men's ideas. Of course, as
a child I didn't know what their ideas actually were, and I offered
few, if any, opinions. I read very little that I did not perceive as a
prescribed and acceptable text, other than those assigned in school. I
read almost no fiction until I was in college, save for *Charlotte's Web*
and the Nancy Drew and Hardy Boys mysteries, which I loved. We
didn't go to bookstores. Instead, my parents brought books home for
me to read. Sometimes I went with my father to the Brooklyn Public
Library. I waited for him in the children's section while he researched
one thing or another that related to the party, but I couldn't check
anything out. He always said he wasn't sure when he'd be back in
the library again and didn't want to risk having books be late. Of
course we were always back with some regularity, so this rule never
made any sense to me. I didn't learn to read for pleasure or to escape
into another world with books until I was well into adulthood.

By fourteen, I was poring over the English-language edition of
the eight-hundred-page tome *Fundamentals of Marxism-Leninism*
and studying my father's books. I felt compelled to merge into him,
win his unconditional approval, take on his cause with unswerving

loyalty. I read Marx again and again until I thought I had mastered something of his theory of surplus value, understanding how the workers were exploited at the point of production while the capitalist owners amassed their wealth. I studied Lenin's *Philosophical Notebooks* and *What Is to Be Done?* Like my father, I believed that only those who were in the Communist Party or closely associated with it were "good" people; others were "bad" or, at the very least, suspect. I was taught that there was no separation between a person's politics and his or her being. When Mrs. Smith, one of my favorite history teachers in high school, announced in class one day that "of course the Rosenbergs were guilty," I shrank into my seat, my heart pounding, and felt personally betrayed. It was five years after their execution. I decided I couldn't possibly like her. Afterward, I challenged everything she said in my mind, wrote polemical essays, and defended the Soviet Union in the Cold War that was then raging. Mrs. Smith must have noticed my shift in behavior from adoring student to spiteful adolescent, but she still gave me an A in the course, much more a credit to her good character than to my behavior.

This was my own private gulag—Stalinism internalized, unmediated, intensified by the madness of McCarthyism, and shot through with the terrible violence of my parents' frequent outbursts. Marxism was all-consuming in my family. Everything was measured against this way of thinking. I was much older before I understood that even within Marxism there were many debates.

When news reached the United States of Nikita Khrushchev's report to the Twentieth Congress of the Soviet Communist Party in early 1956, revealing the extent of the atrocities committed against thousands of Soviet citizens under the rule of Joseph Stalin, these revelations shook the very foundations of Communist life everywhere in the world, and certainly in my home. I have only two fleeting memories of my parents' reactions to this news. One is of my mother saying to me something to the effect that Stalin went crazy, apparently in response to a question I had asked. The other is of my father shouting to my mother about that "cowardly bastard" Johnny Gates, editor of the *Worker,* whose picture I can still see on the front page of *The New York Times,* accompanying an article announcing his resignation from the party. He had resigned in response to the revelations about Stalin.

Some thirteen years later, in 1965, after I was married, living in Berkeley, and a member of the party, my husband, who was also a Communist, tried to talk to me about the atrocities committed by Stalin. Almost reflexively, I shouted at him to stop and became hysterical. I felt that I was holding off a huge wave that would sweep me out to sea and to a certain death. Acknowledging the reality of Stalin felt as though it would crack the structure of my Communist belief system, and with it my loyalty to my father and mother and the world I knew. It terrified me.

While some families embraced religion to believe in and guide their lives, we had Communism. Although my parents were Jewish and I was raised on the border of the Crown Heights section of Brooklyn, they rejected Judaism as a religion with such vehemence that I dared not ever question it. I was raised knowing virtually nothing of Jewish values, traditions, or history. In retrospect it seems as though they substituted their belief in Communist ideals for the Jewish orthodoxy with which they both had been raised.

By the 1950s, large numbers of Chasidic Jews had moved into our neighborhood. The men and boys wore black hats, coats, and trousers, with white shirts. They all had *payes*, the long, curling sideburns characteristic of Orthodox Jews, and many of the men had long, thick beards. My mother hated the Chasids. When she saw one on the street she would sputter and curse, nearly spitting in her rage. Her fury frightened me. She despised even the most reformed expressions of Jewish religion, referring to anything religious with bitter sarcasm and contempt. Zionism was unmentionable. My father shared her views, although he didn't spit at the Chasidim on the street. For a time he edited a Communist Party newsletter called *Jewish Affairs*. It was vehemently anti-Zionist, supported the Palestine Liberation Organization, gave extensive coverage to the Israeli Communists, denounced the Israeli government, and memorialized victims of the Holocaust.

Both my mother and my father were raised in Orthodox Jewish families, and my grandfather had helped to found the first synagogue in Brooklyn. That I didn't find this out until a cousin told me years later, when I was in my forties, only reinforced my sense that my parents were ashamed of being Jewish. There were complicated reasons for this shame. My mother, having been raised in great poverty on the Lower East Side of Manhattan in what was then a Jewish ghetto, equated the religious orthodoxy of the grandmother who raised her with the shame of poverty. The Jewish God had done nothing about that! She still seethed in fury fifty years later, telling me stories about going to the Jewish orphanage uptown, where wealthy Jews lived and gave away last year's fashions for children like her to wear. The first thing my mother did when she got paid on her first job was to buy fashionable clothes.

My father rejected Judaism as a religious practice in the face of the Holocaust, detesting what he saw as the acquiescence of the Jewish people in their own destruction, and the failure of any God (Jewish or otherwise) to stop such a catastrophe. For both my parents it was socialism that provided the promise of liberation from class injustice, and only Communists who could be truly trusted in the resistance to fascism.

In my childhood the only expressions of our Jewish heritage were my parents speaking Yiddish to each other when they didn't want me to understand what they were saying, and their love of bagels and lox. I didn't attend synagogue as a child or young adult, and I had no Jewish education. I was terrified to ask why we never attended synagogue or celebrated Hanukkah, lest I trigger a parental explosion. The Holocaust was the only safe subject, and then only if the Jews were victims and/or the Communists had led the resistance. As we traveled through Europe and witnessed the sites of the Nazi terror, my father explained to me repeatedly the significance of what I was seeing, of fascism unleashed. Only the Communist Party organized any serious resistance, he emphasized, pointing out that the party led the resistance movement all over Europe. Only the party could be counted upon, only the comrades could be trusted. I felt constricted, almost asphyxiated, by the weight of history, by the righteous burden that I was called upon to bear. It allowed for no margin of error. I stumbled among the ruins of Ravensbrück, a concentration camp for women and children, a young girl of fifteen, blinded by fear at the sight of the crematoria.

We celebrated none of the Jewish holidays except Passover, and only then if we were invited to a family Seder. But even this was fraught with danger, since many of our relatives, especially my Uncle Jay, were Zionists. He and my father would argue over Israel's right to exist. It was, after all, the 1950s, fewer than ten years since the founding of Israel. On one such occasion I remember my mother cutting my father off sharply as his voice rose in pitch and volume toward hysteria. Dad stopped in mid-sentence, and my cousin Sonya, who hosted us that evening, admonished both men not to argue at Passover. "Shhh," she said, "we're family. Let's put our differences aside and enjoy ourselves." I knew my mother's intervention had only been a matter of etiquette. She couldn't stand Uncle Jay's politics. Sonya's husband began the traditional reading of the Haggadah, first in Hebrew and then in English, and the story of the Jews' freedom from slavery was told once again.

Many of my schoolmates were Jewish, and in elementary school all of the Jewish students left on Wednesday afternoons to attend special classes at Hebrew school—except for me. There may have been other Jewish children who didn't go to Hebrew school, but I didn't know if they existed, much less who they were. We were shrouded in silence and left to study with our Christian classmates. This reinforced the sense I had from a very young age of being both apart from and above most of the kids I grew up with, as if my father's status as a public figure, whether revered or despised, set us apart from the mundane world of those around me. I didn't participate in any after-school activities and often spent the afternoons with a babysitter (and when I was older, alone) since both my parents worked full-time.

"Aunt Sarah" was my favorite babysitter, playing with me every afternoon for almost five years. But one day she didn't come to take care of me anymore. I was still in elementary school, maybe nine or ten years old. Mom told me a woman named Mrs. Boyle would be there instead. When I asked Mom what happened to Aunt Sarah, she said she had "retired." When I asked Mom again what happened to Aunt Sarah, she said I had gotten "too old for her," meaning that she only took care of younger children. Years later, on a visit home from college, I went to find Aunt Sarah because I thought it would be fun for her to see me all grown up. I had been very fond of her. I learned her name was Mrs. Jackowitz. She lived on Eastern Parkway, near my parents' home in Brooklyn. We had a wonderful reunion. She had aged, of course; she was more hunched over, shrunken. When I told her how sorry I was as a little girl that she had retired, she said, "I didn't retire. Your mother fired me." I didn't understand. I was embarrassed. I didn't know what to say, so I said, "I love you." Now I think about what I might have said to Aunt Sarah as a young girl, what she might have seen or guessed about Father's sexual abuse, what she might have said to Mom that caused so precipitous an action.

My parents also employed women—all African American—to clean our house. The first was a woman named Dora, who worked for my mother for seven or eight years, until the time she had had a run-in with my mother and left. Apparently Dora had quit and told Mom exactly what she thought of her, imitating Mother's voice and intonations. My mother was a demanding employer, and she resented having to pay what she saw as an exorbitant amount of money for cleaning house. By the time I was old enough to understand the concept of wages I was shocked at how little Dora was paid.

I was confused, trying to reconcile Dora cleaning our house for what I thought was very low pay for the hard, hard physical labor she did, with my father writing and giving lectures on African American history, and excoriating those who oppressed black people and continued to deny them true equality. Typical of my father's writings on this subject of equality was a pamphlet he wrote, "The Negro Today," published in 1962, in which he wrote, "To maintain injustice requires that it be rationalized. The greater the injustice and the more prolonged its life, the more fantastic becomes its rationale. In our society, the deepest, most significant, and most atrocious injustice has been the oppression of Negro people. . . ." He had written and spoken words like this throughout my childhood. I felt that hiring black women as domestic workers at such low pay was wrong, and I was sure that my father would too. But when I brought this up to him when I was thirteen or so, he dismissed my objections brusquely, saying that Mother needed the help and that it provided the women with much-needed jobs. Mother paid the going rate, he said. His response was so angry that I understood I was not to bring it up again.

On the other hand, I was enormously relieved when my mother hired an African American comrade to help me sew a dress, and paid her very well for her highly skilled labor. In our elementary school we girls were required to sew our own graduation dresses as a condition for graduating. We were required to work on our dresses in school during sewing period, and to complete assignments on them at home in the evening. (Needless to say, the boys were not required to tailor their own suits as a condition of graduation!)

Mom and I went to a fabric store and bought a bolt of the required lacy material and the assigned pattern. But I couldn't sew if my life depended on it, which at the time seemed to be the case. After long hours at work, and with minimal sewing skills herself, Mother not only couldn't help me but resented being asked. Caught between the terrors of my sewing teacher, Miss Kenney, who stood over me in school as she made me undo every wrong stitch I might have managed to complete the night before, and Mother's temper, I was soon in a state of fearful anxiety. Finally, one night I tearfully pleaded for help. Mom shouted at me that all the other girls had mothers who didn't work full-time and who knew how to sew. This was when I realized that I wasn't stupid. None of the girls were making their own dresses. Their mothers were! Mom then picked up the phone and called this comrade for help. Yolanda was a superb seamstress. She came the next night and in about a week, just prior to the graduation deadline, completed the dress for me. Miss Kenney raised her eyebrows the first day I came to school with an assignment perfectly completed and noted the remarkable progress I had apparently made in one night, but she didn't question me about it. Each night, Yolanda sat at the sewing machine that Mother kept in a kitchen alcove. Her head was bent over the machine, and her hair, worn in a bun at the nape of her neck, was streaked with gray. She was in her mid-forties and had a smile like the sun. To me, Yolanda was a savior sent by God, to whom I had prayed every night for weeks.

The woman who cleaned our house after Dora left was Mrs. Jackson. I insisted upon calling her Mrs. Jackson, although my mother wouldn't tell me her last name and I had to ask her. In her late fifties, she was a soft-spoken grandmother who worked quietly and methodically through the house, but she had neither the physical strength nor the stamina to duplicate Dora's standards. Although Mrs. Jackson cleaned my room, I was uncomfortable with this. I seesawed between my discomfort and Mother's angry warning should I attempt to do anything about it. For example, if I would start to make my bed the morning Mrs. Jackson was coming, my mother would order me to leave it for her. Nevertheless, when I got home from school I sometimes helped Mrs. Jackson with the chores. Since Mom was at work, there was no way she would know.

The first Christmas I was home from college I went to visit Mrs. Jackson. She was still working for our family, and she and I had developed something of a friendship. I had brought a small gift for the holidays. She lived in an old apartment building in Brooklyn, on President Street, not more than a mile from our home. When I rang the bell her granddaughter opened the door. She was about six or seven years old. She was followed quickly by her mother, who stepped back in alarm, throwing a protective arm around her child. Mrs. Jackson came then from the back of the apartment. Seeing me, she called out to her daughter, "Oh, it's fine, hon. Don't worry. She's okay." It was the first time I had experienced myself as a threat, and I knew it was because I was white. Though I understood that Mrs. Jackson's daughter's fear was not personal to me, I wanted to shrink into myself, to become as small and inoffensive as possible, lest I cause any further hurt. But Mrs. Jackson spread a canopy of welcome and we had a nice time catching up.

By the time I reached high school, my afternoons were no longer supervised, and my after-school activities became well-guarded secrets. When I came home from school I gathered up the mail that had been shot through the slot of our front door on Ludlam Place and bounded up the stairs. I was required to phone Mother at work to check in. "Consolidated Tours," rang out the receptionist's voice. "How may I help you?" Mother would always ask if there was "anything of consequence" in the mail. Since our telephone conversations were guarded, with an ear toward the FBI tap we assumed was there, my answer to this ritual question could only have been perfunctory. How was my day? Fine. What would I make for supper that night? I would make something up or she would tell me what was in the refrigerator. She and Daddy would be home late. After a hefty snack I launched myself into an afternoon of adventure. I had a sturdy three-speed Schwinn bicycle, and I rode all over Brooklyn.

Among my favorite places to ride was the path along the East River in an area known as Brooklyn Heights. It was a residential neighborhood with multistoried apartment buildings, one- and two-story houses like ours, and old brownstones with their stone stoops.

Trees lined the streets. Across the river you could see the docks along the Manhattan shore. To get there I rode through miles of homes, candy stores, shops, and grocery stores. I knew the area well because Dr. Du Bois and his wife, Shirley, lived at 31 Grace Court in the heart of it, and we had driven to their home countless times.

Another favorite place to ride was the Flatbush neighborhood, much closer to home, where my high school English teacher lived. She was my first teenage crush, and I managed to discover her address by finding a listing in the telephone book for her father, who was a physician. Miss Fialka was in her mid-twenties, with short blond hair, blue eyes, and blue-rimmed glasses, which made her look very scholarly. She was perhaps five feet tall, thin, with quick movements of hands and body, and a sharp intellect. In her classes we read Chaucer's *Canterbury Tales* and *Beowulf*, and Gregory Eliot's *Silas Marner*. I cared very little about these books because the stories seemed remote to me and with no political cast I could understand. However, Miss Fialka's love for literature inspired me to do my best. She was immensely kind to me, and my diary was filled with descriptions of her. On one of my bicycle trips I actually intended to visit her, but lost my nerve at the last moment.

Upon returning home from a bike ride around the neighborhood, I made myself Mother's prescribed supper, usually some kind of meat, like a hamburger patty, and a frozen vegetable. Then I turned on the TV. I sat in a corner of the living room couch doing my homework and watching *The Lone Ranger, I Love Lucy, Superman, Policewoman Decoy,* and *Dragnet.*

I also spent many afternoons at home alone, especially in the winters. There I sometimes acted out a series of "performances" in which I was director and played all the parts. Mostly, I was either the victim of some violence from which I eventually escaped, eliciting unconditional love from women I knew, or I was a heroic figure rescuing women on whom I had crushes from some terrible trauma. I entered rooms with my arms extended, holding an imaginary weapon as I'd seen the police on television do. I threw myself headlong across the room onto an imagined enemy, pounding pillows with my fist again and again, until I was exhausted. Sometimes I cut myself in places on my body my mother wouldn't see, the pain and blood actualizing the drama I was performing. Much later, I realized that my afternoon plays allowed me to release the pent-up fury that I felt but could not allow myself to express. I was the one who needed to be rescued, and one part of me sought to save the other, dissociated and unable to identify or express emotion.

In the course of these afternoons I might also drink a shot of rye or scotch, sneaking small quantities from the stash Mother kept in the hall closet, or I smoked the filter-tipped cigarettes she kept in a dish on the end table in the living room "for when company came." I drank and smoked very little because I didn't want Mother to notice any depletion in her supplies that might require an explanation. I used the alcohol and cigarettes only as theatrical accessories to my melodramas. Even in college, I did no drugs and drank very little alcohol. I did, however, become addicted to cigarettes.

After my plays, I took great care to clear the room of the cigarette smell by opening the porch door off the living room. Sometimes great piles of snow had accumulated on the porch. The cold air felt like nectar, which I inhaled in huge gulps. I was careful not to let any snow fall onto the polished wood floor, lest my mother discover my activities.

I began lying to my mother just after we moved from our apartment to the house on Ludlam Place. I lied because my father did. He lied about anything he thought would "upset" my mother;

he lied when he had seen or talked with someone of whom she disapproved. But he often told me about it, taking me into his confidence and reminding me not to tell my mother. For example, if he had an argument with someone in the party leadership, or if he was told not to publish something in *Political Affairs*, he didn't tell my mother. Later, when I was older, he still took me into his confidence. For example, he carried on a long correspondence with the historian Eugene Genovese, who was very critical of Daddy's work in his book *Roll, Jordan, Roll: The World the Slaves Made.* Mom felt he should have nothing to do with the man, so Daddy avoided talking about him or his correspondence.

I remember only some of my lies; they were completely inconsequential in themselves. I lied about my grades on school tests, confident that by the end of the term when my report card came I would average up to an A or a B+ in the class. I lied about having practiced the piano, which I was supposed to do every afternoon for an hour. I believed my piano teacher, Mr. Leibowitz, would never notice the difference or report the delinquency. The day before a lesson and the day of it, I practiced like crazy. Mom had high hopes for my potential career as a concert pianist.

Although most of the lies have slipped from memory, I can clearly recall my terror of being caught. I lay awake at night, my mind racing, adrenaline washing over me. I waited anxiously for my father to come home from whatever late-night class he had taught. As I heard his key turn the latch of the front door, I felt a wave of relief. I heard him kiss Mom, and then he always asked, "Is the baby still up?" Sometimes Mom knew that I was, and at other times I called to him. He'd come in to kiss me goodnight. I'd pour out my terrible secret through muffled sobs. He'd always promise to take care of it. He would tell Mom the truth and make everything all right.

"It's fine now," he'd say. "Don't worry about it. It's nothing. Just go to sleep." He'd give me a reassuring pat and a last kiss. My confession completed, I'd fall into an exhausted sleep. The next morning neither Mom nor Dad would say a word, the episode erased as though it had never happened. On February 12, 1957, I wrote in my diary: "I made a new ruling for myself. I will never lie again. So far I've been pretty good." But my resolve didn't last.

By the time I was fifteen I disagreed with everything my mother said. Even if it was raining and she said, "It's raining," I would shout, sullen and angry, "No, it's not!" Finally one day she said to me, "Bettina, why do you disagree with everything I say?" Stamping my foot in exasperation, I yelled, "I don't disagree with everything you say!" Later, however, I thought about it. What she said was true. I felt very annoyed with myself for being so stupid. It was just that it felt so good to disagree with her. I was aligned with Daddy after all. I agreed with him. But I didn't like how clearly Mom saw through me. I stopped disagreeing with her.

In high school I was too old to play baseball as I had with the boys in the neighborhood, who were by then on school teams, which excluded girls. I did have three or four girlfriends in high school, but I almost never played with them after school; I never went to their homes and they never came to mine. I knew my parents would not approve. They wanted me home after school, and they did not want visitors in the house if they were not home to supervise us. Once, though, out of curiosity, I went out with these girlfriends. It was a Saturday afternoon, and we went to see a matinee featuring Elvis Presley. I tried very hard to fit in as my girlfriends giggled, sighed, and swooned, but I didn't get it. When I came home, Mother wanted to know if I'd had a good time. It had been a huge deal for me to go out on my own. Although I was fourteen at the time and other girls did go out on their own, Mother didn't approve. She had fussed about it for at least a week. So I said yes, I'd had a very good time, but I didn't push for another such excursion. It wasn't worth the hassle with Mom. I was suffocating, lonely, isolated, but I had my bike and my fantasies. And, of course, political activism.

Although I had been surrounded by Marxist teachings and books my whole life and had joined my parents in their protests as a child, my own political activism began when I was thirteen. In the spring of 1957, and again in 1958, the first marches on Washington for integration were organized by a coalition of civil rights organizations. I went on these marches as part of a delegation of "red diaper babies" (RDBs). We were the young Communist contingent, and within a few years RDBs a little older than we were helped us organize a socialist youth group called Advance. By designating ourselves as "socialist" we were not officially or organizationally linked to the Communist Party. The Brooklyn club met in the basement of my parents' home. Angela Davis and Margaret Burnham, with whom I was to have a significant connection a decade later, were part of this early alliance. During our childhood the Burnham and Davis families were close friends. When Angela came up from Birmingham, Alabama, on a Quaker scholarship to attend Elisabeth Irwin High School in New York, she was a frequent visitor to the Burnham home. We lived in Brooklyn within easy reach of each other, but I saw Angela and Margaret only in this political context.

Politics mattered above all in our family, and my parents, especially my mother, discouraged me from forming more conventional teenage friendships with girls. Although she and I never discussed it, I think the reason for this was the sense that friendships that were not based on political partisanship were frivolous at best, and suspicious at worst. I think my parents worried about child-informants, or my inadvertent slippage in conversations to which the FBI might have access. Mom did allow me to start dating boys and young men when I was sixteen, as long as they were connected to the party.

Caught up in the heroism of black college students sitting in at lunch counters all over the South to protest segregation in the early 1960s, our socialist youth group organized sympathy picket lines at the Woolworth's store in downtown Brooklyn, urging customers to boycott Woolworth's until they integrated their lunch counters in the South. One afternoon a man, young, white, and very drunk, pushed me off the line, pinned me up against a parked car, and shouted, "What part of the South are you from?" His speech was slurred, his eyes bloodshot, his breath reeking, his body rigid. It all happened so fast, I just answered him literally. "North Carolina," I said, it being my place of birth. I hadn't heard the sarcasm intended by his question. He shoved me harder against the car and raised his fist, as if to strike me in the face. Someone pulled him off me; someone else brought me back into the picket line.

The other focus of Advance activism in the first two years of the 1960s was to urge President Kennedy to sign the atomic test ban treaty. The treaty provided for an international ban on the atmospheric testing of atomic weapons, with numerous on-site inspections of testing sites by scientists from the several nations involved, most prominently the United States and the Soviet Union. Its main purpose was to lessen Soviet-American hostilities and, above all else, to protect the planet from the irreversible effects of radioactive fallout. Participating in the "Ban the Bomb" movement, tens of thousands of people held demonstrations all over the world, especially in Europe and Japan. But the treaty was extremely controversial in the United States because anything that lessened international tensions also shifted the anti-Communist politics of the Cold War, which launched and sustained both Democratic and Republican political careers.

One such demonstration to support the test ban was organized in March 1962, when I was seventeen. I went with my first boyfriend, Gregory Milakos, a twenty-one-year-old Communist of Greek heritage. Thousands of people had converged at Gramercy Park near midtown Manhattan. It was a peaceful, lighthearted, easygoing crowd that gathered on that sunny day, the first hints of spring breaking the grip of winter. Suddenly I heard screams, saw people surging forward and then back, breaking and running in all directions. With shining black boots and swinging clubs, police charged into the crowd on horseback. Their horses snorted, eyes frightened and mouths foaming. I stood there, incredulous and unable to move. One officer, with a distinctive handlebar mustache, swung his club repeatedly through the crowd. Out of the corner of my eye I saw a policeman on horseback coming toward me, and I raised my arms to protect my head. I felt a club crash across my ribs, and I went down. I never saw who had hit me; everything by then was a blur of motion. Gregory picked me up as I struggled for breath, and half dragged, half carried me to the relative safety of a nearby storefront. For a few minutes we watched the swirling, chaotic mass of humanity. "Let's get out of here," Gregory said. As we walked, he kept asking me if I was all right. But I had already left my body, dissociation a well-established escape for me. My mind floating above the sidewalk, I watched a movie of Gregory and me, the revolutionaries in love.

The next day's Sunday *New York Times* headlined the police attack, with a photograph of Julian Beck, a well-known theater director who had been badly beaten and hospitalized. There were charges of police brutality, and an investigation ensued. Soon after, a police officer came to our home to interview me. My father must have notified the authorities of the policeman who attacked me when he learned of the investigation. The officer was in his thirties, uniformed, clean shaven, exceptionally polite. We sat across the kitchen table from each other, while my mother and father sat at each end. It turned out that I was not the only one who remembered the mustached officer swinging his club through the crowd. But I could not provide a description of the officer who struck me. I don't think anything came of the investigation. X-rays showed the fracture in my ribs.

Though I felt isolated and lonely in high school, I was good friends with a fellow red diaper baby named Phyllis Haberman. We saw each other only at school, except once when I went over to her house one afternoon so we could study together. We waited for each other every morning under the rather imposing eighteenth-century archway of gray stone and arcane sculpture that marked the Flatbush Avenue entrance to Erasmus Hall High School. Phyllis was an excellent student with a special gift for mathematics. It was undoubtedly due to her patient tutoring that I passed solid geometry. She was also a sympathetic listener, and gave me healthy and practical advice. But even Phyllis was never privy to my inner life, or the uncertainties and terrors of my home life. She did, however, instruct me in the use of Kotex the first time I got my period. Although I felt all right, I thought I must be very ill when I started bleeding that morning. I took a mass of toilet paper and stuffed it into my underpants. Mom had never told me anything about menstruation, and I had never seen any evidence of hers. I confided in Phyllis, who marched me off to the nearest drugstore for supplies.

As best friends, Phyllis and I were also political allies. We staged our first political protest—against the civil defense drills—together, as high school sophomores. In the 1950s and early 1960s, with the ever-present fear of Soviet "aggression," these drills were regularly held in all of the schools. Special bomb shelter signs were posted in all public buildings, alerting occupants to shelter locations. A siren shrilled, penetrating our very bones. As it sounded, we were required either to crawl under our desks and crouch, hands over our heads, facing away from windows, or to exit classrooms and sit on the floors in the halls, facing the walls in that same crouched position.

Raised on the horrors of Hiroshima and Nagasaki, and the constant barrage of Cold War rhetoric and atomic weapons testing, Phyllis and I believed that such shelters were ridiculous in the face of atomic weapons, and that these fears of attack were unfounded. So we resolved one day to protest the next drill. We decided we would refuse to take cover and instead make our way to the principal's office, where we could lodge our protest. We argued that real protection against atomic weapons could only be achieved through a test ban treaty. These drills reinforced both the fear of attack and the illusion of protection.

Phyllis's father, who was a high school teacher experienced in such political gambits, advised us to involve more students, giving us our first lesson in the practical implementation of the Communist Party's strategy of United Front politics. He pointed out, very logically, that if more students were involved we were likely to suffer less severe penalties. My parents thought that our protest was a great idea. Phyllis and I recruited more students to join us. Since we couldn't know when the next drill would take place and could easily be scattered in different classrooms, our plan was for all of us to meet in front of a particular room as the siren sounded.

The day came, and the siren wailed. Phyllis and I met each other at our appointed spot. But all of our erstwhile supporters had had second thoughts. It was just us, at least until we were confronted by the dean of students. Outraged by our disobedience, she grabbed me by the shoulders and slammed me up against a wall. She yelled at us so venomously that Phyllis and I retaliated by forming a picket line of two around her for the duration of the drill. A recent uprising of progressive students in Turkey inspired me to shout "Remember the Turks" as we circled, likely a non sequitur to anyone within earshot. It never occurred to me that we could really get into trouble for our protest, but we did. Our parents were notified, and our respective fathers (not mothers, mind you) were summoned to see Dr. John McNeil, the school principal.

Dr. McNeil was in his late fifties or early sixties, balding, short, and always dressed in three-piece tweed suits. He spoke very calmly, in an authoritative, resonant voice. I recall his tone, but not what he said. I felt enormous pride as I sat next to my father in his office. Dad told Dr. McNeil about his experiences in combat during World War II, about the destruction from conventional weapons, never mind atomic bombs. He argued that the shelters were a hoax, and had nothing to do with any serious protection from attack. The point, Dad argued, was that there was no possible protection for anyone in atomic warfare. He said, "We both know the kids are right." Dr. McNeil had originally intended to suspend us from school, but my father convinced him to reprimand us instead. Such a reprimand—one that would become a permanent part of my otherwise stellar high school record—seemed inconsequential to me, but many of our teachers were very upset about it. The worst of the McCarthy era was over, but the televised hearings and blacklists were still fresh in everyone's memory. It was 1960, and Phyllis and I were sixteen years old.

Once I started dating, with Mom's permission, young men, always older than I, in or around the party, the sons of comrades, took me out. Mom was satisfied as long as they promised to bring me home by some more or less specified hour, usually midnight. We went to movies, party-sponsored events, restaurants. In darkened theaters, alleyways, and apartments, they kissed and fondled me, pressuring me to have sex. To my parents, going out with a young man meant I was not "on my own," while going out with a group of girls was all but forbidden. This double standard made no sense to me, then or now. But I think my mother may have felt that girls alone, no matter our numbers, were vulnerable to male attentions; if I was with a boyfriend, she thought I was safe.

I started dating Gregory Milakos when I was sixteen and Gregory was twenty-one. He was from a Greek family and worked as a printer. I marveled at his rough, ink-stained hands, so different from the softness of my father's. He was stunningly handsome, dark skinned, with jet black hair and dark brown eyes graced by long lashes. As a member of the Communist Party, he was a dedicated revolutionary who studied pamphlets like "How to Be a Good Communist," published by the Chinese Communist Party and translated into English by their foreign press. We read these pamphlets together and had many earnest, intense conversations about revolutionary politics. Gregory saw his life completely at the service of the party, and I wondered about how this would affect his family life. I had met his mother, an elderly woman shrouded in black, who spoke no English. She smiled at me and seemed very kind. While Gregory lived with her, he was hardly ever home. I thought about how lonely she must have been.

As I hovered between childhood and womanhood, we divided our time between Coney Island and Greenwich Village and its many cafés and theaters. He cut a very dashing figure, as much to me an icon of revolutionary fantasy as a real person with whom I presumed to have a relationship. I liked our kissing and foreplay but wanted nothing to do with intercourse. But Gregory pressured and cajoled and even ridiculed me for my reluctance to sleep with him. When he threatened to end our relationship, I finally consented. I wasn't ready, it hurt a lot, and I didn't like it. I couldn't see what the big deal was, and I worried about getting pregnant. When we had sex I just floated off and watched us from the ceiling like we were in a movie. At the time, I didn't understand this as a process of dissociation, a defense against memories of the incest that had so recently ended.

My cousin Sonya gave me advice about contraception. I stayed overnight at her house one weekend, around the time I was seeing Gregory. She came into the guest room where I was sleeping to kiss me goodnight. In the subdued light, half under the covers but still sitting up, I told her about Gregory. Very gently, she asked me for details and when I told her, she said, "Do you know what to do so you don't get pregnant?" I had no idea. I hadn't learned anything about sex or pregnancy at school or from my mother. Sonya inaugurated me into the world of contraceptive options and Planned Parenthood. However, without parental consent I couldn't be fitted for a diaphragm. And of course, asking my parents was unthinkable. I couldn't imagine asking Gregory to use a condom since I'd already made such a fuss about sex. Like so many young women of my generation, I prayed a lot and waited anxiously each month for my period.

Going out with Gregory didn't change the feeling I'd had about myself for as long as I could remember: I was attracted to women. By the time I was in high school I had had a series of crushes on a succession of women. One of them, Yvonne, was our downstairs neighbor when we lived in our Brooklyn apartment. In her mid-thirties, the mother of two young children, Yvonne earned her living as a waitress. She was tall and sinewy, her face flat with high cheekbones. Her hair was jet black and usually cut shoulder length. Her skin was white, but she turned brown in the summer sun. Her smile lit her brown eyes into a warm and playful glimmer. She had little formal education and took classes at the New York School for Marxist Studies.

I was fifteen the summer Yvonne worked in the kitchen at Higley Hill camp in Vermont. She was a dishwasher and I was a counselor-in-training (we were called CITs). I had assumed that after my long association with Higley Hill and my CIT apprenticeship, I would be a counselor the following year.

Yvonne and I spent much of the summer together. On days off, we hiked or sat around and talked. On workdays, I sometimes helped out in the kitchen. Once, when we were playing around outside, she threw me into the lake with all my clothes on. It seemed like we laughed all summer. Although I felt very sexually attracted to Yvonne, she always steered us carefully into a playful space and kept her energy affectionate but sexually neutral. But once I kissed her on the lips. It was a spontaneous burst, and I was startled by the surge of feeling it released in me. Although Yvonne said nothing and did nothing to push me away, I knew by the expression of unease in her eyes not to do it again.

The following year I submitted my formal application to be a counselor at Higley Hill. Yvonne was also going to return with her children. Having been part of the Higley Hill family for years, I was stunned when a letter of rejection came from Grace Granich, the camp owner, just a few weeks before I was to leave for camp. And the reason for the rejection struck a chord of terror in me. Grace had observed my behavior, she wrote, with a woman on the kitchen staff the previous summer. This behavior had interfered with the successful performance of my duties as a CIT. Such behavior, her letter concluded, was not compatible with camp life. She regretted to write such a letter, but she felt circumstances compelled it.

Mom read the letter and was furious—with Grace. She dismissed the charges, announcing that Grace was either jealous of my affections for Yvonne or mentally unbalanced. Needless to say, I was enormously relieved by her response. Meanwhile, I said nothing about the truth of Grace's observations, however cruel her response. I did show the letter to Yvonne. She was very upset, but also relieved that her job at Higley Hill, which she urgently needed, was secure.

I decided that although I might continue to fall in love with women, it would be my secret. I was never, ever going to get caught again.

So instead of working at Higley Hill, I spent the summer working at the Jefferson Bookshop, the Communist Party bookstore in New York. I spent most of my lunch hours in a nearby park, necking with the Italian waiter who worked in the coffee shop next door to the bookshop. He had to have been at least thirty. He kept saying, "You know what I want," and I said nothing. I just hoped we could stay in the park and away from any private space. At the end of the summer, I was relieved to return to school.

In the late summer of 1961, about to begin my senior year in high school, I went to work for W. E. B. Du Bois. He had asked me if I would work with him and I was honored to volunteer to do so. I was just shy of my seventeenth birthday. He was ninety-three. Dr. Du Bois and his wife, Shirley, had made the decision that year to leave the United States. Emigrating to Ghana at the invitation of President Kwame

Nkrumah, Dr. Du Bois intended to begin work on a project he had long dreamed of, he explained to me, a multivolume "Encyclopedia Africana." He chuckled, his eyes lit with amusement, as he told me about it when I started my work with him. Many volumes, he said. Many years of work. He envisioned an encyclopedia as large and as broad-ranging as the *Encyclopedia Britannica*. This one, however, would be centered on African histories, cultures, tribes, migrations, discoveries, religions, geographies, fauna, and more. He hired me to assist him with the overwhelming task of organizing and boxing up his many papers and books in preparation for the move.

The "Encyclopedia Africana" was the culmination of more than seventy years of scholarship, beginning with the 1896 publication of his doctoral dissertation, *The Suppression of the African Slave Trade*. Dr. Du Bois was most famous for his 1903 book *The Souls of Black Folk*. It was part autobiography and part argument against the politics of Booker T. Washington and his accommodation to segregation, especially in education, a crucial debate in the black community at that time. In 1953, on the fiftieth anniversary of its original publication, a new edition had been published, and Dr. Du Bois had autographed a copy especially for me. Though I was only eight years old at the time, I treasured my special edition of the book.

Dr. Du Bois was also known for his political activism: He helped to found the NAACP in 1909 and edited its magazine, the *Crisis*, for thirty years. In 1950, when I was six years old, Dr. Du Bois was indicted and arrested by the U.S. government for being a "foreign agent" because he headed the Peace Information Center. The center opposed the Cold War with the Soviet Union and advocated the peaceful resolution of disputes between nations. Any organization that affirmed the idea of peace with the Soviet Union was suspect in the eyes of the U.S. government. The center was a continuation of Du Bois's work in helping to found the United Nations in 1945 as part of the U.S. nongovernmental delegation. The charges against him were eventually dismissed by an embarrassed federal judge when he learned who Du Bois was.

Dr. Du Bois and I began work each weekday morning at nine. I arrived promptly; he was extremely punctual. We worked in the study of his home on Grace Court, a few miles from my home in Brooklyn. His desk was large, glass topped over a dark wood, with piles of paper neatly stacked on it, on surrounding chairs, and on the polished wood floor. Drapes covering the windows were pulled back to let in the daylight. The room fronted the street, but it was set below street level so we just saw the sidewalk, the black wrought-iron fence marking the property and the legs of any passersby.

Dr. Du Bois had decided to name my father as the executor of his papers, and all of them were very soon to be moved to our house. The steel filing cabinets full of his papers ended up in our basement, unbelievably in the laundry room under the clothes hanging on the lines to dry. I spent hours in our basement poring over the letters, fascinated by a near century of correspondence, the carbon copies of Du Bois's letters neatly stapled to the original letter to which he had replied. There were letters from Indian Prime Minister Nehru, and Mahatma Gandhi, President Woodrow Wilson, and Henry James, Langston Hughes, James Baldwin, Countée Cullen, Paul Laurence Dunbar, to name only a few of those I remember.

I spent my time at the Du Boises' sorting and filing correspondence, manuscripts, news clippings, and journal articles. He showed me his system of dates and categories and I set to work. Dr. Du Bois was at his desk. There was no conversation as we tackled each day's tasks; we worked in companionable silence.

Dr. Du Bois was a small man. By his eighties and nineties he stood just under five feet. He was mostly bald, with a neatly clipped mustache and goatee. He was always formally dressed in a three-piece suit, usually tweed or dark colored, with a white shirt and a tie. He wore a pince-nez that attached to a black ribbon and tucked into his left vest pocket. His skin was a light pecan color. The pigmentation on the back of his hands, especially the right one, was nearly white. On one hand he wore his Harvard College ring, and on the other a gold wedding band. He was of medium build, but the stoop of age and a small belly gave him a slightly rounded appearance. When not in public he preferred thick rubber-soled soft leather shoes to his polished oxfords. Du Bois's voice combined an almost Southern musical lilt with a clipped British-sounding accent, a paradox that produced an altogether distinct speech. He sang a high tenor and had a splendid voice. He told me with some pride that he was in excellent health.

We worked more or less in silence each morning for three hours. At noon we broke for lunch. Shirley prepared our food, but she rarely ate with us. Dr. Du Bois and I ate outdoors, on a stone patio at the rear of the house. It faced a manicured lawn and flower garden. Even in the summer humidity the patio was comfortable, heavily shaded by trees. Our lunches were delicious: salads and fruit or sandwiches, and always a dessert, something luscious with whipped cream. We drank iced tea. And now, work put aside, we could talk.

In the presence of someone as revered as Dr. Du Bois, I was, of course, on my best behavior. But he was relaxed, often on the verge of laughter. He asked me about school, about what we studied, and about the socialist youth group, Advance, in which I was involved. Recently returned from a trip to China, Dr. Du Bois was thrilled by the social reconstruction he had witnessed. He emphasized to me that all of this was being accomplished by "a colored people," a fact that filled him with pride. I had never thought of race in conjunction with the socialist revolution in China. He told me stories about children he had met, his amazement at the cleanliness and splendor of Peking, the circus he and Shirley had attended, and the opera.

Although in awe of him, of what my father told me he represented, I loved Dr. Du Bois personally, and with strong feeling. I had known him all of my life. He always treated me with respect, answering my questions fully, focusing his attention on me. He encouraged me to share ideas with him. He was affectionate, warm, funny, and very gentle. He seemed to have so much joy about him, and so much delight in life. It was always a pleasure to be around him.

When we finished our leisurely hour-long lunch, we resumed work for another several hours. A few weeks after my employment with Dr. Du Bois ended, I received a check in the mail from Du Bois's attorney for $40, drawn on a special account from Fisk University, where he had taught for many years. I was very surprised and more than a little honored to receive this check. For me, those weeks with him had been a joy, and I thought of him as a model for living a good and purposeful life.

As much as I enjoyed my time with Dr. Du Bois, I loved seeing his wife, Shirley. Thirty years his junior, she stood considerably taller than he, at five feet eight or nine, her hair long and wiry, swept up and back. It was dark, streaked with gray. She was a light-skinned black woman with a round face, large nose, generous mouth, animated brown eyes, and a loud raspy voice that crackled with life. I knew her as Shirley, rather than Mrs. Du Bois. She didn't adopt her husband's formality for herself, but she always called him Du Bois (with the accent firmly on the "Du," and with the anglicized version he used so that the French *"Bois"* was pronounced "boys"). When speaking to him directly she used various terms of endearment; I never heard her use William, Edward, or Burghardt. Very, very rarely she might say "W. E. B."

Shirley was a writer. Among her many credits were the biographies of famous African Americans written especially for young adults. There was, for example, one about the first published African American poet, Phillis Wheatley, another on Benjamin Banneker, a surveyor who helped design the blueprints for Washington, D.C., another on Frederick Douglass. I had read most of them. Later she wrote a definitive biography of Gamal Abdel Nasser, the president of Egypt, whom she knew. She also wrote a singularly affectionate intimate biography of Du Bois, *His Day Is Marching On*, several years after his death. Forty years later, when I wrote her biography for a new edition of *Notable American Women*, I learned of Shirley Graham's career as an operatic composer and playwright in the 1930s. Shirley was astute, witty, learned, and a consummate storyteller. She was also the founding editor of *Freedomways*, a New York–based quarterly that chronicled the birth of the civil rights movement. This journal remains one of the best sources for documenting the black movements of the 1960s.

In my first years in high school I began writing short fictional pieces, many of which focused on racial justice. I told Shirley about my stories. After reading them she asked me for permission to publish one of them in *Freedomways*. I was thrilled, though in the end the story wasn't published. What mattered was her encouragement, her hands comfortingly on my shoulders, the warmth of her hugs, her treatment of me with dignity, as my own person.

My mother thought Dr. Du Bois and Shirley were great fun. I can still see them seated in the back of my father's car. He frequently picked them up to bring them to our house for dinner, to take all of us out somewhere together. I always wanted to ride in the car with him to pick them up. They would sit in the back seat of the Plymouth holding hands, giggling, sparring with each other, using my father as their straight man. "Now Herbert," Dr. Du Bois would say in his British/Southern lilt, "you know how things are. . . ." Shirley would feign a harrumph. "Herbert, let me tell you what he did . . . ," referring to her husband, with her rich, rasping laughter. But they weren't really talking to my father. They were playing with each other, an effervescence of sweet love. I clearly remember the story about Shirley's move to Grace Court, where Dr. Du Bois was already living. Shirley was expecting Dr. Du Bois to show up at her home to help her with the move. It was shortly after they were married, in 1951, when I was six. I still remember the wedding ceremony at Shirley's home in St. Albans, a neighborhood in Queens. "He never came," she said, referring to moving day and feigning outrage. "I waited and waited, and he never came." At this Dr. Du Bois gave a small chuckle, admitting sheepishly that he had escaped this dreaded task by spending the afternoon at the movies. And then Shirley would give her harrumph, and he would chuckle again. Of course, he was eighty-three at the time. The whole thing was ridiculous, and they both knew it.

Our family drove the Du Boises to Idlewild Airport in New York on October 5, 1961, for their flight first to London, and then on to Accra, Ghana. So many friends and reporters were jammed into the first-class passenger lounge, it was like a party, with cameras flashing, champagne glasses clinking, laughter, hugs, and farewells.

I wrote to Dr. Du Bois and Shirley, especially after I got to the University of California at Berkeley and the burgeoning civil rights movement hit the San Francisco Bay Area. A group of us, mostly red diaper babies and other students who identified themselves as

Marxist, formed the Du Bois Club. Responding to this news, Dr. Du Bois wrote back, on February 17, 1963:

Dear, dear Bettina,

Thank you and all members of your Du Bois Club for what you have done to make known the principles for which I have tried to stand. Out of the mist of years I send my love and appreciation and Shirley joins me.

Dr. Du Bois died August 27, 1963, in Accra, at age ninety-five, on the eve of the great March on Washington for civil rights. I was in Berkeley, and read of his death in an obituary in the *San Francisco Chronicle*. My parents had not thought to call me. They never thought to call me because it didn't occur to them that I had my own relationship with Dr. Du Bois. I was together with them on so many occasions growing up, and yet I was invisible to my parents because they saw me only as an extension of themselves, like a shadow.

Following Du Bois's death, Shirley remained in Accra and became director of the national television network in Ghana. In close alliance with Ghana's president, Kwame Nkrumah, she was considered in the early to mid-1960s to be among the most powerful women in all of Africa. Following President Nkrumah's assassination, she fled Ghana and for several harrowing months was stateless and feared for her life because of her close association with the president. Nevertheless, Shirley continued writing, traveling, and speaking, and eventually made her home in Cairo with her son, David, who was a well-established radio journalist. When she came to Berkeley on a lecture tour sponsored by the *Black Scholar* in the early 1970s, I went to hear her. She gave a brilliant talk on the political situation in Africa, one that emphasized the role of the U.S.

government in destabilizing any democratic or socialist movements. Meanwhile, I knew that my parents were cooler to Shirley than they had been because she supported China's Communists in their split with the Soviet Union over whether or not to seek a policy of peaceful coexistence with the West, and the United States in particular. Later, of course, the reality of the Chinese Cultural Revolution and the vast suffering it caused became widely known. I loved Shirley, and nothing about her political views changed that for me. We had a wonderful reunion in Berkeley.

Eventually, Shirley went to live in China, where she died from cancer on March 27, 1977. The poet Sonia Sanchez, who had known Shirley as her mentor, wrote a poem in tribute to her. I loved it the moment I heard Sonia read it. It was called "*Kwa mama zetu waliotuzaa*" ("For our mothers who gave us birth"). In part, it reads:

Call her name again. bells.
shirley. graham. du bois
has died in china
and her death demands a capsizing of tides.

no longer full of pain, may she walk
bright with orange smiles, may she walk
as it was long ago, may she walk
abundant with lightning steps, may she walk
abundant with green trails, may she walk
abundant with rainbows, may she walk
as it was long ago, may she walk.

As I approached my senior year in high school, the prospect of college applications and the SATs loomed ahead. My classmates were mostly the children of solidly middle-class white parents, significant numbers of whom were Jewish. A small number of my schoolmates were African American. All of us were expected to attend college. The competitive fever to outdo each other on the SATs effected many a whispered huddle in the halls of Erasmus. Having never done well on tests in general, and intelligence tests in particular, I was a subdued senior, moving swiftly and diligently between classes, library, lunchroom, and home. Winners of the New York State Regents Scholarships, based on SAT scores, found their names posted one morning at school. I wasn't on the list. But I admit I was relieved to have some modicum of dignity preserved when I found my name posted among the runners-up. My best friend, Phyllis, got a scholarship. I was thrilled for her.

As for colleges, I knew my first choice. I had already announced it to my parents: the University of California, Berkeley. I wanted very much not only to leave home, but to put a considerable distance between me and my parents, although I did not acknowledge this to myself. What I focused on was Berkeley's political draw, its student movement already coming to life. The May 1960 San Francisco protests against the House Committee on Un-American Activities hearings had drawn national headlines. The protests marked the beginning of the end of this congressional committee, which had struck such terror in the hearts of so many people by forcing them to testify about their political beliefs and associations or face imprisonment.

Mom complained about how far away Berkeley was, but my father deemed it a fine school with an excellent history department, which was what he cared about. At the time, I was planning to be a premed major, but I didn't share this with my parents. In the end, I applied to Berkeley, Oberlin, and the University of Wisconsin, Madison, all hotbeds of political activity. I wasn't accepted at Oberlin, but was thrilled to receive acceptances from Berkeley and Madison. Flooded with romantic images of student revolutionaries, a California paradise of spaciousness and sunlight, and a scholar's nook in an ivy-covered building, I wrote an ecstatic letter to Meredith Martin, the daughter of the chairman of the Communist Party of Northern California. She was a year older than I, had grown up in nearby Oakland, and was already enrolled at the university. She in turn sent me a generous letter of welcome. Breathless, I waited for June.

My boyfriend, Gregory, wasn't happy about my impending departure. It wasn't the fact that I was going to college, or even the distance. It was that I hadn't given a thought to him or to our relationship. Deeply hurt, he began dismissing me from his life. However, I was long gone emotionally, not from him so much as from my childhood, from New York, and from my parents' suffocating expectations and restrictions and their tempers. At the time, and for years afterward, I would have said that I had had a perfect childhood, repeating what my father always said about his childhood. I had no access to my emotions, no way to articulate what my father had done to me. I had no memory of it in my head, but my patterns of dissociation and "spacing out" were becoming more and more evident. I knew only my elation as the day of graduation approached and I could at last escape.

As the time of my leaving home grew closer, I announced to my father that I was joining the Communist Party. He was washing dishes at the kitchen sink. He did the dishes by running a constant tiny stream of very hot water, dabbing a sponge onto a bar of yellow soap, washing each dish, rinsing it, and stacking it on a towel. It took him forever to wash the dishes. He didn't look up from his stream of water or his sponge. He just said, "I think you're ready."

two

UPHEAVALS IN BERKELEY

I SWEPT INTO Berkeley a minor celebrity, introduced as "Aptheker's daughter," the appellation delivered in a stage whisper. I was soon ushered into the inner circles of various informal revolutionary councils, including the student activists who had mounted the campaign against the San Francisco hearings of the House Committee on Un-American Activities and others in the Communist and Socialist parties in Northern California. I was one of only a handful of women in these inner circles.

My parents had driven me across the United States, my father's green Plymouth hurtling by the Nebraska cornfields, the Dakota badlands, and Mt. Rushmore, with what I considered its ostentatious facsimiles of the Great White Fathers. We visited the Grand Canyon, gaped at the red pinnacles of Bryce and Zion, climbed Donner Pass, and descended eventually into Yosemite Valley, gazing up at El Capitan and Half Dome. For a few days we stayed in a motel just outside of the park boundary, and I got badly sunburned lying across a rock in the shallow ripples of the Merced River. I left everything in Brooklyn except for the clothes in my suitcase. I was looking for a fresh start, without the daily intrusions of my parents and the isolation of my childhood and adolescence.

Just after celebrating my eighteenth birthday that fall of 1962, my parents left me in the care of Max and Evelyn Martin, a temporary refuge until my housing could be arranged. My father, of course, knew Max from national party meetings. Max and Evelyn were Meredith's parents, and their home was a hub of Communist Party life in the Bay Area. Max was the chairman of the Northern California Communist Party. Evelyn was also active in the party and worked in the kitchen of Herrick Memorial Hospital in Berkeley. The Martin household could not have been more different from the intellectual, sheltered, middle-class world in which I had been raised. It was full of noise, laughter, and a revolving door of party members, community activists, and university students; the atmosphere at the Martins' was warm, comfortable, and accepting. There was always something going on.

Set on the Oakland-Berkeley border in a working-class, racially integrated neighborhood, their house was a rambling two-story structure that reminded me of a farmhouse. A large kitchen, dining room, and front parlor were downstairs, and a well-polished wood staircase led up to a second floor, where an enclosed porch had been built off the room farthest to the back. This was Evelyn's favorite space, with its indoor plants and view of sky and trees. Max's study was in the main upstairs bedroom fronting the street. He had a large desk, piled high with books and papers that spread themselves onto the surrounding floor, the bed, and nearby bookcases. Meredith lived in her own place, but the Martins' two younger children, Ray and Sheila, were still at home and occupied other upstairs rooms. The Martins also had a

German shorthaired pointer I particularly liked. Though Marina was her formal name, we called her "Mimi" for short.

A constant stream of people flowed through the Martin household, and anyone who was around late in the afternoon—friends, comrades, the neighbors' children—was likely to be invited for dinner. A large, oval, polished-wood dining room table was set with thick plastic plates and glasses and piled high with food. It seemed to me that an infinite number of people could eat there, and the family never hesitated to add another setting. After eighteen years of sharing a small dinner table with my parents and on many occasions making dinner for myself, meals at the Martins' were refreshingly fun and joyous times for me. Welcomed into this rollicking household, I was treated as a member of the family. The Martins provided me with a second home, one marked by generosity, kindness, and warm hospitality. Evelyn always seemed to have time to have a cup of tea with me and see what I was up to. I had a standing invitation for dinner and a key to the house.

Raised along the Northern California coast, Max was in his mid-fifties and had been a fisherman when he was younger. He had rough workingman's hands, permanently grooved with grease. He wore workingman's clothes, favoring dark trousers and heavy work shirts. His voice had the tenor of a low growl and he had a thick, hearty laugh. He could fix or build just about anything, "if he got around to it," as Evelyn quipped. Max read a lot, from pop fiction to Marxist theory to the driest of political tracts. Confronted with news of some new "capitalist atrocity," as the phrase went, he would say, "It's a helluva system," or "It's a brutal system," his brown eyes lit with feeling, and then he would think out loud about the best way to approach the problem at hand. For example, in December 1962 Juan Bosch was elected president of the Dominican Republic in the first free elections held in thirty-eight years. He was a socialist and began dramatic economic and social reforms. He was overthrown by a military coup after only seven months in office, and a period of brutal repression followed. This was the kind of "capitalist atrocity" that particularly affected Max, and he followed the events with keen interest. He organized special meetings to educate all of us on the situation in the Dominican Republic and encouraged us to pass resolutions in condemnation of the coup. We were all well aware of CIA complicity in the coup. Two years later, when the United States sent troops to the Dominican Republic to prevent the return of Juan Bosch to the presidency, we held a large protest meeting on the Berkeley campus.

Evelyn was ten years younger than her husband, and she combined the hefty strength of a farm woman with the austerity of a nun. She had a college degree but was very modest about her obvious intellectual abilities. She spent much of her time helping to organize Local 250 of the hospital workers' union. She was also, of course, a member of the Communist Party and extremely active in local politics and the constant fundraising and circulation drives for the party's West Coast weekly newspaper. She was a voracious reader. I remember library books, mostly fiction and biography, piled in her special corners of the house. I adored Evelyn, confided in her, frequently sought her advice as I struggled through my late teens and into my twenties. Evelyn even taught me to drive, on a 1951 Ford sedan that I bought for ninety dollars from Jack Kurzweil, who was to become my husband. She used to say that if I could drive that Ford with the arm muscles required to turn its steering wheel, I could drive anything.

Within a couple of weeks of my arrival in the Bay Area, I moved into a home owned by Vivian and Vincent Hallinan, a well-known progressive couple in the Bay Area. The Martins had generously offered me temporary housing until I could move into a place of my own. Vivian was a peace activist, beginning with her opposition to the Korean War and her support of U.S.-Soviet friendship, and Vincent was a San Francisco attorney who had run for president on the Progressive Party ticket in 1952. His running mate had been Charlotta Bass, an African American journalist and civil rights activist from Los Angeles. Two of the Hallinan sons, both students at Cal, also lived in the house, as did Ken Cloke, another Cal student and one of the founders of Slate. Slate was a radical campus group that had won a series of student elections with a "slate" of progressive, "Ban the Bomb," pro–civil rights, and anti-HUAC candidates. I had my own room in the house, and the boys treated me like their kid sister, giving me much-needed advice on what to do to survive my first semester. They guided me in selecting classes with dynamic and progressive professors, and gave me a new sense of family by including me in their good-natured kidding and more serious political discussions.

I plunged into school with enthusiasm, declaring myself a premed major and tackling my general education requirements. In my last year of high school I had read a biography about the Canadian physician Norman Bethune. This book, *The Scalpel, the Sword,* had inspired me to become a doctor. A Communist, Bethune had traveled with the antifascist brigades in Spain during the Civil War, and in 1938 he went to China and provided medical training and care for the Red Army. I was attracted to the immediacy with which medicine could help people, and with Bethune's example I could see the possibility of being a doctor while still honoring my Communist loyalties and not disappointing my parents—both of which were strong needs I had at the time.

The Berkeley campus was built with solidity across what must once have been, in my mind's eye, a forest of oak trees and grassy meadows. Strawberry Creek descended from the eastern hills and ran through the campus. There were paths along it, draped with weeping willows. The buildings themselves seemed to me to be massive slabs of concrete with little character or design. The campanile at the center of campus dominated the landscape from a considerable distance, and from its tower one gained a spectacular view of the San Francisco Bay and the city itself, gleaming in sunlight. At noon the bells of the campanile were rung, often with beautiful melodies. I was pleasantly surprised many years later to learn that it was a woman, Margaret Murdock, who played them during my years as a student.

This peaceful, bucolic setting fulfilled every fantasy I had had about what a university campus should be, even if my classes were nothing like I had expected them to be. I had imagined myself in small seminars with learned men. In 1962, it never occurred to me that there could be learned women. I'd not yet heard of Virginia Woolf, whom I first encountered in 1966 when I saw Richard Burton and Elizabeth Taylor in the movie *Who's Afraid of Virginia Woolf?* and wondered who she was. I looked her up, but it was another ten years before I read *A Room of One's Own*. My professors were indeed learned men, all of them white, and my classes were enormous. Most of the courses I took as an undergraduate were held in huge auditoriums with five hundred to a thousand students, the professor barely visible at a lectern at the front of the hall, a disembodied voice floating above the rows of heads. Real learning, such as I had envisioned it, took place in small discussion sections taught by graduate students. These were the teaching assistants who graded our midterms, commented on our papers, and answered our questions.

With rare exceptions these TAs were more interested in getting through our papers and discussion sections as quickly as possible than in teaching us. The exceptions were important: a woman in anthropology, another in politics, a man in history. In them I saw a glimmer of an enthusiasm and passion for teaching.

I liked the science courses I took for the premed major, especially physical anthropology, where we pieced bone fragments together to consider human evolution and peeled sedimentary evidence to gauge the age of various rock formations and thus determine the approximate age of villages or cities. But I was also immersed in politics. Having joined the Communist Party in New York before coming to Berkeley, I was transferred into a party club when I arrived. Thrust into a welcoming camaraderie of fellow young Communists, I attended one meeting after another, readily agreeing to serve on party committees and joining the dozen or so earnest students who formed the Communist Party club on campus. I was eager to learn the discipline of organizing and how the boys only a few years older than I could conjure a variety of political strategies in a given situation. For example, there were many discussions about the absence of a Young Communist League, such as had existed in the 1930s, to harness the radical energies of a new generation and train them to become future leaders of the party. The "political estimate" at the time was that it was not possible to organize a YCL with direct ties to and under the discipline of the Communist Party. And our comrades argued that we needed a more open, less ideologically rigid organization where Marxism itself could be debated and discussed. This was a new idea to me, having grown up with my father's dogmatic insistence on righteous truth.

These discussions led to the decision to launch the W. E. B. Du Bois Clubs as a national organization, with the first chapters in

Berkeley and San Francisco. Dr. Du Bois had joined the Communist Party just before his departure for Ghana, and he was an esteemed historical figure in the struggle for civil rights and the Pan-African liberation movements. We felt that naming ourselves after him would announce our revolutionary intentions without officially tying us to the Communist Party. We felt that with the Du Bois Clubs, we could openly sponsor classes on Marxism and plan for participation in a burgeoning civil rights movement in an organized and consistent way, rather than only as individuals. The civil rights movement was picking up steam in the South, with plans to register disenfranchised black citizens to vote, and to integrate all public restaurants, libraries, and sports facilities like swimming pools, basketball and football teams, bowling alleys, and so on.

In the fall of 1962, when I began my studies at Cal, there were a number of crucial historical events playing out on the world stage, the most terrifying being the Cuban missile crisis. With the perceived threat of another U.S.-led invasion of Cuba following the Bay of Pigs in April 1961, Soviet Premier Nikita Khrushchev placed nuclear missiles on Cuban soil within range of major U.S. cities. A "routine reconnaissance" by a U.S. spy plane over Cuban airspace had revealed that the missiles were under construction. President Kennedy was alerted on October 16, 1962, and he announced the presence of the missiles in a national television address on October 22. The mood on campus was tense. President Kennedy had ordered a naval blockade of Cuba to prevent the arrival of any more Soviet ships. On October 26, Khrushchev announced that the missiles would be withdrawn if the United States promised that there would be no further invasion of Cuba. The next day a U.S. spy plane was shot down over Cuba and Khrushchev added to his demands, insisting that U.S. missiles be withdrawn from

Turkey, a country that bordered the Soviet Union. The world held its collective breath.

In Berkeley, none of us were going to classes. We were gathered either at the Terrace, the student coffee shop on campus, glued to the radio, or at home, riveted to the television. I remember being up all night at home with the Hallinan brothers, watching the U.S. naval forces as they steamed toward Cuba, all of us knowing the Soviet ships were also en route. We felt helpless—and betrayed. Many of us on the Left, myself included, hoped and believed that President John F. Kennedy—young, vigorous, and seemingly idealistic— would lead us into a new era of nuclear disarmament and peaceful coexistence with the Soviet Union, especially after the Bay of Pigs debacle. We were young and naive. Protests seemed meaningless to me in the face of such an overwhelming and immediate crisis. I was not sophisticated enough to understand much about the intricacies of power, but there was a part of me, at eighteen, that simply could not believe we were actually going to be led into a nuclear war. The possibility of it felt surreal, even as newscasters reported the escalating confrontation in ever more frantic tones. Everywhere on campus there was this agitated energy that I could not handle. One day, late in the crisis, I entered a kind of stillness, feeling as if I had separated from the world, walking alone on the campus and settling on the grass alongside Strawberry Creek, under the shade of the giant trees that hugged its banks. By the time I came back into myself later that day the crisis was over. The United States promised there would be no invasion of Cuba, and the Soviets withdrew their missiles. However, the United States left its missiles in Turkey and maintained its occupation of the Guantanamo Naval Base. The Cuban Revolution was assured its autonomy from U.S. intervention, and a nuclear world war was averted.

Despite the tenor of the Cuban missile crisis, President Kennedy had, in fact, worked with his Soviet counterparts to seek a peaceful resolution. Many of us held out great hope for a Kennedy presidency that would move the country toward the peaceful resolution of all international conflicts. Equally important, we held out great hope for a president who seemed to support the civil rights movement, and had telephoned Martin Luther King, Jr., as he sat in a Birmingham jail. The assassination of John F. Kennedy on November 22, 1963, in Dallas came as a terrible blow. It was only three months after the first great March on Washington for civil rights had drawn a quarter of a million people, and Dr. King's words still reverberated in our hearts. Many of us associated Kennedy with King, however naive our assumptions.

I was just coming out of class, walking toward Sproul Hall Plaza, when I saw clusters of students grouped around radios. Instead of the normal noon-hour rush, there was an uncanny silence. As word of the president's death spread, I was in shock; we all were. And then I felt a growing sense of foreboding. Many of us on the Left were wary of the "military-industrial" complex of which departing president Dwight Eisenhower had warned just before Kennedy took office. Even as the vice president, Lyndon Baines Johnson, was sworn into office, we wondered if democracy as we knew it would survive the assassination. Many of us feared that a military coup d'etat was the real motive for Kennedy's murder. Our Communist Party campus club held an emergency meeting, as did many other leftist and progressive groups. Our discussions focused on ways to begin massive protests should anything but an orderly transfer of power be attempted. In fact, though, there was a national outpouring of grief, especially in the black community, that made the idea of a coup seem untenable. And President Johnson took over the reigns of government with swift vigor. It was quickly apparent that our fears were unwarranted.

However, I became obsessed with Kennedy's assassination because I never believed that Lee Harvey Oswald had acted alone in his alleged killing of the president. Jack Ruby's murder of Oswald before he could be brought to trial left no doubt in my mind that Kennedy's assassination had been part of a much larger conspiracy. Months later, the Warren Commission's insistence that Oswald had acted alone only confirmed my suspicions. I saw the Warren Commission report as part of a cover-up by the highest authorities of government. By 1965, with the escalation of the war in Vietnam and President Johnson's commitment of large numbers of U.S. armed forces to the conflict, I and many others on the Left concluded that it was Kennedy's decision to withdraw our military's "technical advisers" from Vietnam that had sealed his fate. These "technical advisers" were involved in training the South Vietnamese army in its efforts to defeat a Communist-led insurgency. By removing them, President Kennedy would seem to have decided not to further involve the United States in a growing civil war.

Independent commissions also conducted investigations into the assassination, one of them led by Mark Lane, an attorney and a former member of the New York state legislature. I had known Mark from childhood because he and his wife, Martha Schlamme, the Viennese singer I had long adored, were friends of my parents and had visited our home in the early 1950s. In 1966 he published his book, *Rush to Judgment: A Critique of the Warren Commission's Inquiry into the Murders of President John F. Kennedy, Officer J. D. Tippit, and Lee Harvey Oswald.* I contacted Mark and arranged for him to speak on the Berkeley campus under the auspices of the Du Bois Club. Mark had campaigned with Kennedy in the 1960 presidential

election and felt a deep personal affinity with him. Mark's book had
been widely and sometimes critically reviewed, and he had become
a very controversial figure. Hundreds of students attended his talk.
He raised very serious questions about Oswald's guilt, showing that
it was impossible for him to have acted alone because of Oswald's
presumed positioning in the book depository and the actual trajectory
of the bullets (more than one) that killed the president. Mark also
detailed the many contradictions in the Warren Commission report.

With these crises, and my growing involvement in the Du Bois
Club and the Communist Party, it became apparent that I couldn't
pursue the rigors of a premed degree and continue full tilt in politics.
So many of us believed we were on the brink of progressive radical
change in the United States that every issue, every moment seemed
critical to me. By the end of my second year at Berkeley, I switched
my major to history and minored in cultural anthropology because
these subjects were much less difficult for me and gave me more time
to dedicate to political causes. I studied other cultures and puzzled
over key theorists in anthropology, like Bronislaw Malinowski,
Émile Durkheim, and Raymond Firth. In my first two years at Cal I
returned to New York only twice, brief interludes in the new life I
was struggling to make.

The members of the Communist Party of Northern California
lived primarily in the Bay Area. There were small clubs in what
were then called the outlying areas, like San Jose to the south, and
Petaluma, Sonoma, Chico, and Eureka to the north. Once a month,
comrades met in either Berkeley or San Francisco for an all-day
meeting of the district committee, which set policy for the Northern
California branch of the party.

In my early days at these meetings, we talked about a variety
of issues, some mundane and some more wide reaching. We

devoted a lot of attention to the International Longshoremen's and Warehousemen's Union (ILWU) because it was one of the few independent unions in the United States, at that time unaffiliated with the more conservative and bureaucratic AFL-CIO. The ILWU had its roots in the radical Left and Communist-led organizing of the 1930s. The shipping industry was an economic linchpin in the Bay Area, and the ILWU had thousands of members up and down the West Coast. Actions by the union affected the politics of the Bay Area directly and profoundly, from mayoral and gubernatorial elections to work stoppages protesting the war in Vietnam.

Our district, like others in the party, had special commissions established in such areas as black liberation, peace, youth, and women. Each consisted of a small number of comrades who met biweekly or monthly and assessed the politics of those movements. The women's commission, prior to the emergence of the women's movement, examined the status of women and what was called "women's equality," which referred to discrimination against women in wages and employment. Although the comrades on this commission took their work seriously, their efforts received little attention from the predominantly male party leadership. By my second year in Berkeley I was on the district committee and the youth commission. I also helped to circulate the *People's World,* the Communist Party's official publication on the West Coast, at peace and civil rights protests, although I was very shy and found this extremely difficult. Meanwhile I was attending weekly meetings of the campus club of the party to which I was assigned, and helping to establish the Du Bois Club chapters. While I very much believed in the humanitarian, peace, and social justice goals of the Communist Party, the party also represented my extended family, my root moorings.

Although I was openly a Communist among my friends, among members of the Du Bois Club, and among others within the civil rights movement, there was still an air of secrecy surrounding the party. Until 1967, when the United States Supreme Court ruled sections of the 1950 Internal Security Act (popularly known as the McCarran Act) unconstitutional, the party existed in a semi-legal status. Of course, under the First Amendment we were guaranteed freedom of speech and of association. In this absolute sense it was perfectly legal to be a member of the Communist Party. However, under the provisions of the McCarran Act, all Communist Party members were required to register with the government. Failure to do so incurred a $10,000 fine and five years in prison for *each day* of noncompliance. In addition, the Smith Act of 1940 made it a crime to be a member of an organization that sought to overthrow the U.S. government by force and violence. The McCarran Act defined the Communist Party as such an organization in order to justify its special registration provisions. Thus, if you registered under the McCarran Act, you in effect indicted yourself under the Smith Act. The Smith Act also, of course, subjected people to fines and imprisonment. The Communist Party challenged the constitutionality of these laws, contending that the McCarran Act violated the spirit of the First Amendment and the letter of the Fifth by requiring people to testify against themselves. This challenge eventually succeeded, and these key provisions of the McCarran Act were overturned. The McCarran Act made publicizing Communist Party events a complicated and awkward procedure, and necessitated the fiction of promoting the *People's World* and the Du Bois Club as independent and politically unaffiliated. Mindfulness about FBI tails and wiretaps had always been part of my life in Brooklyn, and it was no different in Berkeley. Max and

I often sat at his dining room table, writing notes to each other as we talked so as not to mention anyone's name or even the subject of our conversation. He was convinced that the house was bugged, a common practice since the 1940s. Names of comrades had been unwittingly disclosed in this way. Max or I would inevitably slip and say a name or subject aloud, then break into laughter.

In addition to Max, three other men gave principal leadership to the district in the early 1960s. They were Archie Brown, Roscoe Proctor, and Al Richmond. Archie was a leading member of the ILWU, a participant in the 1934 San Francisco general strike, and a veteran of the Abraham Lincoln Brigade that fought in the Spanish Civil War a few years later. Archie was something of a legend in the Bay Area. Before speaking in a meeting he would wet his lips, smack them together, smear the back of his hand across his mouth. Then his voice would crackle to life. Archie lived for the class struggle.

Roscoe Proctor was a highly skilled carpenter, who at times did construction work remodeling older homes. He also occasionally worked as a warehouseman and was a member of the ILWU. But the heart of Roscoe's life was in the Oakland ghetto. Through economic and civil rights organizing, he sought to give meaning to the lives of the young black men with whom he worked. Roscoe was a consummate social worker, not in the bureaucratic sense of that profession, but in its literal and original meaning. He inaugurated a group called Youth for Jobs and nurtured the young people in it, often helping them with financial and personal crises, as well as planning political actions. Roscoe brought enormous energy, deep thought, and a passionate commitment to his work. He loved the young people with whom he worked. He wanted, above all else, to spare them the suffering he had endured growing up black in Los Angeles in the 1940s.

The third principal leader of the party in Northern California was Al Richmond, editor of the *People's World*. Al was the most intellectual of the men in the leadership, and a crack journalist. He went after facts, read widely in what was referred to as the "Cap press," by which was meant the mainstream media, maintained cordial relationships with fellow reporters in that mainstream, and insisted upon a high standard of reportage.

Though men dominated the party in California and elsewhere (this was the early sixties after all), there was one woman who wielded power on the West Coast: Dorothy Healy, chair of the Southern California Communist Party. I adored her. She had quick, electric movements and enough energy to launch a space shuttle. Dorothy smoked cigarillos that bobbed up and down in her mouth as she spoke. Her raspy voice crackled and sparked. She was sharp as a tack, witty, and above all else, a consummate organizer. With her charisma she had wide-ranging associations and friendships all over Southern California. Party meetings could swing from the exquisitely boring routine of organizational reports and uncontested policy to passionate and vituperative debate that bristled with hostility. The air in the room became fetid with the anger and tension of too many bodies for too long in a closed space. Comradely decorum might be applauded in the abstract, but when someone's personal stakes were in the pot it was another matter. Ego motivated a lot of this, and when comrades were heavily invested in a movement, a position, or a group, all hell could break loose.

Such meetings were sometimes shocking to me. I was not inarticulate and I did have opinions, but I found it virtually impossible to fight, and certainly not in a public venue. Young and a woman, I was expected to listen and to do a lot of the tedious, grinding work that is the by-product of any political movement. In fairness, many meetings were neither boring nor combative. I learned a lot about the patience required for effective political organizing, and the kindness of comrades who cared so deeply about the suffering in the world. This was what I would carry with me in the years to come.

Although women were an intricate part of party life, "women's issues" were not given any priority. We were one of the few organizations that took "women's equality" seriously, but organizing workers in industry largely excluded women workers, who were clustered in clerical and service work. In traditional Marxist theory they were not part of the *industrial* working class—like the men in auto and steel, for example—which mattered most in a capitalist political economy. Party men gave lip service to the idea that childcare should be a general trade union issue, and believed in equal pay for women, but they never did anything about either in their unions. Not so, party women. Women often organized among their sister workers in hospitals and restaurants and offices, though they did so without much credit or recognition, and usually with an eye toward simply bettering everyone's day-to-day lives. In this way the women and comrades of color shared a decidedly different sense of politics than many of the white men in leadership, one that was rooted in their daily living, not simply in theoretical ideas. Some of the sharpest conflicts centered around these differences.

Sexuality, violence against women, reproductive freedom, and other issues that sprang from the women's movement did not find their way onto party agendas until the very late 1970s, and then only after considerable resistance from those who considered them personal issues that were not the subject for political discussion. This sexist assumption masked many of the privileges men enjoyed. Equally important, party men were not immune to engaging in sexual abuse, sexual harassment, and domestic violence, although they considered themselves progressives and sympathetic to those subjugated on the basis of race or class. Many committed adultery, with society's sexual double standard allowing men's indiscretions far more readily than women's. Several of the older men in the national office were notorious among us younger women for their sexual advances. However, in the 1960s and '70s, we spoke of these matters in hushed tones. And we weren't always sympathetic to each other.

It seemed that most of the party men I knew were deeply sexist. Male supremacy, condescension, and disrespect for women were simply a given, a product of the times that all of us, women and men, accepted as the natural order of things. It was so natural as to be almost invisible, except when it was so obvious that it was unavoidable. It didn't matter that the men were all in favor of racial and class equality. When it came to women it was business as usual. I remember one evening meeting when ILWU member Archie Brown whispered to me, "I'd like to get my hands inside her pants," referring to a tall, blond, exceptionally competent woman, an activist in the peace movement. On another occasion, when I condemned the Soviet invasion of Czechoslovakia at a National Committee meeting, Gus Hall, the general secretary of the party, told me I should always listen to "my pop," who endorsed it. I never forgave Gus his patronizing homilies—this was only one of many. On the same occasion, I overheard Gus talking in loud, hearty tones to another comrade. Deriding Dorothy Healy's opposition to the same invasion, he said, "What she needs is a good lay." I was revolted by Gus's sentiments, even at the time, which I considered vulgar and mean spirited. Later, as a feminist, I saw his comment as profoundly demeaning to women, as if Dorothy's opposition to an invasion was a matter of personal moodiness that a "good lay" could cure.

While sexism was unsurprisingly alive and well, the Communist Party was not, as it turned out, full of FBI agents tripping over each other to expose members of the party, as was fashionable in some liberal circles to believe. Of course, paid informers within the party did surface periodically at congressional and state legislative hearings. I learned, for example, that a man I knew as Alan Prince, the treasurer in my first party club in Brooklyn, worked for the FBI, when he surfaced as a witness in a congressional hearing. But the overwhelming majority of people I met in the party were sincere and hardworking. They were my political mentors, and through them I absorbed the rigors of revolutionary discipline, and watched and listened as concepts and debates whirled around me.

In addition to Evelyn and Max Martin, Decca Treuhaft (a.k.a. Jessica Mitford) provided me with much-needed solace those first years in Berkeley and for many thereafter. "Dear old Dec," as we often called her, lived on the Berkeley-Oakland border and was a Communist rebel from a large, well-known, upper-class British family. By the time I knew her, she had long since left the party because of the Stalin revelations. Her radical politics, however, never wavered. She was married to attorney Robert Treuhaft, who was to be one of the principal defenders of the Free Speech Movement. Tall and gangly, with a thoroughly distinctive gait and crisp English speech, Decca was a marvelous and loving mentor. When we went out for lunch, always in one of Berkeley's finest restaurants, Decca regaled me with stories. She was a supremely fine muckraking journalist, best known then for her book *The American Way of Death*. She had a thousand ways to expose the moneymaking plots and racist schemes

of institutions as diverse as mortuaries and prisons. When working
on her book *Kind and Usual Punishment*, one of the first damning
exposés of the U.S. prison system, she subscribed to a prison-guard
newsletter and read me shocking excerpts about the ways prisoners
might be cruelly and routinely disciplined.

Decca was a generous and loving mentor. She encouraged me
to write, read my writing for many years, gave me serious feedback,
and dismissed anything that struck her as politically dogmatic
or sectarian. She introduced me to literary agents and invited me
to her celebrity parties with the Left upper crust in the Bay Area.
("Upper crust" was not a matter of class or race; it was a matter of
political acumen, good humor, and talent.) It was there I met people
like ILWU president Harry Bridges, poet Maya Angelou, and *San
Francisco Chronicle* columnist Herb Caen. Decca's parties reminded
me, at twenty, of the ones my mother used to give. Meeting these
California-based celebrities felt like a continuation of my childhood,
except now I got to participate in the adult conversations. Though
Decca had little to do with anyone in the Communist Party, a few
others and I were the exception. I think Decca felt very maternal and
protective toward me. I loved her dearly.

Decca bubbled with fun and had a delicious sense of humor.
When my son, Joshua, was born, she went to the infants' section of
Hink's department store in Berkeley and requested rubber diaper
pants designed with a hammer and sickle, the universal symbol
of Communist revolution. When informed by the astonished
saleswoman that no such item existed, Decca feigned shock that
such an obvious bestseller should not be available to Berkeley's
radical population. She bought the unadorned pants and painted on
her own hammer and sickle in red, rewrapped them in their original
packaging, and delivered the gift to me. Given my propensity for

believing what I am told, however absurd, I thought the rubber pants, complete with their unique design, had indeed come from the department store. My gullibility sent Decca into hoots of laughter.

Yet for all of this fun, and despite Decca's outward and often genuine gaiety, I felt in her emotional pain. Once, years later, when I was preparing to leave an evening affair at her home, I searched her out to say goodbye. I found her stretched out on a couch in a darkened back room. We could hear the sounds of merriment from the front of the house. "I love you," I said, bending over to kiss her, my throat swelled tight with emotion. "Always," she said.

However together my outward appearance as a healthy young woman with a growing political acuity, by the beginning of my second year at Berkeley I was a psychological basket case. Swinging from one emotional extreme to another, I was in a constant state of anxiety. Despair dogged me. Sometimes I would drive around Berkeley alone at night in my beat-up Ford, soft rock playing on the car radio, weeping and suicidal. Other times, in the solitude of my room, I would work a knife into my stomach or my leg as I had done in childhood, now occasionally drawing blood. I was externalizing psychic pain from childhood sexual abuse, but at the time I didn't know that. I just knew that the physical pain gave me some sort of psychic relief. I had few social skills, did not know how to dance, felt lonely and awkward at parties. I didn't go to many and I left early. School provided the one steady structure to my life. Naiveté saved me from drugs, and little tolerance for alcohol saved me from excessive drinking. My comrades and I discussed politics until late into the night, but we shared little personal intimacy. The party provided no guidance for personal growth and no tolerance for personal problems.

In my first year at Cal, I moved from one housing situation to another, unsettled, unhappy, often distraught. I fretted over money, of which I felt I never had enough. My parents were supporting me, and my mother had me on a strict budget. My father occasionally sent me a check for fifty dollars from a separate account unknown to my mother. However much I fretted, it never occurred to me to get a job. I ate mostly Cream of Wheat, peanut butter and jelly sandwiches, and hamburgers from Blake's, just off Telegraph Avenue. Friday nights I ate dinner with Evelyn and Max, and sometimes on other days as well if I got too upset or lonely.

Finally, I settled into a small cottage on 51st Street in north Oakland. I lived alone in this racially well integrated residential neighborhood less than two miles from the Martins'. My cottage was bright and sunny, although this seemed to do little to help my mood swings. Emotionally unstable, raised in a bedlam of fear, retribution, sexual abuse, privilege, and exalted expectation, I was now thrust out into the world with virtually no social skills. I had no boundaries, little sense of self-worth, no confidence in my judgment, and no common sense. This was combined with an utter passivity in personal relationships and a childlike, trusting innocence stunning in its parameters. On top of all this, I felt myself to be physically deformed. Not only were my breasts small, but they didn't look anything like the well-formed, supple mounds of my peers'. I became obsessed with my deformity. I decided that I was a sexual freak. I was desperate to appear normal, but I had no idea what normal was. In the public world I was Herbert Aptheker's daughter, an organizer, visible on campus. In my interior world, I was lonely, confused, anxious. I felt crazy at times because I couldn't reconcile the two realities.

I dated men in and around the Communist Party, although I wasn't physically attracted to men. It just seemed the normal thing to do. With two exceptions, these encounters could hardly be called relationships. The first exception was Joey, whom I met in my party club. He was my age, a fellow student at Cal. There was something wholesome and solid about him, and we were as much pals as lovers. We talked about school, politics, and our families, but our short-term relationship was casual, with little intensity. Though we were companionable, eventually we simply wandered off from each other.

The other relationship was with Jack Kurzweil. He, too, was in the party. Jack was seven years older than I, a graduate student in electrical engineering, with a thick New York accent that I found comforting. Born and raised in Brooklyn, he had eclectic tastes, and a good sense of humor, and was a good cook. He also liked the theater and concerts, things I had greatly missed since leaving home. As connoisseurs of James Bond thrillers, we had our own self-styled movie festivals whenever local theaters showed these films. We dated for several months. He was the nicest man I had known, caring and kind. With him I felt safe, protected. Once, early in our relationship, while making love, Jack discovered that I was not using any contraception. He altered our path by giving up on intercourse on that occasion, imitating the stereotypical Jewish peddler in the shtetl to whom all bad luck falls. At that moment I thought he was the most thoughtful and conscientious man I'd known, and I found myself falling in love with him. Within a few months Jack went to New York to visit his family. When he came back to California, he broke up with me suddenly, with no explanation. He told me on the phone. I didn't know why and I didn't ask. I just shrugged, the phone cupped between shoulder and ear, and said, "Okay." I said "okay" because I couldn't think of anything else to say. It wasn't really okay, but I had no way to express my feelings. Much more devastating things were about to happen.

Raul Hernandez was in his thirties, a thin, small, sinewy man with skin the color of a well-used copper penny, very straight black hair, and high cheekbones. He came to live with the Martins in the spring of 1963 and stayed for several months. A San Quentin prisoner convicted of an assortment of property crimes, he had been released on parole after more than ten years. Evelyn had corresponded with him while he was in prison. Having befriended him, she worked diligently to secure his release. To encourage his reentry into civilian life she suggested that I take him on some sightseeing excursions into San Francisco.

Raul and I rattled across the Bay Bridge in my old Ford into the dazzling lights of the city. We drove up the narrow twisting streets to Coit Tower, roamed Fisherman's Wharf, jostled in the crowds at Union Square, and ate at Solomon's Jewish delicatessen. Enacting a fantasy loosely based on the forbidden love of the Broadway musical *West Side Story*, I began a romance with him. Raul was gentle, quiet, his English spoken in a soft Spanish cadence. We slept together once. His lips were cold. I thought he must not have had sex in a long time.

Evelyn became very concerned, sensing rather than knowing the details of our affair. As we washed the dishes together one night after dinner, she said, "I love you. I want you to find someone whose eyes still have light in them."

"Yes," I breathed, knowing already that she was right. Raul's eyes were like two pieces of unlit coal.

I continued to spend time with him, but without the romantic fantasy. It was clear that he was terribly, perhaps irrevocably, damaged by the prison system and whatever had preceded it in his barrio life. He held no violence in him that I could see, only defeat. Eventually he left the Martin household. He lost his job, drifted back into San Quentin on a parole violation, Evelyn told me, months later. Meanwhile, I had just turned nineteen and the one time Raul and I had slept together I had become pregnant.

What to do? What to do? I paced back and forth in my small cottage. Waited for my period. I thought about the people I knew, wondered whom to tell. My parents were out of the question. In the end I told Evelyn. "Are you sure?" she asked. It was 1963 and abortions were illegal. I don't remember that we explored other options, like keeping the baby or giving it up for adoption. Evelyn told Max, and they located an abortion clinic in Tijuana. Together they put up the two hundred dollars I needed to pay for it and I paid them back bit by bit over several months. Evelyn said I shouldn't go alone to Mexico, so she asked Elly, a comrade in my club, to go with me.

Elly and I flew to San Diego. We boarded a bus crowded with women tourists going to Tijuana for a day of shopping, gaudy with fake diamonds, too much makeup, hair spun into beehives. From the Tijuana bus station we took a taxi to the clinic. After that everything was a blur.

A waiting room. It was full. A handsome brown-skinned doctor in a white coat in a white room with silver instruments. Gleaming. Immaculate. "A vacuum procedure," he said in perfect English. A sucking sound. A drawing up. Pain. Blood. A taxi. A plane. Evelyn at the San Francisco airport to meet us. Driving back across the Bay Bridge, trying to lift off the seat to ease the ache as Evelyn's car, a VW bug, rumbled and vibrated. I bled heavily for days, spewing huge clots. I called a Berkeley doctor for advice, a man I knew, close to the party. He said, "Get off your feet and keep them elevated." And as an afterthought he said, "Good luck." I had incredibly good luck. The bleeding stopped. There was no infection.

As I recovered physically, I continued to sink emotionally. Stayed in bed. Closed up the house. Evelyn came with a pot of soup. Sat me up. Told me to get dressed. Opened the windows. Brought in the sunlight. Fall classes began. And so did the civil rights sit-ins at Mel's Drive-In restaurants. It never occurred to me to think of control over my own body as a civil right.

San Francisco and Oakland had substantial black populations, families who had migrated from the South in the 1940s, looking for work and opportunity. A surge in jobs at the shipyards and in the steel plants during World War II promised both. However, once the war was over, black workers and women, white and minority, were laid off. Skilled jobs were scarce. Black women and men found themselves again relegated to janitorial, service, and domestic work.

Youth for Jobs, a community-based activist group from the Oakland ghetto, initiated a series of boisterous, jubilant demonstrations at Mel's Drive-Ins. Mel's was a fast food chain serving mostly hamburgers, fries, and soft drinks to a largely teenage and often minority population who could pay to eat the food but could not get a job there. This was long before affirmative action laws a decade later. There was nothing illegal about the racial discrimination, but we thought it was immoral. Protests began with picketing and posting flyers and quickly escalated into nonviolent sit-ins at the lunch counters, patterned after the sit-ins in the South. Young African Americans and their white supporters occupied all the seats, bringing business to a standstill. Unlike their Southern counterparts, the protesters were demanding not service, but jobs.

Our African American comrade Roscoe Proctor was in the thick of things, with a genius for strategy and timing. Youth for Jobs was soon joined by the Du Bois Clubs, and local branches of the NAACP and CORE (Congress of Racial Equality). The protests were front-page news and continued on and off for several weeks. Support grew. I was thrilled to find myself back on a picket line, militantly shouting slogans. I felt like I had found my voice in the righteous anger of these young black people.

The drive-ins were owned by Mel Dobbs, a well-known San Francisco businessman with connections in the upper echelons of city politics. A Republican, Dobbs was running for mayor against Jack Shelley, a more progressive Democratic Party candidate. As the November 1963 election neared, Dobbs negotiated a settlement with the leaders of the civil rights coalition, providing a percentage of behind-the-counter jobs to minority youth. Dobbs sensed that not supporting the move for fair hiring practices was hurting his mayoral campaign. The agreement was one of the country's first models of affirmative action in hiring practices, coming long before the legal concept was established. Even with the settlement, though, Dobbs lost the election. Fresh from victory, Youth for Jobs and its supporters founded the Ad Hoc Committee to End Discrimination. By continuing its militant protests against discriminatory hiring practices, this coalition would help change the shape of politics in the San Francisco Bay Area for years to come.

Initially, many comrades were hesitant about and even fearful of these new civil rights actions. They didn't follow the "old rules" of political or trade union organizing. These new civil rights protests were unruly, militant, and showed no apparent respect for the old liberal alliances the party had managed to hold on to through the McCarthy years. For many of the party's old guard, the protests moved too fast, swept over the city like a tidal wave. But Max supported the movement, saw in it the weight of a new generation, the coming shift in the political climate.

Max and I often drove to party meetings together. He would pick me up at home and we would talk nonstop on the way to and from our gatherings. I knew he was training me for party leadership and felt he was genuinely interested in my ideas, in my growth. Likewise, I was an avid listener, learning from his years of experience. Max was a practiced organizer with an acute sense of strategy and timing. He was also a learned Marxist theoretician and an especially avid reader of Lenin. I think in training me he didn't consider so much that I was female as that I was young and represented the future for an aging party leadership. Or so I thought.

One night very late, Max didn't just drop me off at my cottage as usual. He came in with me. I thought we were still talking politics. I thought he was just finishing a conversation, getting ready to leave. Instead, he drew me to him, kissed me, caressed me. I went weak in the knees, my heart pounding. I said, "No." I remember I said it very clearly, pushing him away, my hands up against his chest. He laughed then, a funny sound throttled in the back of his throat. He didn't stop kissing me. I felt something inside me collapse. I became passive, completely passive, the way they instructed us to be when the police came during a demonstration. I went limp. Nothing else happened that night, just the kissing. But it was way more than I could handle. I felt dirty and ashamed and thought I must have done something wrong, that I must in some way be responsible. I felt paralyzed with fear and guilt. I thought of Max as my "West Coast father" and had once even said that to him in a joking way. After he left I crawled into the walk-in closet, curled into a fetal position, and cried uncontrollably. What had I done to tempt him? Why was this happening? I was only eighteen and could think of nothing to do except blame myself. It didn't occur to me that he was taking advantage of my youth, inexperience, and trust in him. And he probably knew that I wouldn't protest. Still in the closet, I fell into a deep sleep, as though I were drugged.

When morning came, I pretended that nothing had happened. I thought it wouldn't happen again, that he had lost himself somewhere, that he would come back into himself, that it was all just a dream. But it didn't stop. First, it was only at night after the meetings. Then he would call early in the mornings, come over. I didn't know how to make it stop, and it never occurred to me to refuse to see him. I didn't want to draw attention to myself or anger anyone in his family. And I certainly didn't want anyone to find out. I was sinking, sinking. Nothing was ever consummated, but I felt violated by his touch, and deeply ashamed. Pretending everything was normal. Week after week after week. I began to lose myself somewhere in the folds of his grease-stained clothes, in the musk of his aftershave lotion, in the throttled laugh. I felt powerless to stop it. I couldn't erase it either, but I tried to pretend that everything was normal. I felt crazy, and found it harder and harder to function, to maintain the facade of a healthy family connection and of our friendship as comrades. I had no language with which to explain what was happening between us. I was not in love with Max; I was not afraid of him. But I felt deep shame about what we were doing, afraid that I would be found out and that it was a terrible betrayal to Evelyn.

Somewhere in the middle of this, Phyllis Haberman, my best friend from high school, telephoned me. She had been at college in upstate New York at Binghamton, and she wanted to relocate to Berkeley. Could she live with me, at least for a while? Of course, I said at once and with real enthusiasm. I warned Phyllis that my cottage was small, but I thought we could manage. I thought Phyllis's presence would alter Max's behavior. I was enormously relieved for a while. But Phyllis's arrival did not end Max's sexual advances. It just changed his timing.

I was paralyzed with despair. I could hardly focus on even the most routine schoolwork. I was afraid to make waves, to hurt anyone's feelings. And I didn't know how to make him stop. Once I tried to have a conversation with him, to talk about what he was doing, what we were doing. Sitting in the truck on the coast overlooking the waves. That same throttled laugh. His only words something like, "It'll be all right, honey."

One morning many months after, when Max was still coming over to my cottage, there was a knock on my door. I had a premonition even before I answered it, the adrenaline surging up my spine. I opened the inner door, kept the outer screen door hooked from the inside, peered out through the gray mesh, saw the figure of a man. He was in his thirties, stocky, with a suit, red tie, crew cut, affable face. He was grinning at me.

"Good morning," he said. "My name is Donald Jones. I'm with the FBI." He held up his badge. "May I come in?"

"No," I said.

"You would make it a lot easier on yourself if you cooperated with us," he said, the grin gone now, his face serious.

"I will never cooperate with you," I said, my voice cracked with stress. I closed the inner door very gently, heard the latch click into place, leaned up against it. I waited a few minutes, willing myself to be calm, waiting for my hands to stop shaking. A few minutes later I peered cautiously out the venetian blinds, the front window giving me a glancing view of the door. He was gone.

I thought about calling someone. Evelyn would be at work. Not Max. And that's when I knew that the FBI knew about me and Max. Max and Evelyn's phones were tapped. Surely they monitored the calls that he had made to me. Given the party's semi-legal status and the continual harassment of party members, all of us assumed we were always under surveillance. Surely they were tapping my phone as well, each of us leading the FBI to the other. That they should know about my most private of shames, that they might use it, made me want to vomit.

I thought seriously about suicide, carefully plotting the details.

Then I sat back down at my desk and resumed writing a paper that was due the next day. I was split into two people, the private Bettina, living in desperation, and the public Bettina, going to classes and writing scholarly papers.

Then there was an afternoon a week or two later when I came home from school earlier than usual. The front door was ajar. I knew Phyllis was at work. I knew someone else was in the house. I eased open the screen door. Then I slammed the inner door open all the way with my foot so that it crashed against the wall. James Bond style, I gave a deep-bellied yell and charged into the living room.

He had been standing at my desk, a gray suit in broad shoulders, at least six feet tall. I never saw his face, but I knew it wasn't Donald Jones. As I flung myself into the room, he bolted, ran through the kitchen and out the back door. I ran down the driveway, yelling.

Suddenly I stopped. *This is crazy,* I thought to myself. *What am I doing? Is he with the FBI? A right-wing provocateur? And what if I caught him? Would I beat him up?* It was one of my adolescent fantasies run amok.

I went back inside, looked at my desk. Schoolbooks and papers, notes from party meetings and party reports, files and index cards were scattered everywhere. Some of it was a result of the perpetual mess in which I left my desk, and some of it was as a result of his search. For what?

I knew then, maybe not at that moment, but certainly in the next few days, that I had to get Max to leave me alone. Somehow we were going to be set up, the party crucified. And the shame that I carried, that I must have done something to make Max think I wanted this— even the thought of telling made me weak with fear and guilt. I had tried to say something once to one of the comrades in my club with whom I felt particularly close. I was vague and mentioned something about Max kissing me and he said, "Gee whiz" or something similar, and changed the subject. Counselors and therapists were completely out of the question. My parents, along with virtually all of the party people I knew, had a knee-jerk hostility to anything smacking of psychology. It had something to do with Freud, about whom I knew nothing. I needed to keep it within the party, but even that didn't seem safe enough. *Within the family,* I thought. Meredith, Max and Evelyn's daughter, seemed a possibility. We were friends, of course, but I didn't know her really well, and I couldn't predict how she would respond. We weren't especially close. Plump, rosy cheeked, cheerful and articulate, she seemed to me the epitome of stability and mental health. I couldn't even imagine how to approach her. And Phyllis? I couldn't see how to do it. In the end I told Evelyn. And it was awful.

I picked a time when I knew we would be alone. Dizzy with fear, I blurted it out. "Max is making love to me." Those six words were all that I spoke. It was all so complex—I wasn't scared of Max, but I felt responsible for what was going on between us, even though I knew I had not encouraged him, and that I had pleaded with him to stop. I still thought that it must somehow be my fault. As soon as the words were spoken I wanted to take them back, disappear, float up, dissolve into the ceiling. Evelyn turned so pale I thought she was going to faint. She sat down at the dining room table. There was no sound for several minutes, except for the ticking of the clock on the fireplace mantle. Then she said, "This may seem very cruel to you, but I need you to leave. Now." There was so little intonation in her voice that I could not read the emotion.

"Yes, of course," I said. And added, "I can leave the area. I'll go away."

The faintest hint of a smile brushed her lips. For an instant it reached her eyes and I could see her love for me. She said nothing more. And I left, weeping and driving, driving, driving. Nowhere. Suicide seemed the only option.

The next morning, Max and I and another comrade were supposed to drive to Sacramento together for a party meeting. I didn't know whether or not to go over to the Martin house at the appointed hour. Finally, I decided to keep the appointment, but I didn't go inside the house. Max came out. Just before the other comrade pulled up, he said, "You should say something before you go off and do something like that." To my silence he added, "I denied it, of course. Evelyn couldn't understand why you would want to hurt her like that."

Raw fury swept over me. *You sonofabitch,* I thought. *You goddamn sonofabitch.* I had never imagined that he would lie about it to Evelyn. But looking back now, it seems to make sense that he would deny it. My anger subsided, collapsing into shame. I said nothing.

Days passed. Images of Evelyn haunted me. I looked for some sign that she would forgive me, that she would continue to love me. Obsessed, I took to looking for her on the street, in the hospital parking lot, at the co-op market on Telegraph Avenue. I knew her schedule, thought about trying to run into her. I did, once. In the co-op. She spoke harshly, "Are you following me?" I shook my head. Pushed my cart forward.

I went to the Martin house one morning a couple of weeks later. I knew everyone would be gone, the kids at school, Evelyn at work, Max in San Francisco at a meeting of the district staff. Ostensibly I went to borrow a typewriter. I needed it to finish a paper for school. I really went because I was obsessed with fear and guilt and shame. I still had my key and I had permission to use the typewriter.

Just as I turned to walk up the short path to the front steps of the house I caught sight of a man in my peripheral vision. Before I could turn or otherwise react he grabbed me from behind, threw me into a choke hold, his right arm wrapped around my neck, his other pinning my left arm down and back. Pressing me hard against him, he dragged me toward the curb. I made no effort to resist.

FBI, I thought hopefully. *If he's FBI he won't hurt me.* I meant physically, and I was thinking about my constitutional rights. He said nothing.

An instant later another man ran out of the Martin house, slamming the front door behind him. Gray suit, red tie, broad shoulders, six foot. *Same man,* I thought. *Same man as at my place.*

I was still in a choke hold. He got into a car, started the engine, opened the passenger door. I was released and shoved forward, my assailant flinging himself into the front seat, the car already in motion. I saw him again for an instant: gray suit, gray hair, wire-rimmed glasses, white shirt, red tie, thin, and shorter than his partner, florid face.

I picked myself up off the sidewalk and rubbed my neck and arm.

I hesitated for only a few seconds. Then I got into my car and drove to the hospital to find Evelyn. I parked, ran through the visitor's entrance, down the stairs toward the kitchen, scanning corridors and rooms. I nearly collided with the metal food cart she was pushing.

"Did they hurt you?" she asked. I shook my head. "Okay," she said, "but don't go back there now." And, as an afterthought, "I'll find Max and let him know."

Max picked me up for another meeting. Drove me home. Came inside. Phyllis was out. He began kissing me again and reaching down into my pants as he had done so many times before. I couldn't believe he would do this again. Not after I had told Evelyn. "No," I said, pounding his chest with my fists. I sank onto the floor at his feet, hysterical. "Okay, honey," he said. "No more."

Somehow I knew it was over. It had gone on for a year, and it was finally over.

I was restored to the Martin family circle. Invited again to Friday night dinners. Evelyn's face was no longer taut with grief. Nothing was ever spoken of it again. The silence reminded me of the dynamics in my own family, the fact of violence and abuse subsumed in the etiquette of a family dinner. I felt a sense of enormous relief, like a great weight had lifted from me, but feelings of shame remained.

Early in March 1964, the San Francisco Bay Area civil rights movement resumed its activities with a series of sit-ins at the Sheraton-Palace Hotel and, later, at the Cadillac auto showrooms on Van Ness Avenue. Under the leadership of the Ad Hoc Committee to End Discrimination, these protests were modeled precisely on the ones organized by Youth for Jobs the previous fall. Protesters demanded that the businesses hire minority women and men in all job classifications, including as receptionists, clerks, supervisors, and, in the case of Auto Row, sales personnel. The movement was led by Tracy Sims, an eighteen-year-old African American woman whose portrait of studied determination on the front pages of the San Francisco newspapers belied her youth. Hundreds of students from the Berkeley campus participated in these actions. Three hundred protesters, myself included, were arrested in two days at the Sheraton-Palace.

After negotiations with the hotel industry came to a standstill, we had formed a picket line around the hotel. We selected the Sheraton as the site of the first picket lines because it was one of the largest hotels in town. We thought if the Sheraton capitulated, the rest would follow suit. Management responded to the picketing by obtaining a court injunction limiting the number of pickets and requiring that each stand twenty feet from the next. Anyone who has participated in a strike knows that such an injunction effectively neutralizes the effect of a picket line.

Our failure to comply brought a police order to disperse (which most of us never heard). When we didn't hear the order, the police moved in to make arrests. We sat down on the sidewalk and linked arms. As each of us was arrested, we went limp in the nonviolent tradition of the civil rights actions in the South. We were half dragged, half carried into the waiting paddy wagons.

The women were placed in a large holding cell in the San Francisco Hall of Justice on Bryant Street. A raucous, jubilant crowd of teenagers singing freedom songs, we were released on our own recognizance within hours. Our attorney was a very young African American named Willie Brown, who was soon to be elected to the California State Assembly and later to become mayor of San Francisco. The charges against us were eventually dropped, although others, arrested after us, were tried and some were convicted.

The protests escalated, and the week after I was arrested we moved the protest into the hotel lobby itself, snaking our picket line along the plush carpets and giggling at the astonished faces of high-paying guests. Even with arrests at the hotel entrances, the lobby remained clogged with students. Business was seriously affected. Within days of our move into the hotel, management capitulated. They signed an industry-wide agreement, specifying goals for minority hiring in every job classification. The Ad Hoc Committee then turned its attention to San Francisco's Auto Row, and selected the Cadillac dealership because of its symbolic value. Again, there were sit-ins and mass arrests. The auto industry quickly negotiated a settlement using the formula worked out by the hotels. Although I was excited by our success, I was too exhausted to truly appreciate what we had accomplished.

By the middle of the Auto Row protests my energy was spent. Emotionally and physically exhausted from the political protest and the turmoil with Max and the FBI, I turned my attention back to school, relieved to sink into eighteenth-century British history and cultural anthropology. One Friday night at the Martins' for dinner, I felt extremely ill. Evelyn took a good look at me after dinner and drove me directly to the student hospital on campus. I was burning with fever, and my eyes were bloodshot and glazed. I was admitted that night. The next day I was diagnosed with a severe case of mononucleosis. My spleen and liver were badly swollen. I was hospitalized for about two weeks. My memory is of cool white sheets, regular food, and sunlight streaming through the windows of my room. It was immensely peaceful. Even though he had broken up with me a few months before, Jack came to visit bearing a single red rose.

I finished two classes that semester, and only because of my professors' and TAs' generosity in extending their deadlines for papers and allowing me to take make-up exams. I emerged from my bed cautiously in May, smelling the burst of spring flowers. In June I went home to Brooklyn to visit my parents. A few days after my arrival, word came from Mississippi that civil rights workers James Chaney, Andrew Goodman, and Michael Schwerner were missing. I took the subway into Manhattan and joined the picket line at the Federal Building in Foley Square. Already in mourning, our line was somber. Their bodies had not yet been found, but we knew that Chaney, Goodman, and Schwerner were dead. Still, we demanded federal protection for hundreds of others organizing in the South as part of the Student Nonviolent Coordinating Committee's (SNCC) Freedom Summer project.

The civil rights movement in the South was at the heart of the energy that infused the Berkeley campus and inspired the Free Speech Movement in the fall of 1964. Scores of white students from the North joined their black counterparts in the South in the massive voter registration drive for which Chaney, Goodman, and Schwerner had given their lives. African Americans had been systematically denied the right to vote in Mississippi (and the rest of the South) since the end of Reconstruction. The SNCC-led campaign intended to break the back of the segregationist politics within the Democratic Party in Mississippi, and send an integrated delegation to its national convention in August.

Thwarted by Klan terror, the indifference or hostility of voter registrars in local townships, and the failure of the federal government to provide either physical safety or constitutional authority, SNCC changed its tactics. They focused instead on building the Mississippi Freedom Democratic Party (MFDP). More than sixty thousand people were registered under its auspices, following precisely the legal mandates of official voter registration. The overwhelming majority were black, but there were some whites among them. The MFDP held its own primary, and elected an interracial delegation to challenge the credentials of the all-white Mississippi regulars at the Democratic convention in Atlantic City, New Jersey. The MFDP challenge was defeated. Vice presidential nominee Hubert Humphrey offered a compromise in an effort to save his party's face. Two members of the MFDP delegation could be seated on the convention floor but would not be allowed to vote. He failed to see the terrible irony of such a proposal and, of course, the MFDP delegates rejected it.

The inspiration for the MFDP was a sharecropper from Ruleville, Mississippi, who in 1962 was the first African American to register to vote in the state. For this she was arrested and very nearly beaten to death. Her name was Fannie Lou Hamer. As an MFDP delegate faced with Hubert Humphrey's compromise in Atlantic City, she said, "We didn't come all this way for no two seats, 'cause all of us is tired."

Mrs. Hamer was a short, rotund woman with a dark, freckled complexion and jet black hair cut short and straight. Her head appeared to sit almost directly on her shoulders. She had a powerful voice, and her signature song was "This Little Light of Mine." She sang it outside the convention center after Humphrey's compromise had been rejected. Nobody who heard Mrs. Hamer sing it ever doubted for a moment that her light would, indeed, shine all over Mississippi.

Mrs. Hamer's speech at the Democratic Party National Convention, broadcast on national television, stands as one of the most dramatic moments of the decade. "I question America," was her repeated refrain. "Is this America, the land of the free and the home of the brave, where we have to sleep with our telephones off the hooks because our lives be threatened daily because we want to live as decent human beings?" The MFDP may have failed in its immediate challenge, but it changed the course of Southern politics. Within a few years, tens of thousands of African Americans had registered to vote, and black sheriffs, city aldermen, state legislators, and congressmen were elected to office. Mrs. Hamer was the first woman I'd ever seen giving a speech on national television. We all knew how badly she had been beaten. What struck me most about her was her courage to transcend what I imagined must have been her personal fears, to rise above herself, as it were.

Returning to school in September 1964, in the wake of Mississippi and a year after the March on Washington, many of us felt as though we stood on the threshold of a new epoch in history. In California that fall, two political efforts loomed foremost on the horizon. The first was the campaign to defeat Barry Goldwater, the Republican Party's presidential candidate, who represented the extreme right wing of the party. The second was the fight against Proposition 14 on the California ballot for the same November election. In 1962, under the sponsorship of Byron Rumford, then one of the only black representatives in the California legislature, a fair housing act had been passed, prohibiting racial discrimination in rentals and sales. Proposition 14, if passed, would have repealed the Rumford Fair Housing Act.

The Board of Regents of the University of California had instituted a ban on all political activity on its campuses in 1949, coincident with the enforcement of the loyalty oaths required of all university staff and faculty. The oath stated that the signer was not now and had never been a member of the Communist Party, or of any other organizations that sought to overthrow the government by force or violence. Attached to the oath was a list prepared by the U.S. attorney general's office of organizations that were considered "subversive." It began with the American Civil Liberties Union.

A bitter fight over the oath had ensued, and several prominent professors were fired when they refused to sign it. A few years before my arrival in Berkeley, Clark Kerr had been installed by the regents as the new university president. Politically, Kerr was a right-of-center liberal Democrat, with extensive training in industrial management and labor relations. He had been chancellor of the Berkeley campus since 1952, and although he had signed the loyalty oath himself, he opposed the firing of faculty who had refused to sign it. When he was appointed president of the university, many faculty hoped that this would mark a lessening of political tensions and a healing of old wounds. Under Kerr's initiative, several professors fired in the 1950s were, in fact, reinstated amidst an aura of honor and solicitude.

As the political activism of the 1960s gradually engaged students at Berkeley, the old 1950s ban on politics was still enforced on the campus. However, a strip of sidewalk at the main entrance to the university on Bancroft Way and Telegraph Avenue served as the site of many political rallies. Students also set up tables in front of the kiosks at the Bancroft entrance to the university, where they distributed literature and solicited funds. Permits for the tables were routinely issued by the Berkeley Police Department, which sought only to regulate the unimpeded flow of pedestrian traffic. Everyone assumed that this gateway to the university was the property of the City of Berkeley. As classes resumed in that politically auspicious fall semester of 1964, however, Dean of Students Katherine Towle, acting on orders from higher authorities, announced that this small strip of red brick sidewalk belonged to the regents. The ban on political activity had now been extended to the street.

The student response was swift and dramatic. All of the civil rights organizations, the political parties, the New Left, and the socialist groups arose en masse. We planted our tables on the contested turf and continued our now-illegitimate solicitations and distributions. As the person in charge of the Du Bois Club table, I was immediately launched into the center of the controversy. Large numbers of curious students gathered, many of whom had previously only glanced at our tables en route to classes. Around noon one day at the beginning of the school year in mid-September, school officials appeared and began to issue citations for disciplinary action to those students seated at their respective tables. But as soon as one student was cited, another took his or her place. I never understood why the administration so favored the noon hour for the enforcement of its regulations. It signaled the lunch hour, when thousands of students, staff, and faculty descended on the main plaza in droves. Within two hours the bewildered deans had cited hundreds. They finally retreated into their administrative offices at Sproul Hall.

To contest the university regulations we formed a group we dubbed the "United Front." From the beginning it spanned the political spectrum, from the Young Republicans to the Young Socialist Alliance (YSA) to Friends of SNCC, CORE, SDS (Students for a Democratic Society), and the Du Bois Club. Everyone was concerned about the November elections and eager to reach some reasonable denouement with the administration so that the real work of partisan electoral campaigning could begin. The regents didn't understand the fuss. They were, after all, merely enforcing their long-standing regulations. What they failed to understand until it was much too late was that the status quo had changed irrevocably because of the impact the civil rights movement was having on the country.

In the swirl of this activity I was euphoric. At the United Front meetings, which I attended as a representative of the Du Bois Clubs, I listened, riveted to the unfolding drama. Our first direct action was a sit-in at Sproul Hall, the university's administration building, on September 30 beginning at 3 PM, when students cited by the deans were supposed to have met with the chancellor. Scores of us occupied the first and second floors, singing the anthems of the civil rights movement. We ended the occupation at 3 AM, when it was clear the disciplinary action appeared to be unlikely. It was during this time that I first encountered Mario Savio, who would be heralded by the press as the leader of our burgeoning movement. Mario had been in Mississippi that summer, just after Chaney, Goodman, and Schwerner had been murdered. He was determined to see a more enlightened policy for freedom of speech on the part of the university, especially because that speech was connected to advocacy for civil rights.

Mario was intense and passionate. A junior, majoring in philosophy, he made a forceful argument that night: If we objected to regulations that apparently contravened First Amendment guarantees of freedom of assembly and speech on the campus, then why settle only for the Bancroft strip? Why not move our tables to the very center of Sproul Hall Plaza in more obvious defiance of those regulations and demand their complete revocation? Although some in the United Front initially objected to this escalation in tactics, Mario's commitment to change, coupled with the sheer force of his argument, won the day. I believed in him from the beginning and couldn't wait to implement our decision.

We prepared a leaflet, explaining our intention to set up our tables in Sproul Plaza and declaring that constitutional authority guaranteeing freedom of speech trumped university regulations. Thousands were printed and distributed all over the campus. The next morning we set up our tables in front of Sproul Hall. At noon, the campus police appeared and drove a car into the center of the plaza. The administration, escalating their tactics in response to ours, had decided upon police rather than the dean's authority to enforce their regulations. Two officers approached the table of the Congress of Racial Equality (CORE) and placed Jack Weinberg, who was seated at it, under arrest. Jack was a graduate student in mathematics who was then on leave from Cal to devote himself full time to the civil rights movement in the South. He also had just come back from Mississippi. Good-naturedly, almost jauntily, Jack accompanied the arresting officers to the waiting car. The two officers climbed into the front seat. By now, of course, a huge crowd had gathered on the plaza. I was just to the side of the front fender on the driver's side of the car when I heard someone shout, "Sit down!" Immediately the whole crowd took up the chant, "Sit down! Sit down!" Within seconds we were seated on the ground surrounding the car. I heard the engine start almost at the same moment as the chanting, and I saw the officer's face as he peered out his windshield, saw the size of the crowd, and grasped the situation. He pushed his cap back off his forehead so that it seemed to stand on end, and slowly shut off the ignition. Warily, he reached for his car radio and called in. I started laughing, roaring with laughter. The plaza was electrified as the import of our confrontation with police authority became apparent to us.

We ended up holding the car in the plaza for thirty-six hours, with Jack locked inside of it. With hundreds of us surrounding the car so that it could not be moved, an impromptu rally began. We used the roof of the car as our speaker's platform. I wanted to speak from the top of the car, and I knew that I would be welcomed by the young men helping students up and down from the roof. I paced back and forth as evening descended, rehearsing in my mind what I would say and summoning the courage to get up there.

I had so much I wanted to say about HUAC and loyalty oaths, about the persecution of Communists, about the civil rights movement and freedom of speech. Finally, I took my shoes off and climbed atop the car. (We all took off our shoes to minimize the damage to the roof!) The lights from the television crews blinded me and my knees were quaking. I could not see the people in the crowd, but I could feel their energy. I went through the points I had rehearsed, and then I quoted a line from Frederick Douglass: "Power concedes nothing without a demand." A bellow of approval rolled across the plaza. In that moment the crowd's energy surged through me like an electric current. The tension in my legs disappeared. I felt suddenly grounded, strong, uplifted, and so moved I thought I would weep. At the end of my speech, willing hands reached up to help me down from the car and then turned into congratulatory handshakes and slaps on the back. The next day I was over at San Francisco State for a noon rally they had organized to support us. When I spoke I experienced the same sense of strength and a deep well of happiness.

During those first hours around the police car some students went home and returned with blankets, food, water, and hot drinks, and with this we settled in for the night. Our numbers shrank in the predawn hours, and the police made several attempts to whisk Jack away, but each was prevented by those of us who were left, waking ourselves and bunching up close to the car, surrounding it once again. By morning, University President Clark Kerr was in charge of coping with the situation. He had called the governor, Edmund G. Brown, who had ordered nine hundred police in full riot gear to assemble near the Berkeley campus, with orders to disperse the demonstrators by seven o'clock that night. In the meantime, Kerr agreed to meet with student representatives from among our group, in an attempt to negotiate a settlement.

By six that evening the negotiations were still in progress. Our numbers had swelled to at least a thousand, with hundreds of onlookers standing around us on the plaza. Floodlights from the television crews lit the scene. From the top of the police car the speeches continued, this time by experienced civil rights activists and attorneys who instructed us in nonviolent tactics and our rights when arrested. We could see the police lined up along Bancroft Way, at the entrance to the campus, their face visors still resting atop their heads, clubs at the ready. I could feel tension in the crowd as the time drew near for the police to break up our standoff. At two minutes to seven, Mario was sighted racing toward the plaza, a piece of paper in his hand. He took off his shoes hastily and climbed on top of the police car. His face drawn and exhausted, he announced, "We have reached a tentative agreement with the administration." Cheers went through the crowd. He went on to say he believed it was the best settlement we could hope for. There were three primary provisions: first, that Jack Weinberg was to be booked and released on his own recognizance, and the university would not press charges against him; second, that a disciplinary committee from the faculty academic senate would try the cases of the hundreds of students cited earlier for sitting at "illegal" tables (this placed the discipline out of the administration's control); and third, that a committee consisting of administration, faculty, and students, *including representatives from among the demonstrators* (Mario emphasized this; it had been a key point in the negotiations), was to meet and negotiate a settlement of the contested regulations. In addition, the university agreed to take no disciplinary action against us for seizing the police car. The administration had granted significant concessions, obviously preferring a peaceful ending to the standoff. From atop the police car, Mario continued, "Let us agree by acclamation to accept this document. I ask you to rise quietly and with dignity and go home." After thirty-six hours, we were only too happy to agree. But most of us didn't go home. Instead, we went to the Joan Baez concert that had been scheduled weeks before at the open-air Greek Theater on campus. Renowned for her civil rights partisanship and pacifism, Baez led our triumphant forces in one song after another, our voices soaring into the night. It was an extraordinary closure to the almost unbelievable overture that had launched the Free Speech Movement (FSM). Its official name was proposed by Jack Weinberg and adopted by the United Front at marathon meetings that weekend.

For me, that thirty-six-hour siege marked a critical moment in my life. I gave my first speech from the roof of that police car. I had a deep sense of satisfaction, a happiness I had never known before. Even as the police gathered for their intended assault I remained euphoric. I had a sense of belonging to something, being on the inside of a community of my own making, on my own terms.

Over the weekend, Clark Kerr held a press conference and the *San Francisco Examiner* reported that he had announced that 49 percent of the demonstrators in Sproul Plaza during the siege had been Communists or Communist sympathizers, a ridiculous calculation if ever there was one. (Years later, in a meeting with Clark

Kerr, I learned he had never made such a statement. He attributed the calculation to the purposeful inaccuracy of the *Examiner*, a newspaper owned by Randolph Hearst. At the time, of course, we had no way of knowing that.) As the one actual Communist in the FSM inner circle, I remained silent during the discussion of Kerr's statement. Everyone knew that I was a member of the party. I thought that perhaps it would be best if I took a less conspicuous position in the movement. These thoughts were interrupted by Mario. Slapping his knee with glee, he said, "I've got it! Bettina should speak at the noon rally on Monday!"

It was typical of Mario's tactical humor to fling the one real Communist defiantly into the administration's lap. Michael Rossman, a graduate student in mathematics, laughed raucously, and Jack Weinberg twittered as he deftly curled a piece of his hair, a habit when he was thinking. And so my public role in the Free Speech Movement began. As the drama of the movement intensified, I was catapulted onto national television, into *The New York Times,* and even onto the pages of *Time* magazine. The local press, hungry for news or scandal, insinuated that Mario and I were lovers, and the right-wing news sheet *Tocsin*, published in Berkeley, portrayed me as the evil woman (read also Jew) who had manipulated and plied the fair-haired Mario with sexual favors. In fact, Mario and I were never lovers. We did have a wonderful friendship. For me it was one of the best, most rewarding, and closest friendships I had ever had.

Mario's strength as a student leader was his absolute and transparent integrity. He never wavered from the bedrock principle of freedom of speech. He was never beholden to any political party or ideology; he spoke only from his own conscience. He believed in the intelligence and goodwill of his fellow students, and most important, he was not interested in personal power. I had never seen anything like this in my short political experience because in the party, my comrades were often preoccupied with the "main line" of a report and with a preset ideology. As a friend, Mario was funny, sympathetic, emotionally available, passionately intelligent, endlessly curious. Above all else, he treated me as an equal, not because I was "Aptheker's daughter" (which meant nothing to him), but because he valued me as a human being.

Marathon sessions of the FSM executive committee lasted late into the night. We operated by a consensus process, along the lines of a Quaker meeting. Proposals were made. Opposition, if any, was heard at length. If objections could be incorporated by modifying proposals, they were. Such a participatory process took an inordinate amount of time, but it also encouraged a confidence and trust in each other. Much of how we did things was modeled after the meetings Mario, Jack, and others had attended in Mississippi that summer. This form of participatory democracy contrasted greatly with the centralized structure and hierarchy of the Communist Party.

Mario was often in front of a typewriter, pecking out a leaflet he and I had likely drafted late into the night. I peered over his shoulder as he typed. David Goines, who worked in a local print shop to help pay his way through school, took the final version and disappeared into the predawn light. By 8 AM he had run off thousands of leaflets and delivered them to the student union building, ready for distribution. Using these low-tech, grassroots organizing tactics, the FSM organized thousands of supporters. Eventually, Mario's apartment turned into "FSM Central," where the steering committee met and two women, Marilyn Noble and Kitty Piper, organized us, manning the phones, providing food, preparing mailings to solicit support and money, and in general taking on the thousand and one tasks necessary to sustain a movement of this magnitude. Gretchen Kittredge organized a financial center and became the FSM treasurer. Myra Jehlen, a graduate student in the English department, was in charge of "strike central." Of course, nobody was hired and nobody was paid.

Women staffed all of these essential positions and were key to the movement; however, the sexism in the organization and leadership of the FSM was pervasive and unquestioned, especially in 1964. Scores of women were cited by the deans for sitting at "illegal" tables, and hundreds would later be arrested. Three women sat on the steering committee, and three would later participate on the negotiating committee. Yet men still dominated the meetings. They did most of the talking, responded to each other, and frequently ignored the comments a woman might have managed to insert in the discussion. The Quaker-style participatory process worked—for men only. Though I, too, was often ignored, I still considered myself one of the boys and was perceived that way by many of the men, who treated me as a friend and a buddy. I was never pursued by men in the FSM, though many women were, to which I confess I was oblivious at the time. I noticed the sexism in meetings, although I had no word for it. In fact, I blamed women for their reticence to speak! In short, I was as sexist as the men. I exercised a privilege of speech in meetings and at rallies that the men had sanctioned, not as an act of equality between the sexes, but as an act of political defiance against the administration. (Twenty years later, on the occasion of a very large public anniversary celebration, I apologized for this.) Likewise, Cal was at that time an almost exclusively white, racially segregated institution and our movement reflected those demographics. One Japanese American woman, Patty Iiyama, was a member of our executive committee. Otherwise, we were all white.

After the October 2 agreement that had ended our seizure of the police car, a negotiating committee was quickly established with administrative, faculty, student government, and FSM representatives. Mario, Suzanne Goldberg, a graduate student in philosophy, Syd Stapleton, a member of the Trotskyite Young Socialist Alliance (YSA), and I were elected as the FSM representatives. By the end of October, the administration had agreed to lift its ban on political activity. Rallies could be held on campus, leaflets distributed, funds solicited. This seemed to be a major breakthrough. But there was one subtle but crucial caveat.

The administration maintained its right to take disciplinary action against a student if he or she advocated participation in a protest demonstration that resulted in arrests. In the context of the civil rights movement, in which nonviolent civil disobedience was our major tactic, this provision effectively allowed the administration to prevent advocacy of and mobilization for civil rights. This, of course, was unacceptable to us. The FSM maintained that the administration could regulate only "the time, place, and manner" of speech, not its content. We maintained that freedom of speech *on* campus should be as fully protected by the Constitution as it was *off* campus. The administration would not yield this point, and negotiations came to a standstill.

Meanwhile, we learned that the faculty committee that was supposed to process the disciplinary hearings against students from the September protests did not in fact exist. We were not only angry at the administration's duplicity, but also frustrated by our own ignorance of university committees and procedures. Not wanting to get tangled in an endless bureaucratic mire, FSM no longer recognized the validity of the October 2 agreement. Early in November, student organization tables sprouted again on Sproul Hall

Plaza. Deans reappeared to take the names of students in violation of university regulations. It rained heavily and our spirits sagged. It seemed impossible to keep the momentum going as midterm examinations loomed and the administration, under the auspices of two political science professors, made an effort to split the internal ranks of the FSM by wresting control of it from those of us who were seen as "the radicals." The effort failed.

On November 10, the regents were scheduled to hold their monthly meeting in Berkeley. We had organized a day of protest. It began with a noon rally on the steps in front of Sproul Hall and continued with a march through the campus to University Hall at the west entrance, where the regents' session was in progress. Five thousand students participated. A well-known photograph of that moment shows Mario in the lead as he walked through Sather Gate, the landmark entrance to the campus, flanked by Mona Hutchins, a prominent conservative on campus. and Ron Anastasi, who identified himself as an independent. An American flag is visible in the crowd. We look so conservative by modern standards, the women in skirts, hair carefully groomed, the men with ties and crew cuts, freshly shaved, all of us glowing with confidence. Until that march we had not realized how many students supported the Free Speech Movement.

Three days later we began another sit-in in Sproul Hall in an effort to sustain the momentum of our previous success. We received word that unless we cleared the building by 5 PM, arrests would be made. Out of the thousands we knew to support the principles of the FSM, fewer than two hundred sat in. Meeting in the women's restroom on the second floor of Sproul Hall, the steering committee debated whether or not to end the protest by 5 PM. Stressed and exhausted by weeks of protest, frustrated by the nonresponse of the regents at their meeting, we were seriously split for the first time. In the end, the vote was six to five to vacate the building. There had been no time to work through to a consensus. Profoundly distressed because he felt the decision to be wrong, Mario left Sproul Hall, saying that he could not implement a decision with which he disagreed. I mounted a desk in the main rotunda of the building to address the students. After a long discussion, we all agreed to leave. From this incident, ironically, I enjoyed a reputation in the administration as "the moderate" within the FSM leadership.

Our Communist Party club met regularly as the drama of the Free Speech Movement unfolded. In the beginning, many older members eschewed the significance of the movement in the face of the coming presidential elections, and disputed the advisability of tactics that escalated the conflict. Some also felt unsure about the stability and political acumen of the FSM leadership, particularly because we were all so young. Mario and Jack may have come out of the cauldron of a Mississippi summer, but they had no ideological commitments or Marxist training, or so the argument went. These meetings were very difficult for me because I was already so emotionally invested in the FSM.

By the middle of October, however, people's doubts were erased by the sweep of events. The police car seizure had been international news, and thousands of students were now engaged in the movement. On campus, everyone in the club pitched in to organize support among the students and help with all of the movement's needs. Meanwhile, Max wanted to act as a sort of "special advisor," in his capacity as chair of the Communist Party of Northern California. He and I met regularly and surreptitiously—"or security reasons," as Max put it. The abuse had ended by then. Max and I met in the bleachers of a deserted ballpark in Oakland. He insisted on this location, although it seemed to me that we stood out to an absurd degree. He expressed none of the doubts and hesitations of those in my party club. He said nothing about recruiting or advancing the party. Instead, he urged strategies that would build and sustain the broadest possible support for the FSM, both on and off campus. What he emphasized to me was how much power the regents, the governor, and the police had, and how much support we would need to defeat them.

The day after Thanksgiving, four FSM students received letters from the UC administration requiring them to appear for disciplinary hearings. These students—Art and Jackie Goldberg, a brother and sister, Sandor Fuchs, and Brian Turner—were among those who had led the initial protests in September. I had particular respect for Jackie, who because of her devotion to FSM had been expelled from her sorority, which was traditionally a stronghold of the most conservative politics. The FSM executive and steering committees had no doubt that these initial indictments against the four student leaders were just the opening salvo in an administrative offensive intended to crush us. We countered that unless these charges were dropped and the regulations limiting freedom of speech were altered by Wednesday, December 2, at noon, we would occupy Sproul Hall.

In the seventy-two hours preceding our intended action, none of us on the steering committee slept more than a few hours. FSM Central—Mario's apartment—was bedlam. We flooded the campus with leaflets, arranged sound equipment for Wednesday's noon rally, and planned the sit-in in exquisite detail with floor-by-floor assignments. There were to be classes in history, literature, and philosophy, patterned after the freedom schools of the South, film screenings of Charlie Chaplin classics, and even a Chanukah service in the basement of the administration building. We trained monitors in nonviolence and gave them specific areas of responsibility. We contacted attorneys to witness arrests if any should be made. We asked faculty members to witness the sit-in and prepare a resolution in support of the FSM principles for the next meeting of the academic senate. And the Graduate Students Association planned a strike of teaching and research assistants to begin on Monday, December 7. We knew that if the strike was even partially successful it would paralyze the campus.

Amidst these preparations, Mario and I left Berkeley on Monday morning and drove south to Carmel. In a small café in what was then still a quaint artist's community at the southern tip of Monterey Bay, we met a man named Ira Sandperl. He was a pacifist, a nonviolent activist/philosopher who was Joan Baez's principal teacher and mentor. Mario and I had driven down the coast in hopes that Joan would come to Berkeley and sing at the rally to precede the occupation of Sproul Hall. Ira had arranged for us to see Joan, and was to lead us out the Carmel Valley Road to her home. Ira was in his fifties, a gentle, joyous man, special in a way I'd never before experienced. He had what I would today understand to be a spiritual practice, and this made him very different from anyone I had ever met.

Joan lived in a remote valley off the Carmel Valley Road, surrounded by the misted, often fog-covered mountains of the Big Sur coast, then green and lush from the winter rains. Joan was only a year or so older than we were. I thought of her as much older because her career was already so well established. Her main concern that day was to confirm our absolute commitment to nonviolence, no matter what the provocations of the police. We assured her that this was certainly our intention. Several hours later, Mario and I drove back to the Bay Area uplifted by the knowledge that Joan Baez would be with us in Sproul Hall Plaza that Wednesday. When Joan arrived in Berkeley a few days later she was nervous, not about the protest or the possibility of arrest, but about her performance. I took her into the women's restroom on the second floor of Sproul Hall, the building we were very soon to occupy. I reassured her while she straightened her black tights and combed her hair. We laughed and talked, two schoolgirls waiting for classes to begin, except our class was to be the FSM rally.

By noon, Wednesday, December 2, police conservatively estimated that five thousand people were in Sproul Hall Plaza. It seemed like many more to me. Mario's voice crackled like an electric current through the crowd in a speech that was to become the hallmark of the Free Speech Movement. He said, in the words most often quoted:

> There comes a time when the operation of a machine becomes so odious, makes you so sick at heart, that you cannot take part, you cannot even tacitly take part. And you've got to put your body upon the gears, upon the levers, upon the wheels, upon all the apparatus, and you've got to make it stop. And you've got to indicate to the people who run it, to the people who own it, that unless you are free that machine will be prevented from operating at all.

Joan Baez sang "Blowin' in the Wind." As the sound of her voice swelled into the plaza, more than a thousand students walked into Sproul Hall. We occupied every corridor from the basement to the fourth floor. We sat on the floors up against the walls, leaving room for foot traffic and access to offices. The steering committee remained on the second floor so that we could meet as needed. Joan and Ira sat with us for many hours.

At one point during the evening, Mario and I toured the building. Classes were in session, films in progress. We saw people studying and others clustered in tight groups talking earnestly. Up on the fourth floor I smelled something peculiar. "What's that?" I asked Mario, trying to place the sweet odor of wet grass. "Oh, it's nothing," he said laughing, taking my arm and leading us back down the stairs. Later he told me, of course, laughing at my naiveté about marijuana. He said he'd asked people to stop smoking it and to throw the stuff away lest it become an issue should we be arrested.

At about 2 AM the chancellor of the Berkeley campus, Edward Strong, a former professor of philosophy, flanked by campus police officers, spoke to us. A tall, white-haired man, his shoulders stooped with fatigue, he stood at the entrance to the dean of students' office on the second floor. His face was a ghostly white in the fluorescent lighting, his eyes red-rimmed. His hands shook as he read from a prepared statement. It was an official order to disperse, issued by the governor over the objections (we learned later) of University President Clark Kerr. When Chancellor Strong got to the line that said, "The work of this university has been materially impaired," the demonstators roared their approval.

At 3 AM the arrests began. The police started on the fourth floor and moved systematically floor by floor until the building was cleared. It took them twelve hours. There were 773 arrests, about one-third of them women. It was the largest peacetime arrest in the history of the United States up until that time. The campus and Berkeley police were assisted by the Alameda County sheriff's department and the California Highway Patrol. Each of us had our photograph taken, with a number printed in bold black letters held below our chins by the arresting officer. Then the student/prisoner was either dragged down the stairs or hauled into an elevator and brought to the basement. Here we were searched, placed in a holding area, and eventually driven in police wagons to holding cells in Oakland and Berkeley, where we were officially booked. From there, we were taken to what was called the Santa Rita Rehabilitation Center. It was the county jail, about thirty-five miles south of Berkeley.

Students maintained a remarkable discipline of nonviolence despite provocations, police violence, and selective beatings. My friend Decca's husband, Robert Treuhaft, a well-known civil rights attorney from Oakland, was inside the building to witness the arrests. This arrangement had been previously sanctioned by police authorities. To his and our outrage, Bob was himself arrested. Police taped over the windows in the basement of Sproul Hall so that press and spectators could no longer see into the building. And early Thursday morning a phalanx of club-wielding officers roared up the staircase to the second floor from the main floor rotunda. I saw them clubbing the seated students, who balled themselves up and used hands or books to protect their heads. The sound of shattering glass mingled with screams as police clubs smashed windows overlooking the plaza below. The attack stopped as suddenly as it had begun. I suspected, however, that it took place in retaliation for the roped descent from the front balcony to the plaza of Steve Weisman, leader of the Graduate Coordinating Committee and a member of our steering committee. We had agreed he should not be arrested in order to provide leadership for the impending strike. His rather dramatic descent had occurred about a half hour earlier in full view of the crowd in the plaza and was caught by the press in a well-known photo that captures the spirit of the protest.

I was arrested that morning, just after Steve's descent. I had been moving through the crowd, intending to talk to someone. Arrests on our floor had not yet begun. One officer yelled to another, "Grab her!"

As he did, I went limp and sat down. After being photographed, I was dragged by the arm down the corridor and deposited in front of the elevator. Its doors were open. A booted officer kicked me hard in the stomach. Doubled over, I crawled into the elevator. Removed to the basement, I walked out of the elevator still holding my stomach. I was met by more officers. Two, one on each side of me, held my arms straight out, twisting my skin in opposite directions, while a third pummeled me in the stomach and breasts with his fists. I yelled something like "Hey!" in a surprised protest and the assault stopped as quickly as it had started. I was then taken into a small room where I was searched by a female officer who ran her hands down and between my legs, and up under my sweater and over my breasts. Then I was taken to a holding area. Many other women were already in custody. Some time later, we were escorted to a police van. I was startled by the momentary warmth of the sun full on my face, and the sight of hundreds of onlookers cheering and waving to us. We were then driven to the Oakland jail.

I was very tired, no longer pumping adrenaline, nursing the bruises suffered during my arrest. My ribs in particular were very sore. An officer, blue uniformed, asked me my name, address, date of birth. It seemed a routine booking process. I cooperated fully, answering each question. Then he said, "Nationality?"

I said "American" automatically, without thinking about it. I felt his fury before I saw it.

He snarled, "You're not an American." And then he repeated his question. "What's your nationality?"

"American," I said again, now fully alert.

"You're not an American," he said again. "You're a goddamn Russian! You're a goddamn Russian Jew!" Then he repeated the question in a measured hiss, "Nationality?"

"American," I said again, evenly, carefully, pronouncing each syllable.

He struck me hard in the chest, hauled me back to my feet, repeated the question. "Nationality?"

"American," I said.

He struck me again. Hauled me back up.

I was set now in resistance, no longer aware of anything but my will against his. *American!* I thought to myself, anticipating the next blow.

Another officer came over. He took charge. Sent me back into the holding cell.

I was not denying my Jewish identity, but I was not about to own it on his terms, which would have forced me to deny my identity as an American and my rights as an American citizen. The intervention of another officer was fortunate because I had no plans to give in.

By that Thursday morning, the university was at a standstill. The graduate students were on strike in overwhelming numbers. Faculty cancelled their lectures. On some blackboards appeared emotional, hastily chalked messages: "I will not teach while police occupy the university." By Friday, picket lines were up at all the major academic buildings. A noon rally on Friday drew an estimated crowd of fifteen thousand. Joan Baez was back. Telegrams of support flowed in from all the major civil rights organizations in the country, including the Southern Christian Leadership Conference (SCLC) and its president, Martin Luther King, Jr. At least two state legislators, including Willie Brown, were on campus. The central labor councils in the San Francisco Bay Area sanctioned the graduate student strike. This halted deliveries to the campus as the Teamsters refused to cross the picket lines. And many janitorial, maintenance, grounds, and clerical workers remained at home.

Meanwhile, civil rights and civil liberties attorneys, including law professors from Boalt Hall, flocked to the jail to investigate the charges against us and arrange for our bail. Sympathetic faculty raised more than $80,000 in less than twenty-four hours. They paid the 10 percent bondsmen's fees to secure our release. Some even put up their homes as collateral, and others came to Santa Rita to drive us home as we were processed out. The line of cars stretched for two miles from the prison gates, according to a newscast we heard inside Santa Rita, which brought us to our feet cheering and hugging each other. One of my history professors, Kenneth Stampp, personally provided for my bail.

The women's section of Santa Rita was a dormitory-style facility with special solitary cells at the end of one corridor. The female sheriff's captain in charge of us was a heavy, middle-aged woman whose khaki uniform was too snug for her ample form, causing the skirt to hike up. She was constantly pulling it down as she marched up and down the halls, barking threats at us. She put two members of our group in solitary confinement for some imagined infraction, one of whom was steering committee member Suzanne Goldberg. We snuck down the corridor to provide our confined comrades company and solace. They were in total darkness and became increasingly apprehensive as the hours passed. We assured them we would not leave without them. Eventually, they were released on bail.

Segregated from the regular prison population, we roamed the dormitories awaiting our release. I walked out Friday morning at about seven o'clock, happily breathing the frosty dawn air. A car was waiting for me. I asked to be driven to the Martins'. Evelyn was home, Friday then being one of her days off from work. She fed me a huge breakfast as we pored over the morning papers, FSM news spread across every front page. Then I went upstairs into a guest bedroom and slept. I had intended to get to campus by noon, but I didn't wake up until late in the afternoon. Hastily I showered and dressed and made my way to the university.

It was after five when I got to campus, and it was almost deserted. It reminded me of a stadium just after a ball game—the litter of FSM leaflets fluttering on the ground like discarded wrappers and scorecards, the energy and heat of the crowd, the excitement still palpable. Picket signs rested against kiosks. The plaza itself seemed to still ring with the thousands who had gathered there. I went to FSM Central and found Jack Weinberg, who was sprawled on a couch, twirling his front curl, smiling happily. Our steering committee was reunited amidst jubilant hugs. We set about organizing for the following week.

Saturday, in the student union building, we held our first-ever press conference. Sweat glistened on Mario's face in the glare of the television lights as he patiently explained the issues and our plans to continue the strike and take other "appropriate action" until our demands for freedom of speech were met. We spent much of the weekend in meetings with faculty supporters. They were drafting a resolution for the academic senate meeting that was scheduled for Tuesday afternoon, December 8. Reggie Zelnik, history; Leon Wofsy, bacteriology; John Searle, philosophy; Jacobus ten Broek, speech communication; Jack Schaar and Sheldon Wolin, political science; Joseph Fontenrose, classics; Michele Loeve, mathematics—these professors were among our most trusted allies. It was the faculty who now clearly held the balance of power in determining the outcome of the struggle. We felt certain that a pro-FSM vote at the senate meeting would compel the regents to yield.

In an effort to regain control of the campus and ensure the faculty's support for the regents, University President Clark Kerr convened an extraordinary convocation for all students, faculty, and staff. It was to begin Monday, December 7, at 11 AM in the Greek Theater. Departmental meetings between key administrators and faculty were held just before, and a couple of hundred faculty members were to be seated onstage, marshaling presidential support, as it were.

Shortly before eleven, Mario and I made our way backstage at the Greek Theater, in search of Professor Robert A. Scalapino from the political science department. Known for his conservative politics and hostility to the FSM, Professor Scalapino was president of the academic senate. He was to chair the convocation. We could see that a large number of faculty were already seated on the stage. A podium stood ready, front and center. We had a single request. Mario asked for permission to make a brief announcement at the conclusion of the meeting, to the effect that the FSM would hold a responsive rally at Sproul Hall Plaza immediately following President Kerr's speech. Professor Scalapino denied permission. As we left him and exited across the stage to take our seats, the audience, just assembling, broke into applause as they recognized Mario.

Twenty thousand people filled the Greek Theater. Scores of reporters, television cameras, and crews crowded in front of the stage. Clark Kerr spoke. He called for a restoration of order. He called for faith in the ideas of freedom upon which the university was founded. Only with both order and freedom would the university endure. He promised more enlightened policies. He assured that no disciplinary action would be taken against those arrested. He said that the intended disciplinary action against the offending four from the late September protests would be dropped. On the substantive issue of advocacy that had occasioned the sit-in, he said the university could not and would not yield.

The speech ended. The meeting was adjourned. Many faculty had already left the stage; others were about to do so. The audience was gathering itself together, preparing to leave the theater. Mario mounted the steps to the stage and walked toward the microphone. Art Goldberg, Sandor Fuchs, and I accompanied him. His intention was to announce the FSM meeting, even though permission to do so had been denied.

Mario reached the podium. Before he could speak, however, campus police rushed out from backstage. One threw his arm around Mario's throat and dragged him off, while two others wrestled Art and Sandor to the stage floor. I alone remained standing, no doubt due to my gender. I faced the audience and called out, "Let him speak!" And the words roared back at me. Art and Sandor were let go, and the three of us took up the responsive call. Art, always worried about people's safety, extended his arms out in a placating gesture, palms down, and shouted, "Stay calm! Please stay calm!" Out of the corner of my eye I saw President Kerr. He was alone, stage center at the rear curtains through which Mario had just been swept. The text of his speech was still in his hand. His head down, he stared at his shoes. He must have known that in seizing Mario the police had made an irrevocable error in judgment.

The audience now abandoned any intention of leaving until Mario was released. On its feet, the crowd called, "Let him speak!" Moments later, Mario was released. He strode quickly to the podium. The power, which had been cut to the microphone, was restored. Mario said, "Let us leave this disastrous place. The FSM rally will follow immediately at Sproul Hall Plaza." Then he turned, grabbed my hand, and we raced down the steps and away.

More than twenty thousand people filled Sproul Hall Plaza. The crowd stretched north, south, and west as far as the eye could see. Even the roofs of the student union building on one side and the Golden Bear restaurant on the other were covered with students. Mario spoke, I spoke, Steve Weisman spoke, representatives of the faculty spoke. The strike was to continue. Until the issue of freedom of speech was settled, there could be no resolution of the conflict. Immediate hope lay in the faculty senate meeting. We urged everyone to come to Wheeler Hall the next afternoon. Students would not be admitted to the senate meeting, but we could stand in witness outside.

Monday night and Tuesday morning, FSM students met with faculty. The graduate students were particularly crucial in this effort because they knew their professors personally. Reggie Zelnik was the principal faculty organizer of the "radical 200" who had supported the FSM from the beginning. At twenty-eight, Reggie was a young professor just beginning his career in Berkeley's history department and he laid it on the line. The strike continued. At 3 PM on Tuesday, December 8, 1964, thousands of students stood quietly outside Wheeler Auditorium in the shadow of the old oak tree that had stood as a campus landmark for a century. Loudspeakers outside the building allowed us to listen to the debate. Over nine hundred faculty attended, making it the largest senate meeting in anyone's memory. A resolution supporting the FSM position on freedom of speech was introduced. It was seconded. Faculty spoke for and against, often obviously reading from prepared texts. It was an orderly and immensely moving process. I had never heard such a defense of political liberty, and I felt a sense of wonder at what our movement had apparently unleashed. Many of the speeches provided eloquent testimony to the transcendent wisdom of the freedoms embodied in the Bill of Rights.

Hours later the vote came. Professor Scalapino read the results: 824 in favor of the resolution, 115 opposed. Outside we began to clap. Moments later the faculty emerged through two sets of double doors, descending the steps of the hall, walking toward us. We parted ranks, forming an aisle through which they seemed now to formally march in a different kind of academic procession, past the rising crescendo of our applause. Many of us were crying, and so were many of them, these stolid, mature, often elderly, white men. At this moment many of us, faculty and students alike, understood that the days of the loyalty oaths and speakers' bans and anti-Communist witch hunts were finally over. Six days later, on December 14, 1964, the regents officially announced that henceforth their regulations governing freedom of speech and assembly "will not go beyond the purview of the First and Fourteenth Amendments to the U.S. Constitution." We had won. Within a year, university and college regulations all over the state and in much of the country had been changed to allow for a greater freedom of speech and advocacy.

After the regents' resolution we were exhausted and jubilant, euphoric, giddy with laughter. It was less than a week to Christmas break. Go home, we said to our fellow students. Explain the movement to your parents and relatives and friends. We produced small blue and white buttons that said FSM. Everyone seemed to be wearing one. A group of graduate students recorded FSM Christmas carols and sold the records to raise money to pay off our debts, primarily to the printer and the phone company. We also gave over a thousand dollars to the campus police department to pay for the damage to the roof of the police car all the way back in October. The lyrics on the graduate student record reflected the humor and politics of the

FSM. For instance, these lyrics were sung to the tune of Beethoven's
Ninth Symphony:

> From the tip of San Diego
> To the top of Berkeley's hills
> We have built a mighty factory
> To impart our social skills.
>
> Social engineering triumph
> Managers of every kind
> Let us all with drills and homework
> Manufacture human minds.
>
> Keep the students safe for knowledge
> Keep them loyal, keep them clean
> This is why we have a college
> Hail to IBM machine!

Mario, Suzanne Goldberg, and I flew to New York City courtesy of
ABC television. We used the cross-country airfare to stop at colleges
and universities in New York and New England and in the Midwest
on our return flights. Between us, singly and together, we spoke at
Columbia, Queens College, Harvard, and the Universities of Chicago,
Minnesota, and Wisconsin. Everywhere we were greeted with
standing ovations by hundreds and often thousands of students. It
was as though the FSM had broken the shackles of the body politic,
and a new generation shook off the fetters of the old. In New York I
saw my parents, their faces flung open with pride. I was the prodigal
daughter, returned home triumphant.

Back in my little cottage in Oakland, I buckled down to schoolwork.
I had managed to attend most of my classes throughout the fall

semester, taking copious notes. I now read book after book, completed one assignment after another, wrote paper after paper, and by the third week in January 1965, when the semester officially ended, I had managed a B average. Somehow, in the midst of studying, I also moved. The cottage where I lived was about to be torn down to make room for a new freeway. And sometime in the midst of moving, as I was standing in a pile of boxes in the new house Phyllis and I were to share, Jack Kurzweil arrived. He said, "Let's take up where we left off," referring to our prior months of dating. It was very abrupt; we had not been seeing each other. He offered no explanation for breaking up with me. Jack just burst out with it.

"Okay," I said, knowing already that I would marry him.

three

A WEDDING, A TRIAL, AND A WAR

THE FSM BROUGHT me out of personal crisis, allowed me to focus on the political exigencies of the moment. With Jack providing refuge, I felt more comfortable in myself. I had gained a modicum of self-confidence. But I still processed nothing of what I had been through with my father and with Max. I was still split in two, and I had suppressed my attraction to women deep, deep down and out of immediate consciousness. Instead, I piled the debris in a corner of mind and gut and turned my attention to our pending trial.

Arraigned before Berkeley Municipal Court Judge Rupert A. Crittenden, demonstrators at the Sproul Hall sit-in were charged with trespassing, disorderly conduct, and resisting arrest. We received the latter charge because we had gone limp and had to be carried out. We pleaded not guilty. Our trial began on April 1, 1965—no April Fool's for us. There were just fewer than eight hundred defendants. In order to accommodate our numbers, the trial was held in the auditorium of the Veterans Administration Building across the street from the Berkeley City Hall park. All defendants were required to be in court every day.

No reading or writing was permitted. This was a punitive action designed to cripple our ability to study. The trial lasted for six weeks.

Our first strategic problem was whether to have one trial, all of us together, or eighty separate ones. In the San Francisco civil rights cases the previous spring and summer, defendants had been split up and brought to trial in groups of ten. Some had been convicted and others acquitted, depending upon the sympathies of the jurors and the instructions of the trial judges. Based on this experience, most FSM defendants wanted to be tried together, in solidarity with one another. Our civil disobedience had no meaning except as a collective act. Moreover, the legal expenses of eighty separate trials were prohibitive.

Judge Crittenden ruled that we could be tried en masse, but only if we waived our right to a jury trial. He alone would hear the case, convict or acquit, and sentence us should we be convicted. With great reluctance, and only after all arguments to the contrary had been denied, did we agree to this provision. (A few defendants decided to opt out of the joint trial. In later jury trials, several won acquittals.)

In order to resolve this and other issues of trial strategy we held defendants' meetings to which everyone arrested was invited. Our attorneys laid out their ideas, and people responded. We adhered to the participatory process FSM had always used, and meetings went on for hours. Again our steering committee was most deeply involved in the day-to-day workings of the trial.

Although we pleaded not guilty to the charges against us, the FSM defense in no way denied our participation in the Sproul Hall sit-in. Our strategy was to argue the merits of the case. The prosecution began by laboriously detailing each arrest. One officer after another testified to having taken so-and-so into custody, the appropriate photograph and number entered into the record, its accuracy stipulated by the defense. The prosecution then called university administrators as witnesses to show that the "work of the university had been materially impaired." Best among them from the defense's point of view was Dean of Students Katherine Towle. In her early sixties, tall and thin, austere, with short gray hair, wire-rimmed glasses, and a military bearing (she was a retired army officer), Dean Towle accurately and precisely recounted our presence outside her office on the second floor of Sproul Hall. Asked by Prosecutor Jensen if we had disrupted her work, she said, "No." On cross-examination she described us as an orderly and disciplined crowd, and agreed with defense attorneys that we had left aisles in the corridors and at the entrance to her office. Chancellor Strong also appeared and affirmed his reading of the "lawful order" for us to disperse.

The defense strategy in the FSM trial was to show the sit-in as a justifiable act of civil disobedience in defense of constitutional principle. The technical legal term for this is to show "the state of mind" of the defendants. Ours was to be a two-pronged approach. First, we were to show our frustration with administrative ploys to undermine or suppress the movement despite our "good faith" negotiations. Second, we were to explain the substantive issues of freedom of speech. Despite the prosecution's objections that our "state of mind" was irrelevant and immaterial, Judge Crittenden allowed the defense. We were overjoyed because regardless of the outcome of the trial, it meant we had another opportunity for a public rendition of the issues. Several of us on the FSM steering committee testified, including Mario, Jack Weinberg, Michael Rossman, and me. Each of us was responsible for articulating a distinct aspect of our collective "state of mind."

The great danger in calling me as a witness was my membership in the Communist Party. This was not publicly known, nor was the relationship between the Communist Party and the Du Bois Club, which I had represented in the FSM. We knew that on cross-examination the prosecution would seek to establish this link. Once established, and my membership in the party acknowledged, I could be asked to name party members as had happened so often in HUAC and related congressional hearings. Of course, if I refused to answer these questions I could be held in contempt of court and imprisoned. My attorney, Henry Elson, intended to object to any such links the prosecution might try to make. We believed Judge Crittenden would sustain these objections as "irrelevant" to the present case, thus closing this avenue of interrogation.

I was on the witness stand for two and a half days. The direct examination went well. Edwin Meese (who was later Ronald Reagan's attorney general) conducted the cross-examination. He kept me on the stand for a day and a half. He began in exactly the manner attorney Henry Elson had feared, asking about my membership in the Communist Party. Henry objected. The judge sustained the objection. Then Meese tried to link the Du Bois Clubs to the party. Each question was followed by an objection from Henry. Each objection was sustained. Finally, Meese abandoned the effort. For the next hours he worked to impeach my testimony by asking me to repeat the sequence of events, places, and people, and by deliberately scrambling them. I corrected, repeated, reordered. At the end, Meese showed me a photograph of the sit-in and established that it had, indeed, been taken during the occupation of Sproul Hall.

"Are there any aisles visible in this photograph?"

"No," I said, looking over toward the defense counsel to catch Henry's eye, since I was about to violate his cardinal rule and elaborate on a response. Then I turned to the judge.

"May I explain, Your Honor?"

He nodded. When I turned back toward Meese, I caught sight of Henry. He was grinning.

"I was standing next to the police photographer when this picture was taken," I explained. "It was on the second floor, early Thursday morning. The police had just charged into the crowd. Everyone was bunched together then, but that was the reason."

Meese said, "I have no further questions."

FSM defendants roared their approval. The judge banged his gavel.

Attorney Norman Leonard prepared Mario to testify. Together they presented an often subtle and intricate analysis of the First Amendment, and the rights of freedom of speech and of association. Crucial to Mario's testimony was the idea that freedom of speech has little significance as an abstract philosophical concept. Speech is invested with meaning precisely when it results in action, precisely when it is connected to advocacy and to social movements, such as those for civil rights. Tolerance and protection of *this* speech is the crucial test of political liberty. It was intolerable, Mario concluded, that the university should have denied such protection.

Expanding on our "state of mind," about a dozen other defendants testified. Each was asked to explain his or her reasons for participating in the sit-in. As a final gesture of solidarity and appeal, all the defendants wrote personal letters to Judge Crittenden, setting down their thoughts and feelings about the FSM and the reasons they had joined the demonstration.

One wrote: "The world is perhaps not everything we would want it to be. And we live really only a very short time. Whatever we can do to make things better for our children and their children, I think we should do. Surely we must be free from fear; free from want; free to believe; free to act."

Another wrote: "In our high school civics and American History courses we learned that democracy is the finist [*sic*] political form, that it is the participation of people in political affaires [*sic*], and that the most important reason why we established public education was to raise the general level of education so that ordinary people could participate in democracy and make the decisions that affect their lives. We believed all this and thought it was good."

Still another asserted: "By restricting the political freedom of students to organize, solicit funds, and advocate political causes, the University loses sight of what education really is. As a member of the University community, I had an obligation to maintain these standards of education and to rebel against and negate the decisions of those who were turning the university into a human factory."

Another said: "I found the call [to sit-in] to be a call against injustice, arbitrariness, deceit and simple stupidity. I found the call to be a call for principle. . . . A choice so drawn leaves little room for debate, and on December 3 I sat in Sproul Hall with unreserved commitment to that principle."

During the course of the trial we held several rallies in support of FSM defendants in the municipal park across the street from the Veterans Administration Building. In an effort to sustain the political coalition that had made FSM a reality, we included the civil rights movement and the burgeoning movement against the escalating war in Vietnam on each rally's agenda. Each was also intended to keep the campus and community informed of the trial proceedings, to maximize public attention and support.

On one such occasion I was just beginning my speech when my soon-to-be-husband Jack Kurzweil hurried to my side. I bent over to hear his whispered confidence. FBI agent Donald Jones, who had come to my cottage on 51st Street more than a year ago, was present. He was on the periphery of the crowd, way in the back. As Jack took up a position next to him, I began my speech again and continued for a while. Then I said, "There's someone here in the crowd today I would like to introduce to you." An expectant hush, a turning of heads to see who it was. "His name is Donald Jones, and he is an FBI agent. He has been following me for more than a year." The crowd laughed, more heads turning, craning to see.

"There he is!" I called, as Jack pointed him out.

"Come up here, Mr. Jones! Come and speak to us! We believe in freedom of speech."

A chorus of two thousand took up the chant: "Speak! Speak! Speak!"

Donald Jones melted away from the crowd, but not before several photographs of him had been taken.

A few days later, I was walking up the long concrete steps that led into the Berkeley post office when I heard a voice shouting, "There she is! There she is! There's the Communist!" Startled, I looked around. I saw Donald Jones across the street, pointing an accusing finger. A woman I had never seen before put her arm around me and led me into the building. "Some men are just crazy," she said. "Are you all right?"

"Oh, yes," I said, grateful for her kindness. My initial adrenaline rush gave way then to giddy laughter. Later I heard that Donald Jones had been reassigned to San Francisco. I never doubted, though, that another agent had taken up his Berkeley beat.

On another occasion as I was leaving the court proceedings, I was met by a phalanx of reporters, microphones shoved under my face, cameras on me. I could not imagine what the uproar was about and could not distinguish one question from another in all the shouting. Finally, I understood. Mario Savio had announced his engagement to Suzanne Goldberg. How did I feel about that? Was I jealous? Outraged? Hurt? Suzanne was a graduate student in the philosophy department, a member of our steering committee, who had flown to New York the previous December with Mario and me. I saw at once, then, that the undercurrent of right-wing propaganda about Mario and me as lovers held considerable sway.

I smiled, radiating the genuine happiness I felt for both Suzanne and Mario. "Isn't it wonderful news?" I said. And added, "I have been engaged for several weeks now to Jack Kurzweil. We're going to be married this summer."

"Who's that?" they wanted to know in chorus, pens poised, flashing in the sunlight.

Judge Crittenden found us guilty on two out of the three counts against us. He dismissed the charge of disorderly conduct. Although I expected the verdict, I was disappointed. During the weeks of the trial I had grown to like Judge Crittenden. He presented the stereotypical image of a "most distinguished jurist." He was in his early sixties, hair white, face pleasantly round and lined, voice resonant. He bent over his magisterial desk, shoulders hunched in his black robes, often writing, alert to testimony and argument.

Verdict reached, court was adjourned for several weeks, during which we were summoned individually before Alameda County probation officers for interviews and appraisal. The recommendations of the probation officers were intended as a guide for sentencing. I have only a vague memory of Jackie Townsend, the officer assigned to me. I recall feeling embarrassed that Jack and I were already living together, "to save money," I hastily explained, this being contrary to the sexual mores I was raised with in the 1950s. The sexual revolution of the late 1960s and '70s had not yet begun.

Judge Crittenden pronounced sentences. Mario Savio, Jack Weinberg, Art Goldberg, and Michael Rossman were each to serve four months in the Alameda County jail, no fine, and two years' probation. Suzanne Goldberg and I were to serve six weeks in the Alameda County jail, no fine, and two years probation. As women, we got less jail time. All other defendants were sentenced to fines of between $100 and $200, and to one year's probation. None of us was required to report to probation officers. The provision for probation was a form of harassment intended to prevent us from committing further acts of civil disobedience in the prescribed period without incurring additional penalties for a prior offense.

Our attorneys filed an immediate appeal of the conviction, determined to exhaust every possible avenue of judicial review. We remained free on bail pending final adjudication of our case.

However much the trial had occupied our attention, campus politics continued to simmer in the aftermath of the Free Speech Movement. Foremost among these FSM-related events was the administrative establishment of a "rules committee" in the fall of 1965. Its purpose was to designate the "time, place, and manner" of speech on the campus, in accordance with university policy, which now allowed for a free range of speakers and programs. The administration appointed representatives from its own ranks and from the faculty. The student participants were to be elected in a general, campuswide election. I agreed to run as a highly visible representative of the FSM.

Campaigning was vigorous. I visited student dormitories and nearby student co-ops, and even a couple of sororities. Likewise,

I was invited to speak to student organizations, many but not all of which had been part of the FSM. I was impressed by the support of even the most conservative of students for free speech issues. Many expressed the feeling that freedom of speech was a hallmark of our democracy and felt pride in our country for affirming it.

Toward the end of the campaign I decided I wanted to make my membership in the Communist Party a matter of public record. Accused by so many in the media of being manipulative and secretive as a Communist, I wanted my political affiliations known. I was supported in this decision by the former members of the FSM steering committee, by the party leadership in our district, and by my party club, whose members on campus would be most affected by my action.

I wrote an open letter to my fellow Berkeley students, which, accompanied by a front-page story, appeared in the *Daily Californian,* the student newspaper, on Tuesday, November 9, 1965. It read, in part:

> It has been argued by some respectable and not so respectable people that I came to the University of California in the Fall of 1962 as part of an insidious Communist plot to corrupt the minds of my fellow students. . . .

> I am awed by the power I am alleged to have; but surely it must be clear that revolt is resultant from unjust and intolerable conditions. . . . And more specifically, the FSM revolt was made by the students on this campus. It would have occurred whether or not I was at Cal. FSM involved thousands of students. . . . Its power came from its Principle. And you made its Principle. . . .

> There has been speculation . . . as to whether or not I am a Communist. Due to the attempt to outlaw the Communist

Party it has been difficult to answer that question. I have, however, always affirmed that I am a Marxist and a socialist. . . .

I wish, however, to take this occasion to go further. I have been for a number of years, I am now, and I propose to remain a member of the Communist Party of the United States."

I won the election with the highest vote ever cast in a student election at Berkeley. All of the student representatives elected to the rules committee supported the principles of the FSM. The work of the committee was essentially pro forma. We negotiated our way through stipulations that prevented the disruption of academic and administrative work, while maximizing access to Sproul Hall Plaza and campus facilities in general. Literature could be freely distributed and student groups could set up tables to solicit funds and information, as long as they did not impede the flow of pedestrian traffic. The Communist speakers' ban and the rules prohibiting or circumscribing electoral speakers were rescinded. Likewise, it had been university policy to require an adversarial debate format with "both sides" represented in the case of a "controversial" speaker or issue. An administrative/faculty review committee had determined what was "controversial," effectively curtailing or preventing many programs. This requirement, too, was eliminated. The Berkeley regulations, or a facsimile of them, became the norm on all nine of the University of California campuses.

My open letter to the Berkeley students generated an enormous public response. It prompted the *San Francisco Examiner* to run the front-page banner headline "Bettina Admits It: She's a Red!" accompanied by a factual if somewhat sensationalized story and a flattering photograph. Although not as dramatic, accounts of my party membership ran in other Bay Area and national media. I was heralded as a kind of "folk heroine" in the Communist world. The Chilean poet Pablo Neruda, for example, a sometime journalist for the Soviet-run Novosti Press Agency, wrote of me as a "good looking and courageous girl," and described the election.

Shortly after the election, I flew back to New York to speak at a mass meeting publicly organized by the Communist Party. Hundreds of gray-haired comrades and a smattering of younger ones welcomed me with a standing ovation. I saw my former boyfriend Gregory, and my parents introduced me to all their friends who had seen me grow up.

Back home in Berkeley, I was deluged with mail. Well-known Bay Area figures, like ILWU president Harry Bridges, my friend and writer Decca Treuhaft (a.k.a. Jessica Mitford), Soviet analyst William Mandel, folksinger Malvina Reynolds, artist Emmy Lou Packard, my friends Vincent and Vivian Hallinan, and dozens more sent beautiful, warm letters of congratulations and support. A profoundly moving letter came to me from my English professor, Thomas Parkinson, on sabbatical in the south of France. Professor Parkinson had refused to sign the loyalty oath in the 1950s, and was the victim in 1961 of an attack by a crazed gunman who had put together a hit list of "Communist sympathizers" he intended to execute. Bursting into Professor Parkinson's office, he opened fire and killed the graduate student with whom Professor Parkinson was conferring. Tom was shot in the face and seriously wounded. He wrote, in part:

> My feeling about you, from knowing you as a student and, later, as a friend, is that you too are an aspirant toward the community of the just and that fundamentally we are in accord. But I hope that you will not find yourself embittered

either by the troubles that you will have from an ignorant and malicious public or from disappointment in the policies of the Communist Party. Bitterness creates nothing but blindness and the interests of justice are served only by those who can see.

Many warm and loving letters also came from strangers in the Bay Area and from all over the country. I answered as many of them as I could. I also received loving if despairing letters from Christians, with prayers for my conversion and redemption. These were frequently accompanied by small pamphlets, and occasionally a large package containing the Holy Bible. If these letters were signed I answered them with gratitude, reassurance—some way of saying I am not the stereotype you think I am.

More difficult, if fewer in number, were the hate letters. Some of these were unsigned, and all were filled with violence, often with explicit threats of rape. They were also almost always anti-Semitic.

Miss Dirt in the Backhouse

With a Face like yours its [sic] no wonder you hate the World as you do yourself. There's only one Place for you and that's Russia. And I don't think they would let you in. You and your Russian Jew Friends should be put on a Chinese Junk and set adrift in mid Atlantic. You and your Family are no good to yourselves or our Country. There's no place for your kind in the United States. So you and your kind should be thrown out of Berkeley.

I am a True 4th Generation American.

Thank you

More serious were the death threats. In the months following my open letter, there were many. Members of the American Nazi Party, in full uniform complete with swastikas, picketed the main entrance to the Berkeley campus with signs reading BURN APTHEKER. One death threat was received by the university president's office, which neglected to inform me. When I read about it in a newspaper gossip column, I went to see President Kerr, who confirmed the letter and gave me a copy. Other letters were sent to my home or to the university and forwarded to me. The one I took most seriously was on a card with pink trim. On the inside was the crosshair of a rifle sighting, with the date November 21, 1965. It was signed "The Minutemen." This was a right-wing paramilitary organization much in evidence in those years. The message said I would be killed on that date, which coincided with a very well publicized march against the war in Vietnam.

When I took this and other threats to the Berkeley police, they informed me that nothing could be done unless an actual attempt was made on my life. My auto insurance company cancelled my policy because I was a "Target Person," a category of public figure they didn't insure. On another occasion, when the ACLU of San Bernardino County in Southern California invited me to speak, a full-page advertisement shrouded in black borders appeared in the local paper denouncing me and the ACLU. The night before my appearance, rifle shots were fired into the public library where I was to speak. Although shaken by the vehemence of these threats, I felt not so much afraid as defiant. I never believed I would be assassinated. During the November 21 peace march through Berkeley to the army induction center in Oakland, I rode standing in the back of a pickup truck.

However, there was an attempt on my life in the spring of 1966. Driving home to Berkeley after a speaking engagement in San Jose, I noticed my gas gauge showing a rapid loss of fuel. Too rapid. I was by then driving a 1960 Volvo, having finally given up on the old Ford. I exited the freeway at the first opportunity and pulled into a gas station. The mechanic on duty inspected the engine. He showed me the frayed edges of a hose. A fuel line had been cut. He said I was very lucky not to have had a fire. The car was easily repaired, and I resumed my drive home. I did not bother with the police.

For a time, comrades thought I should be armed and they loaned me weapons. One was a .38 caliber automatic. It was of little use, however, because I did not have the physical strength to load the clip. I wouldn't let Jack do it for me because I didn't want a loaded gun in the house. Then someone else loaned me a .22 caliber pistol. It was easily loaded, one bullet at a time. I gave it back. I couldn't fathom shooting anyone. Jack owned an old 30-ought-6 rifle, and Bob Kaufman, a comrade, took me out to teach me how to shoot it. He strung a can or a bottle from a tree branch, showed me how to load the chamber and cock it. I did these things, aimed like he showed me, and squeezed the trigger. The force of the kickback into my shoulder knocked me down. The bullet, however, hit the string. Bob took me home, and Jack put the rifle away.

Jack and I had planned to be married in the summer of 1965. As part of the FBI shenanigans that had so marked my time in Berkeley, an envelope addressed to me arrived in the mail that summer before our scheduled departure for our New York wedding. It was a newspaper clipping, the relevant paragraphs circled in red pencil. The Mexican clinic where I had had the abortion two years before had been raided by the police and its files confiscated. It was a small clipping. Nothing else was in the envelope. There was no return address. *FBI,* I thought. I told Jack about the abortion. "Was it mine?" he asked.

"No," I said. He shrugged, sorry I had been hurt, resisting the urge to ask who the father was.

We drove across the country, reaching New York in three and a half days. I met Jack's parents, Rose and Sam, for the first time in their seventh-floor Brooklyn apartment in the Luna Park Co-ops, a few blocks from Coney Island. Friday night at the Kurzweils' was Shabbat dinner. It was done without the ritual of prayer, but with the assemblage of family: Rose's sisters and brother, and their respective spouses. Sam read his Yiddish-language newspaper in the living room while Rose bustled in the kitchen, calling out dinner preparations or random thoughts to everyone in general and no one in particular.

"Rose, Rose, calm down," Sam would shout from the living room, his large hands patting the air. His shoulders slightly stooped on his solid six-foot frame, Sam had thick black hair, a long firm jaw, and a large nose. He was very modest. "Me?" he'd say, shrugging his shoulders in self-deprecation. "I'm just a worker." Sam worked in a leather factory making bags and suitcases.

Both Rose and Sam spoke with thick New York accents, tinged with Yiddish and hints of Polish, their first languages. Fleeing anti-Semitic hatreds and searching for a better life, they came to the United States in 1929. "In October," Sam used to say, shrugging again, "just before the stock market crash," as if this fact summed up the luck of his life with the irony of a Sholem Aleichem story. I adored Jack's parents. Right away I was part of the family, Rose slipping her arm through mine, whispering confidences to me about her "Jackie," telling stories, sharing family gossip. "Us girls" went shopping for silverware (that is, for real silver) and a formal dining set.

A few days before we were to be married, Sam shoved wads of money into Jack's pockets and sent us off to buy a wedding ring. We took the subway from Brooklyn into lower Manhattan and walked up and down Canal Street, renowned for its jewelers. I wanted a simple gold band. The first store in which we looked had a ring I liked very much. With some trepidation, Jack asked how much it cost. "Seven dollars," the proprietor replied. Jack whispered to me, "That's not enough money. My father will kill me!" So we thanked the man and wandered on down the street looking for something I liked that cost more. In the end we bought the gold band for seven dollars and gave the rest of the money back to Sam, who quavered at Jack. "Seven dollars?! You spent seven dollars for a wedding ring for her?"

"It's okay, Sam," I said. "It's exactly what I wanted. I made him do it."

"Okay," Sam said, with his characteristic shrug. "What do I know? You're happy, that's all that matters."

Although we had been living together for six months, Jack and I honored tradition while in New York. We each stayed at our respective parents' homes. Both were in Brooklyn, about a half hour away by car or subway. Jack already knew my father from numerous political encounters, so my mother had quizzed my father about the prospective groom. For his part, however, my father had noticed very little. "Well," he had said, Mom reported to me in exasperation, "he's an electrical engineer. He seems very nice."

Reserved and formal, Jack's initial meeting with my parents was strained. My mother was especially class conscious, and although Jack's aspirations were clearly middle class, his origins were too close to her own. More to the point, there was no fame or status attached to Jack or his parentage. It was some years into our marriage before my parents accepted him. This came largely as the result of his own good heart and gracious effort.

Jack and I were married on August 29, 1965, four days shy of my twenty-first birthday. The ceremony took place in the spacious backyard of my cousin's home on Long Island. Phyllis's lawn was festooned with flowers. There were long tables with white linen tablecloths and dozens of chairs. A formal dinner was catered. Our parents shared the expense of our wedding.

We were married by a rabbi under a canopy known as a *chuppah,* in a formal Jewish ceremony. Our parents stood behind us at the altar, forming a semicircle, along with Jack's best man, "Dynamite," one of the Hallinan brothers with whom I had lived when I first arrived in Berkeley, and my matron of honor, our friend Sue Witcovsky from San Francisco. In deference to our politics, a "progressive" rabbi had been retained to perform the service. After he read the traditional marriage vows, and while we stood holding hands, the rabbi spoke at considerable length about peaceful coexistence between the United States and the Soviet Union, scientific exchanges, and orbiting space laboratories. Then Jack slipped the gold band onto my finger and the rabbi pronounced us man and wife. Jack smashed the traditional wine glass wrapped in a white napkin, with a decisive stamp of his foot. He kissed me, cautiously, as he was staving off a major hay fever attack brought on by the extensive floral arrangements.

It was a large wedding. All of Jack's extended family attended, as well as my aunts and uncles and cousins. We ate, and drank a lot of wine. We pushed tables aside and danced the hora as a musician played the accordion. I pretended it was a movie set; I was present and not present at the same time, floating, and feeling increasingly warmed by the wine.

After the wedding we headed west with our friend Carol, also from San Francisco. Just outside of Cheyenne, Wyoming, on

Interstate 80, our Ford Pinto collided with a five-ton truck. People stopped to help us, including a nurse who was especially helpful. Both Jack and Carol were injured. Meanwhile, I scrambled around in the back seat of the car stuffing the Communist newspapers and pamphlets into one or another of our bags, fearful of what the state police in Wyoming would make of us should they find the papers.

An ambulance arrived and sped the three of us to the Cheyenne hospital. I visited with Carol in the ER, and then stayed with Jack, holding his right hand, cold and clammy with shock, while a doctor stitched up his left. In his forties, with a blond crew cut, clean-shaven jovial face, a stethoscope around his neck, and wearing a white shirt open at the neck, the doctor chatted amiably with me while he worked on my husband. He asked where we were from. I said, "Berkeley." He said, laughing, "You're not one of those Communist rabble-rousers, are you?"

"Oh, no," I said, smiling, my heart pounding, lying shamelessly while Jack squeezed my hand.

Safe in our anonymity, we were treated with exceptional kindness by the hospital personnel, the owner of the motel where we spent the night, and the state police, who kindly brought our luggage to the hospital. Although the car was totaled, Jack's and Carol's injuries were not serious. Someone offered to drive us from the hospital to our motel. The next day, the motel owner drove us to the airport. We boarded a flight for San Francisco. A few days after our return I was hospitalized with a blood clot in my left leg, a result of the accident. The attending nurse, who recognized me, started up a conversation, announcing herself to be a Republican. As she bandaged my leg I winced. She said, "Oh, I may be a Republican, but I wouldn't do anything to hurt you!"

Jack stood a shade over six feet, had broad shoulders, and with a determined effort kept his weight under two hundred pounds. He had thick curly black hair, receding in front, and soft hazel eyes, at times luminous with emotion. Though clean shaven for our wedding, he alternately sported a mustache or a full beard (of which his mother despaired) during our marriage. Jack's complexion was dark enough that when he was in Paris in 1962, the French gendarmes often mistook him for an Algerian, and he was constantly accosted and harassed.

Jack was widely read in literature, philosophy, and history. He loved classical music and the theater. He could sing Yiddish songs whose origins lay in the shtetls of Eastern Europe in ways that moved me beyond words. He was, above all, a decent and caring human being, sometimes lonely, and often pained by emotional forces he dared not bring to the surface. He used a rather banal humor to deflect intimacy or to conceal emotion.

Ours was a marriage of mutual relief and refuge. Jack was viewed by many of our contemporaries as something of an eccentric and he perceived himself as an outsider. His marriage to me secured entrée into the political and social circles that mattered most to him. My marriage to Jack provided me with a sanctuary from sexual pursuit, and at least the illusion of heterosexual normality.

Ours was also a good marriage, certainly in its first years. I had no idea what it meant to be in love, of what passion and intensity I was capable. Sex was comfortable. We had a host of friends and comrades with whom we had dinner, went to movies, spent an evening. We lived in a small rented house on Roosevelt Way, less than a mile from the Berkeley campus, a few blocks from the shops, coffeehouses, and bookstores typical of a university town. Our lives were bounded by our commitments to the party and to school. The war in Vietnam was raging and we were both deeply committed to ending it. In the first years of our marriage, Jack was struggling to complete his dissertation for his doctorate in electrical engineering. I had two years left to complete my bachelor's degree. We were mutually supportive. This was our common ground, a structure upon which to build a life. This was how it was on the surface of things, how it could have been, might have appeared, how we thought it would be.

In a photographic essay by JEB (Joan E. Biren) titled *Eye to Eye: Portraits of Lesbians,* there's a wonderful picture of a woman named Dot. She is, it says, fifty-seven years old. In the picture she's caught in mid-motion, about to pull a dish from the oven. Her spectacles are dropped along the bridge of her nose and her eyes are peering up over the top of the lenses. Knees bent slightly, with a hand waving a spatula, she's wearing a white apron with a bib. The accompanying text quotes Dot: "I came out when I was five." I love this portrait because it speaks so directly to my experience. I was always falling in love with women from as far back as I could remember. I loved their breasts and bellies, curves, and warm, safe smells. And so, predictably (certainly in retrospect), I fell in love a few months after I was safely married. Her name was Gerri Jacobs. She was a graduate student at Berkeley, pursuing a master's degree, married to a handsome, blond, blue-eyed Midwesterner with a doctorate in mathematics, Orin Williams. Gerri was Jewish, had grown up in Greenwich Village, a red diaper baby whose father I remembered from my childhood.

We met at an antiwar meeting. The connection was mutual, immediate, and intense. We had lunch together a few days later. Munching sandwiches and downing chocolate ice cream sodas, we exchanged childhood stories. We became best friends, at times inseparable. We walked endless miles through Berkeley and along its marina, rode horses in the foothills of Mt. Tamalpais in Marin County, hiked in Muir Woods, roamed the backwaters of what was then still the small, quaint community of Sausalito, with its houseboats, art galleries, and cafés. A sophisticated intellectual with a sharp wit and a solid critical knowledge of the Marxist classics, Gerri spent hours discussing politics, economics, philosophy, and history with me. She nurtured my still-nascent intellectual abilities. By the late 1960s, she had weaned me from the pure orthodox Leninism of my father's house and introduced me to the world of European Marxists, most notably in France, England, and Czechoslovakia.

Three years after we met, Gerri and her husband left Berkeley to live in Europe. Orin wanted to pursue his research free from the constraints of federal grants, which inevitably compromised the integrity of his work because they were almost always tied to a U.S. military agenda. Gerri's absence from my daily life was a devastating loss. We had never been lovers, but Gerri was central to my emotional life. We corresponded for the four years she lived abroad. I waited for her letters with breathless anticipation. She wrote long, graphic, often hilarious epistles with astute commentaries on European politics and culture. And I made two trips overseas to see her, one with Jack and one alone. Whether I met her in Paris, or later in Copenhagen, it was as though we had never been separated, strolling arm in arm through streets and gardens and into museums and cafés, talking, endlessly talking.

Almost coincident with my marriage and my first intense encounters with Gerri, I went to Chicago to attend a national conference against the war in Vietnam. And it was there that I met the woman with whom I was to have my first affair. As was the practice in all such movement conferences, housing for participants was made available by supporters in the host city. I was given a name and address on the north side of Chicago, scrawled on a scrap of paper, along with a few hastily jotted directions. Clutching the paper in one hand and a small suitcase in the other, I made my way on the subway, exited as instructed, and walked, slowly searching the street signs for North Southport. I found it, and eventually the proper number. The entrance to the apartment I sought, however, was through a side alley and to the rear of the building. This I negotiated with my usual excessive caution in dealing with anything new. I rang the doorbell still uncertain that I had found the right place. I was greeted by a woman only slightly older than myself. She was tall and willowy, swaying in the door like pampas grass in a gentle breeze. We shook hands. Her name was Martha Kirkland.

Martha brewed us a pot of tea and invited me to join her at the kitchen table. In the space of an hour she chronicled the essential details of her life, to "get us acquainted," she said. She had been raised on a farm in southern Illinois, where her parents still lived and worked. She had, as I recall, two brothers and a sister. She worked at Alexian Brothers Hospital, on the graveyard shift. Her best friend worked there too, and I would certainly have to meet her. Martha was the devoted caretaker of a very elderly man of special spiritual qualities who lived alone and in poverty. She called him Friar John. I could see that she loved him a great deal. She had only recently left a convent, she announced. After seven years in training she decided not to take her final vows.

"Now," Martha commanded, pouring us still another cup of tea, "tell me about yourself." I started to review some of the facts of my life when she leaped up from her chair, halting my narrative in mid-sentence. She was late for work. She grabbed various necessities and rushed off, shouting to me to make myself at home, to sleep on the couch in the living room or in the bedroom if I wanted since she'd be at work. There were clean towels, and food in the fridge.

I slept fitfully on the living room couch. She woke me at first light, brimming with enthusiasm. She fixed us some breakfast and invited me to finish my life narrative. This I did. Finally spent, she went to bed, and I headed into midtown Chicago for my conference. We met again that afternoon. She came to attend some of the conference workshops. She was pulsing with energy. And so it was for the duration of my visit to Chicago. We promised to write to each other, certain that we would see each other again.

I returned home. Her letters came regularly, as mine were sent. She forwarded a picture of herself, which I kept, along with her letters, in the top drawer of my desk. Our second meeting was in Washington, D.C., a short time later, occasioned by an antiwar encampment near the White House. Lyndon Johnson occupied it, and the fighting in Vietnam had escalated into a full-scale war. I can remember few details of the protest itself. What I do remember was that Martha had set our sleeping bags side by side in the grass under a gorgeous star-studded sky. As we lay there she leaned over and kissed me.

After we left Washington, the flow of letters resumed. I returned to Chicago for the next available conference. This time when Martha went off to work the graveyard shift at the hospital, I chose to sleep in the bedroom. She woke me at first light, and we made love. For a long time afterward neither of us moved or spoke. Sunlight streamed into the room, filling its corners and walls, dancing across the ceiling and down onto the sheets. I felt an indescribable joy, as if this light that filled the room had entered into me everywhere.

I cannot tell how many trips I made to Chicago in the next year and a half, but they were all for antiwar or party meetings, which I was more than willing to attend and to which Jack easily assented. I do recall one determined occasion during an airline strike when I rode the Southern Pacific from San Francisco. The train was so many hours late that I missed the intended meetings altogether. In our days together Martha and I roamed the parks along the shores of Lake Michigan, romped through old streets and shops, and guffawed loudly in restaurants. We got into our share of trouble too, escaping men's advances on two young, unescorted women largely through Martha's wit and streetwise ways. Martha took life as it came, set her priorities and plans with the resources and skills she had available or those she could fathom in her versatile imagination.

One Christmas, we visited her family on their Illinois farm. They were very hospitable to me, imagining us, I think, to be just friends. I loved the snow-covered expanses of fields, and the smell of burning wood from the huge fireplace in their living room. Martha and I shared a rustic, antique-filled upstairs bedroom. I got my first speeding ticket on the drive back to Chicago. On another occasion, Martha came home with me to Brooklyn. My parents were warm and cordial; my mother especially liked her.

Amidst the joy I felt with Martha, however, I had times of uncontrollable panic and self-revulsion. Once back in my "real" life in Berkeley and away from Martha, I would be consumed with guilt—not for having been unfaithful to my husband, but for having indulged what I construed as my "baser" self. I did not know how to hold or balance the contradictions in my life. I was a married lesbian, having a celibate but passionate relationship with one woman in Berkeley, and a sexual liaison with another in Chicago. As for my despair, it was housed in the dark recesses of my mind, my self-mutilation a well-hidden secret.

Between the end of the Free Speech Movement trial in May 1965 and my graduation from Berkeley two years later, most of my political energy was directed toward ending the war in Vietnam. Beginning on May 21, 1965, Berkeley had its first "teach-in." Organized by the Vietnam Day Committee—primarily faculty and graduate students opposed to the war, and calling themselves the Vietnam Day Committee—the teach-in included speakers on all sides of the debate, although opposition to the war was the predominant view. Among those who spoke were the renowned, and by then elderly, European intellectual Isaac Deutscher and the pediatrician who had raised my generation, Dr. Benjamin Spock. I remember no women and no people of color among the speakers.

The teach-in was my first sustained exposure to information about Vietnam. It provided a crash course on the thousand-year history of the Vietnamese people's struggles for independence, first from China, and in modern times from France and the United States.

Of great urgency to us was the utter, unmitigated horror of the war. Reports of routine torture and rape by U.S. and South Vietnamese troops, of the mass killings of civilians, of the razing of villages, the slaughter of livestock, the burning of crops, the use of napalm and chemical defoliants, the incessant, apparently indiscriminate bombings of "suspected Vietcong," and the mounting toll among U.S. soldiers, dead and maimed, intensified antiwar sentiment in the United States. Mainstream media outlets, from *The New York Times* to the CBS evening news, confirmed these atrocities daily.

Washington officials consistently lied to the American people about the war. They lied about the number of U.S. troops committed to battle and the number of U.S. casualties; they lied about the use of chemical defoliants and about the many escalations in the fighting. Much of this was revealed when Daniel Ellsberg released the so-called "Pentagon Papers" to *The New York Times.* Coming from a former state department official with impeccable credentials, Ellsberg's public statements deepened the crisis in U.S. foreign policy, even among those formulating it. Likewise, when former green beret Donald Duncan appeared on the rostrum at antiwar rallies in the full dress uniform of a special forces soldier, he revealed further details of U.S. military operations. Similarly, the testimony by returning Vietnam veterans added immeasurably to the credibility of the antiwar movement. That the government chose to prosecute Daniel Ellsberg, Benjamin Spock, and Yale Divinity School's Reverend William Sloan Coffin for encouraging young men to resist the draft did nothing either to diminish the movement or to intimidate the opposition. All of these prosecutions ultimately failed.

By the late 1960s, annual spring antiwar mobilizations in San Francisco and Washington, D.C., were garnering half a million and a million protesters respectively. The first of many Chicano Moratoriums occurred in Los Angeles in 1969. These antiwar demonstrations linked police violence against people of color in the United States. to a war against people of color in Vietnam, and publicized the fact that a disproportionate number of Chicano soldiers were among U.S. military casualties. The moratoriums brought scores of thousands more into the streets, uniting a coalition of Chicano and Anglo peace activists. The Student Nonviolent Coordinating Committee (SNCC) condemned the war in a statement by its executive committee in 1965. Two years later, Dr. Martin Luther King, Jr., added further prestige to the antiwar movement by speaking out strongly against the U.S. presence in Vietnam. Thousands of African Americans from the civil rights movement, the churches, and the labor movement joined the peace marches.

In Berkeley, our initial protests focused on the U.S. military induction center in Oakland. Trains and buses loaded with young recruits passed through Berkeley and into Oakland, where soldiers were processed and eventually loaded onto planes headed for Vietnam. We sat down on the tracks of the Southern Pacific railroad in west Berkeley to stop the trains, marched to the Oakland induction center, threw up picket lines around it, leafleted soldiers, and counseled young men to resist the draft. A humorous antiwar pamphlet was published listing dozens of ways to "beat the draft." Among the suggested methods was to "marry Bettina Aptheker." Indeed, my husband, when called up before his draft board, was rejected for military service because of his relationship to me and, more important, because Herbert Aptheker was his father-in-law. An official letter to Jack from the United States Army announced this rejection and offered a process of appeal should he wish to challenge it. "Appeal the decision?" Jack roared. "Never!"

To qualify for graduation, Cal students were required to write a senior essay of at least fifty pages in our major. I wrote mine for my U.S. history major on the student peace movement of the 1930s. Engaged in research at Berkeley's Bancroft Library, I came upon boxes of uncatalogued archives from the student movement. Pamphlets, leaflets, and other memorabilia had been collected by some enterprising librarian, dutifully stamped with the date, and dropped into a box. No one seemed to have looked at them since. Imagine my amazement as I found leaflets dated 1935 proclaiming "Italy out of Ethiopia!" much as we proclaimed "U.S. out of Vietnam!" thirty years later. Among these archives I also found leaflets and documents relating to national student strikes for peace organized in the mid-1930s.

Inspired by this example, I set up my typewriter and wrote a letter to students I knew on campuses across the country. I proposed that we organize a one-day student strike against the war in Vietnam. Favored with an immediate and enthusiastic response, I wrote a strike statement and sent it out for endorsement. Although I must have discussed this idea with comrades in my party club, I have no recollection of doing so. For a Communist, I acted in a singularly anarchistic and individualist manner.

Literally hundreds of individuals and groups signed the call, and in the spring of 1967 the Student Mobilization Committee to End the War in Vietnam successfully organized the first such annual strike. An estimated one million students participated nationwide in actions ranging from noontime rallies to picket lines at military installations to informational leafleting in public malls and city plazas to sit-ins at induction centers.

As an FSM, civil rights, and peace activist and a "self-proclaimed" Communist (as the press put it), I was invited to speak at dozens of campuses, in churches, and to Communist groups all over California and in much of the country. Invited to Tuskegee Institute in April 1966, I had my first encounter with racial injustice, Southern style.

Routed through Atlanta, I was met at the airport by Gwen Patton, then president of the student government at Tuskegee, and two other students, both young men. We piled into an official college car, the Tuskegee emblem on its door. I was the only white person. Gwen was in the front passenger seat, one young man drove, and the other sat with me in the back. We headed for the Alabama state line, talking animatedly about politics in Berkeley and the civil rights movement in Alabama. A few months earlier Sammy Young, Jr., a Tuskegee student, had been shot as he exited the "whites only" restroom at a local service station. Organizers held many protests in the aftermath of his murder. The struggle was far from over, and Sammy's death was still widely and personally mourned.

As we crossed from Georgia into Alabama, our driver noted the presence of a state police car behind us. Carefully observing all traffic and speeding laws, he fell silent, concentrating on his driving. Conversation halted and tension filled the car. The police followed us for miles. Then a siren sounded, a red light flashed. Our driver pulled over. Gwen turned around to face me. Pointing her finger, she said, "Aptheker! No matter what happens, keep your mouth shut!" She wasn't kidding. Hearing her voice in that moment, I understood how much danger we were in.

The driver rolled his window down halfway and then put his hands on the steering wheel at ten o'clock and two o'clock, just like they teach you in driver's ed. He looked straight ahead. One officer was behind the car, the other approached the driver, his hand resting on his holstered gun.

"Nigger," the officer began, "where the hell do you think you're going?"

From that opening line his dialogue deteriorated, hurling insults and four-letter words like they were going out of style. Our driver answered, "Yes, sir," and "No, sir," never moving his hands, never raising his voice, never turning his head.

The officer looked back at me. "Your name, ma'am?" I was so furious I could hardly speak, but I remembered Gwen's warning.

"Mrs. Kurzweil," I said, invoking the anonymity of my married name.

He continued to question us for several more minutes, but then moved on. The police car followed us all the way to Tuskegee. Relief swept over us as we reached the campus.

At all the campuses where I spoke, audiences were warm, engaged, enthusiastic, supportive. I was never heckled, not once, anywhere. Sometimes questions were sharply worded, hostile to the Soviet Union and to Communism. Even in these cases the hostility was never directed at me personally. Once, for example, in the mid-'60s, a young man on a campus somewhere in Southern California made a long speech against Soviet interventionist policies in Eastern Europe. Finally he asked, his voice rising and cracking in a highly rhetorical vein: "And what about Bulgaria in 1922?" The question was so completely unexpected that I blurted out: "Bulgaria in 1922? I thought you were going to ask me about Hungary in 1956!" The audience roared with laughter. I admitted that I didn't know anything about Bulgaria or what had happened in 1922.

This incident, however humorous, is revealing. First, as a Communist I was held responsible for all of the Soviet Union's foreign and domestic policies. People may not have believed that U.S. Communists were "foreign agents" in a sinister sense, but they certainly thought that we should be able to explain everything about socialism wherever it existed. Second, it had never occurred to me that anything my father had written or said was not the absolute truth. Relying on his research, his documentation, and his rhetoric (which I knew virtually by heart), I simply repeated my father's arguments when asked about Hungary, or East Germany (where there was an uprising in 1953), or Jews in the Soviet Union, or the lack of democracy and freedom of speech in socialist countries. I exuded precisely the same confidence whether I spoke from my own experience (as in the case of the civil rights and antiwar movements and the FSM) or my father's, which was seamlessly imprinted upon my consciousness. There was no separation between us; I exercised no critical, independent judgments. I had no self-awareness, even that such an imprinting had occurred. It was a terrible irony that while I was heralded as a leader of Berkeley's Free Speech Movement I simultaneously justified the Communist suppression of freedom of speech and freedom of the press in the Soviet Union, East Germany, Hungary, and elsewhere. I attribute this imprinting to the way I survived my childhood, the sexual abuse in particular: I dissociated from myself and merged with my father, making us one, indivisible.

In June 1966, the U.S. Communist Party held its eighteenth national convention, in a hotel in midtown Manhattan. I attended as a delegate elected by the Northern California district committee. In the hotel lobby, on the bulletin board where events and rooms were listed, the party convention was described as an "education committee." This obscurity was intended as a security measure, although it seemed absurd to me. Of course the FBI knew when and where we were meeting.

The convention was held in the hotel ballroom. White-clothed tables had been set up. On each table was a placard naming the state delegations, like a mini version of Democratic or Republican Party conventions. There were hundreds of delegates and observers. My father, of course, was also a delegate. Gus Hall, recently elected general secretary of the party, was to give the main report. A former steelworker of Finnish heritage, born and raised in the Midwest, Gus exuded confidence. Looking at him you would never have guessed he had spent eight years in a federal penitentiary. Gus was a handshaking, slap-you-on-the-back politician with a booming voice.

Max, as chairman of the Northern California district, headed our delegation. He encouraged me to speak. I talked about the successes of the student and antiwar movements, exuded confidence in the party and in the struggle, mimicked Gus's style and rhetoric. Comrades grinned at me with benign indulgence. There was applause, and my father was pleased. He patted me on the shoulder later: "That was good, baby." By the end of the convention I had been elected to the party's National Committee. The committee had 120 members. It met twice a year in New York and was the highest policy-making body of the party.

I was twenty-two years old. I was oblivious to the responsibility membership in the National Committee implied, to the policies we were setting or endorsing, especially in the international arena. All that mattered to me was my personal achievement as heir to the Aptheker covenant.

Even as I came into my inheritance, the realities of party work soon dampened my enthusiasm. In the summer of 1966, just after the party convention, I attended the national convention of Students for a Democratic Society (SDS) in Clear Lake, Iowa. Based largely on East Coast and Midwest campuses, SDS epitomized the New Left. It was radical, activist, highly critical of capitalism, vaguely socialist, and unaffiliated with any of the Old Left parties. I remember little of the conference grounds, except that there was indeed a large beautiful lake, and lush green grass stretched as far as the eye could see.

The Communist Party and the Socialist Workers Party (SWP), with its Young Socialist Alliance (YSA) affiliate, had been battling each other for decades. At the Clear Lake conference we struggled with each other for control over Students for a Democratic Society. The battle at Clear Lake was part of a larger struggle in which each party sought to enhance its prestige and influence in the antiwar movement, and in the Left in general. I was part of the Communist Party contingent, but in my mind, in my image of myself and of the party, I saw only virtue and principle. In reality I was part of a faction that was attempting to manipulate the conference agenda and divest SDS of its autonomy. Despite our actions the SDS leadership refused to deny us participation in their organization because they did not want to be a party to red-baiting. They worked with us to reach compromises, and SDS prevailed as one of the most important radical sites of student activism in the 1960s.

Meanwhile, the realities of war were all-consuming. Deaths mounted daily. While the FSM had been a serious movement, it was also joyful and effervescent. The political stakes were modest and nobody had been killed or even seriously hurt. We stayed pretty much within the protective wings of the university. But this struggle against the war was of enormous magnitude, the suffering unimaginable. Here we were, I raged to Jack one night, all of us with our privilege and security arguing about slogans for our antiwar actions. "What difference do our slogans make? We just need millions of people in the streets!" I ranted. However much I disliked one or another political process or decision, it did not occur to me to question my membership in the Communist Party or, more to the point, my inherited status in its national leadership. I rationalized, excused, dismissed anything that might threaten the structure of my world.

Even as we fought each other for dominance, we fought the police for survival. The Berkeley campus seethed with a radical, defiant activism that often garnered national media coverage as students and police battled each other. Two such confrontations occurred with the

Oakland police, in part a consequence of the Oakland authorities' obstinate abuse of power, and in part a result of growing student frustration and impatience with the failure of the antiwar movement to achieve more tangible and rapid results.

While Berkeley police routinely issued us permits to march (negotiating only routes and traffic control), Oakland police denied us a permit for our proposed march to the U.S. Army induction center to protest the draft. We did march, of course. And when we reached the border between the two cities, we were met by hundreds of Oakland police in full riot gear preventing our passage.

The first confrontation at the Oakland border took place southwest of the campus at a very broad intersection where several major streets converge. Traffic had been diverted on both sides of the border. Oakland police were massed before us. We halted the line of marchers, planning to hold a rally in the street on the Berkeley side of the border. About forty or fifty of us were in front, standing with linked arms, forming a human shield and signaling those behind us to stop. Berkeley police were just behind us and to our sides.

Assessing our situation, we were shocked to see twenty or thirty Hell's Angels in leather jackets wielding metal chains. The Hell's Angels stood directly in front of the Oakland police line. At a prearranged signal from the Oakland police, gang members, swinging their chains, charged into us. Our arms remained linked. We did not break ranks. Someone turned and yelled to the crowd behind us, "Sit down! Sit down!" They did, filling the streets for as far as the eye could see.

The Hell's Angels made a second charge. This time they broke through our lines, with club-swinging Oakland police directly behind them. Those of us who had linked arms turned and ran, covering our heads with our hands as chains and clubs swept through the air around us. Mustering astonishing discipline, the crowd of thousands remained seated; those of us running found safety amongst them. Meanwhile, the Berkeley police defended their border against the invaders. In the end, several Berkeley officers were seriously injured, but the assault was turned back. Our rally proceeded at the border between the two cities. Protesting the obvious attempt to provoke a riot, antiwar speakers vowed to take legal action against the City of Oakland to guarantee our rights of assembly and speech.

Among the speakers that day was the poet and Zen practitioner Allen Ginsberg. At his turn he rang a small metal triangle, which he held in his hand. In rhythm with the chime, he chanted, in a language I did not know, words that appeared to have no meaning. Some in the crowd listened respectfully. Others laughed, shuffling nervously. But many of us were outraged. We believed that the apparent meaninglessness of his chant, coupled with his disheveled appearance and full beard, would give us a bad public image and diminish the seriousness of our protest. Of course, what I didn't know then was that he was chanting the Buddha's "Prajnaparamita," the Heart Sutra, which spoke to a spiritual understanding of the causes of war, the delusions that make enemies of "Others."

The second confrontation at the Oakland border took place a month later in the early evening. Our march left the Berkeley campus and proceeded south, along Telegraph Avenue. Again, a group of us in front led the march. Again, the Berkeley police were around us. A few of us ran ahead to the border, where a heated, tense conference began. Jerry Rubin, an activist from the East Coast recently arrived in Berkeley, was one of the leaders of the Vietnam Day Committee, and was present, along with the Berkeley chief of police, several other students, and me. It was clear that the Oakland police were not going to yield. Jerry wanted us to lead the march across the border and into Oakland.

We had made alternate plans for a rally at the Berkeley municipal park, in the eventuality that we were blocked at the border. Steve Weisman, a former member of our FSM steering committee, was being driven in a car behind us that slowly led the antiwar procession. Behind him, walking, were many other FSM students and a few of my comrades.

Several of us said to Jerry, "We must turn the march."

"No!" he said. He was adamant.

"Someone will be killed if we try to march through this!" I insisted.

His reply flabbergasted me: "Imagine the funeral procession we could have!" Jerry seemed to be only interested in a media extravaganza. There was nothing left to say.

Grabbing a couple of other students, I ran back toward the approaching crowd. Steve leaned out the car window looking for directions. I yelled, "Turn the march!" Immediately the car swung a right turn. The call was taken up by Jack Weinberg on a bullhorn. The marchers turned west, away from the border. I never forgave Jerry Rubin for that moment, and from then on I did not trust him.

As the war escalated and the fighting grew more intense, our activism grew more desperate. The day after the United States began bombing North Vietnam, I spoke at an illegal rally on the campus—that is, a rally that defied the regulations of "time, place, and manner" that I had helped write as a member of the Rules Committee. Several of us were brought up for disciplinary action. We were tried before an administrative committee, at least one of whose members, John Searle, had actively supported the FSM. In the end, we were found guilty and placed on academic probation. This was the lowest penalty that could have been exacted. Although I was defensive about our action, I knew the rally had been a mistake. Even so, I thought it was wrong for the university to prosecute us for what was, in fact, a minor infraction. It reflected the growing polarization of the times, as well as the rightward turn of some formerly progressive faculty, like John Searle.

Antiwar protests in general were growing more militant and defiant. Battles continued between police and students. When the leadership of the Vietnam Day Committee voted in its majority not to apply for a Berkeley police permit to hold a street demonstration, tensions erupted. The strategy was intended to show solidarity with South Vietnamese students, who were battling the police in Saigon, so the argument went, where no permits for antigovernment activities were ever issued. I did not agree with this decision. I thought it would simply provoke police violence. Still, I participated in the protests because ending the war was my overriding concern.

The failure of the Vietnam Day Committee to obtain a permit did result in police violence. The Berkeley police called for reinforcements, most notably from the Alameda County Sheriff's Department. Hundreds of officers poured into Berkeley in full riot gear. We would begin a march and the police would charge into us, firing tear gas, swinging their clubs. We scattered, regrouped. The police charged again. Some among us picked up hissing tear gas canisters and lobbed them back at the police.

For three successive days and nights, police and students roamed the campus and its periphery. When I went out I dressed for the occasion. I taped my ribs and padded my stomach, ribs and breasts with newspapers, over which I wore a battered brown suede jacket. The jacket had belonged to my mother and I thought of it as a protective shield. I smeared my face and neck with Vaseline, which dispelled the worst effects of the tear gas. I took several blows from police clubs, but they were glancing, and my padding worked well. There were virtually no arrests, but there were injuries, mostly head wounds from police clubs. I tended one boy, for example, a Berkeley high school student who was about fifteen. Thin, red haired, and freckled, he was bleeding profusely from a head wound. We carried him into a nearby bookstore and laid him on the floor. Someone called an ambulance. I applied first aid. The boy was terrified but conscious. He kept asking me if he was going to die. I assured him that his wound was not serious. Eventually the paramedics arrived, and I was relieved of my emergency tasks.

This experience moved me greatly. I knew the violence was unnecessary. Both weary and wary of Jerry Rubin's tactics to provide the media with an "event," I drifted away from the campus antiwar protests. Instead, I put my energies into building the national mobilizations against the war. And it was in these months that the contradictions in my personal life reached a terrifying climax.

A national antiwar conference was scheduled for Washington, D.C., in the fall of 1966 to plan for the spring mobilizations the following April. I took the opportunity to rendezvous with Martha. We met first in Chicago. She was also to attend the Washington conference. After a day or so of romping in Chicago, we took a flight to Washington. We retrieved our bags from the claim area and proceeded by subway to the conference headquarters. We were assigned housing at the home of a Washington activist, and went to get settled. Appropriately greeted, fed, and then sequestered in our room, we began to unpack.

As I opened my suitcase, a chill passed from the back of my neck down to the tip of my spine, where it froze in a hard knot. Spread across the top of my clothes were several layers of slick magazine pages. They were pornographic pictures of women. I never doubted for a moment who had planted them. It had to have been the FBI. I knew then that they knew that Martha and I were lovers. However discreet Martha and I had been, they were on to us. I told no one of my discovery. I hid the photos at the bottom of my suitcase and never fully unpacked it. I hid everything from Martha because I already knew that this was going to mean the end of our relationship.

I went home to Berkeley a few days later and asked Jack what he thought about having a baby. He readily agreed. We had talked about having children, and Jack was waiting for me to take the initiative. We stopped using contraception and by January I had conceived. Motherhood, I prayed, would wrap me more securely in a cloak of heterosexual normalcy. The next time I visited Chicago I was four months pregnant. If Martha had any qualms about my decision to have a baby she did not speak them. We made love for what I knew would be the last time. It was a gentle, quiet loving in the first of the spring thaws.

I was on the road for weeks before and after the April mobilizations, speaking about the war. As my belly began to protrude and the baby began to kick and move vigorously, I squashed anxiety with frenetic activity and finished up the last of my academic requirements for my bachelor's degree. It never occurred to me, my parents, or my husband to attend the graduation ceremonies. Several months later my diploma arrived in the mail.

That same spring of 1967, my mother was diagnosed with breast cancer. Dad telephoned me at home in Berkeley, just as she was going into surgery. "Do you want me to come?" I asked. "Would you?" he responded. Feeling emotionally flat, I caught a red-eye flight to New York that night, and Dad met me at the airport at about six in the morning. By nine I was at Beth Israel Hospital on the Lower East Side, bending over Mom and gently summoning her from sleep.

"You came," she said, bewildered, thrilled to see me. I squeezed her hand and felt a rush of love for her. Dad said, "You're going to be all right, baby." The surgeon, Dad reported, was confident that he had gotten all the cancer. He had performed a radical mastectomy, removing Mom's left breast and several lymph nodes from under her left arm. He recommended no further treatment. Radiation and chemotherapy were not standard protocol in 1967. Dad was exuberant. "He's a comrade," Dad explained to me, referring to the surgeon. "He fought in Spain." With these credentials Dad had total confidence in his prognosis. Mom, in fact, made a rapid recovery and lived for more than thirty years after that. The cancer never recurred.

I went to the hospital every day, tending to Mom's immediate needs. I was well into my pregnancy, and she was just joyous about the baby. I read her *The New York Times,* and she did the daily crossword puzzles to my continuing amazement, as I could not do them at all. She said nothing to me about the loss of her breast. Later, long after she had healed from the surgery, she fretted about the redness and swelling in her upper arm. She thought it was from the removal of the lymph nodes. She was meticulous about her appearance, and she felt the redness and swelling were unseemly.

In the hospital, Mom shared a room with another patient. I soon learned this woman was Ruby Doris Smith Robinson, the executive secretary of SNCC. All of us involved in the civil rights movement knew of Ruby; she was a legend. She had been diagnosed with cancer. Ruby and I were almost the same age and she already had a two-year-old son. I tended to her needs as well as Mom's, and got to know her a little. Ruby was so worried about her son and missed him so much. I learned of her death a few months later, and my grief was all rage. "Why?" I stormed at Jack. "It's so unfair!"

I returned to Berkeley as soon as Mom was released from the hospital. Our time together was the best I'd ever had with her. All my fears of her from childhood seemed to disappear, at least temporarily, as I sat with her, providing small comforts and hearing her voice softened by the fatigue of illness.

Early in June 1967, just before graduation, the United States Supreme Court refused to hear the appeal our attorneys had filed on behalf of the FSM defendants. It was our last recourse. Sentences were to be executed by the end of the month. We made frantic legal and personal appeals to Gregory Brunn, the Berkeley municipal court judge who had been assigned to carry out the sentencing when our trial judge died. Mario and Suzanne had an infant son, Stefan. We pleaded that they not be imprisoned at the same time. Judge Brunn converted Suzanne's jail time to a stiff fine, which was promptly paid by supporters. Mario, however, received no such reprieve, and neither did Jack Weinberg, Art Goldberg, or Michael Rossman. In solidarity, several other FSM defendants refused to pay their fines, forcing Judge Brunn to sentence them to an equivalent jail time, usually between one and two weeks.

Great effort was made to convert my sentence to a fine. I was six and a half months pregnant, my supporters argued, and should not be subjected to such punishment. Supporters flooded Judge Brunn, and even the governor, with letters. My mother sent a blazing protest. My friend Gerri Jacobs and her husband, who had not yet left the United States, wrote an eloquent appeal. Judge Brunn felt compelled to reply to them. Dated July 7, a week after my internment, he pleaded his innocence. He did not impose these sentences, he wrote, but was charged, as an officer of the court, with carrying them out. Pointing to the failure of our appeals, and the modifications in sentences he did grant, Judge Brunn wrote:

> The one exception [to the sentence modification] involved Miss Aptheker whose sentence was carried out after I had obtained information that she would receive adequate medical care, that her own doctor would at all times have access to her, and that in the event of a premature delivery she would be removed from jail and be placed into a hospital.

I surrendered myself to the Alameda County Sheriff's Department at the Berkeley municipal courthouse on Friday morning, June 30, 1967, along with Mario, Art, Jack, and Michael. In a beige and orange maternity dress, matching low heels, my long hair brushed back from my face and put up in a bun, I looked like a typical young, middle-class wife. Press and supporters surrounded the five of us. Michael Lerner, a fellow former FSM protester, later to become the editor of the progressive Jewish journal *Tikkun*, was there to see us off. Michael had baked a chocolate cake with a saw protruding through it, a joke intended to convey his chagrin and outrage at our imprisonment. When he hugged me, I could feel his fear for us. We were to serve our sentences at the same facility where we had been sent upon our arrest two years before: the Santa Rita Rehabilitation Center, located south of Berkeley, in Pleasanton. The euphemism of "rehabilitation" for prison and the ironic juxtaposition of the facility and its location were not lost on any of us.

With several other women (not involved in FSM) I was transported from the Berkeley court to a holding cell in the Oakland jail. We joined more women awaiting transport to Santa Rita. One of them, an African American woman, was very upset and I asked her what had happened. She had gone to the supermarket and come out, both arms laden with bags. Two boys came tearing out the doors just after her, a security guard in hot pursuit. Each tossed candy bars into her bags as they fled. *She* was arrested! She had not been permitted to make a telephone call. I sputtered in disbelief and outrage about her constitutional rights. My sister inmates looked on, amused by my naiveté. Threatened with solitary confinement should she dare further protest, she begged me not to say anything. "Of course," I nodded in compliance. "However," I said, "my husband will visit me on Sunday. If you give me your name and the number to call, he will do it." She did. I committed both to memory. Sunday Jack visited. Sunday evening the woman was bailed out. Jack told me that her family had been frantic with worry. From their vantage point she had simply disappeared. Her bail was fifty-two dollars. The women's section of Santa Rita rocked in celebration.

Arriving at Santa Rita early that Friday afternoon, we were stripped of all personal belongings and clothes. Even my wedding ring was taken from me. Naked, we were told to squat in front of several matrons. In lieu of a physical examination, Santa Rita officials enforced this squatting position because it made it almost impossible to hide drugs or other contraband in our vaginas. Then we were escorted to nearby showers, issued towels and our prison clothing, and ordered to bathe. Matrons remained in the communal shower room. Newly clothed in a green prison dress, bra, panties, socks, and slippers, with my hair wrapped in a towel, I was informed by a matron that the lieutenant in charge of the women's facility wanted to see me. I padded down the hall after her. The matron said, "I'm not leading you to a gas chamber. The lieutenant really wants to see you!"

The lieutenant had replaced the captain we had met two years earlier. Middle-aged, heavily made up, hair set and sprayed, khaki uniform perfectly fitting and snappily creased, she motioned for me to sit down in front of her large wooden desk. She said, "I know who you are. If we have any trouble in here, you'll be in solitary faster than you can say it!"

I said, mindful of my recent holding cell encounter, "If there are no violations of our constitutional rights, you won't have any problems."

She said, "I won't tolerate protest."

I said, "If there are no violations of our constitutional rights, there will be no need for any."

She said, "Do I make myself clear?"

I nodded. I thought she needed to have the last word.

Returned to the shower area, I finished with my hair. Then I was escorted to the dormitory and assigned a cot and cubby. A couple of other FSM protesters were still left at Santa Rita serving the last days of their sentences (in lieu of fines). We hugged, chatted easily. They gave me a tour of the women's facility, showed me the outdoor courtyard between the two dormitories where we were periodically allowed to congregate, the rec room with its TV, couches, tables, and chairs, and the library with its assortment of murder mysteries, romance novels, and *Reader's Digest* condensed fiction. I saw the locked cells, four bunks each, where felons and those accused of violent crimes awaited trial, and the solitary and isolation cells. They introduced me to a few of the other inmates.

A siren sounded, a whistle blew, a matron yelled, "Count." Everyone stood in front of her assigned cot. I followed suit. The matron walked down each side of the dormitory, counting as we called out our last names. Everyone was present. We lined up for dinner and filed into a nearby building with a large dining hall. It had rows of wooden tables and benches. Adjacent to it was the kitchen. We each picked up a metal tray, indented with what I thought of as separate puddles. We filed past a broad-windowed counter that gave access to the kitchen. Sister prisoners served food into the puddles. Our only eating utensil was a spoon. The food was oily, "stewy," with a lot of potatoes and little flavor. After eating we deposited our trays in an assigned space for the dishwashers, lined up, and were escorted back to the dormitory. We had about an hour and a half of "free time," most of us congregating in the rec room. Lights were out at 9:30 PM.

We were awakened at 6:30 AM. Siren. Whistle. Count. I stood in bare feet. "Medicine call." Trundled off to take my vitamins. Got dressed. Stripped the bed. Stood on line. Breakfast. Made the bed. Seven AM. Whistle. Count. 8:00 AM. Saturday. No work. We spent the morning straightening up the dorm. At 10:00 AM the deputies began a bed-by-bed check. Each of our possessions was carefully examined.

Noon. Siren. Whistle. Count. Lunch.

Afternoon. I went outside into the courtyard. I played a game of Ping-Pong. Others were knitting, sewing, reading. Inside there was a flurry of activity. Sunday was visiting day. Saturday was spent in preparation. There were long, elaborate showers. Uniforms were cleaned and pressed and carefully hung in the one mutually shared closet. Shoes were polished. Hair was cut and set. Frankie, a thirty-year-old African American, was the beautician, her occupation before Santa Rita. She was issued scissors, creams, and curlers for this specific task.

Three PM. Siren. Whistle. Count. 4:00 PM. Supper. 6:00 PM. Siren. Whistle. Count. Mail. Television. Reading. Jigsaw puzzle. 9:00 PM. Siren. Whistle. Count. 9:30 PM. Lights out.

Seven AM. Sunday. An extra half hour in bed. Siren. Whistle. Count. Medicine call. Dressed. Stripped the bed. Stood on line. Breakfast. Made the bed. Siren. Whistle. Count. I spent most of the morning in the library, hopeful that I might find something to read. I was amazed to discover amongst the mysteries and romances Hemingway, Dickens, and Jack London. Then my eyes fell on Jessica Mitford's *Daughters and Rebels* and Shirley Graham Du Bois's *Your Most Humble Servant*, a biography of Frederick Douglass. These books had a special stamp on the back denoting their origin. Unbelievably, they were donated to Santa Rita by the United States Navy. I returned to the dorm with my books. In the weeks that followed I read them again and again.

Noon. Siren. Whistle. Count. 1:00 PM. Visiting hours. Jack came. We had thirty minutes, standing on either side of a metal screen. I felt self-conscious in my prison uniform. We had to shout to hear each other. All the visiting was done simultaneously in the same room. Prisoners were allowed only one visitor per week. There was no privacy.

Four PM. Siren. Whistle. Count. Supper. Siren. Whistle. Count. No mail. Sunday. Movies. We were lined up, taken to a bus driven by an armed male deputy to the men's compound, five minutes away. We were escorted into the auditorium, up the stairs to the balcony. We could hear the male prisoners below us. A heavy curtain had been drawn across the balcony to block our view of them. It was not opened until the lights were out and the movie began. As our eyes adjusted to the darkness, the women scanned the crowd below, looking for friends and lovers. I spotted Mario and Art easily because they were so tall, bushy haired, and white. The movie was a crime thriller. When it was over the heavy curtain was again draped across the balcony. We were escorted to the bus and driven back to the women's side.

Siren. Whistle. Count. 9:30 PM. Lights out.

Six thirty AM. Siren. Whistle. Count. Monday. A work day. I was assigned to work in the supply room. My co-worker was Barbara, a light-skinned black woman in her early thirties. She was four months pregnant. We established an easy rapport. We were the first prisoners new inmates encountered. We handed out their clothes and toiletries. We did a lot of counseling, trying to ease fears, to make a woman feel welcomed. We kept a stash of cigarettes with us. Almost everyone smoked and our offers were always gratefully received.

Prisoners were overwhelmingly young, and most were women of color. They were not serving sentences but awaiting trial, not having enough money to post bail. The major alleged offenses were drugs, prostitution, and an assortment of property crimes ranging from stolen credit cards to petty theft. Our daily routine was a monotonous blend of working, eating, relaxing during a quiet hour, and sleeping. Work in the jail meant the supply room, the kitchen detail, the housekeeping detail, laundry, and gardening. Gardening was the favored assignment as it put one out of doors. Kitchen work was rotated. The facility's strict discipline meant there was no sitting on beds during the day, no sitting on each other's beds ever, no touching between prisoners for any reason. Discipline also meant standing at attention at the foot of our beds for "count," and being sent to solitary confinement or isolation for rule violations. Eating was called "feeding time." Medical attention was available from a man the inmates called "Nurse Nellie." Nobody went to see him. He had a reputation for sexual abuse and incompetence. Moreover, the matrons punished a claim of illness by putting the sick in isolation or solitary.

I was lovingly cared for by my fellow inmates. They smuggled me containers of milk and extra food, "for the baby." The penalty for such smuggling was solitary, but we were never caught. They arranged it so that I never rotated into the kitchen. They had decided that washing dishes in the 120-degree summer heat would cause a miscarriage. In turn, I used my commissary funds, swelled by donations from friends, to buy my companions cigarettes, toothpaste, candy, thread, yarn, stationery, and postage. We shared stories, jokes, and recipes. I got lots of tips about raising children.

Incoming and outgoing mail was read by the matrons and censored. No mention of names was permitted. Jack wrote about "Igor," and everywhere this name was used it had been cut out of the letter with scissors. "Igor" was a joke. It was the name we had given to the baby in utero. I was permitted to write and receive one letter a day. Each day I wrote to a different person: Jack, Evelyn, my parents, and so on. If my letter wasn't received, family and friends were to contact our lawyers.

Sometime in mid-July, one of our attorneys, Mal Burnstein, came to see me. Escorted to an interview room, we sat at a table next to each other. There were no screens. He hugged me. I could touch him whenever I wished. I was so grateful for the physical contact. At the end of the third week in July, my personal physician, Ephraim Kahn, came to see me for what was intended to be a routine examination. By then I was not feeling well. I was running a fever, vomiting, and having trouble holding down any food. I was managing water and vitamins. Eph did a very thorough exam, encouraged me not to be upset, and promised to be back. The baby's heartbeat was strong and regular.

July 18, 1967. Dawn. Siren. Whistle. Count. Medicine call. I got dressed, stripped the bed, stood on line. Breakfast. I made the bed. Siren. Whistle. Count. 8:00 AM. Work. A regular day. Until 6:00 PM.

"Bettina Aptheker. To the booking room. Bettina Aptheker. To the booking room." The message came over the loudspeaker. I was informed that Judge Brunn had issued an order. I was to be transferred "forthwith" to the county hospital. My possessions were gathered and put in a bag supplied by the prison. I was transported in the back of a sheriff's car, caged in, in my prison uniform, in handcuffs, by a female deputy.

We arrived at the county hospital about seven o'clock. We went directly to the emergency room. I was still in handcuffs, escorted by the deputy. It was a Friday night. The waiting room was full. Patients and their families, sprawled, sitting, reading, pacing. People stared at me, cuffed and pregnant.

The deputy informed the nurse at the desk of our arrival. I was told nothing, knew nothing. I kept hoping that Eph would appear. There was a clock on the wall of the waiting room. I watched the hours pass. The emergency room was flooded with the Friday-night wounded. Knife wounds, bullet wounds, burn wounds, head wounds. After several hours the deputy offered to remove my handcuffs. She cautioned me not to try to escape.

At one o'clock in the morning, I was finally summoned into an examining room. The deputy waited outside. The doctor introduced himself as the hospital's chief obstetrician. I learned then that the court order specified that only he was to examine me. He asked for permission. I gave it. He was in his thirties, white coated, brisk, and efficient. Sitting on the table before the exam, I leaned over to see what he had written on his chart. Under my name it said: "Female. White. Twenty-two. Alert." His examination was routine, painless. He asked me a few questions, went out, leaving me on the table, came back in.

He said, "I am recommending that you be hospitalized. You have a kidney infection. The baby is fine, but you would do better in here than in Santa Rita." He spoke without affect, gave his diagnosis. I asked for permission to call my own doctor. He went out, came back, said that was fine. It was after two o'clock in the morning. I dialed Eph's home number. He came on the line, sounding amazingly alert for someone awakened from a sound sleep.

Eph had also diagnosed the kidney infection. Mal had gone to Judge Brunn, pleading that the last two weeks of my sentence be commuted. The judge refused. (I did get a week off, however, for "good behavior.") Working with this intransigence, Mal had succeeded in at least getting the court order for hospitalization. The food would be better. I could rest. Still, I felt a terrible anxiety at leaving the protection of my fellow prisoners in Santa Rita. Eph calmed my fears. He urged me to consent to hospitalization. Paperwork completed, I was taken to a dark room somewhere on what I assumed to be the maternity ward. The deputy now relinquished her charge, remanding me to the custody of the hospital authorities and reminding me again that I was still a prisoner. I was exhausted. I wanted only sleep.

Sometime within the next hour a man entered the room. He wore a white coat. In the darkness I could see only the contours of his face, and the outline of a crew cut. In a whisper he instructed me to put the heels of my feet together and to spread my legs. I whispered back that I had just been examined by the chief obstetrician and he was the only one authorized to examine me. Suddenly it occurred to me that this wasn't a medical examination. The room was pitch black, he wore no surgical gloves, there was no nurse present. I started then to sit up. His left arm came down hard across my chest. Holding me this way, his right hand fought to control my legs. I struggled furiously, but I did not scream. I didn't in the first moments because I feared I would awaken other patients, and in the second moments, because I understood the lethal consequences of a direct blow to my stomach. I was pinned down. I ceased any resistance. I was penetrated. Pain shot up my spine and into the base of my skull. Then he was gone.

I lay rigid. My first fear was that I would lose the baby. Slowly I moved my hand down the length of my body so I could feel for blood. There was none. I waited a few minutes. I felt myself again. Still none. The pain lessened. I got up. I found a bathroom. I turned on the light. There was no blood. I shut off the light, fearing discovery. Alternately, I crouched in a corner of the bathroom and paced back and forth, pounding my right fist into the waiting palm of my left hand. "How much can I take?" I whispered hoarsely between sobs. Finally I got back into bed. I was overwhelmed with despair, sinking fast.

The baby was not moving. Usually I felt him moving all the time. I had even made up a game for us, pretending to grab his "foot" up near my waist; he would move "it" and I would chase "it." Of course, I had no idea what part of his body it was, or if he was really responding to my touch.

For hours there was no movement. Then just before dawn the baby moved. As the room became lighter I could make out beds. I was in yet another dormitory-style accommodation. The room was very long and empty except for another pregnant woman over at the other end, also presumably a prisoner. I began silently to weep. A nurse's aid came in to check on me. An African American woman in her thirties with a light complexion, a round face, and round eyes, she gave me a bright beautiful smile. "Don't you cry now," she said. "You'll be out of here soon enough." She wrapped me in her arms. I cried even harder. But I said nothing. I did not speak of this night to anyone for years, I wasn't sure anyone would believe me. More importantly, I saw in this assault a continuation of the police violence begun months earlier with the pornographic pictures in my suitcase in Washington. Disclosure of the one, I felt certain, would lead inexorably to disclosure of the other. If I accused, they would retaliate. The results would be worse than the rape I had already survived.

Jack was permitted to visit me in the hospital on Sunday. And a few days later, I was startled awake by Gerri, who, dressed in a white coat, had snuck in to see me. "Mrs. Kurzweil," she said in her most official-sounding voice. "Gerri!" I shrieked. She shushed me quickly. We visited for several minutes in hushed, hastily conspired voices. Then, her nerves shot, Gerri fled before we were caught. I was released on Thursday morning, August 3. Jack came and took me home.

A few weeks later, hoping to give me a breather from my summer nightmare, and still not knowing the extent of it, Jack drove us to Yosemite. It was a glory to be high in the Sierra, to see the gleaming granite, snow still patching the very highest peaks. We drove up to Tuolumne Meadows and got out of the car to walk. I was gasping for breath after only a few steps. We were at nine thousand feet and I was almost nine months pregnant! Laughing, we got back in the car and slowly descended to the valley floor. It was many, many years later that I told anyone, including Jack, about the rape.

Joshua was born on October 19, 1967, at 11:54 AM, on the Thursday of the Stop the Draft Week protests at the army induction center in Oakland. I had marched at the induction center on Monday and Tuesday, and gone into labor on Wednesday morning. Someone telephoned on Wednesday afternoon and asked me to speak at a noon antiwar rally at the Berkeley campus on Thursday. I hesitated before saying no, and then I explained my condition.

I watched a good part of the birth in a mirror positioned above and in front of the delivery table. My arms and legs were strapped down. The doctor put the baby on my belly just after he was born and, I think, before the umbilical cord was cut. The feeling of his body against mine, still swimming upstream as it were, was the most beautiful sensation I have ever experienced. My father, who happened to be in the San Francisco Bay Area on a lecture tour, was outside the delivery room when I was wheeled out. I told him it was a boy. He took out the white hanky he always carried in the back pocket of his trousers and wiped the tears from my face.

A week after Joshua's birth, I hemorrhaged. Part of the placenta had been left in the womb. Jack stayed at home with the baby, while Gerri came and rushed me to a hospital. It was the middle of the night. The doctor performed a D and C without anesthesia, an unheard-of lapse in established protocol. A nurse stayed with me through the agonizing procedure, the two of us clinging to each other. About eleven o'clock that morning the doctor came to my hospital room to apologize, without ever explaining why he had done the procedure without proper anesthesia. I shrugged, managed a smile. I was no longer in pain, and too traumatized to feel any emotion.

Six weeks after the birth, I swung into a full complement of political work. The following March, I collapsed. It could have been called postpartum depression. More accurately, it was a nervous breakdown precipitated by all I had been through: the prison rape, the ongoing FBI harassment, my terror that my lesbian identity would be made public, and the sexual violence I had experienced since childhood. I had no safe ground. For weeks I refused to see a doctor, any kind of doctor, not even an internist. I didn't want to visit with anyone except Gerri. I could tolerate my husband. However, the ringing of the telephone, an unexpected visitor, any break or change in our routine threw me into a terrible panic. Flooded with anxiety, I could hardly eat. I slept very little. Walking the baby in his carriage down the streets of Berkeley, I was plagued with fear: of other pedestrians, of passing motorists, the mailman, a bus driver. Suffering from acute paranoia, I was just barely able to distinguish between reality and delusion. Caring for my son helped to provide daily structure and purpose. But it wasn't enough, and I couldn't always do it. Rose, Jack's mother, came for a week to take care of the baby. Her presence, cheerful and competent, helped me a great deal.

As one part of my mind watched the other, I knew I was slipping more and more toward madness. I began to inflict wounds on my body again, cutting myself with knives and razors. Externalizing the pain brought some relief. I thought seriously about suicide. My mind would spin into a vicious self-loathing: *I am so perverted, so damaged, so evil, I should kill myself to protect others from being contaminated.* One day I almost shot myself to death. I was acting out a suicide fantasy. I did not realize that the rifle, Jack's old 30-ought-6, was loaded. I was lying on the floor with the rifle resting along the length of my body. It was pointed at my head. A second before I squeezed the trigger I moved the barrel. The sound of the shot reverberated in our small house. The bullet tore a mammoth hole in the wall of my study. Joshua, in his crib in the bedroom, slept through the whole thing. Just after I fired the rifle I telephoned Gerri. She was at work. She promised to come as soon as she could. Meanwhile, she begged me, "Call Eph." Her voice rang with panic. "Please call him." I did.

Eph Kahn was a superb doctor, and infinitely kind. I described only a few of my symptoms, refusing to elaborate even with his gentle probing. He did a routine physical examination. I remember that he asked me to hold my arms straight out in front of me and he watched my hands for several minutes. He said, "You should be hospitalized." Seeing immediately that I was becoming frantic, my trust shattering, he switched course mid-sentence. "Let's try you on some tranquilizers first," he said. He prescribed a heavy dose of Valium and asked to see me again in a week. I took the Valium and

kept my appointments with Eph. I took care of Joshua. I related more
to Jack, who was frightened and worried and very unsure what to do
to help me. Gerri stayed steady, loving, a veritable anchor to which
I moored my reality. When I got upset or started to feel suicidal, the
Valium seemed to trigger in me an overwhelming desire to sleep.

Gradually as spring turned into summer I improved. Eph cut
back the Valium dosage. I improved some more. I began to write,
first a pamphlet about the student uprising at Columbia that spring
and then the outlines of a book that was to become *The Academic
Rebellion in the United States: A Marxist Appraisal,* which was
published in 1972. With Gerri's counsel and encouragement I
studied the work of contemporary European Communists, including
Alex Dubcek's revolutionary texts about democratizing socialism
in Czechoslovakia, and Maurice Merleau-Ponty's *Humanism and
Terror* on the Stalin purges. I read Roger Garaudy's re-visioning of
Marxism in France, and Herbert Marcuse's synthesis of Freudian
and Marxist paradigms, marking my first serious encounter with
psychoanalytic theory. It was a period of great intellectual ferment
for me, and both Gerri (in letters from abroad once she had left)
and Jack helped me process and synthesize an enormous body of
Marxist literature. Never before in my life had I read with my own
intentionality and purpose.

Stronger in myself, I challenged my father for the first time.
When the Soviet Union invaded Czechoslovakia in August 1968, the
U.S. Communist Party's National Committee called an emergency
meeting. I went. It was the first public activity I had engaged in since
my breakdown in March. Armed with my reading of Dubcek and
other Czech comrades, I denounced the Soviet invasion. I argued
privately with my father, but he remained immovable in his defense
of Soviet policy. When the vote was taken, only three of us—out of

120 comrades on the National Committee—opposed the invasion: Al Richmond, Dorothy Healy, and me.

After this National Committee meeting I thought about leaving the Communist Party. Emotionally I couldn't do it. It was one thing to argue with my father as part of a loyal opposition. It was quite another to fathom myself disinherited. Still wearing the Aptheker mantle, I decided instead to work from within to change the party, to make it into a vibrant, democratic, revolutionary, loving movement, and to embody within myself its "perfection."

Jack completed his dissertation in the spring of 1968 and was awarded a PhD in electrical engineering. Having taught at San Francisco State for two years, he secured a tenure-track position at San Jose State for the following fall. News of his appointment reached the *San Jose Mercury News*. It ran a story under the headline "SJS Hires Bettina's Mate." There was a small political flap, which became the source of sophisticated jokes at the faculty cocktail parties to which we were invited.

With my mother's generous assistance, Jack and I put a $3,000 down payment on a large, pre–1906 earthquake house near the San Jose State campus. (In 1968 the cost of the house was $26,000. To us this seemed an unimaginable sum.) The house had redwood beams, a fireplace, and a spacious yard. We got a puppy, an Australian sheepdog. We named him "Igor." Joshua was approaching his first birthday, a cheerful, curly-headed, gurgling baby whose first words were an approximate sounding of "apple juice," his favorite drink. I nestled into the safety of being a faculty wife and mother. I thought, *Who would suspect that beneath this striving middle-class conformity, even with its Communist quirk, there lurks a past of perversion and madness?*

four

COMMUNIST LIFE AND THE MOVEMENT
TO FREE ANGELA DAVIS

IN 1968 SAN JOSE was still far from the rapid growth that was to transform this small agricultural community into the hub of Silicon Valley. San Jose State College was situated in the heart of the old town. Originating as a normal school in the nineteenth century, its oldest buildings were overlaid with ivy, its lawns immaculate, its trees luxurious. However, the newly built School of Engineering, where Jack would be teaching, had a slick glass facade presaging the electronic age. The campus was flanked by a pleasant, tree-lined residential neighborhood to the east, where we lived, and a downtown business section to the west. San Jose was a rich, fertile valley; its fruit orchards were still much in evidence and the sweet fragrance of apple and peach blossoms marked the beginning of each spring. There was a large Chicano community, its barrio pushed up against the eastern hills. Jack began his teaching career that fall of 1968, and I found private childcare for Joshua three days a week in the home of a nearby family, allowing me to pursue my career as a writer.

Emotionally spent after my nervous breakdown, bereft of the intensity of my almost daily contact with Gerri, who had by then left for Europe, I spent my first months in San Jose curled into the public library, where I found refuge. It was housed in an old brick building downtown, the musty smell of the stacks comforting. I found solace in research as I pored over Moody's Industrial Index, banking and real estate listings, and lawyers' directories, reconstructing the financial interests and interlocking directorates of the men who sat on the University of California's Board of Regents. The research was preparation for a book I was planning to write on the student movement. I had a small study in a back room of our house, adjacent to Joshua's room and overlooking the yard. Books lined its walls, and I worked at an oak desk Max had given me from one or another party office. Except for party meetings, he and I never saw each other, another part of my life sealed and shelved.

I took my life as a writer very seriously, fashioning myself at twenty-four as part of a revolutionary intelligentsia that was to transform the orthodox Marxism-Leninism of the nineteenth and early twentieth centuries into a vibrant force for a democratic and humane socialism. This was the hope many young Communists shared. We believed in the promise of the Prague Spring of 1968, when tens of thousands of people participated in a movement to democratize socialism, and the almost simultaneous uprisings in Paris, led by students and later joined by the various trade unions comprising the French working class. Ferment in the French, Italian, and Czech Communist parties measured the vibrancy of that moment in party history.

I wrote for a variety of small radical presses, the Communist Party's monthly journal, *Political Affairs* (which my father no longer edited), and more mainstream publications like the *Nation* and the *California Law Review*. I also aspired to write for more intellectually prestigious journals like the *Atlantic Monthly* and the *New York Review of Books*. With the assistance of Jessica Mitford, my submissions at least made their way onto various editorial desks. I was, nevertheless, repeatedly rebuffed. I think now that my writing was much too precious and self-conscious. With my father writing at a phenomenal rate (one may say, in retrospect, perhaps a fanatical one) I felt enormous pressure to "produce." In telephone conversations with my parents the most urgent question was "What are you working on?"

Shortly after we moved to San Jose I needed to rent a typewriter. After helping me find a suitable model, the clerk asked me to fill out a card with my name, address, telephone number, and occupation. Under occupation I wrote "writer." The clerk then reviewed the card. When he got to the space for occupation, he crossed out "writer" and wrote in "housewife"! Normally hesitant to make a scene, I exploded. The clerk's hands literally trembled as he tore up the first card and issued me a second with which he dared not tamper. Though it would be a few years until I called myself a feminist, I knew that such an incident would not have happened had I been male.

It was in these months and the coming year that I wrote *The Academic Rebellion in the United States.* Whatever other pretensions I had, this work came directly from the heart of my experiences in the student movement. I focused on the new post–World War II relationships between the university, industry, finance, and government. The universities, I maintained, had become crucial to a scientific and technological revolution that was destined to change the face of capitalism. I drew diagrams of the inner workings of computers as I explained the implications of the electronics revolution. Whether in Berkeley or New York, the student uprisings were in response to this new "objective reality," meaning, in Marxist terms, the material conditions that were transforming the students' potential as agents for revolutionary change. I loved working on this book, and felt myself to be on the cutting edge of arguments then taking place within Communist and, more broadly, Marxist student and intellectual circles.

My book reflected the debates then raging in Communist circles about the potential of the New Left, including groups like Students for a Democratic Society (SDS), to be a revolutionary force. Although many of my older comrades welcomed the change in the political climate since the 1950s, wrought at least in part by the New Left, most of the elders in the U.S. Communist Party remained deeply suspicious of it. Intellectuals were seen as unreliable allies to the working class, with the potential to corrupt Marxism. As I began to publish, Gus Hall, the party's general secretary, asked me to submit my work for prior approval. I refused. The whole struggle for a democratic socialism was about precisely this—the freedom to express oneself with no fear of censure. Right from the beginning of my time on the National Committee, I was in trouble with the party leadership, both because of my writings and because I had opposed the Soviet invasion of Czechoslovakia. My father, however, approved of my work, and this was all that mattered to me.

Shortly after Jack and I moved to San Jose, Martha wrote to me from Chicago. Her letter was forwarded from our Berkeley address. She asked if she could visit us and see Joshua. Her letter made me very nervous. All my paranoia about our relationship and the FBI intrigues returned. Martha arrived full of good cheer. She was humorous, pleasant, at ease with Jack, delighted with Joshua. I was a wreck: physically distant from Martha, tense, and largely silent. She stayed the weekend. I did not see her again for eleven years. I had sealed off the traumas I had survived in Berkeley, and Martha's presence brought them all back up to the surface. I was so relieved when she left and I could shut it all away again.

Jack and I joined the Communist Party club in San Jose as soon as we settled into the area. It was an enclave of older comrades, survivors of both the McCarthy era and the revelations about Stalin's persecutions in the Soviet Union. We were the only members under fifty. The comrades were set in their ways, and they interacted with each other in habitual patterns, like partners in an unfortunate marriage that had gone on for too long. For all of this, however, this small group of a dozen or so comrades cared deeply about the state of the world, diligently sold the *People's World*, marched against the war in Vietnam, and agonized over police violence in the barrio. I liked a couple of the women comrades very much; they were kind to me and gave me maternal advice. But I felt no connection to the club's concerns, which were so far removed from my experiences among students. Jack was getting his political bearings on the San Jose State campus, and my activist heart was still in Berkeley. In the spring of 1969 that campus exploded again, this time over what was to become known as People's Park.

A vacant lot a few blocks from the campus was taken over by community residents. They built a children's park with flowers, sandboxes, and swings. No sooner was the park completed than the regents laid claim to the land. Planning to pave it over and make a parking lot, they ordered a chainlink fence be placed along the perimeter of the property. When residents and students protested, heavy police reinforcements were called in. The police then systematically uprooted the flowers and dismantled the play areas. Soon, the relatively routine skirmishes between police and protesters erupted into a major conflagration when police opened fire using shotguns loaded with allegedly nonlethal pellets. James Rector, a young bystander observing the fighting from the roof of a building, was shot and killed; another observer, Alan Blanchard, was shot in the face and blinded; 110 students were treated at local hospitals for gunshot wounds. Most of them had been shot in the back fleeing the police. The governor called in the National Guard.

Horrified by this news, I resurrected my suede jacket, padded my ribs, shoved a bottle of Vaseline into my pocket to protect against the tear gas, and drove to Berkeley to participate in the continuing protests. Police roamed the campus and the surrounding streets, firing tear gas at will. Students were unarmed, but many had become adept at hurling smoking tear gas canisters back at the police who had fired them. A helicopter made repeated sweeps over the campus, bombing us with "CS gas," a form of tear gas more potent than the conventional police arsenal. It was so thick that many local residents and patients at Cowell Hospital on the Berkeley campus had to be evacuated.

Police with riot helmets and clubs, their faces covered with gas masks, repeatedly charged into us. We would disperse, dash for cover, regroup. At one point I took shelter in the student union building. From the third floor, I watched the battle in Sproul Hall Plaza below me. As the police helicopter hovered directly outside the window, I imagined hurling a chair through the glass to catch in its propellers and bring it down. At another point a group of us walked on the western periphery of the campus and entered it from that direction in an effort to reach the chancellor's residence to register a direct protest with him. As we approached University House, helmeted and masked police charged us, firing tear gas. We scattered. I ran toward the center of campus only to encounter yet another police charge. As

I jumped off a small stone parapet, a tear gas canister exploded in my face and I fell to the ground. Three or four officers began beating me with their clubs. I curled into a ball, my hands over my head. I was rescued by a student in a white coat with a Red Cross arm band. He half-carried, half-dragged me into the Life Sciences Building.

I hurled myself into the People's Park protests as much from personal fury and despair as from political outrage at the injustice of the regents' decision. It was a fury born from my time in prison and a despair born from unacknowledged sexual violence and abuse. I welcomed the combat, although I was never armed and never fought back. Curled in a fetal position while being beaten with clubs was an astonishingly literal metaphor for my emotional state. Afterward, in retelling the story of People's Park, I could enact my ongoing fantasy of the revolutionary intellectual. The experience also satisfied a deep psychological need to be physically abused. I had a deep self-loathing fueled by my sense of myself as a sexual pervert. The beatings acted as a cathartic release, both a punishment and a purification.

By the time the riots at People's Park took place, Ronald Reagan was governor of California, Richard Nixon was in the White House, and the political climate had moved significantly to the right. The People's Park protests occurred a year after club-swinging police routed antiwar protesters at the Democratic Party National Convention in Chicago. Fred Hampton and Mark Clark, leaders of the Black Panther Party, would be murdered in their sleep by police later that year. And the next year students at Kent State in Ohio and Jackson State in Mississippi would be killed. By May Day 1971, some thirteen thousand people were detained by police in Washington, D.C., for protesting the war in Vietnam in a peaceful demonstration at the White House organized by SDS. To me, this indicated the growing use of police repression to quell dissent. The battle for

People's Park was not about a park. It was about the University Board of Regents, the governor, and the police reasserting dominion over the Berkeley campus and its environs. It marked the symbolic end of our insurgency. Thirty years later, in 1999, "People's Park" was still just a vacant lot surrounded by a chainlink fence.

In that same spring of 1969, the University of California Board of Regents fired Angela Davis from her teaching position as a lecturer in the philosophy department at UCLA because she was a member of the U.S. Communist Party, and so began Angela's long defense of her beliefs, her character, and her very life. Her membership had been made public in a letter to the *Daily Bruin*, the campus newspaper, written by William Divale, who was a member of the party and a paid FBI informant. Divale's letter announced his informant status. Angela had already been the object of sharp attack because of her support of the Black Panther Party (BPP) and her activism against the war in Vietnam.

I flew down to Los Angeles to see what I could do to help. I had not seen Angela since our childhood in Brooklyn more than a decade earlier, but we had stayed in touch through our party connections and mutual friends. Angela had retained counsel and a hearing was in progress. This was not a court hearing, but a proceeding on the UCLA campus before a faculty committee. Meanwhile, hundreds of students gathered at support rallies. The issue seemed straightforward to us. The firing of Angela Davis violated her rights of free speech and free association under the First Amendment, and her rights of academic freedom as a university instructor. The hearing turned in Angela's favor and the regents were forced to rescind their order. The philosophy department was then allowed to continue Angela's employment as they had wished to do.

Angela was rehired as a lecturer for the 1969–70 academic year. In the fall of 1969, two thousand students came to hear her first lecture on Frederick Douglass.

It was wonderful to see Angela again. We reconnected with the intensity and ease that had marked our childhood friendship. She was a graduate student at UC San Diego, working toward a doctorate in philosophy and teaching as a lecturer at UCLA. In the intervening years, Angela had completed her undergraduate studies at Brandeis, and had studied in both France and Germany before returning to the United States for her doctoral work. She had recently passed her qualifying exams and was in the process of writing her dissertation. The chair of her dissertation committee was Herbert Marcuse, a Jewish refugee from Nazi Germany. As one of the founders of the Frankfurt School, a Marxist circle of European intellectuals, Marcuse was one of the best-known philosophers of his time. His book *One-Dimensional Man*, one of the first cultural analyses of capitalism from a Marxist perspective, deeply influenced many on the New Left.

Angela was living in Los Angeles and becoming a well-known activist in the black community. She was a member of the Che-Lumumba Club of the U.S. Communist Party, an all-black club named after Cuban revolutionary Che Guevara and the leader of the Congolese national liberation movement, Patrice Lumumba, whose assassination had been arranged by the CIA. She was also closely allied with the Black Panther Party, which had begun in Oakland and quickly spread to urban ghettos across the country, including, of course, Los Angeles. While the media sensationalized the Panthers' advocacy of armed self-defense against police violence in the black community, the BPP also provided many important community-based services, including breakfast-for-children programs, freedom schools, and health clinics.

In late June 1969, I went to Helsinki, Finland, to attend a World
Congress of Women sponsored by the Women's International
Democratic Federation (WIDF). I was part of a U.S. delegation headed
by Charlene Mitchell, an African American comrade who had recently
moved from Los Angeles to New York. Charlene and Angela were
close friends. Charlene was in her late thirties, a vivacious woman
who was one of the best organizers in the Communist Party. The
WIDF was based in the socialist world, and all of the delegates who
attended this congress were representatives of either Communist
parties or democratic, progressive, or national liberation movements
in their respective countries. All were aligned with the position of
the Soviet Union on international issues. There was a cheering, foot-
stomping welcome for the Cuban and Vietnamese delegations, and
the star delegate was Valentina Tereshkova, the Soviet cosmonaut
and the first woman in space.

From Helsinki I was to fly to East Berlin, where I would meet
up with Jack. We were to be guests of the Free German Youth (FDJ).
This was the official youth organization of the Socialist Unity Party,
which governed the German Democratic Republic (GDR), known in
the U.S. press as East Germany. In other words, we were to be guests
of state. From the GDR we were to fly to Paris for a rendezvous with
Gerri and her husband, Orin. From Paris we were on to England for a
holiday. We were to be gone for six weeks. It was a heady time.

As I planned this trip, I asked my mother if she would take care
of Joshua, who was nineteen months old. After her bout with breast
cancer, Mother had retired from her work at the travel agency. Her
health was good and she was pleased to agree. My in-laws, Rose
and Sam, were also thrilled to share in childcare. My parents still
lived in Brooklyn in the house on Ludlam Place, where I had spent
my adolescence. Although my father went to work every day, he

was home on weekends and was happy, he said, to have Joshua
with them. Still with no memory of my own childhood abuse, I
thought my parents afforded the safest place in the world to leave
my son. I felt guilty for leaving Joshua for such an extended time,
but I was also desperate for emotional space. I needed to be away
from family responsibilities, to be either alone or with people to
whom I had no obligation. Helsinki afforded that. And Paris would
bring me to Gerri.

Although slated as a World Congress of Women, the Helsinki
gathering was certainly not a feminist one. If anything, the congress
was hostile to the feminist movements burgeoning in the United States
and Western Europe. It considered them passing bourgeois fancies.
There was no acknowledgment or discussion of rape, domestic
violence, sexual abuse, reproductive freedoms, the international
slave trade in women, or sexuality. Congress issues focused on
gaining equality for women in literacy, education, health care, and
employment. The party considered issues relating to reproduction,
sexuality, and violence to be "personal" and not relevant to bona fide
working-class struggles. Other resolutions focused on support for the
national liberation movements in Vietnam, Mozambique, Angola,
and South Africa, and condemnations of racism and U.S. imperialism. Charlene and I helped to draft the resolution on racism.

At the time, I had no feminist consciousness and no historical
understanding of the struggles of women in various socialist and
communist movements to gain autonomy and define their own
agendas. And, of course, what was on the congress agenda was of
great significance to women. The problem was not what was on the
agenda, but what was omitted from it. It obscured any definition
of or struggle against male domination, and the ways that women

internalized their own subordination. These were the issues most animating the women's liberation movements in the West.

I was thrilled to be in Helsinki, awed by the vibrant energy of the hundreds of women in attendance. In fact, I could not have imagined so many beautiful and purposeful, competent women in one place. Charlene and I met with the Vietnamese delegation. Their firsthand descriptions of combat and of the U.S. use of napalm and chemical defoliants were horrifying. No translators were available who spoke Vietnamese and English, so we worked with two translators moving from Vietnamese to German to English. When we were joined by Duana, a woman of the Montagnard people (an indigenous group in Vietnam, so named because they lived in the mountains), we moved from Duana's language to Vietnamese to German to English. Duana was more open in her emotions than her Vietnamese counterparts. She described caves and other shelters deep underground and the terrible heat and pounding as bombs fell. At one point, eyes brimming, she voiced surprise at how young the American soldiers were. "They are just boys," she said, expressing her anguish in being forced to kill them.

In East Germany, as guests of the government, Jack and I were accompanied by a guide and translator, Ursula Beitz. Jack, who had been raised in a family much more consciously Jewish than my own, had great ambivalence about visiting Germany, even its eastern, socialist sector. He had many relatives murdered in the Holocaust, and although we did not encounter anti-Semitism, the pall of memory hung over both of us. Our most traumatic experience was our visit to Buchenwald. The former concentration camp was now a memorial. As we walked up the hill toward the gates of the camp, a dramatic cast-iron statue came gradually into view. In the unmistakable style of the social realists, it depicted a cluster of men in varying postures of suffering and defiance. The camp itself was left exactly as it had been, complete with its buildings, barracks, and crematoria.

Although Ursula accompanied us throughout, our guide in Buchenwald was an elderly man, white haired and shrunken, who was a camp survivor. He spoke English and had a brother who lived in Brooklyn. He explained that he was among several survivors who took people on tours of the camp, each having vowed to bear witness to this place where nearly three hundred thousand people were imprisoned and fifty-six thousand were murdered. Many were Jews, but the majority of victims at Buchenwald were political prisoners, among them Ernst Thälmann, the head of the German Communist Party. A wreath marked the spot against a brick wall where he had been shot. Buchenwald was the only camp to liberate itself. When U.S. soldiers entered it in 1945, all the Nazi guards, the commandant, everyone running the camp were either dead or had fled. Exhausted and starving prisoners provided each other what solace they could. Our guide showed us the rooms where people were hung from meat hooks to slowly strangle to death. (Later, in Paris, I could not bear to look at the windows of the butcher shops where animals were hung on display.) He showed us where people were shot under the guise of a medical examination. He showed us the ovens. He described people he had known. He told us how the resistance inside the camp was organized, and how the uprising was planned and executed.

As we walked through the camp, Ursula became overwhelmed with guilt, repeatedly expressing her personal anguish to me. She pointed to a mound of earth, a mass grave, she said, of Jews. It was unmarked. In the commandant's quarters she struggled to explain to me that he was insane. He forced women to have sex with him and then strangled them and put their bodies under his bed. In her distress, Ursula could not think of the English word for "strangle," so to illustrate she put her hands around my throat. The physical sensation was jolting, and terror shot through me so that I felt suddenly nauseous and dizzy. I tried to hide this from Ursula so she would not get any more upset than she already was. Later, as we sat in our hotel room sipping drinks, she told me how her father had forced her to join the Hitler Youth. He was a mathematics teacher in a small village school, and he was afraid he would lose his job if she did not join. "I was twelve," Ursula said, weeping.

On another occasion, I asked Ursula to take me to the Nazi archives, housed in a multistoried brick building in the heart of Berlin. Here historians combed the meticulous records kept by the Gestapo and SS, in part to continue the painful reconstruction of the Third Reich, in part to help relatives in different countries who were still searching for loved ones. Ursula translated for me.

I was astounded at the record of the German resistance to the Nazis, hundreds and thousands of people who refused to acquiesce. I asked specifically about Jewish and student groups. The Baum Gruppe was prominent among the Jewish groups. They operated in Berlin, and among their many activities they blew up an anti-Soviet exhibition in June 1941. This was just after the Nazi invasion of the Soviet Union. A student group called the White Rose was most prominent in Munich. They distributed anti-Nazi materials, including appeals to young men to resist induction into the Wehrmacht, the German army. It was easy to see the parallels to our own activities in the United States in opposition to the war in Vietnam. I read the leaflets of other student groups in the anti-Nazi resistance. One was headlined, "What Is to Be Done Soldiers?" and contained the following text: "The soldiers who you are fighting are not your enemies, but they are the enemy of our enemy, i.e., Hitler."

Another headline read, "The Way Out?" and offered this advice: "Direct your rifles against the grave-diggers of the German people. Death and misery to Hitler and his gang! The Best Germans are the deadliest enemies of Adolph Hitler!"

I read the names of the Jewish fighters, studied the accompanying photographs: Heinz Rothholz, 21; Heinz Birnbaum, 21; Hella Sara Hirsch, 21; Hanni Sara Meyer, 21. All were beheaded.

On another occasion, Ursula accompanied Jack and me to a meeting with the leadership of the Free German Youth for a discussion of the youth movement in the United States. Ursula and I were the only women in attendance. The group thought Jack and I were exaggerating when we spoke of racism, poverty, and police brutality in the United States. I tried to talk to them about the causes of the student rebellion and about the new writings in the Western European parties. I was met with pleasant but resolute opposition. Their utopian projections about life in the United States were so incongruent with the rigid, pro-Soviet dogma about U.S. imperialism; we couldn't connect these diverging views. It was very frustrating. At one point, our dialogue was so intense that Ursula, exhausted, had to ask for a break. She was translating with such fluency and speed that we had forgotten she was there.

Our exit from East Berlin was dramatic and fraught with danger. The reason: U.S. passports were not valid for travel in East Germany. When we had arrived our passports had been taken. They were returned to us with special visas attached, but the passports themselves remained unstamped so that U.S. authorities would have no documentation of our trip to East Germany when we reentered the country. Additionally, I was carrying a 16mm film given to me by some Vietnamese women visiting the GDR who asked me to bring it back to the United States. It documented and explained the

1968 Tet offensive in which U.S. troops had been routed. So Jack and I needed to cross the border into West Berlin undetected by the Western authorities.

Although it made no official stops in East Berlin, the Berlin subway system was controlled by the East Germans. At about five o'clock in the morning on the day of our departure, the streets deserted, Jack and I, with all our luggage, were escorted by Ursula, Grace Arnold, a U.S.-born comrade whose mother still lived in Berkeley, and several party officials to a small, hidden opening in the Berlin Wall. We entered a subway station. Armed soldiers were everywhere. At the entrance, seated behind a tall wooden desk, was a soldier who took our passports. Ursula and the others spoke to him in rapid-fire German. The soldier was young, unsmiling, and unruffled by the officialdom. He carefully checked our passports, then our faces, comparing them to the photographs in our passports. Finally, he lifted out the special visas, stamped them, returned our passports, and waved us on. We said goodbye to our German friends, who were not permitted down the stairs leading to the train platform. Ursula hugged me tightly and wept silently into my neck, bidding me over and over again to take care and be well. Over the next several years we corresponded, but we were never to see each other again.

Hearts pounding, Jack and I clambered down the steps. When we reached the platform we saw many more soldiers, all of them armed with automatic weapons. They also patrolled the catwalks on both sides of the platform. A few minutes later a train came. It made its unscheduled stop to pick us up. I searched the faces of the West Berliners, who were undoubtedly commuters on their way to work, and they searched mine. As we exited at the station for the West Berlin airport, we appeared as two American tourists, indistinguishable from hundreds of others. Later that morning we boarded a flight for Paris, and from there I mailed the contraband Vietnamese film home to myself in San Jose.

After this experience at the Berlin Wall, I knew in my heart that it was wrong, and that it served only to imprison people in their own country. Hostage to my aspirations within the Communist Party, and within my father's house, however, I said nothing.

Paris was glorious. Gerri and Orin were generous hosts. They had secured a small hotel room for us near their apartment on the Left Bank, and we often took meals together. We went to museums, cafés, the Sorbonne, the countryside. All I wanted was to be with Gerri. Whatever else we did in those two weeks, what I remember now are the endless walks Gerri and I took together, the conversations, debates, dialogues we had—in cafés sipping coffee, in bakeries where we bought treats, the odor of freshly baked bread perfuming the street. Jack seemed content to visit the museums and take long hikes through the city. I loved the small shops, the bicycles, the students, the narrow streets, the river Seine, the gardens. I loved Gerri and my heart was full. We talked about Berkeley and Berlin and Dubrovnik (where she and Orin had lived), about the philosophical manuscripts of the young Marx, theories of alienation, Marcuse, Sartre, de Beauvoir (whom I had not yet read).

One evening, the four of us stood in a large crowd gathered around a television set in a shop window and watched Neil Armstrong step onto the moon. It was July 20, 1969.

Perhaps the best period of our married life was our time together in England that summer. Jack and I spent ten days there before our return flight to New York. We walked everywhere in London and Oxford, savored restaurants and bookstores, and visited old estates.

In Oxford, we went to Blackwell's bookstore, by far the largest, most extensive bookstore I had ever seen. I opened an account with them so I could order books once we were home. Then for a few days, we hopped a bus each morning and visited a different village in the Cotswolds. These were charming places with their high streets and village greens and pastoral tranquility. Later, back in London, we caught a performance of the antifascist play *The Resistible Rise of Arturo Ui,* by Bertolt Brecht. We talked a lot, real conversations, about Germany, about the party. We laughed, ate good food in old pubs, and remembered how much we liked each other.

We arrived at Kennedy Airport in mid-August, tanned, relaxed, and refreshed. Waiting to claim our baggage from the carousels, which had not yet begun their rotation, I looked up to see if I could catch a glimpse of my parents and Joshua. I saw them almost at once, behind the giant glass walls surrounding us. My father was holding Josh, waving and pointing him toward us. All I saw was a mop of blond curls. I felt a tremendous rush, and could hardly wait to get upstairs. We cleared customs and bounded to the upper floor. Josh was still in my father's arms, slack jawed, unsmiling, eyes wide. I extended my arms out to take him but he turned away. With some coaxing he finally went to Jack. Mom said, "Oh, he just needs to get used to you again!" and she laughed heartily. She was so glad to see us, she said, all safe and sound. It was several days before Josh would let me hold him without fussing, and several more after we were home before he began to laugh again. His reticence and somber countenance left me worried about my lengthy absence from him, and reinforced my sense of guilt that I was not a very good mother.

Jack came up for tenure in the electrical engineering department at San Jose State just after we returned from Europe. It was the fall of 1969, a year after we had moved to San Jose. His department voted in its majority for tenure and forwarded its recommendation to the appropriate faculty committees and administrative personnel. A minority within the department opposed his promotion on political grounds. Inventing academic reasons, they also wrote incriminating memos to higher authorities that evidenced their true political motives: They didn't want to grant tenure to a member of the Communist Party. Eventually, despite his department's recommendation, the administration denied tenure.

Jack and I were consumed with his case for months. Jack was ostensibly denied tenure because, according to the minority within his department, his laboratory work was "deficient." Even though Jack knew that his was a political case, he agonized over this obvious fabrication, incessantly revisiting the issue, reviewing his lab notes and course reports. This moment was further complicated because, although Jack wanted tenure and the security of employment that went with it, he was also ambivalent about pursuing an academic career. He longed, he said, for a different life that was "more directly in the working class," as he put it. In the throes of this deeply personal and agonizing struggle, Jack and I were brought closer together than we had ever been before or would be again. We talked at length about his options. I encouraged him to explore other employment if that was what he really wanted. I had no fears about our economic situation because my experience had always been comfortably middle class, even though my father had never held an academic position. I had always been provided for, and it never occurred to me that we would not be perfectly all right. Jack, however, remembered years of poverty during his childhood, and in the end economic security held sway. Jack was absolutely firm in his political commitments, and he rose to this challenge with great personal courage.

Jack decided to file a grievance. The grievance committee found in Jack's favor and recommended that he be awarded tenure. However, the college president overruled the committee on direct order from the chancellor of the state colleges. Jack was given what is unceremoniously called a "terminal year of employment." He was very distraught. I, however, had no emotional response at all; I just focused on the political tactics and the steps we needed to take to win his case. I telephoned Doris Brin Walker. With a long history of defending Communists, she was the best lawyer I knew for a case like this. Dobby, as we affectionately called her, was a law partner with Bob Treuhaft, one of the FSM attorneys, and I had known her since I arrived in Berkeley. She told us not to worry about the money to pay her; we could raise it as the case progressed. In any event, she largely donated her services, convinced that this case could be won and would set a vital legal precedent.

Dobby asked me to write the brief for the case, and so, holed up in my study for ten days with the chicken pox, contracted from Joshua, I wrote. I had a transcript of the grievance hearing, a copy of all the college's rules and regulations, Jack's file, and myriad other documents. Jack considered me the legal expert in the family. Whether because of my fevered condition or some actual talent for the law, Dobby pronounced the finished brief excellent. She made the necessary modifications and revisions and filed Jack's appeal directly into federal court, judging it best to bypass the state courts altogether.

The final hearing occurred early in August 1971, two years after the original denial. At the time of the hearing both Jack and I were out of the country. However, a jubilant Doris Walker telephoned some weeks later to inform us of the court's decision. Outraged at the written evidence of political intrigue in violation of Jack's First Amendment rights, federal judge Alfonso Zirpoli had ordered that he be awarded tenure. Dobby explained that this was an extraordinary decision. In most cases where there was a favorable decision, a judge would have ordered the college to grant a new hearing at the departmental and/or administrative levels. Not so in the *Kurzweil* case. The federal court's ruling set the precedent Dobby had hoped for, making it clear that membership in the Communist Party no longer constituted grounds for dismissal. We were thrilled. The university made plans to appeal Judge Zirpoli's decision. At Doris's suggestion, Jack filed a civil suit and asked for significant damages. University counsel telephoned. If Jack would drop the suit, the university would drop its appeal. We agreed. Jack's tenure and continued employment was assured.

Jack's joy was overwhelming; he was giddy with relief. I rejoiced about the political victory and looked forward to a greater sense of domestic ease. Jack and I held a press conference and he read a statement that we had jointly written. We appraised the significance of the case for Communist and radical teachers, and applauded the courage and principle of the court's decision. We ended our prepared statement with what may have seemed a rather incongruous appeal for "the freedom of all political prisoners." But by September 1971, Angela Davis was in jail awaiting trial, and we were in the throes of her case. Newspapers reported the decision in the *Kurzweil* case with astonished headlines, and Jack was flooded with telephone calls and letters from well-wishers.

Shortly before we left for Europe in the summer of 1969, I attended a series of party meetings with Max and other Bay Area leaders. The purpose: to draft me into becoming the West Coast editor of the *World* magazine, inserted into the California-based *People's World,* our Communist newspaper. There was much political wrangling, and in the end the party thought that with my experience in the student movements, I could bring more varied and stimulating coverage. I had never been a big fan of the magazine, and though I knew it would be a thankless position and I would likely be restricted in what I could say, I took it on anyway. Privately I bristled; publicly I complied, as I had for as long as I had been in the party. I almost never permitted myself any expression of anger, and this was no exception. Anger terrified me because I associated it with my father's raging and my mother's unpredictable explosions. I had an image of myself to maintain as a good and trusted comrade, so I agreed to the position.

My tenure lasted only a year. The highlight was asking for an interview with the folksinger Malvina Reynolds. Malvina, a well-known performer who lived in Berkeley, had been an early supporter of the Free Speech Movement, and she often donated her time to raise money for antiwar and civil rights organizations. Malvina was in her sixties, and sang a rugged alto with her raspy, thick voice. She wrote all of her own music. Her most famous song was "Little Boxes," which Pete Seeger eventually popularized. Later she wrote another famous song, "The Judge Said," a fierce rebuke to a Wisconsin jurist who sanctioned the rape of a high school girl. The judge was eventually recalled by an outraged feminist community; Malvina's song was their anthem during the campaign. The first time I heard Malvina sing another of her songs, "We Don't Need the Men," a hilarious take on male privilege, I happened to be sitting next to my longshoreman comrade, Archie Brown. His voice crackled in my ear: "What is this feminist shit?" I sat doubled over with laughter. Her song "The Little Red Hen" was about a hen who gets to eat what she helped to sow, a very sweet ode to socialism. The verses in all of Malvina's songs were seemingly ridiculous ditties. Yet strung together and sung to her clever tunes they provided a sharp political commentary.

Though we corresponded for a while and talked about the possibility of an interview, in the end she wrote to me:

Dear Bettina:

I had it, years ago, with beating my poetic head against the party's rigid formulations . . . and while I am moved to help you personally in any way I can, and I think you are trying to change this rigidity, I'm afraid you'll have to count me out. . . .

I was stunned by her refusal, mostly because I was rarely refused anything by anyone. Also, I had no idea former party people felt so much anger toward the party, not because I hadn't seen it before, but because I hadn't allowed myself to register it. Malvina's refusal was a good lesson for me in breaking through some of my denial about how sectarian and isolated the party was. Yet I couldn't acknowledge this fully without threatening my personal belief structure.

In those same months, Jessica Mitford invited me up to Berkeley for one of our regular tête-à-têtes. Decca was close friends with Al Richmond, who had been one of the principal leaders of the party in Northern California. It quickly became apparent that she wanted to talk to me about his resignation—not only from his position as editor of the *People's World*, but also from the party. Al had traveled to Czechoslovakia the year before, in the fall of 1968, and had ferreted out what he saw as a much more complicated truth than the party leadership in New York would or could allow. No longer able to abide the party's uncritical support of the Soviet invasion, he resigned. After resigning, he was gratuitously expelled by the national leadership (of which I was, shamefully, a part, although I abstained in the vote on Al's expulsion). I explained as much as I knew to Dec, but she was furious. "How can you stay in the party?" she shouted into my face. Seething with frustration and nearly weeping, she shouted again, "How can you?"

How could I? How did I? In my mid-twenties, I was still loyal to the party because I was still loyal to my parents, especially to my father. I was bound to him in ways I did not understand, but when I thought about leaving the party—and I certainly did—the blood drained from my head, my heart began racing, and, depending on how long I allowed myself the fantasy, adrenaline pumped through my body. Leaving the party meant abandoning my father, or, more precisely, leaving the party meant being abandoned by him. It meant I would no longer be the "perfect daughter," and I had invested my whole life into honing that perfection. When you left the party you were, by definition, a renegade. The party allowed no middle ground of reprieve. I had heard my father rail against "that sonofabitch" renegade all of my life and I was not about to become one.

I don't know how I would have continued to cope with all of these contradictions, but I never had the opportunity to find out because Angela Davis was arrested on October 13, 1970. She was seized by FBI agents on a fugitive warrant from California. The FBI took her and her underground associate, David Poindexter, into custody at the Howard Johnson Motor Hotel on Eighth Avenue in Manhattan. She had been on their Ten Most Wanted list, following an attempted escape by African American prisoners from a courtroom in Marin County, California. A grand jury had indicted her on charges in connection with the escape attempt. Angela had fled for her life as media reports of a shoot-out between prisoners and police and the death of the judge had whipped up a frenzy of racist and anti-Communist hatred. A very different set of facts would emerge much later in Angela's trial, but this initial media portrayal was what would remain in the minds of most white people.

I was in my study when I heard news of Angela's arrest on the radio. Hands shaking, I telephoned Jack at work. We had already talked about what I would do if Angela was captured because I knew she had fled. I resigned my position as West Coast editor of the magazine, dropped everything else I was doing, and boarded a plane for New York. Jack took charge of Joshua's care. He would soon be turning three, and I promised him I would be home in time for his birthday, maternal guilt and political commitment vying with each other in my mind. In fact, we delayed Josh's birthday party until I did get home. As I became immersed in Angela's defense I had only the most limited and routine time with my son. I never doubted my choice, but emotionally it was hard to make, and I promised myself I would make it up to Josh when the case was over.

Angela was being held at the Women's House of Detention, an old, drafty, dirty, once–red brick building with barred windows near Greenwich Avenue and West Tenth Street, an eyesore in the otherwise charming, chic environs of Greenwich Village. At the prison Angela and I stood facing each other, separated by a Plexiglas barrier, talking over a telephone. She looked exhausted. Fighting extradition to California, Angela's attorneys were John Abt, the Communist Party's general counsel, and Margaret Burnham, our childhood friend. A California grand jury had indicted Angela on charges of first-degree murder, first-degree kidnapping, and conspiracy to commit both. She was accused of having knowingly supplied the weapons used in the escape attempt. She was never accused of actually being present in the courtroom in Marin County or taking part in the escape attempt.

Her co-defendant, equally charged, was Ruchell Magee, a San Quentin prisoner. There was no bail. Both faced the death penalty. Angela was only twenty-six years old.

Seeing Angela like that, behind the Plexiglas in a drab prison uniform, slammed home the reality of her arrest. Initially, there had been a part of me that could not believe any of this was happening, a part of me that felt I was still a kid, that we were both still kids, and that none of this could be real. It was as though we had gotten into a really bad scrape and our parents would soon rescue us. But as I looked into Angela's face, riven with grief and tension, I knew the reality. I could barely hold my own panic at bay. I, too, was only twenty-six; neither of us was many years out of Advance, the socialist youth group that had met in the basement of my parents' home in Brooklyn. And yet so much had happened to both of us in the intervening years.

Angela was already working out political strategies, studying the transcripts of the grand jury hearing, honing legal arguments. She wanted me to circulate an article I had written about the case that had been published in a leftist, non-Communist newspaper, the *National Guardian*, and to speak at rallies in her defense. She had a list of things for me to do, people to call, organizing to pursue. I left New York to help establish her defense committee on the West Coast. I came home feeling weighted and sobered, my rage razor sharp.

Angela's flight from California and the subsequent manhunt and arrest had caused a sensation. The black community rose to her defense with such a unanimity of purpose that I felt this was the only reason she had not been shot to death by the FBI agents at the time of her arrest. Had she been killed, the ghettos would have exploded again, as they did after the assassination of Martin Luther King, Jr. Angela's picture was on the front page of every newspaper in the country; she was on the covers of *Newsweek* and *Time;* television stations vied with each other in their coverage, replaying again and again photos of the terrible shootings at the courthouse in Marin County.

On August 7, 1970, a seventeen-year-old African American named Jonathan Jackson entered a Marin County courtroom armed with a rifle and a shotgun. The weapons hidden, he took a seat. The trial of a San Quentin prisoner, James McClain, was in progress. Another San Quentin prisoner, Ruchell Magee, was on the witness stand testifying for him, and a third prisoner, William Christmas, was waiting to testify. All were black. McClain, who was acting as his own attorney, had been charged with assault in the attempted stabbing of a San Quentin prison guard. This was his second trial. The first had ended with a hung jury. The jurors, district attorney, and judge were white. Gary Thomas, who was presenting the case, was the nephew-in-law of the judge on the case, Harold Haley. Judge Haley, of course, should have recused himself, given his family connection to the prosecution.

Jonathan Jackson took over the courtroom, arming McClain, Christmas, and Magee and taking the judge, the district attorney, and three jurors as hostages. He then led them from the courtroom, through the corridors of the courthouse, and out into the parking lot to a van, where the hostages were forced inside. Though the Marin County sheriff's deputies drew their weapons, they held their fire. But because San Quentin prison guards had standing orders to shoot to kill escaping prisoners, they opened fire. Within seconds Jonathan Jackson, James McClain, William Christmas, and Judge Haley were dead; prosecutor Gary Thomas and Ruchell Magee were seriously wounded, and one juror was wounded.

Within days, police investigators announced that several of the weapons used by Jonathan Jackson were registered in Angela's name. Jackson was from Los Angeles, and he and Angela knew each other from their mutual efforts to build a political movement to free the so-called Soledad Brothers, one of whom, George Jackson, was Jonathan's brother. In the media-whipped hysteria following the events at the Marin County Courthouse, Jonathan Jackson's particular experience and the reasons for his actions were never reported. We tried to tell the story.

When Jonathan was six years old, his brother George Jackson was arrested for the armed robbery of a gas station. The amount stolen was $70. George was a passenger in the car used in the getaway. Nobody was hurt. In a plea bargain, arranged on the very bad advice of an attorney, George Jackson was sentenced to one year to life imprisonment under California's indeterminate sentencing law. By August 1970, he had been in prison for eleven years, seven of them in solitary confinement.

At the time Jonathan took over the courtroom in Marin County, George Jackson and two other black prisoners, Fleeta Drumgo and John Clutchette, had been charged with first-degree murder in the death of a white prison guard at Soledad, a state prison in Monterey County, about 250 miles south of San Quentin. The killing of the Soledad guard was in reprisal for the murder of a black prisoner a few months before. The families of the men had organized the Soledad Brothers Defense Committee. They insisted that Jackson, Drumgo, and Clutchette were innocent. Their families maintained that they had been charged with the murder because the three were leaders in a movement for prisoners' rights. Angela Davis was a member of the Soledad Brothers Defense Committee, she had spoken widely on their behalf, and she had attended preliminary hearings in their case at the Monterey County Superior Court in Salinas. That spring of 1970, the Soledad Brothers won a change of venue. Their trial was to be held in San Francisco, and they were moved to San Quentin. That same spring, the University of California regents fired Angela for a second time, now citing her support of the Soledad Brothers. They said her advocacy constituted "unprofessional conduct."

On that Friday in August, San Quentin prisoners Magee, Christmas, and McClain, armed by Jonathan Jackson, made their bid for freedom. There was some speculation that Jonathan had planned to go to a radio station to broadcast an appeal for the Soledad Brothers. Whatever his intentions, Angela felt Jonathan's death as an acute personal loss.

Jack and I were away on a summer holiday with Joshua when we heard what had happened at the Marin courthouse. We were camping and just happened to come into town for supplies. When Jack and I saw the newspaper headline, we gave up the rest of our camping trip and came home. Both of us had been involved in the defense of the Soledad Brothers, and were very disturbed by these events.

A few days later, we attended Jonathan's funeral. It was held in West Oakland at a small church, a white ramshackle building, in the heart of the black community. Actually, we never made it into the church. When we arrived hundreds of people were spilling out from it and onto the street. They were mostly young, mostly black, women and men, dressed in Sunday best, milling in quiet tribute. I saw the casket emerge through the church doors, the pallbearers making their way through the crowd and placing their burden in a gray hearse. Jonathan's mother walked out of the church, her face veiled, her eyes hidden behind dark glasses, clutching a white handkerchief to her mouth. Overcome with grief she was physically assisted by a cluster of family and friends.

We knew by then that Angela was implicated in the Marin events, but she had not yet been indicted or placed on the FBI's Most Wanted list. We saw Franklin Alexander at the funeral. A black comrade in his early thirties, he was one of Angela's closest friends and chair of the Che-Lumumba Club. Seemingly invisible in the huge crowd, Franklin told us he was probably under surveillance. He stood close to us in the natural crush of people, but he faced forward so that it was not immediately apparent that he was talking to us. He spoke hurriedly, and in a hushed voice told us that Angela had gone underground. He thought, but wasn't sure, that several of the guns Jonathan had used were registered in her name. A week or two later, with Angela now a fugitive, FBI agents accosted me on the sidewalk in front of our house. Jack had gone to his office at San Jose State and I had just come back from taking Joshua to daycare. They showed me their badges and asked me if I knew where Angela Davis was.

"I have no idea," I replied.

"If we find out that you knew and didn't tell us we'll put you in prison for twenty years," they threatened.

"Go to hell," I growled. I turned away from them and walked up the steps to my front door. They got back into their car and I watched them drive away. My hand shook violently as I inserted my key into the door. I thought about telephoning Jack, or Max, since he was chair of the party and should probably be informed. I decided against both because I knew our phone was tapped. My mind raced with potential scenarios of arrest and imprisonment. How would I care for Joshua? I began pacing, slamming my fists into any available object, like the living room couch and the dining room wall. Then I breathed deeply, made a cup of tea. I took the tea outside to our backyard and sat on the steps. Our dog, Igor, came and muzzled my hand. I looked at the flowers, I looked at the grass, I looked at the sky. I finished my tea. I went back inside, sat down at my desk, picked up my pen, and started writing about Angela's case.

Weeks later, as Angela and I stood facing each other in the New York Women's House of Detention, the task of winning her freedom seemed overwhelming, the odds impossible. But I put one foot in front of the other and did whatever had to be done. We all worked ten, twelve, sometimes fourteen and sixteen hours a day, seven days a week, in a struggle that was ultimately to last for almost two years. Our strategy was to build massive support by educating the community and generating public intervention to guarantee some modicum of due process and a fair trial. I knew Angela would never have given guns to Jonathan; she would never have counseled or supported such an action. I made scores of telephone calls and wrote letters and held countless meetings with individuals and groups, helped with the preparation of leaflets and pamphlets, circulated petitions, and attended dozens of meetings, both in the party and in the Free Angela Davis committees we were in the process of establishing. Focused on this, everything else in my life faded away. Jack and I worked as a team to keep up our care of Joshua. I worked out a schedule to take him to and from daycare during the week, and Jack did most of the household tasks, like shopping and cooking and taking care of Joshua on the weekends. We functioned as a political unit in our family setting.

Many seasoned criminal lawyers told us that if Angela had not been a prominent member of the Communist Party and associated with the Black Panther Party, she would not have been indicted. She was never accused of being in Marin County on August 7. The evidence against her was entirely circumstantial. However, under California conspiracy law a person need not be present at the scene of a crime in order to be charged with it.

Late on the night of December 22, 1970, under the pretense of a telephone call from her attorney, Angela was summoned from her cell in the Women's House of Detention. Wrestled to the floor by attending officers, handcuffed, a coat hastily thrown over her shoulders to protect against New York's winter freeze, she was placed in a car and driven to McGuire Air Force Base in New Jersey. The car drove onto the runway, which was lined with soldiers, shoulder to shoulder, bayonets at the ready. Angela was placed on a military plane and flown to Travis Air Force Base. From Travis, under a military escort, she was driven about thirty miles south, to the Marin County jail in San Rafael. Her attorneys were notified of her extradition the following morning.

As soon as I could I visited Angela. The jail was part of a civic center complex designed by Frank Lloyd Wright. From a distance, the buildings appeared to be nestled into the surrounding hills; their domed roofs were painted bright blue. Up close, the buildings appeared more ordinary, with parking lots, indoor foliage, and lots of glass—that is, except for the jail at the northern end of the complex, which reminded me of a concrete bunker. Angela had put me on her visitors' list. With the assistance of her attorneys, our group of five comrades named by Angela were permitted to see her daily during visiting hours.

Entering the jail, walking its corridors, hearing the whine of its steel gates, the scraping of metal on metal, smelling that medicinal odor typical of jails tinged with the scents of fear and too many bodies in a windowless space, I braced myself for the body search I had been warned to expect. My arms and legs extended, I stood as a matron patted me down, running her hands the length of my arms, under my armpits, along my ribs, over and under my breasts, down my legs, and then up again along the inner thighs. None of this had been required at the Women's House of Detention in New York. But here in Marin I had more direct physical contact with Angela.

She was kept in isolation, separated from the general jail population. Visits with her were held in a small room, a visitor's booth usually reserved for lawyer-client consultations. The booth was divided in half by a Plexiglas barrier, a table shared between prisoner and visitor at waist height. The Plexiglas barrier ended an inch or so above the table so that papers could be passed back and forth. Once I was seated on my side of the glass a guard brought Angela in. We sat facing each other and because of the gap in the barrier we did not need a telephone to hear each other. I was allowed a legal pad and pencil. She was allowed whatever books and papers she wanted to bring in. Still looking exhausted but with less tension in her face, she asked, with her characteristic crooked half smile and Southern cadence, "How're ya doin'?" I was very glad to see her, and under the circumstances I was doing just fine. We were all gearing up for the struggle to win Angela's freedom.

In March 1971 I attended a meeting of the Communist Party's National Committee in New York. The party had supplied Angela with initial counsel, but it was in fact badly divided over her case. Although muffled in their dissent, some comrades wanted the party to separate itself entirely from Angela, and a few actually (privately) advocated her expulsion on the grounds that she was a terrorist. A majority of comrades on the National Committee had never heard of the Soledad Brothers, and many others who had nevertheless denied that Angela had been involved in their defense. Many wanted Angela to disavow herself completely from Jonathan Jackson and the Soledad Brothers. Because the party had so often been accused of advocating and organizing the violent overthrow of the government, comrades who were survivors of the 1950s feared that Angela's very association with Jonathan would rekindle the anti-Communist purges if the party allowed her to remain a member. Thus, in an effort to force the issue at the meeting, many, including the party's national chairman, Henry Winston, an African American comrade, likened Angela's case to that of Georgi Dimitrov, a Bulgarian Communist living in Berlin in the 1930s who was imprisoned by the Nazis. Dimitrov was accused of setting fire to the Reichstag, the German Parliament building. In fact, the fire had been set by a hapless youth named Marinus van der Lubbe, whom other party members believed was in the employ of the Nazis. Those of us whom knew Jonathan Jackson bristled at the analogy. Jon, as friends and family knew him, was neither hapless nor a police agent.

Back in September, when the hunt for Angela was at its height, several of us working with African American community activists had organized a rally in Berkeley in her defense and in protest of the police dragnet. In a carefully crafted speech that was directly contrary to Winston's line, I analyzed Jonathan's action, with particular reference to the long history of African American resistance. I drew a parallel between the response of slave owners to slave rebellions, and the modern-day FBI response to these prisoners' bid for freedom. At the end of my speech, Alex Hoffman, a longtime Berkeley activist, asked me which line would prevail in the party, mine or the national leadership's. I was a little startled by his question; I hadn't really allowed myself to see how serious our differences were. I was still naive and unaware of the reverberations of my words, especially given my father's place in the party, and what I knew to be his agreement with my position in Angela's case. The text of my speech was published early in October 1970 in the *National Guardian*. This was the text Angela had asked me to circulate when she was still in the Women's House of Detention. At the beginning of the National Committee meeting, Max had admonished me: "You should consult me before publishing something like that," he said softly. I was infuriated by his patronizing attitude, but I didn't say anything.

Kendra and Franklin Alexander, Angela's comrades from the Che-Lumumba Club in Los Angeles; Charlene Mitchell, who led the U.S. delegation to the Helsinki congress; and I, among others, spoke again and again at the National Committee meeting, laying out the facts of the case, explaining the Soledad Brothers' defense and Angela's involvement. We insisted that Jonathan could not simply be condemned as a terrorist. His personal history, his feelings for his brother, his frustration with the criminal justice system, his knowledge of the certain humiliations and beatings of black prisoners by the guards had to be taken into account. None of us endorsed or advocated what Jon had done. But we understood it. We saw the continuity between this prison revolt and the ghetto uprisings after Martin Luther King, Jr., was killed. Moreover, we argued, Angela was a co-defendant with Ruchell Magee, the surviving San Quentin prisoner. We could not do anything that would endanger his life. Finally, we said, Angela's defense would not be credible if we accepted the prosecution's version of August 7 as though it were nothing more than a criminal act, as though Jonathan were a gangster. We needed to show why it had happened even as we proved Angela's innocence.

This was perhaps the most democratic of the National Committee meetings I had ever attended because no definite line was set. In the end the party's support for Angela was assured even as the political direction of her defense remained contested. And thousands of comrades everywhere in the country bent their efforts to build the National United Committee to Free Angela Davis (and "All Political Prisoners," Angela insisted), affectionately known as NUCFAD. The party never resolved its strategic differences about Angela's defense, that is, between repudiating Jonathan and honoring his memory. Those of us intimately involved in shaping the case never forgot that it was Angela's life that hung in the balance, and so we conducted the defense as she wished it to be.

I threw myself into this work with a passion I had not felt since the Free Speech Movement. In part, I was haunted by the memory of the Rosenbergs' execution. On a deeper level, however, I was fighting for my own life. Since my breakdown three years earlier, I had managed to patch myself together, but emotionally I was still extremely fragile. Although no longer taking the tranquilizers Eph Kahn had prescribed, I had done no healing, seen no therapist, had no way to recognize or process the sexual abuse at the root of my recurring despair and self-loathing. Angela's arrest brought me out of myself. I was politically committed to her defense, of course, but it was my love for her that sustained me. This love was mutual. The intimacy and trust Angela and I developed were sources of great healing for me, especially in my continued bouts of depression and paranoia. I was fighting for Angela's life, but she helped me to save my own.

Five of us were appointed by the court as "legal investigators." This gave us the right to visit Angela in jail every day without regard to normal visiting hours and without the presence of an attorney. We were Angela's sister, Fania Davis, Kendra and Franklin Alexander, Charlene Mitchell, and me. Charlene Mitchell became the executive director of NUCFAD. We could not have had a more skilled or experienced leader.

Fania Davis was several years younger than her sister. When Angela was arrested Fania had just returned from Cuba, where she had been part of a summer Venceremos Brigade. The brigade had been initiated in the 1960s to protest the U.S. government blockade against Cuba. Many hundreds of Americans went every year to help with the sugar harvest and build schools and medical clinics. Fania was married, living in Philadelphia with her husband, and pregnant. Eventually she made her way to California to work full-time on Angela's defense. She gave birth to a daughter, Eisa, and then, in October 1971, she went on an extensive international speaking tour for Angela.

In its first year, NUCFAD devoted itself to political education; we wanted people to know about Angela's case, the Soledad Brothers, the racism of the criminal justice and prison systems. We focused our campaign on the demand that Angela be released on bail. She had been denied bail under Section 1270 of the California penal code, which said bail could be denied in "capital offenses in which the presumption of guilt is great." We knew that if we went to trial with Angela still in prison with that "presumption of guilt," conviction was likely. We campaigned for Angela's release on bail to restore her constitutional right to a presumption of innocence. We also raised huge sums of money through the extraordinary generosity of thousands of donors. One day, for example, I was sent to the home of a wealthy white woman. She served me tea, chatted amiably if somewhat self-consciously, and then gave me an airline bag with $10,000 in cash for Angela's legal defense.

NUCFAD asked every imaginable organization in the United States, from professional and educational associations to trade unions, from sports leagues to high school clubs to the Congressional Black Caucus, to pass a resolution in support of bail. We circulated petitions addressed to the court urging Angela's release on bail. Within a year we had hundreds of thousands of signatures. Likewise, protest statements, petitions, postcards, and letters poured in from England, France, West Germany, the Scandinavian countries, Japan, Mexico, Argentina, Chile, and from the socialist countries: Cuba, the GDR, the Soviet Union, Hungary, Czechoslovakia, North Vietnam. We received an open letter to the judge from Florence Mophosho, Women's Secretariat, Women's Section of the African National Congress in South Africa:

> 12 October 1971

> We strongly protest [Angela Davis's] continued indefinite detention and demand her immediate release in respect of world opinion. We equally demand the release of all political prisoners who are opponents of racial discrimination in the U.S., which has been condemned by various resolutions and declarations, of the United Nations, and indeed by humanity.

Prominent individuals made pilgrimages to the Marin County jail to see Angela: Maya Angelou, Nina Simone, Toni Morrison, Herbert Marcuse, Jane Fonda, Julian Bond, Reverend Ralph David Abernathy. Aretha Franklin offered to put up any amount of money for bail. James Baldwin wrote the stirring "Open Letter to My Sister Angela" from his home in Paris, published on the front page of the *New York Review of Books*: "We must fight for your life as though it were our own—which it is—and render impassable with our bodies the corridor to the gas chamber."

Baldwin was a source of tremendous support in garnering the signatures of many prominent European intellectuals for a statement that Herbert Marcuse had helped us draft. I corresponded with Baldwin at some length because he wanted to attend court (the trial had not yet begun) but was under tremendous pressure from his publisher to finish a book. He had to postpone his trip from Paris twice, and then he wanted to visit his sister in New York, further delaying his arrival. He was agitated and apologetic when I picked him up at the airport. I assured him that his timing was impeccable and his very presence was an immeasurable gift. I found him to be soft spoken, intense, fiercely intelligent, and alert to every nuance in the court proceedings. He was thrilled to meet Angela.

And I was thrilled to meet James Baldwin, not only for his writings, which I loved, but because he was gay. Nobody talked about that, but Baldwin was evidence to me that a gay person like myself (I dared to breathe the thought) could be productive, respected, and well loved.

As the case gained momentum it felt as though we had to do everything all at once. We put together a stellar legal team. Many attorneys generously gave of their time, did research on case law, drafted preliminary briefs for pretrial motions. One of the first things the attorneys had done was to ask that all Marin County judges be disqualified from trying Angela's case. They cited prejudicial grounds, since all of the Marin judges were at least acquainted, if not friends with, the deceased judge, Harold Haley. Judge Richard Arnason from a nearby county was appointed in their stead. He proved to be a skilled jurist. Whatever his personal views, his goal was a fair trial. Should Angela be convicted, he wanted no serious grounds for appeal because of a technical ruling on his part that could violate her rights. I came to like and respect Judge Arnason a good deal.

Among the most difficult pretrial decisions we faced was whether to sever Angela's case from Ruchell Magee's. The grand jury indictment had bound them together, but Angela had not been present on August 7. The joint indictment made it seem as though she had. On the other hand, Angela felt a deep political commitment to Ruchell, and they met together on several occasions. Problems with a joint defense became apparent when Ruchell objected to many of our pretrial motions. In particular, he was intent on moving his case into federal court. Eventually, Ruchell Magee and Angela Davis made a joint motion for severance and it was granted.

In jail, Angela devoted herself to study. She read voraciously, engaged in developing her legal defense, and wrote three long essays. The first of her essays was entitled "Reflections on the Black Woman's Role in the Community of Slaves." It was published in the *Black Scholar* in December 1971. Widely read, it helped to inaugurate the field of black women's history. She wrote the second essay at the invitation of the Society for the Study of Dialectical Materialism. Affiliated with the American Philosophical Association (APA), the society proposed to sponsor a symposium called "Marxism and Feminism" at the annual APA convention in December 1971 in New York City. Angela's co-presenter was to be Juliet Mitchell, a British socialist feminist whose essay (and subsequent book) "Women: The Longest Revolution" had stirred tremendous interest in the fledgling women's movement. Angela wrote a sixty-five-page philosophical treatise critically appraising the texts of white feminists from both Marxist and African American perspectives. I eventually presented this paper on Angela's behalf at the New York meeting.

Angela and I also collaborated on a project proposed by a British publisher that resulted in the publication of our co-edited volume, *If They Come in the Morning: Voices of Resistance.* We borrowed the title from James Baldwin's open letter. Angela's introductory essay argued that the traditional definition of a political prisoner as one whose intentionally political act had resulted in incarceration was no longer adequate to embrace the tens of thousands of prisoners of color in the United States. Many of them, like George Jackson, had become political prisoners by virtue of their in-prison organizing against racism. I contributed an essay called "The Social Functions of the Prisons in the United States" to complement Angela's. I argued that under the pretext of criminal prosecutions, prisons were used as bulwarks of racial and class oppression. People of color were disproportionately arrested, tried, convicted, and sentenced to much longer terms than their white counterparts. This function, I argued, gave such prisoners an inherently political status. Our book then presented essays, letters, and poems by political prisoners, including those whom we had newly defined as such: each of the Soledad Brothers, Ruchell Magee, Ericka Huggins (a leader of the Black Panther Party framed on murder charges in New Haven, Connecticut, who was eventually exonerated), and others.

Collaborating with Angela was a logistical challenge, as we had to constantly circumvent prison regulations. While I could see Angela on any day, we were restricted in our access to each other. Placed in the visiting booth, we could not exchange books, papers, or manuscripts. Angela needed to read and correct manuscripts, to see what editing I had done, to review the proposed order of selections and the many details that go into writing and editing a book. We turned to the attorneys for help. They were unrestricted in their access to Angela and could bring to her any materials "needed to prepare her defense." Working at a feverish pace, we had *If They Come in the Morning* in print in England by September 1971, and in the United States by December, published in a hardcover edition by the Third Press, owned by Nigerian-born editor Joseph Okpaku, and in a paper edition by New American Library.

Commuting time between San Rafael and San Jose was about two hours, depending on the traffic. I usually dropped Joshua off at his daycare by eight in the morning, got to the jail by ten, was out at four and home by six, day after day. Reviewing each other's manuscripts, soliciting others, deciding on the order of things, addressing myriad political and theoretical issues, we spent hours and hours together and I sometimes lost all track of time, until a matron arrived at four o'clock to tell me I had to leave. I dragged myself away, always feeling despair at leaving her, still feeling disbelief that she was in prison.

Jack had dinner prepared by the time I came home with Joshua, and our little family buzzed with news of the day. One of us played with Josh and bathed him while the other cleaned up the kitchen. Whichever one of us didn't have a meeting that night read him a story and put him to bed. Josh was the sweetest, most good natured and accommodating toddler one could ever have imagined.

When the national party leadership heard about the book Angela and I were writing, General Secretary Gus Hall proposed that we include a long essay by national chairman Henry Winston, entitled "The Meaning of San Rafael." In it, he argued for the repudiation of Jonathan Jackson, restating the same position we had contested at the National Committee meeting two months earlier. Angela and I both made an effort to convince him that this position would be a disastrous one for the defense to take. I spoke with Winston personally in New York at great length in June 1971, before the book was published, and Angela wrote him a twenty-two-page letter/essay to which he did not respond. We felt it was impossible to include his essay without changing the whole tenor of our work.

Our British publisher, Michael Chambers, invited me to come to England to help lay the groundwork for promoting the book, and

Angela encouraged me to go. Once in London, she said I should go on to Germany and France. There were strong "Free Angela" movements in both countries. I could speak on behalf of the defense, and arrange for European editions of our book. Herbert Marcuse was to be in the South of France that summer and offered assistance. I was to leave at the end of June.

Meanwhile, Jack was to be in Cuba for several weeks that summer. He had been invited by the Departmento de Electrónica of the Cuban Academy of Sciences to help modernize their electrical engineering curriculum and he was thrilled. We agreed that I would take Joshua with me to Europe, and Jack and I would meet up with each other in Prague in August.

I booked my flight to London. I was thrilled with the sudden prospect of more European travel. Gerri and Orin were by then living in Munich. They generously invited Joshua and me to stay with them. I was also hoping to see Ursula again. I thought if I could get to West Berlin I could just walk across the border at the U.S. checkpoint. Tourists were permitted into East Berlin with a one-day visa.

Joshua was a marvelous traveling companion, and at three and a half, with his curls, blue eyes, and dimples, he melted the hearts of everyone we met, from airline stewardesses and waitresses to party comrades and "Free Angela" activists. He was easy-going and cheerful. Even his manners were impeccable. We traveled extensively throughout England. I spoke several times in London, then in Manchester, Essex, and Birmingham. I met with Bernadette Devlin, a young partisan for Irish freedom who had just been elected to Parliament. I also spoke with actress Vanessa Redgrave. Both willingly lent their names in support of Angela's freedom, and Devlin agreed to speak at the "Free Angela" events.

The media frenzy over Angela's case was intense. I had interviews with reporters from London's *Sunday Times,* the *Observer,* and the *Guardian.* I had lunch with Anthony Lewis, London correspondent and columnist for *The New York Times*, and did several television interviews. I also met with the editor and staff of the Communist Party's daily newspaper, the *Morning Star.* In each instance, I reviewed the details of the case, hoping for more accurate and factual coverage. At a reception held at a private estate in London I was introduced to ambassadors and diplomats, many from Africa. Here, the support for Angela was overwhelming.

Joshua and I had a wonderful time playing together in London. We rode the Underground, with which he was endlessly fascinated. He also loved cruising the city atop double-decker buses. He stood open mouthed and at attention for the changing of the guard at Buckingham Palace. We visited the London Zoo and Hyde Park, and went boating on the Thames. Our friends provided gracious accommodations, ranging from a modest working-class home in Birmingham to a grand estate in London.

I was shocked by the extreme class differences within the British Communist Party. The coal miner's family we stayed with in Birmingham was very poor. For example, their five o'clock tea was also their dinner. Aware that they had gone to extraordinary lengths to feed me and Joshua, I felt very self-conscious about eating anything at all. They were a large family, the children ranging in age from toddlers to teenagers. They appeared for tea scrubbed and shining in very new clothes. Josh and I shared a bed, displacing some of the children from what was otherwise their room. I had never met people with such a high level of class consciousness and I felt more than a little uncomfortable with my American middle-class existence.

In contrast, the London estate where we stayed was palatial, with extensive lawns and gardens, several guest rooms, multiple bathrooms, and servants' quarters. Tea was an elaborate assortment of small cucumber or cheese sandwiches and creamed pastries. A formal dinner was served at eight o'clock. My hosts, both attorneys, and their guests were intensively interested in U.S. politics, especially in the legal strategies we intended to use in Angela's trial. I found it difficult to reconcile such differences in class within the party, a function of my experiences in the United States, where class lines were less distinct and also were distinctly colored by race.

In Germany, using Gerri's house as a base, I met with "Free Angela" activists in Munich and traveled to other cities, including Bochum and Düsseldorf. At a large public meeting at the university in Bochum, I noticed a man standing in the rear of the auditorium. His back against the wall, his hair in a crew cut, thick arms crossed against his barrel chest, I guessed him to be in his fifties. His energy was so hostile that I leaned over to my translator to ask who he was. "Oh," she said. "He was a member of the SS. He comes to all our meetings." A cold fury passed through me, and my body went rigid. How was it, I wondered, that he could be walking around? And how could my translator, a young German college student in her early twenties, be so casual about it?

In Düsseldorf, Josh and I strolled along the banks of the Rhine. I imagined the city as it might have looked in 1945. My father had fought there. "My outfit took Düsseldorf," he always said, launching into his war stories.

Angela and I wrote to each other frequently during my travels. Her letters were filled with details of the case and her feelings as it progressed:

Your letters have been arriving regularly. I've enjoyed every one of them and would have written long before now if things hadn't been so terribly hectic around here. As a consequence of all the fuss we've been making lately there have been a number of significant changes. Not only do I now have what the sheriff's people have characterized as the largest typewriter in the Civic Center (it's electric, too), but a radio, even a clock on the wall—all these things they insisted before could be used as weapons. . . .

Other news: the judge ordered the jailers to permit us a series of eight-hour meetings with Ruchell and the Soledad Brothers. . . . There were . . . a number of unanticipated pleasures. A trip to San Francisco for me was the best thing about the whole affair. Though they took me in chains, my hands cuffed to a chain around my waist, I had a clear view of the countryside between here and the [Golden Gate] bridge—I didn't know that the area was so beautiful. . . .

All this to say: this rather tenuous routine I had established for myself has been rather explosively disrupted. I assume it must be the effect of prolonged confinement, but every time something extraordinary (outside of the ordinary unfolding of things in this cubicle) occurs, it takes a great deal of energy and concentration for me to pull things back together again. . . .

It was good that I thought to take a look at the addresses and dates you left me. You must already be on your way to Munich! You know my orientation in time is virtually nonexistent: things just don't appear to occur in any kind of logical, temporal sequence in here. . . .

Less subtle manifestations of racism have occurred around here recently. While Mother was speaking at a rally in New York, there was a bomb scare. No bomb, but the hall had to be immediately evacuated. The next day at another rally,

precisely the same thing occurred; this time they decided
to carry on outside until the time designated as the time of
the explosion by the caller had passed. As she was sitting
on an outdoor platform, one of the organizers of the rally
came over to announce that in three minutes they would
return to the hall. Three minutes passed and a small bomb
exploded a few yards away from Mother. Fortunately no one
was wounded and I was impressed that she stood up to the
whole thing quite strongly. But, then, she has had decades
of experience with that type of thing. You know the area
where we lived in Birmingham was for a long time called
Dynamite Hill.

Tuesday in court saw no more than the inept presentation
of the Grand Jury motion. Wednesday was my day—after
an initial and extremely rigorous resistance by [California
State Assistant Attorney General Albert] Harris when he
was informed that I would argue the co-counsel motion.
I got started and continued through most of the session.
Actually it was very funny—Harris' position was that
the judge should not allow me to make my presentation
because he was certain that it would consist of a series
of irrelevant, politically inspired statements. I began by
handing to him, the judge and the court reporter a table
of cases which I would be citing during the course of the
argument. . . .

Angela telephoned me twice while I was in Munich. She was
permitted to call from the judge's chambers. The second time, in
mid-August, she asked me to come home; she needed my support
in preparing for the trial. I had not yet been to Berlin to see Ursula
or to France, but there was nothing to be done about it. I cancelled
remaining commitments, left word for Jack in Prague via a circuitous
route, hoping that it would reach him, and Josh and I flew back to
New York. I stayed for a few days. Jack arrived in New York and took

charge of Joshua while I flew on to California. A day after I returned all hell broke loose.

Saturday, August 21, 1971. I woke up early, showered, dressed, grabbed a cup of coffee, and drove to San Rafael. I got into the visitors' booth about ten o'clock. Angela and I were so glad to see each other, and we had so much news to share. We were deep in conversation when attorney Howard Moore arrived. With Howard present we could move into Angela's cell. It was midafternoon when several deputies appeared at the door to Angela's cell. They ordered me and Howard out. This was highly irregular and Howard protested vehemently, but they were adamant. Under their watchful eyes, Howard and I were taken to an elevator usually reserved for prisoner transport, and escorted out of the building. We had no idea what was going on. We both thought it was some kind of a power play, a flexing of police muscles, as it were. Howard said he would stick around. I decided to drive home to San Jose and see Angela again the next morning.

I was at home when Kendra Alexander telephoned. She said, "George has been shot," referring to Soledad Brother George Jackson, Jonathan's brother.

"What?" I asked.

She said, "George is dead. They said he was trying to escape. We can't get in to see Angela. . . ."

"Wait a minute. Wait a minute. Tell me again, I don't understand," I interrupted her. Adrenaline was shooting through me and my heart was pounding and my head felt all fuzzy like my ears were stuffed with cotton. Howard and I had been forced to leave, and they said they couldn't get in to see Angela, and Margaret was there too, at the jail . . .

I saw Angela the next morning, Sunday, August 22. We were all crowded into her cell, lawyers and investigators. Devastated, her face ashen with grief, Angela sat with her head pitched over the typewriter, her fingers pounding the keys as she hammered out a public statement denouncing the assassination of George Jackson in the prison yard at San Quentin. Our immediate fear was for Angela's safety. The lawyers were in one corner of the cell strategizing legal motions to guarantee it, and the rest of us were in another corner talking about how to mobilize U.S. and world public opinion.

For Angela, George's death was an incomparable personal loss. Through her acquaintance with the Jackson family, attendance at court appearances, and letters exchanged with George, Angela's feelings for him had grown from those of a concerned sister in struggle to a loving and devoted friend. That she survived the weeks and months following his death was a testament to her stamina and strength. That the prosecution intended to use the intensity of her feelings for George as an apparent motive for her alleged involvement in the August 7 carnage spoke to such cruelty, I could hardly fathom its depths. The prosecutor had his stereotype of the aggressive, wanton, ruthless, calculating black woman and he fully intended to use it.

In the weeks following George's murder, Angela was swamped with grief, hopelessness, and despair. Confined to her cell except for brief interludes, she had little outlet for her feelings, and her statements in meetings reflected the rage in her grief. Max suggested to me that the party would "be forced to abandon her" if she persisted in her "line." *What "line"?* I fumed to myself. She was grieving. I could not imagine abandoning Angela, no matter what she said. I was terribly disturbed by Max's pronouncement. I knew it reflected the sentiments of many in the party and in the national leadership. Emotionally it echoed my longtime fear that my father would abandon me if I ever held the wrong "line."

I went to the jail virtually every day to be with Angela. We sat in the visitor's booth, she on one side of the Plexiglas, me on the other. I didn't know what to do, but I felt that it mattered that I come, even if we just sat quietly. Finally, Angela began writing again. We condemned George's death and redoubled our efforts to win her release on bail.

The first real legal break in the case came when Judge Arnason agreed to a change of venue. We had wanted the trial moved to San Francisco. Instead, it was moved to San Jose. Although it had only a tiny African American population and was a center of white conservative agricultural interests, we were at least out of the immediate vicinity of San Quentin and the emotional swamp of Marin County, where Judge Harold Haley, his nephew-in-law Gary Thomas, and other principals in the case had grown up and currently resided, and where Judge Haley had died. In December 1971, after the court-ordered change of venue, Angela was moved from the Marin County jail to a small holding facility in Palo Alto. It was very poorly equipped, and for the first days the toilet in her cell overflowed so that the cell floor was continually flooded with water. When we finally got in to see Angela, she was perched on the upper bunk in her cell, arms hugging her knees to her chest, with a thin wool blanket wrapped around her shoulders. We protested the conditions and in short order the toilet was repaired and she was given access to an adjoining cell. She remained in isolation, but this facility's one advantage was that the legal investigators were allowed into Angela's cell—no screens, no Plexiglas, no telephones—with or without the attorneys being present.

Since Jack and I lived in San Jose, our home became a hub of defense activity. Fania Davis and her infant daughter, Eisa, moved in with us. Mrs. Davis, Angela's mother, moved in with our friends David and Gloria Newman, who lived nearby. NUCFAD rented a new headquarters on a neighboring street. The trial date was set for December, then postponed until January, and then delayed again. Meanwhile, we were given the names of hundreds of prospective jurors.

Palo Alto, a few miles north of San Jose, was an extremely wealthy community, home to Stanford University. East Palo Alto boasted a small black community that, despite its size, rallied heroically to Angela's defense. Meanwhile, officials put into place extraordinary security measures at the San Jose superior court building. A six-foot-tall chainlink fence was erected, video cameras were installed, and metal detectors were set up so that the public attending Angela's trial could be duly searched.

The presiding judge of the superior court banned all demonstrations in support of Angela anywhere in the vicinity of the courthouse. We protested this ruling vigorously. It not only violated our First Amendment rights to lawful assembly and freedom of speech, but it also seriously compromised our pretrial mass actions. About two dozen of us picketed the courthouse. We were promptly arrested and hauled out to the county jail. Deputy sheriffs handcuffed us in pairs, but we were an odd number, and so our last sister was being cuffed with her hands behind her back. Paris Williams, a young black woman working on Angela's defense committee, had come down from Oakland for the day's protests. I objected to her singular cuffing, and much to my surprise, the deputy stopped himself in mid-motion. Paris was cuffed to me on one side, and my comrade Ginny Proctor was on the other. A reporter from the *Oakland Tribune* snapped a picture of the three of us, our cuffed hands upraised in the black power salute, as we were led away. We women spent a raucous night in the drunk tank at Elmwood, the Santa Clara County jail. We refused release on our own recognizance because it was conditional upon our agreement not to picket the courthouse again. Bail was set at $350 each, and we were released the following morning.

This was my first arrest since the traumas at Santa Rita, and somewhere in the early hours of the morning I felt a rising panic. Fania, sensing the shift in my energy, put her arm around me and led me to her corner of the drunk tank. She studied my face carefully. She didn't ask me what was wrong, but as we settled down for the night she spread my jacket next to her on the concrete floor. Under her protective wing I fell into a restless sleep. Days later Angela had a few choice words for our "reckless" actions, since Kendra, Franklin, Fania, and I were her "legal investigators" and the core of her political defense. "What if they hadn't released you?" she admonished us sternly. "Then what?" We didn't care. I knew for myself, I *needed* that kind of militant action. I was tired of just pushing papers and attending meetings. We were brought swiftly to trial and duly convicted by a wholly sympathetic jury that nevertheless felt we had broken the law. We were sentenced to six months' suspended sentences by a Japanese American judge who told an astonished prosecutor in chambers that the next time they came to round up his people and send them to internment camps, they had better come well armed.

In mid-January 1972, the California State Supreme Court overturned the death penalty. Stanford law professor Anthony Amsterdam had argued the case, and we had not expected him to win it. The implications of this decision for Angela's case were immediate and overwhelming. First and foremost in all of our minds was that, even given a worst-case scenario of conviction, Angela could no longer be executed. That alone was a source of enormous relief. The decision also changed the jury selection process because a potential juror's views on the death penalty were no longer relevant. We knew that the prosecution would have challenged many a liberal juror had he or she expressed even the smallest reservations about capital punishment. Most thrilling, however, was that the court's decision potentially nullified the section of the penal code under which Angela was still being held, paving the way for her release on bail. As a free woman pending trial, the presumption of innocence could be restored and the whole ambiance of the trial itself would be changed.

Our attorneys immediately petitioned the court for bail. The word went out to our support committees around the world. All those months of campaigning had paid off. Judge Arnason was flooded with letters, telegrams, and telephone calls by the thousands. Amidst the deluge, and despite the attorney general's opposition, Judge Arnason granted bail, set at $102,500. A white dairy farmer from Fresno, California, named Roger McAfee and his wife, Darlene, braving death threats and daily hostility from people in this conservative farming community in California's San Joaquin Valley, put up their farm as collateral. Months before, Roger had called our office and volunteered to put up bail should it be granted. I was in charge of raising Angela's bail money, and when word of the supreme court decision came, I telephoned Roger to set the process of bail money in motion. On February 23, 1972, five days before her trial was set to begin, Angela was released from custody. She was driven from the Palo Alto jail to our home. More than a hundred people were packed inside and spilling out onto our front lawn and into the street. Jack, ever a proper host, had bought food and champagne. Others came with more. We feasted and toasted this miraculous moment, none more beautifully than Mrs. Davis, whose radiance filled the house.

The trial began on February 28, 1972. Angela had been in jail for almost seventeen months. Jury selection was an arduous and delicate process. We had a pool of 150 prospective jurors. Only one was African American and four were Chicano. We knew we had liberal people in the pool because of the extensive community network we had established to investigate potential jurors. The question was, would their names come up, and when? In questioning prospective jurors, our attorneys focused on race issues and Communism. Did people have personal or social relationships with black people? Did they work with black people? Had they read a lot about this case or formed an opinion? Did they understand the concept of a "presumption of innocence"? Could they be fair? What did they think about Communism? Did they know anything about the Communist Party? I was so agitated by the selection process that I found myself frantic to get to court in the morning, and then frantic to get out again as soon as I had arrived.

Every prospective juror could be a loaded cannon. How could you tell about a person? How could you know? Taking extensive notes during voir dire, Angela seemed absolutely calm, as though she were attending a graduate seminar instead of her own trial. After court we met for hours, debating, digesting, reviewing our notes, our impressions. It was so good that Angela could be with us now in these discussions, and that we could talk in comfort and privacy. Sometimes we met at the lawyers' offices near the courthouse, but mostly we met at my home or at the home of the recently deceased Emma Gelders Sterne, where Angela and Margaret Burnham were living. Emma, white, Southern born and bred, and very radical, had been one of the original organizers of the Soledad Brothers defense committee.

In the end, we settled on a jury of eight women and four men. One of the men identified himself as a Mexican American. This was the designation he said he preferred. Everyone else was white. Still, it was a relatively young jury, and we knew we had forward-thinking, progressive people among them. The selection process had taken just under two weeks. The jury and alternates were sworn and seated. Then the judge ordered a ten-day recess to allow the jurors time to put their lives in order. The judge did not sequester the jury. He just asked them to refrain from reading or listening to any news accounts of the Davis case.

We returned to court on March 27. Prosecutor Albert Harris delivered his opening statement to the jury. He would, of course, detail everything that had occurred on August 7. Then he would trace Angela's actions, establishing her connection to Jonathan Jackson, to the weapons he used, to the events themselves. Finally, he said, he would show Angela's motive. Her motive was not prison reform, or to free political prisoners. Her motive was to free George Jackson, the one prisoner whom she loved. He proposed to introduce into evidence letters Angela had written to George, copies of which had been found in an FBI search of her apartment after she had left Los Angeles. Prosecutor Harris said he would also introduce into evidence a diary Angela had written, a very personal diary, in which she made clear her real feelings for George Jackson. Harris said, "Her own words will reveal that beneath the cool academic veneer is a woman fully capable of being moved to violence by passion." That opening day in court I found myself truly hating Albert Harris. His voice sounded to me like helicopter rotors whirring at a distance.

The next day, Angela, as co-counsel, delivered our opening statement to the jury in a reasoned, calm voice; at moments she was almost conversational, and at other times she conveyed the demeanor of a scholar delivering a carefully informed lecture. Although she responded to each of Harris's allegations, her statement also contained historical and political information useful to the jury. Angela disputed the idea that "uncontrollable passion" should have propelled her into a conspiracy with Jonathan Jackson. She affirmed her sisterly relationship with Jonathan, her concern for him. She challenged the stereotypes of black women upon which the prosecution rested its case. These stereotypes, she explained, were rooted in slavery; they projected black women as aggressive, domineering matriarchs, as sexually promiscuous and without moral judgment. They were both false and cruel depictions.

Angela also offered a clear and reasoned account of the Soledad Brothers case, of prison conditions in general. Jubilantly she observed that only a day earlier a San Francisco jury had found the two surviving Soledad Brothers, Fleeta Drumgo and John Clutchette, not guilty:

> Members of the jury, we were correct in our understanding of the case of the Soledad Brothers. Monday morning . . . the ultimate fruits of our labors were attained. The twelve men and women, who for a period of months had listened to all the evidence which the prosecution could muster against the Brothers, entered a courtroom in San Francisco and pronounced the Soledad Brothers "not guilty." If George Jackson had not been struck down by San Quentin guards in August of last year he too would have been freed from that unjust prosecution.

We printed Angela's opening statement as a pamphlet and distributed it all over the country.

It took Albert Harris almost three months to present his case. He called 104 witnesses and introduced 203 items in evidence. He presented his case in two parts. In the first he intended to show every detail of what happened on August 7. He called Marin County sheriff's deputies, San Quentin prison guards, forensic specialists, the Marin County coroner, a pathologist, a reporter and a photographer from the *San Rafael Independent Journal*, prosecutor Gary Thomas, now confined to a wheelchair, and a juror, Maria Graham, who had been wounded on August 7.

As much as possible, we focused on the facts of the case. But in cross-examination, our attorneys repeatedly sought to establish two basic things. The first was that all of the dead and wounded were shot by San Quentin prison guards and/or by prosecutor Gary Thomas, who had grabbed a weapon and begun shooting; neither Jonathan Jackson nor the escaping prisoners had fired a shot. The second thing the defense worked to establish was that no (serious) demand had been made to free the Soledad Brothers. This was key to undermining Harris's theory that Angela had engineered a plot to free George Jackson. One reporter, for example, said he heard "Free the Soledad Brothers!" shouted by one of the prisoners as they entered an elevator on their way out of the courthouse. He wrote this down in his notebook, he said, but he didn't tell anybody about it. Another witness, this one from the Marin County sheriff's department, also claimed to have heard the "demand." When asked to specify exactly what he had heard, he said, "Free all our black brothers in Folsom!" When asked to repeat what he had heard at the volume at which he heard it, he squirmed uncomfortably in the witness box and then shouted, "Free all our black brothers in Folsom!" I was sitting very near the front of the courtroom on that day. As defense attorney Leo Branton, who had conducted this cross-examination, turned from the witness to return to his seat, I heard him hiss under his breath, "Right on, brother!"

Angela, Fania, Kendra and Franklin, Charlene, if she was in town, our lawyers, and I continued to meet most days after court, and late into the night. We debated about witnesses, evidence, cross-examination, trial strategy. We ate all manner of fast food and pizza, guzzled sodas, and talked and paced and swept our hands through our hair and shouted at each other and carried on until exhaustion compelled us to sleep. Sometimes someone would say something very funny, or what seemed to be very funny. We'd become hysterical, as you do when you are very tired. I often crawled into bed at three or four in the morning. Jack was always up at six to get ready for work. He did what he could to get Joshua up and dressed before he had to leave, and then I would take over. Joshua's daycare was not far from the courthouse. He and I had breakfast together, and then I'd drop him off and race to the superior court building, where I would stand on line to be searched. Court began promptly at nine. Most days I could hear Fania rummaging around upstairs as she also pulled herself and Eisa together for the day. Often we ate together. Sometimes Angela or Mrs. Davis would meet us at the house, en route to the court, and we'd all be in such a rush to get into cars and off to the courthouse on time; it seemed like a slapstick comedy. We were so distracted by the tension that it was hard to focus on the mundane.

In the second half of the prosecution's case, Harris sought to show Angela's complicity and motive. He called as witnesses sales clerks and airline ticket agents, gas station attendants and motel owners. He called Angela's neighbor in Los Angeles, and the owner of a pawnshop in San Francisco. He read Angela's letters to George into the record. We put up a fierce fight to have the diary excluded from evidence because it was such an invasion of Angela's privacy. It had been found in George Jackson's cell after his death. It had been written, we argued, more than a year after the August 7 events, and was not relevant to the case. Our appeal was only partially successful. The judge edited the diary and permitted the prosecution to enter this edited version into evidence.

This part of Harris's case was the most critical. Every shred of paper, sales receipt, gun registration, every alleged identification of Angela, every photograph, was scrutinized and its significance contested. On cross-examination, over and over again, defense attorneys sought to raise a "reasonable doubt." Never alleging that Angela participated on August 7, Harris sought to show that she was with Jonathan in the preceding days, including at the Marin County Civic Center and at San Quentin. He tried to show that she lived with Jonathan in Los Angeles in the preceding months, and that she spent the night of August 6 with him in a San Francisco motel.

Harris's case was entirely circumstantial, so his strategy was to build a preponderance of evidence, piling one witness on top of another to create an impression of overwhelming complicity. He had two major problems. All of his eye witnesses were white people who had little or no connection with African American people and great difficulty in identifying them. The general description of Angela that they all had heard was that she was a tall, light-complected black woman, wearing an afro, and that she had a space between her two front teeth. They chanted this like a mantra on the witness stand, and the very monotony of it cast doubt on whom, if anyone, they had seen. One witness even said that he "couldn't remember about the teeth."

Harris's second major problem was that Angela had never made any attempt to hide her identity. Four of the guns Jonathan had used were registered in her name. Three had been purchased over a period of several years in Los Angeles at a Western Surplus store where Angela was well known. The fourth, a shotgun, was purchased in San Francisco two days before the courtroom takeover. Again, Angela had used her own identification. When the San Francisco clerk had recognized her and asked for her autograph she had cheerfully obliged and chatted with him. Surely anyone plotting a revolt in which the shotgun was to be used would not have been so open about her identity.

Harris called Angela's neighbor in Los Angeles to try to show that she and Jonathan had been living together. However, Mrs. Young, an elderly African American woman, said she had seen Jonathan only once or twice when Angela was moving in, and hadn't seen him since, except that she'd seen his picture in the paper and knew he'd been killed. She gave Angela a neighborly wave as she left the witness stand. Harris called another witness, this time to show that Angela was at San Quentin in the company of Jonathan Jackson on August 6. The witness, a white woman, said she had gone to San Quentin to visit her stepson. She saw a "young Negro couple" walking up the ramp. She recognized Angela Davis because she'd seen her on TV. Asked to identify her in court, she said she wasn't sure that she could. She asked if Ms. Davis could smile so she could see her teeth. She walked over to the defense table, hesitated, and then pointed to Angela. "I think it is this girl here," she said. I thought it was obvious that she was lying. The hilarity and absurdity of these moments in the trial—Leo hissing "Right on, brother!" and Mrs. Young waving at Angela, and the San Francisco gun-shop clerk having asked for Angela's autograph—made everything surreal. I would be guffawing one minute and on the edge of weeping the next.

When Harris read Angela's letters and diary into the record, a complete hush fell over the courtroom. To my ears the letters sounded like part of an ongoing conversation about history and slave revolts and South Africa and nonviolence and the California penal system and freedom struggles and the position of black women within them. . . . The diary sounded like a long poem, even read in Harris's monotone. The letters and the diary showed that Angela had loved George Jackson.

I spent hours on the weekends, when I wasn't in meetings or otherwise directly engaged in the political campaign, writing letters. Writing helped me to maintain some semblance of emotional balance. At times, my feelings for Angela were so huge, so overwhelming, that I felt driven to commit violent acts of retribution. Instead I wrote, and the writing forced me to focus, to clarify and sharpen my understandings. I wrote letters to Gerri in Munich, to Ursula Beitz in Berlin, and to my parents. My parents, of course, supported Angela unequivocally. Mom had a particular gift for sarcasm, which I enjoyed when it wasn't directed at me. Her commentaries on the FBI, the prison guards, and the prosecutor were very satisfying. My father agreed with Angela's and my political views on Jonathan's actions as a prisoner's revolt; drawing upon his knowledge of slave revolts and African American history in general, he wrote several articles and spoke at "Free Angela" events. Finding myself in such complete congruence with him provided a perfect and familiar anchor.

The prosecution rested its case. The tension for us was almost unbearable. Should we present a defense at all? Should Angela testify? How weak was Harris's case really? How much were we projecting from wishful thinking? How accurate were we in our assessment of the jury's response to the prosecution? Margaret Burnham and Doris Walker had been preparing an affirmative defense. They had scores of witnesses prepared to testify: criminologists and psychologists who would talk about the prison system; Angela's colleagues at UCLA; Reverend Ralph David Abernathy, who had taken over from Martin Luther King, Jr., as the head of the Southern Christian Leadership Conference; Herbert Marcuse; California State Senator Mervyn Dymally; actress Jane Fonda; the surviving Soledad Brothers; members of Angela's family; witnesses to her whereabouts in the days immediately prior to August 7.

What to do? If we put on the full measure of our defense, it might look as though we gave too much credence to Harris's case. But we needed to counter the myriad half truths, innuendos, and misrepresentations he had presented. It was the conspiracy charge that worried us the most. There was no way, we thought, that Harris had any kind of case for conviction on the murder and kidnapping charges. But the conspiracy law was so vague and amorphous. I hardly slept those nights before our decision. Every witness, pieces of transcript, pieces of evidence whirled in my mind. I could feel a raw fury in the pit of my stomach, a fury at the prosecutor for what he had done, at the FBI, at the police and sheriff's deputies and San Quentin guards. I was impatient with Joshua, yelled at him, slapped him. I snarled at my husband. I was under such intense pressure, and I struck out in inappropriate ways and then felt an overwhelming sense of guilt and regret.

In the end, we decided on what's called a "pin point" defense. We presented twelve witnesses in two and a half days. We focused on Angela's whereabouts between August 3 and August 7. Our witnesses testified as to when and where they saw her. We called a psychologist to confirm the difficulties in eyewitness identification, especially across racial lines. We called the office manager in the administrative offices of the philosophy department at UCLA to describe the volume and content of the hate mail and death threats Angela had received. This testimony was especially important in explaining Angela's decision to purchase guns for self-defense. We called witnesses to account for the weapons, where they were kept, and how almost anyone could have access to them. We called Fleeta Drumgo to testify that he knew James McClain, and that he knew of no plot to free himself or the other Soledad Brothers. Then the defense rested.

Harris called two witnesses in rebuttal. The first was an ophthalmologist, an expert to dispute our psychologist's estimate of eyewitness accuracy. The ophthalmologist, however, confirmed the opinions of our psychologist. Then Harris called Lester Jackson, the father of George and Jon. It was hard to believe he would do such a thing. He wanted Mr. Jackson to confirm the date that Jonathan went to San Francisco in order to impeach one of our witnesses. Mr. Jackson refused to testify. He told the judge he'd had only two sons and they were both dead and he couldn't "participate in these proceedings." It didn't matter what question the prosecution asked. The judge held Mr. Jackson in contempt of court and fined him $100. News reporters covering the trial raised the money among themselves to pay his fine.

After a one-day recess, closing arguments began. It was Thursday, June 1, 1972. Leo had labored over his statement for days. We had all contributed bits and pieces—made that point, suggested this argument, don't forget that witness. He had many notes, but he did not read his closing argument. He spoke from the heart. Leo gave an impassioned account of African American history. He placed Angela in the context of her people. Point by point, he refuted Harris's case. Then he read excerpts from Angela's diary that the judge had agreed to place in evidence, and which he had had composed into a poem. He asked that justice be done. I sat in the courtroom listening to Leo with my heart jumping and my body swaying back and forth to the rhythm of his voice.

Harris gave his closing argument. It was long, precise, and predictable.

The judge read his instructions to the jury. Carefully, he clarified the meaning of the law in each instance and explained that Angela could be found guilty of lesser offenses. For example, instead of first-degree murder the jury could find her guilty of second-degree murder or manslaughter; instead of first-degree (aggravated) kidnapping (for extortion) they could find her guilty of simple kidnapping. He explained the conspiracy law. He reviewed the standard legal definition of "reasonable doubt": If there are two equally reasonable explanations for a defendant's behavior, you give her the benefit of the doubt. Somehow I had forgotten about the possibility of conviction on lesser offenses, and as the judge read these instructions I felt a terrible panic; I became tremendously anxious.

The case went to the jury on Friday morning, June 2.

We sat outside on the lawn in front of the superior court building to wait for the verdict.

Jury deliberations took place in a room designed for that purpose inside the superior court building. When the jury had not reached a verdict by 5 PM that Friday, they adjourned for the day. They were sequestered in a hotel near the courthouse. They resumed deliberations on Saturday. By 5 PM there was again no verdict. We stayed together with Angela and her family. We ate. We talked. We played games. We went to the home of a community activist for a barbecue on Saturday night. We heard that Mary Timothy was foreperson of the jury, good news in our minds. She was one of our best jurors, we thought. We also learned that the jurors had asked to see all of Angela's letters to George, the visitor's record at San Quentin for August 6, and one volume of the hate mail Angela had received.

At 10:30 AM on Sunday, Franklin strode toward us from the courthouse. "They've reached a verdict," he said. We gathered ourselves together and lined up to be searched before entering the courtroom. I was alternately weak with fear and flushed with euphoria. Mrs. Davis didn't want to go into the courtroom. "Mama, you have to come in," Angela said. I took Mrs. Davis's hands in my own. "It's going to be okay," I said. "Everything's going to be okay." Mrs. Davis came in with us.

We were seated. It was now 12:30. The room was completely still. Security was very heavy. The judge entered. We all stood. We sat down. The jury filed up the center aisle of the courtroom, through the spectators' section. I scanned their faces in rising panic. They looked ashen and worn. The judge asked Mrs. Timothy if the jury had reached a verdict. She said, "Yes, Your Honor." He asked to see it and she handed the forms to the court clerk, who handed them to the judge. As he read them, his face betrayed no emotion. He handed them back to the clerk and told him to read the verdict.

"First-degree kidnapping . . . not guilty."

"First-degree murder . . . not guilty."

Of this much we had been reasonably certain. Franklin had already begun to sob. I think I stopped breathing before the final charge was read.

"Conspiracy . . . not guilty."

Kendra screamed. Fania stood, arms upraised, tears streaming down her face. Attorney Margaret Burnham collapsed in her chair. Angela reached for her mother. The judge banged his gavel for order. He declared, "This trial is adjourned."

The jury stood. We stood, faced them. We started to applaud in a rhythmic clapping until it was an ovation.

We left the courtroom. Before exiting the building we brought Angela into a small private alcove. Weak with emotion, she had one arm flung heavily over my shoulder and her other arm over that of another comrade. She was near to a dead weight. Her head flung back, face twisted in agony, she wept. Then Angela recovered herself. She looked down at me, smiling. She said, "Find the jury; tell them about the party." I nodded.

We all went outside. It was a bright, sunny Sunday afternoon. Hundreds of people had gathered outside the courthouse, and hundreds more arrived as word of the verdict spread. Angela spoke to the crowd. Then Leo spoke. Then someone else, and someone else. Hundreds of people of every hue hugged each other, swept into a bouquet of happiness.

I circled around to the back of the courthouse and saw Mrs. Timothy and other members of the jury emerging from a side door. I walked toward them smiling, waving my arms. Captain Johnson from the sheriff's department rushed forward to block me. Mrs. Timothy said, "Please. It's okay. We're friends now." The captain moved aside, and Mrs. Timothy and I shook hands as other jurors crowded around. I touched each of them. I stammered out our feelings of gratitude. I said, "There's a victory party, and you are all invited." I gave Mrs. Timothy the address. And then Franklin appeared. Would the jurors be willing to hold a press conference with Angela? They agreed. We drove to NUCFAD's San Jose headquarters. As cameras flashed and people smiled, the press flung their questions at Mrs. Timothy, who, as foreperson of the jury, answered them. Then we gathered at David and Gloria Newman's home, where Mrs. Davis had lived for the duration of the trial. Their spacious lawn and garden were filled with people. Angela sat on the grass near Mary Timothy and other members of the jury. We all had so many questions to ask each other. I sat on the grass a few feet away, my arms wrapped around my son.

Everyone scattered at the end of the trial, and I could at last be at home. I took Joshua out of daycare. We spent all day, every day together. We went to the park and to the zoo and to a place called Happy Hollow in San Jose. We ate ice cream and rode our bicycles and played. After that I took off by myself for a little while. I needed so much to be alone. I drove north along the California coast, walked the cliffs overhanging the ocean, smelled the surf that pounded the rocks below me. It was only then, relieved of performance and the drive toward perfection, that I could be at ease. However much I wanted to resist the kind of anger I had witnessed in my parents, I was often filled with an indefinable rage. I could feel that tension building in the base of my neck and across my shoulders, becoming more difficult for me to control. When I was alone I could settle it down again, become more the person I wanted to be.

On June 29, 1972, under the auspices of the Communist Party, a huge rally was to be held at Madison Square Garden in New York City to celebrate Angela's acquittal. The party had arranged to fly our West Coast NUCFAD contingent to New York. Angela telephoned. "See you in New York," she said at the end of our conversation, referring to the upcoming event.

"I was not invited," I said.

"What?!" she fairly shrieked into the phone.

I explained that while the party was flying everyone else on the staff to New York, they had not offered to pay my way and I could not afford to pay it myself. Jack and I were fairly broke by the end of the trial.

"Nor should you!" Angela exploded. "NUCFAD will pay your fare! Get your ticket! I'll see you in New York!"

My feelings had been badly hurt by the party's action, but after I spoke with Angela I felt better, thinking maybe it had been an oversight. After all, everyone was very excited and it could have been a simple mistake. As always, I stayed with my parents when I arrived in New York. Angela telephoned me at their home. She wanted to be sure I was coming to the Communist Party's reception before the big event. She gave me the location at a hotel in mid-Manhattan. I went. Comrades were very warm to me. There were greetings and hugs. I hadn't seen most of them since the party's convention in February. Then Louise Patterson clanked a spoon on a glass and asked for our attention. The party, she said, wanted to thank everyone who had worked so hard to set Angela free.

An African American woman, Louise had worked closely with my father. She and her late husband, William L. Patterson, had been among my parents' most esteemed guests at their many parties. I had known Louise all my life. She was smiling, effusive, in her element as she began to read the names. She went through the NUCFAD staff and then went on to comrades in other parts of the country. But she did not read my name. I could not believe it. Mrs. Davis also registered the omission. She called out to Louise, whom she'd known for thirty years, "What about Bettina?" When this drew no response, Mrs. Davis called again, louder, "Louise! What about Bettina?" Peering over the rim of her glasses, Louise caught Mrs. Davis's eye and said, "Oh, yes. And Bettina Aptheker." And then she went on with her reading. I knew then that the party's failure to send me an airline ticket had not been an oversight.

I was devastated. This wasn't about recognition or fame or being slighted. It was much bigger than any of those things, much more

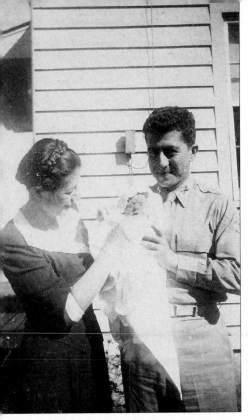

◄ My mother and father holding me soon after my birth, Fort Bragg, North Carolina, September 1944.

▸ Me, at one year old.

▾ Sporting a Brooklyn Dodgers t-shirt; nine years old.

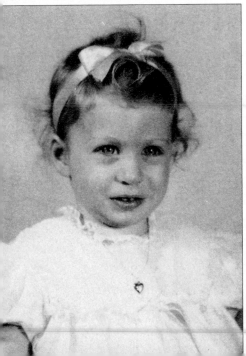

▲ My father, testifying before the Joseph McCarthy Senate Committee, May 6, 1953.

▼ The *New York Times* article that appeared soon after I declared my membership in the Communist Party.

◄ Speaking at an antiwar rally, UC Berkeley, age 23, 1967.

▼ Outside the Veterans Administration Building, Berkeley, CA, after a day at the Free Speech Movement (FSM) Trial, May 1965.

▲ Addressing an FSM rally early in the 1964–65 school year.

▼ Josh and me, 1971.

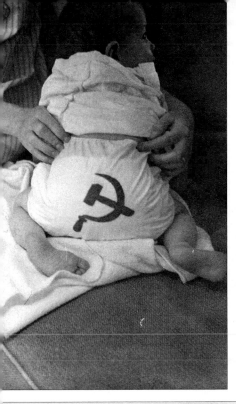

◄ Joshua, a few months old, with a hammer and sickle diaper, a gift from Jessica Mitford.

▼ Jack and Josh, March 1968.

▼▼ Josh, Jenny, and me, Brooklyn, summer 1975.

▲ Angela and me, Oakland, September 1998.

▼ Mary Timothy, foreperson of the Angela Davis jury, who became a close friend, 1974.

▲ Teaching Intro to Feminism at University of California, Santa Cruz, 1981.

◀ Teaching Intro to Feminism at UCSC twenty-four years later, fall 2005.

▲ My father and mother at her ninetieth birthday celebration, in San Jose, 1995.

▼ Kate and me, Santa Cruz, summer 1995.

threatening. It was about who I was, how I saw myself in the world. It was about my identity, my reason for being. I was a Communist. I was Aptheker's daughter. It was one thing for *me* to think about leaving the party; it was another thing entirely to be told I was no longer a trusted comrade, no longer part of the inner circle, much less without warning and in a public venue. I think I stopped breathing. Mrs. Davis was so sweet, so gentle, so sure it had been a simple oversight. She must have seen how stricken I was because she put her arm around me in a maternal way and hugged me to her. I hugged her back, fought my tears, and tried to push down the terror rising at the outer edges of my consciousness. I forced myself to regain the euphoria of the moment.

The rally at Madison Square Garden was thrilling. Fifteen thousand people attended. This was the new garden, renovated since my childhood excursions to the circus with Aunt Leona. The audience was mostly black and mostly young. People whistled and stomped their feet. A bulletproof Plexiglas screen had been erected around the speaker's platform. Nina Simone appeared, bowing deeply to the audience. Her voice, a rich contralto, reached to the very farthest corners of that vast arena. Party chairman Henry Winston introduced Angela. As Angela appeared the audience rose, beside itself with joy. She thanked everyone for all that they had done to save her life. Then she talked about the Soledad Brothers, prison conditions, racism, and the need to stay united and build a broad massive movement to free all political prisoners.

Angela's acquittal came at a moment when much of what had been won in the 1960s faced the test of terrible reprisal. Police assaults on the Black Panther Party and the black community more generally in the late 1960s and early 1970s had left scores dead, wounded, or imprisoned. The whistle-stomping crowd at Madison

Square Garden came to celebrate Angela and her day of freedom.
But we had also gathered as a political testament to the strength of
community, for a renewal of the spirit that had kindled the fire of
a decade.

I went home to San Jose, exhausted. I was filled with gratitude
for Angela's freedom. And I was overwhelmed by the party's stinging
rebuff. Although all of us on the NUCFAD staff had shared the same
position regarding Jonathan Jackson's August 7 prisoner revolt, in
opposition to the party's national leadership, Angela and I were the
ones who had most visibly acted upon it. And I was the one who had
secured publication of our book, *If They Come in the Morning*. The
U.S. paperback edition, published by New American Library, had a
first printing of four hundred thousand. The book had been translated
into more than a dozen languages. I had not gone through party
channels to secure these editions. Neither had Angela and I included
Henry Winston's article, "The Meaning of San Rafael," in the book;
we had disagreed with its argument and he was unwilling to revise
it. My actions in Angela's case came on top of my "unauthorized"
National Guardian article about the August 7 revolt and my equally
unauthorized book on the student movements of the 1960s. I had
also condemned the Soviet invasion of Czechoslovakia. These were
sufficient grounds for a fall from grace, even as my father continued
to be a prominent member of the party.

Four years later NUCFAD leader Franklin Alexander and I were
formally removed from the party's newly created Central Committee,
a smaller body that was to replace the National Committee, on
which we had both served. We were to serve instead on the National
Council, a titular body with no authority that was to meet once a year.
At the convention that year the party held an election for the Central
Committee that was strictly pro forma. The national leadership put

forward a slate of candidates. Other nominations could be made
from the floor, but everyone just voted the slate. When I protested
my removal from the slate to Max he smiled condescendingly, patted
me on the head, and said it was because I was too "individualistic."
When I asked my father why I'd been removed, he cleared his throat.
For the first time I felt a surge of real fury at my father, followed by
fear. What I had always thought was true: I was expendable to him.
I could be jettisoned if the party required this of him. I didn't push
him any further for an explanation. He had shared the same position
on the Marin prisoners' revolt as Angela and I had. I felt the party
had betrayed me. I was taking the fall for Angela (through no fault of
her own) and for my father, both of whom were too important and
too famous to be renounced or rebuked.

Angela's trial marked a watershed in my life. Things shifted for
me in its aftermath, imperceptibly at first and then with increasing
clarity. The student movement at Berkeley had had to it a youthful
effervescence. I had been carried along by political events, acting
out of the expectations and mores of my childhood. But by the
end of Angela's trial I had matured. I was approaching only my
twenty-eighth birthday, but I felt well beyond my years. I felt
accountable for my actions in ways that I had not previously.
And others held me accountable too. I also became obsessed
with issues of recognition and fame, wishing to wend my way
back into the party's good graces. I was jealous of Angela, of her
acclaim and her status as a worldwide symbol of revolution,
of her place in the party's inner circle, its heroine. I also loved
Angela, and I knew that the closeness we had shared during her
incarceration was over, as it had to be, as her life went on. And
even as I struggled emotionally with all of these things, I wrestled

with my own ongoing ambivalence about the party and its many contradictions.

With the end of the trial Jack and I resumed some semblance of family life. Throughout the trial he had been teaching full-time; his salary had supported us. Jack also had worked methodically on Angela's case, especially within the academic communities he knew so well. He had assumed more than his share of parenting Joshua. So in August 1972 we took Joshua and our dog, Igor, and went on vacation. We had had so little time together in the previous two years, it was almost as though we were each spending time with an old friend. We both knew there were serious problems in our relationship, but we thought with the strain of the trial over that things would sort themselves out. At the time I was very aware of my sexual feelings for women and still very much in the closet, fearful of any possible relationship.

In September Jack went back to work and I began writing about the trial. I hadn't planned to write a book, but in those weeks and months after the trial I needed to channel my rage and grief about the trial and the prison system, my love for Angela, and my devastation with the party into some kind of constructive action. Fania and Eisa moved out of our home just after we returned from our summer holiday, and I turned their room in the attic into my new study. It had a small window that opened onto a portion of the roof. I could climb out and sit there overlooking our yard with its old walnut tree and giant cactus, and the fruit trees and flowers that Jack had planted.

I began clipping dozens of articles about Angela from newspapers and magazines I had saved. I read them, sorted and pasted them into what would become a giant scrapbook. I reviewed and organized all of my notes from the trial and from our meetings. One of our lawyers supplied me with a complete transcript of the trial, which included all of the proceedings in the judge's chambers. It was thousands of pages, bound in more than twenty volumes. I studied. I read. I began to write and the book poured out of me. The following January I piled everything into our car and went up the Northern California coast to a cabin belonging to a friend of a friend. It was in the town of Jenner, just across the road from Goat Rock State Beach. I took the dog with me. I wrote all night, slept a few hours in the morning, walked the beach with Igor in the afternoon. I had ten days alone and I savored every moment. I was into my own rhythms, away from everybody. I did call my mother once from a pay phone at a grocery store across the road from the beach. She noted that I was unusually talkative, and then laughed when I explained that I hadn't spoken with anyone except the dog in more than a week. I returned to San Jose and kept on writing. I typed pages over and over again, until I was satisfied with what I had written and with how the words looked to me on the page. I finished the book in a year; it was a six-hundred-page manuscript.

Upon hearing about my manuscript Henry Winston wrote a formal letter to Max, in his capacity as chair of the Northern California Communist Party, requesting a copy of the manuscript so that he and Charlene Mitchell could approve it for publication. I had already sent the manuscript to Max, Angela, and others because I felt that their comments would be critical. In October 1973 Max forwarded the manuscript to Winston, sending me a copy of his accompanying letter. I wrote to Max on October 20, a long letter in which I stated categorically that:

> I do not give you or [Winston] or Charlene or the political
> committee or anyone else the option to *approve* this book
> for publication. . . . I do not want your approval. I want

> your ideas. This is the difference between censorship and
> criticism. It is a vital distinction in spirit and in fact. . . .
> There must be a basic trust and rapport between the writer
> and the prepublication critic, there must be sensitivity
> to the feelings, passion, political commitment of the
> writer. . . .

I asked Max to forward these views to Winston and Charlene, and I further objected to Winston's formal process in requesting the manuscript through party channels rather than directly from me.

The Morning Breaks: The Trial of Angela Davis was finally released by International Publishers in 1975. I had tried unsuccessfully to secure a commercial publisher for it. Toni Morrison made a great effort to help me. She had edited Angela's autobiography, which met with critical acclaim upon publication in 1975. Toni and I had become friends when she visited Angela in the Marin County jail, and she had given me a copy of *Sula* when it was published, with a beautiful inscription. Toni felt strongly about my book and was keenly disappointed at her failure to secure a contract for me. I felt sure the manuscript was turned down at both Random House and Doubleday because of the conservative politics of their top executives. It was one thing for Random House to publish Angela's autobiography. She was a Communist, but she was also a celebrity, guaranteeing them a sizeable market. It was quite another thing to publish a partisan account of the trial.

Since International was the Communist Party's press, I expected to have to negotiate over the political "line" of the book. In fact, very little was said. Lou Diskin, who headed International, thought it would sell very well in tandem with Angela's autobiography, and it did. It went into a second printing very quickly, and was later translated for publication in Hungary and Russia.

I had hoped for a commercial publisher because I wanted the story of the trial, the case of Ruchell Magee, and the general horrors of the prison system to reach the largest possible audience. When I finally and reluctantly submitted the manuscript to International, I was told that Gus Hall, the party's general secretary, wanted to know why we needed another book on the trial since Angela's autobiography was already in press. Given its Communist publisher, *The Morning Breaks* was not reviewed in the mainstream U.S. press at all because, from *The New York Times* on down, they never reviewed Communist publications.

The most exciting thing that happened for me after the book's release was the launch party held in the student union at San Jose State. Arranged by comrades in the San Jose party, the event featured Angela and Maya Angelou as the main speakers. Kendra and Franklin arranged for a slide show featuring vivid photographs of the Soledad Brothers, "Free Angela" protests, San Quentin and its prisoners, and trial scenes. Hundreds of people attended, including Mary Timothy and several other jurors from Angela's trial.

My mother flew in from New York for the event. I had dedicated the book to her. Since her breast cancer surgery, I had continued to make efforts to feel more comfortable in our relationship, less fearful of her outbursts, more respectful of her views. With growing awareness of the women's movement I saw that Mom had a life independent of my father's, that she had been a union and party organizer in the 1930s and 1940s, and that she had a long history of political engagement. She was much more grounded and practical in her politics than my father, and she made intelligent and authoritative sense of the world and her place in it. Though I was still somewhat fearful of her eruptions of anger, I had lost much of my own anger toward her.

At our home before the event Jack prepared a beautiful dinner for the NUCFAD staff, Mrs. Davis, Angela, and Maya, and some of our oldest friends, including Gerri and Orin, who had recently returned from Europe. In a post-celebration party back at the house, Maya continued to perform for hours, dazzling us with poems and songs, my mother singing along or dancing in rhythm to her voice. Maya said that Mother reminded her of her grandmother. Having read Maya's autobiography, *I Know Why the Caged Bird Sings*, in which her grandmother is featured, I knew that Maya's feelings for Mom were an extraordinary compliment. My heart was full. I had never experienced so much love in all my years in the party; I was profoundly moved. After so much hassling with the party leadership in New York, I realized that Angela, Kendra and Franklin, and my comrades in San Jose had come through in a way that was deeply healing.

Ruchell Magee, the surviving prisoner of August 7, went on trial for first-degree murder and aggravated kidnapping in San Francisco on November 27, 1972. By then, I was deeply involved in writing the book on Angela's trial, but I followed Magee's case closely. Albert Harris again acted as prosecutor in the case. Defense counsel Robert Carrow, appointed by the court, served over Magee's objections. Magee wanted to defend himself. Ramsey Clark, the former U.S. attorney general under President Lyndon Johnson, offered to assist and, after some wrangling with the trial judge, was appointed co-counsel. In this trial Albert Harris withdrew the conspiracy indictment with which Magee had originally been charged. He dropped any allusion to the Soledad Brothers, since both they and Angela had been acquitted. Ruchell Magee's trial lasted for almost six months. The jury was unable to reach a verdict. The judge declared a mistrial. We learned afterward from jury members in sworn affidavits that they had acquitted Magee of aggravated kidnapping but could not agree on a lesser charge, and they hung eleven to one for acquittal on the murder charge. In their overwhelming majority they did not believe that Ruchell had killed Judge Haley. On May 7, 1973, Magee was brought back into the San Francisco courtroom. He was informed that the attorney general had dropped the murder charge against him. He was to be retried for the aggravated kidnapping only. Magee requested and was granted a change of venue for his second trial. It was moved to San Jose. Early in June 1973 Magee was transported from San Quentin to a maximum security cell in the San Jose jail and I went to see him.

After being searched by a female deputy sheriff, I was brought back to a cell. Ruchell was seated behind bars that were covered with a wire mesh. He was in chains. One of his hands was shackled to a chain around his waist, and his legs, too, were shackled with a chain leading up to his crotch and fastened to the one around his waist. Ruchell was of small stature, soft spoken with a Louisiana drawl. I sat down on a bench outside the cell. We shared a table slipped through the bars, half on his side, half on mine. I introduced myself and offered to help with his defense. We talked for about half an hour, and I took notes.

Later that month, on June 26, Ruchell sent a history of his prison life to me and to others who had worked on Angela's case. He titled it "An Open Address to the Public." It was written in pencil with printed letters and a distinctive style of curlicues and fancy script. Ruchell had taught himself to read and write using the U.S. Constitution as his primary text. I thought the lettering might reflect the particular printing of the text he had used. His "open address" told the story of his incarcerations, beginning in Louisiana at the age of sixteen.

He was accused of the aggravated attempted rape of a white woman. I knew enough history about lynching to make a good guess about this case. He was tried as an adult, despite his age, convicted, and sentenced to twelve years. He served almost seven at the Louisiana State Penitentiary in Angola. He was released on the condition that he leave the state of Louisiana, and his parents arranged for him to live with relatives in Los Angeles. Six months later he was involved in an altercation with a man over ten dollars, which the man said Ruchell had stolen. They were in this man's car. Although Ruchell was unarmed, he was arrested and charged with kidnapping committed during a robbery. He wanted to plead not guilty. A court-appointed attorney, however, entered a guilty plea over his most strenuous objections. He was sentenced to life in prison. He filed numerous appeals acting as his own attorney, his conviction was finally overturned, and a new trial was ordered. He stood trial again before the same judge. A court-appointed attorney entered a plea of not guilty by reason of insanity. Ruchell objected very strenuously. He wanted to represent himself and he wanted to plead not guilty. Instead he was bound and gagged in the courtroom. Again he was convicted and sentenced to life imprisonment. This is where he was on August 7, and this was why, he said, he decided to take his freedom. His "open address" also included the names of many other black prisoners in San Quentin, the charges against them, and the legal appeals Ruchell had written on their behalf. He documented their mistreatment by prison guards, giving names, dates, and details.

I worked intensely on Ruchell's case throughout the summer of 1973. He wrote to me periodically, and I visited him in jail. I helped with publicity for his case, contacting many of the same prominent community people in the Bay Area who had supported Angela. We arranged for Ruchell to be interviewed by the *San Jose*

Mercury News. Angela continued to speak in his defense, and we reported the truly remarkable "non-verdict" in his first trial for the events of August 7.

As I got to know Ruchell, it became apparent to me how much trauma he had gone through. He seemed paranoid and was given to emotional outbursts, which certainly seemed consistent with the conditions of his existence. But he was also brilliant. I had great compassion for him, but I found it very hard to maintain a working relationship with him because he was so erratic. In December 1973 I went to see him and he refused the visit. Then he wrote to me and asked me to come again, apologizing for his earlier refusal. When I went back to see him again, he refused my visit again. At that point I stopped my active engagement in his case, but I was still extremely involved in its outcome. Ruchell eventually pleaded guilty to the kidnapping charge. In January 1974 he was again sentenced to life imprisonment. He was returned to San Quentin to continue serving his two life sentences. Ruchell Magee is still in San Quentin.

On September 11, 1973, the democratically elected socialist president of Chile, Salvador Allende, was overthrown by a military junta. It quickly became apparent that the United States government had played a significant role in the coup, through a series of covert actions. President Allende was assassinated, and a fascist reign of terror was unleashed. In November I received a telephone call from Patricia Bell, a comrade from New Mexico who had been in Chile during the coup. Pat was a journalist, the *Daily World* correspondent in Santiago. She had been sent to report on the progress of the new socialist government.

Arrested within hours of the military takeover, Pat talked her way out of prison, denying her Communist affiliations and waving her U.S. passport. She was deported. She told me that a Chilean woman, Fernanda Navarro, was going to be in the United States in the coming months. Would I like her to come to San Jose? Yes, I said, without hesitation.

Fernanda arrived in May 1974. She stayed with me and Jack for a week. She was personal secretary to Hortensia Bussi de Allende, widow of the slain president. Fernanda had escaped certain death by seeking refuge in the Mexican embassy in Santiago. She had raced through the streets, dodging machine gun bullets. Mrs. Allende had also survived, and both of them were now temporarily living in Mexico City.

Fernanda was in her early thirties, a small, wiry woman with an intense manner. Consumed by the events that had shattered her life and her country, she worked incessantly, hardly eating or sleeping while she was with us. I traveled with her and we talked with each other late into the night. The story she told that I most vividly remember was of the murder of Victor Jara, a much-loved Chilean folksinger. He was publicly and sadistically tortured and executed in front of tens of thousands of prisoners housed in a stadium in the capital city in the days immediately following the coup. I had recordings of Victor Jara, and I played them again and again, feeling the grief of his murder.

Our comrades arranged for Fernanda to meet with dozens of individuals and groups, especially in Chicano/Latino communities. They embraced her, offering emotional and political support. She spoke to trade unions and with congressional representatives. She was also the featured guest at our annual *People's World* banquet. In those first few months after the coup, there was hope that the intervention of world public opinion might bring about a swift and effective reversal. It was not to be.

Fernanda and I corresponded for years afterward. She wrote to me from Mexico City, and then from London, where she and Mrs. Allende established a more permanent residence-in-exile. I remained active in the Chilean solidarity movement, doing whatever I could to help. My time with Fernanda brought home to me the immediacy of fascism and, in a much more personal way, the utter ruthlessness of its U.S. imperial agents, who seemed to have no hesitation in assassinating a democratically elected head of state because his policies potentially interfered with corporate profits.

When I finished my book on Angela's trial, I decided to return to school. I was at loose ends, feeling isolated in my little attic room, and still deeply conflicted about the party. Graduate school seemed like a terrific option. It would provide structure and intellectual stimulation, and it was outside the control of the party. And, I thought with growing enthusiasm for the idea, I would have a good excuse to stop attending so many meetings.

Jack helped me to explore my options at San Jose State. I was nervous about returning to school after seven years, and I was very nervous about taking the required Graduate Record Exam (GRE). I had never done well on those kinds of aptitude-IQ tests. I finally settled upon a master's program in the speech-communication department under the generous auspices of David Elliott, who was then department chair, and Philip Wander, who was among the more radical of the younger professors on campus. By the time I took the GRE, I had already been provisionally admitted into the department.

I really wanted to teach, and the department offered me a position as a "graduate teaching associate," a title they invented for me since there were no provisions for teaching assistantships at the state universities. While many of the faculty were enthusiastic about my arrival, a few others in the department were less so, given my Communist affiliation. Nevertheless, a majority of the department supported my admission and approved my appointment as a teaching associate. Appropriate papers were duly forwarded to the dean of social sciences. He promptly rejected the teaching appointment on political grounds. Given my brand-new status as a graduate student, the department asked me if we could wait a year and put forward the appointment in the following September. I readily agreed.

I loved graduate school. I loved my seminars. I loved studying. I loved writing my papers. I was in the rhetorical criticism track in the department, as distinguished from communication theory, but I took classes in both fields. I veered toward surveying the speeches of sundry historical public figures, treating them as subjects for critical analysis. For example, I wrote a long paper on the African American orator Sojourner Truth. I learned that her first language was Dutch, not English, because she had been a slave on a plantation in upstate New York owned by the Hardenburghs, a Dutch family. I realized that Sojourner Truth had to have spoken English with a Dutch accent, rather than in the Southern idiom attributed to her. She had never actually spoken the phrase "Ain't I a woman?" for which she was so famous. By the end of my first year I was hooked on graduate school. Members of the party were not happy with my decision; as Max put it, he couldn't see "the point."

My parents, on the other hand, were thrilled with my decision to return to school. Both conveyed their sense that my *real* life had finally begun. In the mid-1960s, my father had founded the American Institute for Marxist Studies (AIMS). A sort of leftist coalition of U.S. intellectuals in and around the party, the institute organized symposia and published monographs and a monthly newsletter. AIMS was headquartered in New York City, in the same general downtown area where my father had always worked. He had been "removed" as editor of *Political Affairs,* the party's "theoretical journal," as its masthead announced, and would not explain to me what had happened. When I asked he would grunt and snap his head in the air as if shaking off a fly. From these gestures I gathered he was removed as a result of political differences with the party leadership, but I never learned what they were.

My father loved AIMS, with its library and archive (Elizabeth Gurley Flynn, for example, left her papers to him) and the routine he had established for himself. He produced a newsletter, which was largely his compilation of and commentary on new books and articles on or related to Marxism published in English in the United States.

Though he didn't directly say it, I knew he wanted me to assist him and eventually head a West Coast AIMS center. With more academic training and an advanced degree I would be appropriately credentialed. This was, in fact, the inheritance for which I had been carefully groomed since childhood. I could imagine myself as an AIMS director and indulged in the fantasy for several years. It felt safe and predictable. The only problem was how emotionally hard it had become for me to be around my father. I did not understand why; I just knew a sense of tension and suppressed anger.

I published two "occasional papers" with AIMS. The first was "Higher Education and the Student Rebellion in the United States," a bibliography related to my book on the same subject, and the second was "Lynching and Rape: An Exchange of Views," reproducing and commenting on a 1901 debate between Ida B. Wells and Jane Addams. The latter was very much a result of my graduate research. In the same period I also edited a volume of my father's essays entitled *The Unfolding Drama: Studies in U.S. History,* published by International (with no mention of the need for party approval whatsoever). My father wanted me to include some of his more contemporary political polemics, but his vitriolic style made me too uncomfortable. I told him the essays didn't fit with the historical pieces, and he accepted my editorial judgment.

While I was in graduate school at San Jose State, my father sent me a constant stream of letters. He had a little formula for them. He would list the articles he had written, the lectures he had given, the books or essays he had read, and then, "Regards to Josh and Jack. Love, Pop." Sometimes he included news clippings or articles that he thought would be helpful to me in my work. It was as though my father and I were sharing this AIMS director fantasy. His letters reinforced his plans little by little, and I appeared compliant, contributing to AIMS as I pursued my graduate studies. But there was always a part of me that was profoundly ambivalent. Graduate school opened up new ways of thinking for me that were not exclusively or primarily entrenched in Marxism. There was a whole world of ideas out there about which I knew almost nothing because my reading had been so (self-)censored. Unspoken, yet increasingly present, was my pressing desire for an independent life, but I couldn't even begin to imagine how to define it.

Now secure in his position as a tenured faculty member at San Jose State, Jack pursued active involvement in the teachers' union and eventually became its president. He had helped me secure my place in the speech-communication department, and he encouraged me in my studies. Meanwhile, Joshua was turning seven in the fall of 1974, already entering the second grade. He attended Horace Mann Elementary School very near our home. The school was housed in "temporary" buildings that had been temporary for a very long time. Joshua loved several of his teachers, most especially Mrs. H, a

Japanese American woman who introduced him and us to Hidden Villa. This was an organic farm and summer camp run by a Quaker family in Los Altos Hills, near Stanford University. Mrs. H took her classes on field trips to the farm, and Joshua was eventually to spend several very happy summers at the camp. Josephine Duveneck, who founded the camp in 1945, was committed to making it a haven for children of all races and economic circumstances.

Good to its word, the speech-communication department put forward my teaching appointment again in the fall of 1974. Again, the dean denied it. The faculty now set aside all of their political differences and put their appointment letter forward unanimously. Even the most conservative members of the department supported my appointment. It was denied again. This time the dean cited my arrest record. In frustration, I threw up my hands and called our attorney, Doris Brin Walker, who had handled Jack's tenure case and was also co-counsel in Angela's trial. She called the university president. "Bert," she said, "are we going to go through this again?"

That was all it took to get my appointment approved. Courageously, Karen Borden, who did not yet have tenure in the department, offered to co-teach a class with me. Later, another colleague in women's studies, Mollie Rosenhan, also offered to co-teach with me. With them I gained valuable teaching experience during my graduate studies. Meanwhile, I was introduced to the feminist faculty on campus. Under their mentorship I gained confidence in myself in a university setting, and I began work on my master's thesis. It was to be a comparative study of Ida B. Wells-Barnett and Mary Church Terrell, African American women whose leadership helped to shape the modern civil rights movement at the turn of the twentieth century. A graduate seminar on African American history with the meticulous scholar and extraordinary teacher Gloria Alibaruho introduced me to Afrocentric ways of thinking. Billie Jensen introduced me to women's history.

I spent two years doing the research for my thesis. African American women's history was a new field then, and only a handful of us were working in it. We corresponded with each other and excitedly shared our "finds." The interlibrary-loan staff at San Jose State and the staff at the manuscript division of the Library of Congress in Washington, D.C., were extraordinarily generous with their time. I was thrilled to be doing this research. My department gave me a small office on campus. Really it was just a soundproofed room only slightly larger than a booth used for speech therapy; it didn't even have a window. But I was content to seclude myself inside and write. I received my master's degree in June 1976. That fall I began teaching in women's studies and Afro-American studies, a course called "History of Black Women." Since I had a degree now in speech-communication, I also picked up occasional classes in public speaking at San Jose City College. For the first time in my adult life I was gainfully employed. I was thirty-two years old, which seems to me a very late start to employment that most certainly reflected my class privilege, albeit with its peculiar Communist twist.

Although women's studies co-sponsored my course on the history of black women, I was initially ambivalent about my association with the program and decidedly condescending toward the women's movement, which by then had been in full swing for about seven years. The party considered the women's movement a "petit bourgeois formation," and its women's commission, of which I was a member, spent a lot of its time, in the rare meetings it held, attacking the movement for its attention to "personal" issues like abortion and rape. As a counterpoint to the "bourgeois" radical feminists, the party initiated Women for Racial and Economic Equality (WREE).

Located in New York and staffed by a younger party cadre, WREE focused on the ways that class and race impacted women's lives. It rejected theories of male domination in favor of instances of male chauvinism and believed that capitalism was solely responsible for "women's inequality." Its program centered on issues of childcare, pay equity, and racialized job segregation, which kept black, Puerto Rican, and other women of color in the most menial and poorly paid jobs. The issue of reproductive freedom was addressed primarily in a campaign against the forced sterilization of black, Puerto Rican, and Native American women. There was no discussion of sexual violence, domestic violence, lesbian and gay rights, or the newly won right to abortion. Had the women's liberation movement not emerged, it is unlikely that the party would have initiated WREE. Nevertheless, the issues WREE spoke to were real. I joined and subscribed to its newsletter, using many of the articles in my classes.

The real reason I was so hostile to the women's movement (and suspicious of women's studies), however, had nothing to do with ideology or party loyalty. The real reason was that I was a lesbian, although a highly closeted one. I couldn't explain the connection between lesbian life and women's liberation, but I knew it existed and I felt very threatened by it. Nor was I the least bit willing to look at issues of sexual violence. No way; not yet. Racism, on the other hand, was safe and familiar ground for me. WREE was about as far as I was personally willing to go on women's liberation in the mid-1970s. However, I had an inkling that the women's movement was much more significant than I wanted to acknowledge because Angela took it very seriously. In fact, she had given me my first introduction to feminism a few years earlier.

It was in the Palo Alto jail in December 1971. Since I was to present her paper at the philosophy association convention in New

York, I had to understand what I was to read. Sitting on the floor of her cell, our heads bent forward over her paper, Angela explained each of the philosophical concepts embedded in her discussion of Hegel, Kant, Leibniz, and Marx and Engels. I was already familiar with Engels's *The Origin of the Family, Private Property, and the State,* but we went over Marx's theories of precapitalist economic formations and alienation very carefully. Angela had read and studied the early white feminist writers that the party spurned, like Shulamith Firestone, Robin Morgan, Erica Jong, Kate Millett, and Juliet Mitchell, and she took them seriously. She took sexual violence seriously. She took male domination seriously. She challenged the racism in the work of these early feminist writers, but she did it in a respectful and thoughtful way. Even as I feared feminism and continued to shy away from it, Angela taught me that it was a philosophy and a politics with which to reckon.

In the fall of 1977 the women's studies program at San Jose State asked me to co-teach a course called "Sex and Power." They also continued to co-sponsor my course on black women's history. I told Sybil Weir, a professor of English and coordinator of women's studies, that I didn't know anything about sex and power. She said that I knew more than I thought I did, and besides, a graduate student in the program, Tonia Harvey, would teach it with me. I agreed to do it because by the fall of 1977 my ideas had begun to shift, and more important, my emotional space had widened. Tonia had ordered our book, a standard introductory text, and we designed the syllabus together. Since my strengths were in race and class I emphasized those issues in the syllabus. I asked Tonia to teach the unit on homosexuality (as it was called in the text). She was straight, and I was afraid to touch it. Teaching women's studies accelerated a personal transformation that was already in progress. I was one chapter ahead of the students, but in my heart I was already traveling at light speed.

Every day during Angela's trial all of us had watched the jury intently. We paid special attention to Mary Timothy. She was our bellwether on the jury because our community folks had told us she was progressive. We knew for sure that she was against the war in Vietnam because she and her husband had supported their son when he had been arrested in an antiwar protest. When Mrs. Timothy and I met on the lawn at David and Gloria's home on the afternoon of Angela's acquittal, we chatted easily with each other. She had seen me in court, too, and wondered who I was. She'd never met a Communist before. We exchanged addresses and a few days later I had a letter from her. Would Jack and I come to dinner at her home? This was the beginning of my long and intimate relationship with Mary Timothy. She may never have known a Communist, but I found her just as unfamiliar; my connection with Mary was my first close friendship with someone who was not in any way associated with the Communist Party. It was a revelation to me. The world in which I had been raised was so insular. I had been taught to believe that the only "good people" were Communists or their supporters. This is what my father always insisted. In my late twenties at the time, I still believed this.

Following our first dinner together Mary and I met often. We talked about many details of the trial. She had so many questions. One night we talked until two or three in the morning. "Thank you so much," she said. "I think I needed to talk to you for that long." I, too, was immensely curious about the jury's deliberations. Mary said they had truly abided by the judge's instructions. None of them had read about the case in the newspapers or listened to

TV newscasts, and they had not talked to each other about it. She said they spent most of their time in the jury room talking about the experience itself. The night before the case came to them, many of the jurors couldn't sleep. Some of them, Mary included, threw up. Individually they each thought they were the only ones to believe in Angela's innocence, and each was preparing to hold out against the others. They discovered all of this in the jury room that first morning of deliberation. They decided then to take a secret straw vote on each of the three counts. Mary had already been elected as foreperson by acclamation. On the first straw vote the tally was kidnapping, twelve to zero for acquittal; murder, twelve to zero for acquittal; conspiracy, eleven for acquittal and one "undecided." Mary said they didn't want to box anyone into a corner, so they didn't ask who was "undecided." The juror came forward herself and put her questions on the table. Mary said everyone worked together to be sure not to "blow it." They all felt the weight of Angela's life hanging in the balance.

When I met Mary she had just turned fifty-two, and she had been struggling with breast cancer for eleven years. She had had two radical mastectomies, the second one seven years before Angela's trial. A bout with hepatitis, contracted at work the year before we met, had seriously compromised her health. For a long time Mary had been convinced that cancer was connected to the immune system, and she thought the hepatitis would trigger a return of the cancer. Sometime in the middle of Angela's trial, Mary knew the cancer had recurred. Even though she knew, she stuck with the trial because she felt it was so important.

In those first months when we were getting to know each other she was in and out of the hospital for tests, and eventually for surgery and radiation treatments. Mary investigated every possible avenue of treatment. Once, in a darkened hospital room shortly after the surgery, she squeezed my hand. "Sometimes," she whispered, "I get so frightened." Tears welled and rolled down over the crow's feet at the corner of each eye.

Mary fought the "Big C," as she called it, with all the intelligence and courage at her command. She was a research assistant in the urology department at the Stanford Medical Center, and she used her considerable medical knowledge to consider alternative cancer treatments. She experimented with several non-Western, nontraditional methods of treatment. Finally, the cancer went into remission. She enjoyed a period of four years in relatively good health.

She used these years to the fullest advantage. "You are what you do every day," she used to say to me. "You have to set your priorities, do what's really important." This was a whole new concept to me. Mary wanted quality time. She believed in taking accurate stock of a situation, sizing it up for what it was, and then choosing between your options. She was sure the cancer would return. Her strategy was to stay in the present, take each day as it came, and do those things she loved most. She continued to work at Stanford because she loved it. She went to football games because she loved them. She spent time with her family and friends because she loved us. She read books, attended lectures, went to movies and the theater, took long walks, because these things contributed to the richness and fullness of her life.

Sometimes we met on her lunch break from work and picnicked in the hills above Stanford. We saw each other every few days for a while, and at least every week or so for years. I took Joshua with me on special occasions. She and her husband, Art, had bought a piece of land on the beach at a place called Salmon Creek just north of Bodega Bay. They had put a trailer on the spot and talked about building a retirement place for themselves. Mary and I went up to the trailer together, and sometimes I stayed there by myself. It was a wonderful place to write and walk for miles along the beach. Mary taught me to really listen to the surf, to see beauty in a small stone, to watch the sun rise, to stand in awe of a full moon. I had been so "busy" making a revolution, it had never occurred to me to do these things. Mary also introduced me to football and to the Oakland Raiders. She was a devoted fan. I became such an enthusiast that one Sunday afternoon at the Oakland Coliseum I found myself standing on my seat, waving my arms, and screaming at the Oakland quarterback to "Pass . . . pass the fucking ball!" just before he was sacked by the opposing rush. Mary gazed up at me, a grin spread across her face, and I slithered self-consciously back into my seat. Once, we went to San Francisco and rode the Powell Street cable car to Ghirardelli Square. I tasted crab for the first time and decided I liked it a lot. "Stick with me, kid," she used to say, knocking me gently in the ribs with her fist, "and you'll have a great time." I did, and I fell in love with her.

Tentatively at first, and then with growing confidence, I began to tell Mary about things that had happened to me. The biggest risk I took was telling her about being raped while in police custody at the hospital; I never thought she would believe me. She told me that in-hospital rapes were common. She didn't tell me how she knew this, but I was both relieved and astonished. These conversations with Mary were the first evidence I had that healing was possible. It was the first time I understood that you could talk to someone about something so painful that it was almost unbearable, and that if they received your story and held your pain and loved you, you could feel better.

We shared many stories from our lives. Mary was an independent woman long before it was fashionable. She had enrolled at the University of the Pacific to finish her bachelor's degree once her kids were old enough to be more on their own. This was long before women's "reentry" programs were established. She majored in biochemistry with the intention of going on to medical school. She took the MCAT exam and scored well. But she was forty-three and female and nobody would take her. Then her youngest daughter developed a urinary tract infection that didn't respond to traditional medical treatments. Mary began making frequent trips to Stanford's medical center with her daughter. Nothing seemed to work. Frustrated by the failure of the Stanford doctors to find a cure for her daughter, she took matters into her own hands. Mary applied for and secured a job as a technician in the urology lab at Stanford. She commuted to work, often staying in Palo Alto so she could, once her shift was over, work late into the night, testing her own ideas for a cure. Eventually, she discovered a vaccine that she thought would work. She checked with the supervising doctor, who said, "Try it." She did, and her daughter was cured. This was how Mary began her work at Stanford, and the family moved from Stockton to Palo Alto to accommodate her now-full-time employment as a research assistant. She showed me her lab notebooks. Smaller than standard college notebooks, they had blue covers and light green paper. Hers were filled with formulas, mathematical equations. Her notes were written in pencil, in a small, neat hand. Ironically, it was while working in the lab that Mary was exposed to the hepatitis that she believed precipitated a recurrence of her cancer.

Nourished by Mary's love and by our relationship, I sprouted. My writing became less academic, and I drew upon personal experiences and experimented with poetry. I kept a journal for the first time and began reading novels, which I had previously shunned as my father had. When I asked him why, he told me novels were "trivial" relative to the "serious philosophical and historical" texts he studied. Only the Russian novelists were worthy of serious attention, he said: Tolstoy, Dostoevsky, Gorky. Under Mary's tutelage I stopped rushing around so much, observed more of the details of a moment. I paid attention to my body. I stopped smoking. (I had stopped before, but had started up again during Angela's imprisonment, when I smoked her cigarettes and then kept her supplied!) I started lifting weights, and I jogged several times a week.

Falling in love with Mary, I was at once exhilarated and terrified. I wanted her to know and not know at the same time. Then one day in a bookstore, I saw a paperback title that caught my attention. It was *Lesbian/Woman* by Phyllis Lyon and Del Martin. It was the first time I had consciously seen the word "lesbian," and I knew without a doubt that this was what I was. I picked up the book, flipped through its pages, but with my heart thumping I was too distracted to read anything. I put the book back. It took me weeks to summon the courage to buy it, which I finally did in a bookstore where I hoped I would not be recognized. After I bought the book I hid it in my study. I didn't read it for weeks. One day I left it out, casually, on the stairs leading up to my study where I often left books. Jack had already left for work, Joshua was in school, and Mary was coming to visit. I left it out so she would see it. She did, but made no comment, although I had hoped she would. I needed so much for us to talk.

It was at about this time that I became reacquainted with the work of the German graphic artist Käthe Kollwitz. I had seen reproductions of Kollwitz's lithographs and sketches when I was in Berlin, and now second-wave feminists in the United States were rediscovering her work. A socialist, Kollwitz had nevertheless remained in Germany throughout the Nazi period. She was so popular an artist that even the Nazis did not dare to arrest her. They did ban her work, however. Her husband, Karl, was a physician and shared her political views. She often sketched the poor, working-class women she saw in his waiting room. Kollwitz's life spanned the last decades of the nineteenth century and the first half of the twentieth. She died in a temporary refuge in the countryside near Berlin a month before the collapse of the Third Reich.

One day, in the context of my recent and cautious acquaintance with the women's movement (inspired by Mary's enthusiasm), I read this paragraph, written by Kollwitz in 1922:

Although my leaning toward the male sex was dominant, I also felt frequently drawn toward my own sex—an inclination that I could not correctly interpret until much later on. As a matter of fact, I believe that bisexuality is almost a necessary factor in artistic production; at any rate, the tinge of masculinity has helped me in my work.

Earlier, in a journal entry she had written: "I am continually falling in love with women, but I never tell them. I draw them instead."

I had many books with reproductions of Kollwitz's work. I pulled them from my shelves. I looked again on the familiar figures of the women and children she had drawn. I studied the women with renewed interest—the muscles in their arms, the curvature of their worn bodies, the way they surged and swayed. I considered the sparseness of lines and the careful workings of shading and contrast, the method itself bearing witness to the gaunt, emaciated forms of her subjects. There was, it seemed to me, an odd mixture of despair and strength that informed each drawing. One felt the intensity of the suffering, and yet did not turn away from it because the subtlety of strength prevailed. Love had been a motivating force in this woman's work. I gasped audibly with new insight into the biblical scene in the lithograph she titled "Elizabeth and Mary," the two women in profile, facing each other in a tender, almost whispered passion, the hand of Elizabeth on Mary's pregnant belly. I was so excited. Certainly Käthe Kollwitz was not a pervert. Maybe I wasn't either. Maybe I, too, just had this "tinge of masculinity," or whatever it was.

Sure of my feelings for Mary, and taking courage from Kollwitz's journals and drawings, I wrote Mary a note. In the most poetic language I could summon, I told Mary I was in love with her. I wince a little now when I think of how it must have read. In any event, my courage prevailed only through the writing. The delivery was less than heroic. I stuffed the note into her hand one afternoon at the end of a visit, and fled. To my great relief, Mary called a few days later. She didn't say anything about the note, but she asked if we could have lunch together soon.

Finally, we talked about our feelings for each other in the privacy of her garden. The conversation was explicit. This, in itself, was an enormous relief. I was scared, but Mary stayed calm and loving and assured me that there was nothing wrong with "homosexuality." We never mentioned the twenty-year difference in our ages, and we never mentioned the problem of adultery. After a long time she said, "I am at the end of my life. You don't want to fall in love with someone who's going to die on you so soon." I was completely overwhelmed by the prospect of her death, which she talked about all the time, as a matter of course. But she went on: "Besides," she said, "you're a writer. If we have an affair you'll surely put it in your memoirs!" She laughed uproariously, anticipating what she had taken to calling "your great American novel." Mary thought she would never see me again after she turned me down, but I was so grateful to her for our conversation. I tried to explain to her what it meant to me to have my feelings acknowledged and validated after so many years of denial and fear.

However nourished I was in the beauty of our intimacy, old fears lingered. They arose occasionally and pushed me back into terror and despair. When this happened I would allow a lot of time to elapse before calling Mary just to "prove" to myself that the relationship was inconsequential. When we reconnected after one such episode, she told me how much she had missed me. I resolved not to disappear again. Her life was too precarious, our time together too precious.

Every morning I awoke to the sound of Jack yelling, usually at Joshua, who was never deserving of it. Jack was intensely unhappy. He did not like his job. He worried about money. He was tense and often depressed. We had sex, but much of the time I think it held little meaning for either of us. It certainly did not produce intimacy. I was often anxious, I had periodic bouts of paranoia, and I was irritable. One or both of us had meetings almost every night and often on weekends. We were mired in domesticity on one hand, and political obligations on the other. As our relationship deteriorated, we both made an effort to hold things together. We went to concerts and the theater; we went on vacation. We tried to communicate our feelings, but neither of us had appropriate skills. I had learned to suppress my feelings in childhood. Often, I didn't even know what I felt, much less how to communicate it. I can look back now and see that much of what I felt was an inarticulate, consuming anger. While Jack and I had an abiding friendship, my real passion lay with women.

Jack was supporting us financially, and it never occurred to either of us that he shouldn't. The party frequently exploited the labor of its women members, assigning us to staff positions while our husbands supported us and our children. Even when I began teaching, my part-time salary only supplemented his income. Emotionally I was often absent from Jack, and he knew it. He felt very insecure, with good reason. Later, after we had separated, he told me about the affairs he had had, almost from the beginning of our marriage. I felt relieved because I didn't think I'd been a very good wife. I was certainly having affairs with women, even if only one was ever consummated, and I had had two one-night stands with men. On both occasions I had had too much to drink. I felt guilty about both. As hard as I tried not to see it, I understood that my marriage was disintegrating and we were both responsible.

David and Gloria Newman, our closest friends, tried to help us. David, as director of psychological counseling services at San Jose State, was a skilled therapist. Gloria, a Chicana, was an elementary school teacher and had worked hard to establish bilingual education in San Jose. Once, when the four of us and Joshua went camping for a weekend, David and I stayed up talking for much of the night. A connoisseur of good brandy, David had brought an ample supply. We had long since put Joshua to sleep, and Gloria and Jack soon crawled into their sleeping bags. A group of teenagers was camped near us, and David worried that they would be noisy. Actually, they were very quiet and went to sleep early. David and I were the ones up late, sipping our brandy and trying to keep our voices down.

One day not long after our camping trip, I met David on campus by chance. I had a terrible headache, one of a series that had gone on for weeks. "Come see me," David said. I hesitated. He said, "Well, you can keep having those headaches, or you can talk to me." I went to see him; we met in his office at San Jose State. I'd never seen a therapist before, and even though David was a close friend and the visit was unofficial, I was nervous. David seemed very far away from me in the room, as though he were seated at the end of a long tunnel. He eased me into conversation and I relaxed my grip just enough to begin to talk. I saw David several times. He let me guide the sessions, and I focused on the party and my feelings of ambivalence, anger, and betrayal. Finally, what came out was my catastrophic relationship with Max my first year in college. David said Max's actions were "entirely inappropriate." It was a certain pronouncement. David's acknowledgment was enormously helpful to me, as it was the first confirmation I had of my own feelings about how sordid and wrong the whole thing had been. It was still a few years before I had a feminist understanding of the power dynamics between men (especially older men) and women (and girls), and later still when I acknowledged more clearly the abusive qualities of the experience. I mentioned nothing about my childhood to David. I did not remember the incest, but I did know how ambivalent I felt about my parents, and how tense I was around them. Yet I was too weighted in denial, too anxious to project a different reality, and there was no way I was going there with David. I am not sure I even knew where "there" was.

Meanwhile, Jack saw David more often, if in a less formal way. Understanding the benefits of therapy for the first time, I suggested to Jack that we seek counseling together, and that he pursue more formal therapy, with David or with someone else. But Jack refused both. He said he could not bear the pain of it.

Early in June 1974 I took Joshua and went to New York, ostensibly to visit my parents and Jack's. Jack and I both knew, however, that the time apart was a trial separation. I stayed in New York for six weeks. Mom helped to take care of Joshua, as did my mother-in-law, Rose. This allowed me time to seek solace in research and writing.

I also spent time with Joshua, taking him to all the places of my own childhood, to Coney Island, Prospect Park, and the Brooklyn Botanic Garden. I returned to San Jose having resolved to make a go of our marriage.

Decisions like this one are always convoluted and subliminal. I hadn't even sat down to reason out my options. I had just come home. The marriage was the cornerstone of the structure I had built in the panic of my early twenties. Marriage provided economic security and, most important, what I thought of as a foolproof cover for my lesbian fantasies and impulses. My parents, I thought, would certainly disapprove if I were to leave Jack. I do not know to what extent I was ever in love with my husband, but I certainly had affection for him. I thought if I made a renewed commitment to the relationship, returned to him with determination to make our marriage work, it could be salvaged. Jack met me and Joshua at the airport, scrubbed and glowing and bearing a bouquet of flowers. I became pregnant almost immediately, in a motel room on Van Ness Avenue in San Francisco, where Jack and I had gone for the weekend.

I told Mary Timothy that I was pregnant one afternoon as we stood in line to pay the cashier at the Stanford University cafeteria we then frequented for lunch. She looked up sharply from her food tray and studied my face. "I didn't know you were thinking about having a baby," she said. "Do you want one?" I nodded a vigorous ascent. "A girl," I said. "I really want a little girl, and I'm going to name her Jenny." Mary said nothing, but her expression led me to believe that she did not think the pregnancy was a good idea.

In the fall of 1974 I was pursuing my graduate studies at San Jose State and teaching one class in the speech-communication department. I was pregnant. And I had agreed to become chair of the Communist Party in Santa Clara County. This could well be considered an act of personal stupidity, if not insanity. But it makes sense in this context: In my intimacy with Mary and with my return to graduate school, I had begun to break free. I was exhilarated, but I was also consumed with guilt because I didn't think I deserved so much happiness. So I became agitated and despondent. The internal sense of being perverted and evil was always with me. By assuming the chairmanship, I doubled or tripled my responsibilities into an impossible load. I punished myself with work, and satisfied both my father and Max in their respective opinions about my career options. I was so busy I didn't have time to think.

During my three years as local party chair, we worked on several major campaigns. In one we tried to organize the thousands of mostly immigrant women who formed the underbelly of the electronics industry in Silicon Valley. The United Electrical Workers Union sent an organizer into the area, an energetic young man who worked very, very hard. The women were mostly Filipina and Mexicana. Their wages were minimal, and their working conditions, especially their contact with acids, violated many state and federal safety and health regulations. We were heartbroken when a campaign at one plant came within a few votes of union recognition. Management had done everything it could to alternately threaten and cajole the workers. We also focused our work in the Chicano community, supporting struggles against police violence and for bilingual education. We supported local Chicano and Chicana candidates. In addition, Jack launched a campaign to become the county tax assessor, which was an elected office in our county. Research into the public records exposed a lot of shenanigans between corporations, the assessor's office, and real estate speculators. Jack garnered 15 percent of the vote. We were astounded. Usually Communist Party candidates managed 1 to 2 percent of the vote, and I often thought some of that was due to voter error.

In December 1974, as the fall semester came to an end, Jack returned to Cuba, again under the auspices of the Departmento de Electrónica of the Cuban Academy of Sciences, which had sponsored his trip three years earlier. He was due home at the end of January. I piled into our car with Joshua and Igor for a much-needed holiday. Joshua had just turned seven. We drove to the town of Gualala, along the Northern California coast, where our attorney and friend Doris Walker owned a cabin. It was beautiful, with one large room and picture windows facing the ocean. When Josh and I sat up in the morning we looked out to a breathtaking view of sea and sky.

Since October I had had intermittent vaginal bleeding. The doctor told me not to worry about it; he assured me that the pregnancy was normal. After a few days at the cabin in Gualala, however, the bleeding grew much worse. Christmas Eve I passed what looked like a complete but undeveloped fetus, and later I felt like I was passing water. I could feel the baby moving around so I knew it was still alive. I also knew my condition was very serious. Christmas morning I packed Joshua and Igor into the car and drove fifty miles north along the coast road to the town of Mendocino. There was a hospital nearby in Fort Bragg. I took Joshua to the movies and bought us tickets to ride the "Skunk Train" the following day. The train ran between Fort Bragg and the inland town of Willits through a beautiful redwood forest that was part of Jackson State Park.

Christmas night we stayed at the Mendocino Hotel, a building with an Old West–style wooden porch and pillars, and rooms refurbished in red velvet. In the middle of the night I bled very heavily; the baby was still moving. By morning I still couldn't decide what to do. Josh and I had breakfast. Then I took us to Heeser's Point, a particularly rugged site overlooking the ocean. Josh and Igor scrambled around in the rocks and I sat perched in the cliffs, sipping brandy. This was my drink of choice and it helped to calm me down. I was trying to reason out my options. But I couldn't reason out much of anything, paralyzed by the memory of the last time I'd been pregnant and in a hospital. I could not wrap my rational mind around the fact that I had been raped under entirely different circumstances. It was not until I grasped that I was going to bleed to death unless I got help that fear propelled me to the hospital. I told Josh that something was wrong with the baby, and I needed to see a doctor.

The physician on duty in the emergency room refused to examine me because he was not trained in obstetrics, and instead advised me to see an obstetrician whose offices were only a half block away. I told the obstetrician, Dr. Michael Goodman, about the fetus and he said, "I don't suppose you saved it?" No, I said, laughing at the ever-rational scientific mind.

Dr. Goodman completed a gentle examination. After I had dressed and was seated in his office, he told me I needed to be hospitalized at once. Seeing my distress he said, "I know who you are. My aunt used to be in the Communist Party. I will take very good care of you." He then went on to describe my condition in detail. The fetus was most likely a twin. I was hemorrhaging and I had already lost too much blood, but the baby was alive and he thought it was fine. The condition I had was known as "placenta previa," that is, the placenta was below the baby. He thought also that the placenta was torn, causing me to bleed so heavily. He recommended an unusual surgical procedure he called a "McDonald suture." The idea was to stitch the cervix closed, and then use an alcohol IV to relax my muscles and prevent the onset of labor. If the baby was born now, he said, at six months, it was very unlikely that it would live. Since my blood type was rare and I was Rh-negative, he would call Stanford University Medical Center and ask them to airlift blood to the hospital. I would need several transfusions. He would also arrange for a helicopter to stand by. If the baby was born, and alive, he would have it transported to the premature ward at Stanford because it was the best facility available. He said it was probably good that I had been sipping brandy, as this had relaxed my muscles and probably prevented the onset of labor. Dr. Goodman asked if I had medical insurance. Kaiser, I said. Good, he said. Kaiser would cover everything in such an emergency, except the blood. (Later, I learned that the nurses at the Fort Bragg hospital donated blood to cover these charges.) I said I couldn't allow myself to be hospitalized until I found someone to take care of Joshua. He asked if I had someone I could call, and I nodded. I felt close to hysteria, but I pushed it back.

I called Mary Timothy; she said she'd get there as fast as she could. In the meantime Josh and I walked the dog. I was not in pain, but walking increased the bleeding. Then we drove the half block back to the hospital and waited for Mary. I put my feet up while we played tic-tac-toe. We read stories and I explained to Joshua what was going to happen. Mary arrived in less than four hours. I'm not sure how she did it, because the normal driving time from Palo Alto should have been six. I kissed Joshua, hugged Mary, and signed in to the hospital. A couple of hours after nightfall I was in surgery.

When I awoke, Mary was in the recovery room. We started to speak, and then suddenly I came up off the table in a quick, unexpected agony. I was in labor. Mary disappeared and the doctor reappeared. He began an alcohol IV, which was the only remedy he had to stop the labor; it was before doctors knew about fetal alcohol syndrome. One of the nurses brought a stethoscope so I could hear the baby's heartbeat. It was steady and sounded so loud. I was thrilled. Mary came back in, bringing Joshua with her. I kissed him, and I told him everything was going to be all right. He looked very pale and small. Later, when he was older, he told me that he remembered the green netting over my hair, and that he thought I was dying. He said he was very nauseous, and vomited in Mary's car.

I asked Mary to call Doris Walker because I had left the heat on in the cabin and I was worried about it. We agreed that Mary would spend the night in Fort Bragg, see me again in the morning, and then return to Palo Alto with Joshua and our dog. She would also call David and Gloria. I asked that my parents not be called. I didn't want to talk to them or see them; I had enough to deal with without their being upset. Dr. Goodman spent the night at the hospital and checked on me periodically. By the next morning I knew him simply as "Mike." By the next afternoon David and Gloria had arrived in Fort Bragg. David called Jack in Cuba. At my insistence he told Jack that the crisis was over, and that he should finish out his commitments in Cuba. This was a great relief to me because Jack found it hard to be around a crisis situation, and I didn't have the energy to keep him calm and functioning.

Unfortunately, my mother had been telephoning the cabin in Gualala. When she got no answer over several days, she called Evelyn, who called Doris Walker, who told her I was in the hospital. So despite my wishes my parents also arrived in Fort Bragg. They thought I was dying. Nevertheless, my father stayed for only one day and then flew back to New York. "I have to get back to work," he said. I nodded, feeling sad that he was going, but I was concentrating whatever energy I did have on staying alive. Later, after it was all over, I thought my father had left because he couldn't deal with the situation.

Doris Walker telephoned me, and when I reported that the baby was still alive she said, "Oh, that's great! Good going, kiddo!" Hers were the first cheering words I had heard and she boosted my spirits enormously. I was still bleeding, but not heavily, and I was no longer in labor. My condition was stable. Exhausted physically and emotionally, I asked Mike Goodman to allow me to stay in the Fort Bragg hospital for as long as he could. I was there for a week. Then David and Gloria drove me home to San Jose. It was a stressful journey. We all worried that I would go into labor again. We made it, and Mother was there waiting for me; Mary had driven her there. Igor was unequivocally overjoyed to see me. Joshua was happy to have me home, but his little face was pinched with fear.

Mom stayed with me for a week. She took care of Joshua and all of the household chores. But she was tense and nervous and it felt as though she was yelling at me every time I got out of bed. We all feared that I would go into labor and lose the baby. I decided I had to ask her to leave. She was driving me crazy. She got upset, as I knew she would, and I made her sit down and talk to me. I told her how her anxiety was impossible for me to handle, that I felt she was holding me responsible for the baby's life. I couldn't take it. "I don't care about the baby," she said. "It's you I'm worried about!" That's when I learned that her sister Tillie had died in childbirth, from an aneurism. She was thirty years old, the same age I was then. Mom was terrified that the same thing would happen to me.

Talking brought us both relief. It was the first time I could remember being emotionally forthcoming with her. She stayed on for a few more days and we slept together at night. Nighttime was always the hardest, so we didn't really sleep very much. Instead she regaled me with family stories. We guffawed into the wee hours of the morning over Tante Sonny and Uncle Midvinsky. Once Mom left, Joshua, who was only seven years old, began cooking for us and taking care of the house. I would sit on a kitchen chair and direct his efforts. He was no longer so frightened, and he provided amazing emotional and physical support. He was a beautiful child, resourceful and loving.

Labor resumed a few days after Mom left. Coincidentally, Gerri telephoned. She was at home in San Francisco and just had a feeling that something was wrong. I told her the story and said that labor had started up again. She said she was on her way. I called David and Gloria. David drove me to Kaiser Hospital, and Gloria took Joshua home with her. Gerri arrived at the hospital, and I felt relieved to see her. I was in labor all day Saturday, but nothing much was happening because the surgical stitches in the cervix had not been removed. I was given an alcohol IV, but still labor persisted. By now a day had passed and I was hooked up to a machine that monitored my contractions. I told the doctors their frequency and duration, while the machine registered nothing. The doctors thought I was exaggerating and I insisted that I wasn't. This was my second child, I said, and I knew how labor felt. This went on for hours, until finally a nurse had the good sense to check the machine and saw that it was malfunctioning. They finally removed the surgical stitches. Two days had passed.

David telephoned Jack again and told him to come home. The one flight a week from Havana to Mexico City left later that day. Jack made the flight. It was full, but Cuban airline officials asked if a passenger would give up a seat to accommodate this *compañero* whose wife was dying. Immediately a seat was vacated. It took Jack another day and a half to negotiate his way back into the United States because hostile U.S. Customs officials would not allow his reentry, since he had come from Cuba.

The problem at Kaiser Hospital was that no single doctor was in charge. There was no "birth strategy," as Michael Goodman had devised in Fort Bragg. By Monday night I had been in labor for more than thirty-six hours, continually bleeding, without sleep. I thought I was dying, not just because everyone was saying so, but because I felt myself to be losing ground physically. I told Gerri and she thought so too. She never left my side. David was, I learned later, storming up and down the hospital corridors. I thought if I could hold out long enough the baby would live. I set my sights on that. A new shift, another doctor. He was very young. He said, did I know the baby would probably die? I screamed at him.

Tuesday morning, January 14, 1975. A woman in a white coat with a stethoscope around her neck entered the labor room. I lifted my head. "Are you a doctor?" I asked. "Yes," she replied. I started to cry. She stayed with me for more than an hour. She administered a shot of Demerol to temporarily ease the pain, the only such relief I had had because none of the male doctors would stay with me long enough to monitor the baby's heartbeat while the drug took effect. Then she left to complete her rounds.

Some hours later I felt the baby's head pushing through at the cervix. I rang the emergency bell. A nurse came in.

"It's coming out!" I shouted.

"That's impossible!" she said.

"Look!" I said. She looked and flew out of the room and down the corridor. Moments later, I was wheeled into the delivery room. My female doctor was there, at the other entrance, putting on her surgical booties, and calling encouragingly to me, "Don't push! Don't push! I'll be right there!" She arrived in the room in time to catch the baby. It cried and I launched myself up on both elbows, shouting jubilantly, "It's alive!" The doctor peered joyously over my

spread-eagled legs: "It's a girl!" Another doctor, a pediatrician, swept
the baby up for me to see, and then away to another side of the room,
where she plunged to work. Jennifer was nine weeks premature and
weighed only three pounds.

The delivery nurse at my side jabbed my shoulder with a playful,
solid punch: "You did a great job, kid!" I fell back onto the table,
exhausted. Jennifer was born at 3:14 PM. I had been in labor for fifty-
seven hours. Dr. Harriet Korakas delivered her, and Dr. Mary Gable
was the pediatrician who took charge of her after the birth. She was
alive. I was alive.

I woke up sometime later, back in the labor room, with a nurse
on one side of the bed, Gerri on the other, talking quietly across my
body. Suddenly a wild-looking man flung open the door, knocking
over the IV as he came bursting into the room. "Who's that?"
exclaimed the nurse, about to strong-arm the intruder. "Oh," replied
Gerri softly, having deftly caught the IV stand in her hand, "he's the
father." They slipped quietly from the room. "We had a little girl,"
I told him. "That's the royal 'we' if I ever heard it," Jack said, tears
rolling down his cheeks.

I was sent home from the hospital a few days later. A nurse
shoved the ritual, complimentary six-pack of baby formula into my
otherwise empty arms. Jennifer was still holding her own, but she
was to be lodged in the preemie ward at the hospital until further
notice. The following morning the pediatrician telephoned us at
home. She was obligated to inform me that Jennifer was dying.
They were doing everything they could. It wasn't hyaline membrane
disease; the lungs were all right. It was something else. She had a
hunch about it. There wasn't time to run a proper test and grow
the cultures, but she thought the walls of the intestinal tract were
not fully formed and the baby was infecting herself. She wanted

my permission to try massive doses of antibiotics in a last effort to save her. "Of course, try," I agreed. "Try anything you think might work." Depressed, exhausted beyond all reason, I went to sleep. It was a Friday. My husband dutifully called the hospital at periodic intervals, and then woke me up to say that she was still alive. On Monday morning, January 20, the pediatrician called and informed us with cautious cheer that she was pulling through. I was beyond words with relief, joy, gratitude, and an overwhelming love for Dr. Mary Gable. I went to the hospital every day for six weeks. I entered the preemie ward, donned a surgical gown and mask, and cuddled a slightly jaundiced, shrunken-limbed little creature. We took her home at a hefty five pounds, with normal coloring and limbs finally proportioned to size.

Jennifer's mid-January birth coincided with our semester break at San Jose State. I was scheduled to resume teaching the first week in February, and I did, even before we brought Jennifer home from the hospital. I went back to work on my master's thesis, and resumed my responsibilities in the Communist Party. I couldn't allow myself any space to think. I had to stay busy, busy, busy, lest I have another nervous breakdown. I was functioning, but I was in a frenetic state.

About a week into the new semester I started to hemorrhage again. I knew what it was. A piece of placenta had been left in the womb during the delivery, just as it had after Joshua's birth. I sighed. I had a class to teach. I went to class. In retrospect, this decision was crazy, but at the time I didn't think so. I felt compelled to adhere to my schedule, rigidly hold onto my structure, or I wouldn't be able to hold on to myself. Though I generally stood to give my lectures, I conceded to sit down, on a chair behind the teacher's desk at the front of the room. A small pool of blood formed under the chair.

No one noticed it, or at least none of the students said anything about it. After class ended I walked to my car, picked up Joshua at daycare, drove him home, and asked Jack to drive me back to the hospital, to the emergency room. I was whisked into surgery almost at once. I woke up from the anesthesia with Gerri and Orin and Jack all grinning at me happily. Gerri stayed for a few minutes after Orin and Jack had left the room. She took my hand. "I love you," she said. "You look very beautiful."

I wrote a letter to Michael Goodman, sharing the good news and thanking him for saving our lives. A year later I drove back to Fort Bragg to see him, with Joshua and Jenny in tow. Mike peered into the car, where Jenny sat snug in her little seat. "She has a full head of hair!" he said, laughing. Then I took the kids for a ride on the "Skunk Train" through the redwoods to Willits.

Two weeks after Jennifer's birth, Ursula Beitz, my dear friend from Berlin, committed suicide. Ursula and I had corresponded with each other ever since my trip with Jack to the GDR. She was scheming to visit the United States on one or another scholarly pretense, and I had been angling to return to Berlin ever since my unsuccessful plan in the summer of 1971, during the lead-up to Angela's trial. I had intended to go the summer after Jennifer's birth, primarily to see Ursula.

To their horror, early-morning commuters discovered Ursula's body in an underground train station. She had hung herself. I felt as if I had witnessed her death. I had a dream in which I heard the roar of a swiftly moving train as it whipped through a station, and I saw the blur of its lights. I woke up with a start, sweating and agitated. Two weeks later a letter arrived from Ursula's mother. It was dated February 1, 1975. It was handwritten, in English:

My dear Tiny Aptheker,

I'm sorry to give you following news. I'm the mother of Ursula Beitz, geb Frost. My dear child, my sunshine, my friend and comrade is dead. The death, her hour of dying had come in the night of 30–31 of January, 75. We all, my son and his family are very dreary. . . . In her notice book I found some, no many, addresses and I do know you by your last letter. Ursel was very happy about it and showed me your letter. . . . We cannot still believe in it. . . . It is cruel and horrible for us. We ask: Why?—must it be?

In Love, Yours ever sincerely
Elizabeth Frost
geb Lemeke.

I could not believe it. I paced the living room, reading and rereading Mrs. Frost's letter, images of Ursula coursing through my mind. Then I remembered the dream, looked again at the date of Ursula's suicide, and sank into a chair in grief. I thought, *So that was the exchange, Jenny's life for Ursula's life.* I had been so close to death in childbirth, and Jenny had come so close to dying that Ursula's death seemed in some way our payment for having survived.

The last word I had had from Ursula was a postcard, sealed inside an airmail envelope and dated January 6, 1975. It was a New Year's greeting. She had heard of an impending visit by my father to Berlin and she hoped to see him. She was anxious for a copy of my book on the trial, which was then in production. She planned to review it. And would I please remember to send her a copy of Angela's autobiography?

Although our letters were occasionally playful, they were, for the most part, devoted to ideological and political issues, each of us feeling at ease with the other to explore and question in ways not always otherwise safe. We discussed Marxist texts, literary criticisms, and Leninist politics. She wrote to me about religious philosophy, about Jews in the GDR, about socialism, ecology, and African American culture, in which she had a keen interest. There were also observations like this one, from a letter dated February 10, 1972:

> I find too often I have to take refuge in Lenin, explaining why the best Leninist scholars (here in particular) do not live according to much what they say and I find him always convincing showing that the bulk of even the most progressive scholars live the isolated work-life that with all the tensions the necessary polemics bring about are not so conducive to foster personal qualities like warmth, etc. which I have come across more often among the non-intelligentsia than among intellectuals. So this [thought] is instead of a branch of nice yellow flowers which they sell here this moment.

Ursula's first suicide attempt was in April 1972. She jumped from the window of her apartment to the concrete pavement below and broke just about every bone in her body, including the third disk in her lower spine. I didn't know all of this until much later. There was a long break in her letters, but I was wrapped up in Angela's trial, and it didn't really register. Then Ursula wrote to me in care of the *People's World,* instead of to my home address, and I knew something was wrong. The letter was handwritten and barely legible, dated July 29, 1972. She said she'd had "an accident" cleaning the windows of her apartment. My mother, who was in touch with friends in the GDR, told me it was a suicide attempt.

I continued to write to Ursula. More letters came from her, from the hospital, and then a very long handwritten one from a sanitorium, April 7, 1973, fully a year after the fall. She was receiving extensive physical therapy. She described the rigid rules and schedule of the sanitorium, which she found very difficult to abide. She offered a critical appraisal of my book, *Academic Rebellion*, which had finally reached her. At the end of the letter came this: "When I regained [*sic*] my health I will have to face the unpleasant procedure of a divorce. . . . Willi got to know a student 20 years younger and we will part as good friends. He was very nice while I was in the clinic." And this: "Outside snow and sunshine intermingle. But I have too much pain to join a walk." Whatever the enormity of her physical suffering, I knew it was her grief at losing Willi that was the immediate cause of her despair. I kept up a continuing stream of loving support and newsy commentary. By the spring of 1974 she began writing to me about her psychological pain, a "psychosis" about Willi, her doctor had called it. She also observed with her usual scientific objectivity that while the GDR had excellent medical and rehabilitative programs, it had virtually nothing to heal psychological wounds. A weakness in socialist practice, she said.

Through all of this Ursula was also working on her dissertation for a doctorate in American and English-language studies. She asked me to send books, pamphlets, etc., to her university address. The East German government postal regulations did not allow for such material to go to private residences (or its delivery was delayed for months). I sent her a steady stream of material. Whatever criticisms either of us had of socialism, we were both loyal party members.

In the early 1970s I had only the first inklings of a feminist consciousness, and virtually no psychological tools. I knew enough, though, to tell Ursula that she was not alone in her experience with Willi. Men frequently left their wives for younger women. I also knew enough to encourage her to talk about her feelings, and to extend to her my unconditional love. I see now in rereading her letters that she had internalized Willi's rejection of her into a furious self-loathing. She was so critical of herself that at times she could not commit a sentence to paper without tearing it (and herself) to shreds. I thought that her self-loathing was also connected to a gnawing guilt about her role in the Hitler Youth, and perhaps to her class as well. Under socialism her entrance into the university had been delayed for ten years, she told me, because she was from the wrong class. Those from working-class and peasant families were given first entry. She had accepted this policy as a "necessary and correct measure," as she put it, but I thought she also felt very angry about it, and then guilty for being angry. I remembered our trip to Buchenwald, her hands around my throat, the rows of hooks upon which victims were hung. There was a part of me that believed her suicide by hanging was planned as a very public execution, as a final act of punishment for her role in the Nazi era, and as a renunciation of the socialism that had failed her.

I thought if I could have seen her, if we could have had time together, conversations, it could have made a difference. At her death I harbored grief and guilt: I should perhaps have gone to see her sooner; I had not written often enough; I had been too self-involved. These things were all true. And equally true, I understand now, it was only Ursula who could have saved her own life. She died just after completing her dissertation.

I wish now for a "branch of nice yellow flowers" with which to mark her life.

In the midst of the chaos attending Jennifer's birth, I received a letter from Fleeta Drumgo, a surviving Soledad Brother. He was still in San Quentin, serving his original sentence and awaiting trial in yet another murder case. The "San Quentin 6," Fleeta among them, were accused of murdering a prison guard on the day George Jackson had allegedly tried to escape and was killed in the prison yard. These six were Luis Talamantez, Willie Tate, David Johnson, Hugo Pinell, John L. Spain, and Fleeta. All were African American or Latino. In his note to me, Fleeta said he had just visited with Fania, who had given him my address. He thought perhaps in writing to each other it would "help . . . counter the agony of this concrete and steel casket."

I answered immediately, and so began a brief but intense correspondence. Fleeta asked for pictures of my family, which I sent. He told me how "clear" he had found my book on Angela's trial. "It touched me deeply," he wrote. This was, without a doubt, its finest review. I told Fleeta about my research on Ida B. Wells-Barnett and Mary Church Terrell. Just after Jenny's birth came this sweet note:

> I'm glad to hear from you and to here [*sic*] that you're doing better. Right on to comrade Jennifer, Extend the brothers and my revolutionary favor to all the comrades, you know like when I was born I was so small they had to carry me on a pillow, I think that how I got the name Fleeta. I was a little tiny baby they say—I don't know, like at present I'm trying to lay cool, in the midst of the very tense and foul atmosphere here. . . .

The San Quentin 6 went on trial in San Francisco. Their trial lasted for sixteen months, the longest trial in California history. The jury reached a verdict in August 1976. Three of the brothers were convicted—John Spain of murder, Hugo Pinell of felonious assault, and David Johnson of simple assault. Having completed his original sentence, David was released on probation. Willie Tate had been released on $100,000 bail pending the trial because he had completed his original full sentence. He was found not guilty in the "6" case and exonerated. Luis Talamantez was found not guilty and released, also having served his full sentence for his original offense. On August 26, 1976, five years after George Jackson's death, Fleeta Drumgo was freed. He, too, had served the full time on his original sentence, and had been found not guilty in the "6" case. The other surviving Soledad Brother, John Clutchette, had been released two years earlier. The Soledad Brothers case, which had propelled such an eruption of government violence and personal tragedy, was finally over.

Despite increasing hardships my parents continued to live in Brooklyn. My mother had been mugged twice on the way to her neighborhood supermarket. Both times she had yelled and fought back and run after her assailants. She was seventy years old. My father was held up across the street from their home. When he produced only a dollar (he never carried more than a little cash), the enraged mugger slashed at him with a razor. My father lay on the ground, vainly attempting to shield his head and face from repeated blows, when a neighbor, out walking her dog, drove off the attacker by yelling and hitting at him with her purse. She saved my father from serious injury. Even so, he was bleeding profusely. The police were sympathetic but ineffectual. Knowing of these episodes, I suggested to Mom that they move to California. She was ready; my father wasn't. However, she had made up her mind and told me to go ahead with plans to find them a house in San Jose.

I located a place for sale two blocks from where Jack and I were living, and I borrowed money from David and Gloria for the down payment even before Mother had seen it. When she did, she loved it. With swift decision she arranged for renovations and determined what of her furniture to transport across the country and where it would go in their new house. Within a few months escrow had closed, they had sold their home in Brooklyn, and they had moved. Everything fit into the new house exactly where Mother had envisioned it. Within two days it looked as if my parents had lived in San Jose for years. It was the summer of 1977.

My father, then sixty-two, relocated his library and his office to downtown San Jose. Within a couple of years he began teaching at Boalt Hall, the UC Berkeley law school. Fania Davis, who was a student there, initiated a campaign to make him a visiting lecturer, and a reluctant dean bowed to student pressure. My father taught classes on racism and the law for years. He loved it.

When I was around my parents for more than an hour, my chest tightened and I had the feeling of a lead ball weighted into my gut. Whatever these physical symptoms of distress, I represented to everyone that I loved my parents, that I wanted them nearby, and that I had had a "perfect childhood." Daddy always said he had had a "perfect childhood," and I repeated the words like a mantra.

With graduate school, the near-death experience at Jenny's birth, and my gradual introduction to the ideas of the women's movement, the center of my life was shifting. Terrified by this shift from the old and familiar structures of my existence, I deliberately and with fierce determination set them more firmly into place: the return to my marriage, the decision to chair the party in Santa Clara County, and, finally, the relocation of my parents to San Jose.

In the last year of her life Mary Timothy gave me extraordinary and sustaining gifts. Mary had an estimate of her illness, of its progression, of her own strength, of how much time she had left. First she had to resign from work. Then she could no longer attend football games. Eventually she became too weak to go outside, later she couldn't walk unaided, later still she couldn't hold a pen and sign her name. She marked each passing, noting it to me, as one would mark a trail. This was now her place on the journey toward death. When she decided that the cancer was out of control she stopped the radiation treatments and the chemotherapy. She had always considered these as a last resort and did not see the point of continuing treatments whose side effects were worse than the cancer.

Mary arranged to say goodbye to each member of the family, to friends, to more distant relatives. From the bedroom I could hear bursts of laughter, or the heave of her straining to sit up to give someone a hug. She sought and obtained permission from each of us to die. Then she let go. It had been her wish to die at home, and the family honored this. With advice from hospice volunteers the necessary equipment was installed. Each of us took a shift so that she was attended twenty-four hours a day. The pain was kept under control with a morphine-based drug. She called it her "cocktail." I knew the end was upon us when Mary no longer bothered to put on her eyeglasses. The familiar wire rims rested on the night table next to her bed.

In the last week of her life Mary gave me her copy of Adrienne Rich's *Of Woman Born.* It was the last book she read. She told me to read it. She said it was a great book. She said she was sorry she had learned the ideas of the women's liberation movement so late in her life. I had never heard of Adrienne Rich. I didn't know her poetry; I didn't know she was a lesbian.

A few days later I was sitting with Mary. Suddenly she opened her eyes. "Oh, it's you," she laughed. Then, "How are you holding up?"

I said, "I'm okay," which was true.

Then she said, "Why are you still married?" I groped for an answer. She waved her hand to dismiss the question.

"Oh, never mind, never mind," she said. "You know what's best." Her voice trailed off into a sigh, and her eyes closed. She died the next afternoon, January 10, 1978, at 3:37 PM.

I had arrived at the Timothy home at 12:30 that day. Mary's husband, Art, ushered me into the house. "She won't know you're here," he said, "but come in and see her." The bedroom was dark except for a small light on the night table casting a glow across her face. Ellen, her eldest daughter, was stroking her face and hair. Her breathing was labored, irregular. Her mouth was open and as the air struck her vocal chords it made a rattling, almost cavernous sound. I put my hands on the top of the covers over her body. Finally, I took her hand.

Ellen wanted a stethoscope. There was one somewhere in the house. Ellen searched through drawers and in the closets. "Come on, Mom. You know where it is. Come on and tell us." Art didn't see why she wanted a stethoscope. Ellen said, "She'd want to know. Her mind is floating around here someplace and she'd want to know her heartbeat." I thought this was probably right. We found the stethoscope. One hundred and twenty beats per minute. The heartbeat sounded strong. It was very loud. But we couldn't find a pulse. The moment of death was almost imperceptible. We noticed the silence when she stopped breathing.

It was raining and as darkness came I went outside. Water soaked my hair and dripped down my face. Alongside the house was a small tree. I hugged it. I wondered why I could still hear the normal sounds of an evening, of traffic, of car doors slamming, of voices in the distance, of the neighbor's television set.

The family waited for some time before telephoning the attending physician, who was needed to sign the death certificate. They waited until the following morning to call the mortuary. For the rest of the day and the night we took turns sitting with her, rotating in and out of the room. Mary's daughters, Ellen and Laura, and I changed the sheets on the bed, and we changed her, gently bathing her body. We put on her favorite brown silk pajamas. Her body was warm and flexible, and a restful countenance marked the still-softened contours of her face. Mary's husband sat with her for much of the night, even as the rest of us came in and out of the room. Music filled the house. I remember a sixteenth-century violin concerto, and Bach's B Minor Mass. By morning the coloration of the body and the countenance of the face had radically changed. She was gone. My father called the Timothy house, saying that I should come home now to attend to my own family. That was enough, he said. I told him I'd come home when I was ready. He hadn't even offered me condolences. I was furious at him and at his presumption in telling me what to do.

In a poem called "A Woman Dead in Her Forties," Adrienne Rich once wrote of her desire to touch the wound left by a mastectomy, to mark upon it some measure of tenderness. When I read the poem a few months after Mary's death I remembered this longing in myself. When we were on a beach with relatively few people Mary would open her shirt, or take it off altogether. "Always wanted to do this," she'd exclaim, meaning that she had always wanted to take her shirt off like the boys could and let her breasts, her body, soak in the warmth of the sun. The surgical wounds, cut deep into her chest, had whitened, leaving only the grooved sweep of the slice.

Three weeks after Mary's death I asked my husband for a divorce. "You are what you do every day," Mary had said. The reality of her death, the reality of my own finite life finally and irrevocably cracked the old structures. This was Mary's gift to me. Several months later, alone in bed, reading, a small lamp on, I felt a strong presence in the room. I lowered the book onto my chest and looked up toward the ceiling and to my left. There was the glow of a radiant white light. I felt suddenly very, very warm, as though I were bathed in the light. I connected this feeling and light with Mary and I felt a sense of complete happiness.

During the years of our friendship I always spent some portion of the Christmas holiday with the Timothy family. I loved their rituals, the play of lights on their tree, the careful exchange of presents. Christmas 1977 was Mary's last. We all knew it. We had helped her into the living room, and laid her out on the couch. We flopped down on the floor around her. We took lots of pictures, drank hot rum. That Christmas is now a mist of memory, a fairytale of lights and laughter.

The Christmas following Mary's death I invited her family to join me and my children and my parents for the day. Everyone came. Still grieving Mary's death, I wrote this poem, the closest I came then to acknowledging our love:

Your lights on our
decorated tree blinked
delirious in
anticipation of
their coming
laughter; crisp
fragrant memories of maternal
love. Your glow
christened un-
spoken tears. Your touch
dwelled unful-
filled in a lover's
arms. Your sorrow
swelled, lingering in the
shadow of our un-
shed grief. Your voice

hovered at the
edge of
memory.

Still, they
danced; reveled in the
icy grass; tussled in the
crush of childhood
rivalry; anointed my
children with sweet-
scented oil; clothed my
spirit in comic
relief.

Above the dinner
chatter my
mother's voice
rose
singing. And then
later, much later
when I walked in the
frozen night I heard your
rugged tune
whistled gaily from the
naked branches
of wintered
trees.

five

COMING OUT AND COMING HOME

WHEN I ASKED Jack for a divorce in February 1978, three weeks after Mary's death, he started to cry. By this time I was too angry to allow other emotions to emerge. A steel door had closed over my heart. It opened a few years later, and I could see then what really good friends we were. Some years later, too, Jack acknowledged that the divorce had been a good thing, and had allowed us both to get on with our lives. But at the time it was extremely difficult for him. He said he had imagined us growing old together. We had been married for thirteen years, and I felt like my life was just beginning. I didn't know if I could live openly as a lesbian, but I was alive with new ideas, caught up in the strength of the women's movement.

Jack moved out on April 1, 1978. With a bittersweet irony he said he liked the idea of leaving on April Fool's Day. He rented an apartment in the same neighborhood and we agreed to share in the care of the children. Jack and I both wanted to maintain a solid, loving base for them, no matter what else happened between us. The divorce hit Joshua especially hard. At ten, he was well aware of the change, and he was worried and subdued. Several weeks before Jack left we sat down with Joshua and explained our decision to separate. We said that Jack would live close by and that Joshua and Jenny would live with me, but they could see their father whenever they wished. Joshua, his face drawn with tension, couldn't understand why his life had to be so disrupted. He cried and he kicked the living room couch. Then he slammed out of the house. He got on his bicycle and pedaled furiously out of the driveway and down the street. I got on my bike and followed in the direction I'd seen him go. I caught up with him easily, and for a long time we just rode around together in silence, up and down the neighborhood streets. Finally, I asked, "Do you want to get some ice cream?"

Seated facing each other in a booth at our favorite ice cream parlor, we shared a banana split. Once reassured that his life would not be radically changed, that we would still live in the house, and that he would continue at the same elementary school, Joshua felt considerably relieved. In the coming months he was especially affectionate and loving toward both Jack and me, and very protective of his little sister. This was a measure of his maturity and deep kindness. We told Jenny also, but she was only three and it was hard for her to understand. She and Josh continued to see Jack on a regular basis, and their relationship remained strong. I maintained the children's routines so they would feel a sense of security and continuity. However, shortly after Jack moved out, Jenny developed a chronic cough, diagnosed as asthma, which I attributed to stress. At night the sound of her labored breathing conjured the trauma of her birth and I couldn't bear it. I would bring her into bed with me, spoon her little body into mine, my arm around her. I felt her steady heartbeat in the palm of my hand and the wet drizzle of her breath. I slept only intermittently, waking to a surge of adrenaline every hour or so until I was reassured that she was still breathing.

In the months following our separation I was on an emotional roller coaster, and I could go from a state of euphoria to a state of panic in less than sixty seconds. In the first week after Jack left, all of my anxiety about caring for myself and the children became fixated on taking out the garbage. Our two large cans at the back of the house had to be placed curbside the night before pickup. This was in the days before cans were on wheels and uniformly issued by the city. I thought about it very carefully. I determined that I could use gardening gloves to get a good grip on the metal, and I imagined how I would do it. I managed it easily when the evening arrived, which led to a feeling of triumph out of all proportion to my small achievement. It was a measure of how dependent I had been on Jack, and of the pressure I felt managing my life as a single parent.

Jack and I were very angry with each other for about two years. In the beginning he resisted divorce, even proposing at one point that we both stay in the house and live as roommates. Of course this was untenable, but I think he feared the loss of his structure, the comfort of family, however limited its emotional health. Despite our anger, we went through a relatively amicable settlement and we talked a lot about what we each needed and wanted for ourselves and the children. I came out to Jack, telling him that I was a lesbian and that I felt I had been much of my life. He couldn't have been more understanding, assuring me that he would never contest custody of the children on those grounds. Jack was very progressive and very accepting.

We agreed to joint custody of the children, but they were to live with me. Jack also agreed to pay child support until Josh and Jenny each reached the age of eighteen. It was a fixed amount and would not increase with inflation, which I felt was unfair because Jack's income would rise with the automatic cost-of-living increases provided by the state universities. I refused alimony, which Jack wanted me to take to afford him the additional tax break; I didn't want it because I didn't want to be personally dependent on him. We agreed that I would not leave Santa Clara County or an adjacent county for a period exceeding six months without Jack's prior approval. There were no such restrictions on Jack's movements and I bristled at his continued right of intrusion into my affairs. I understood the necessity for such an arrangement since I had physical custody of the children, but I felt it was unfair that Jack could come and go as he pleased and live wherever he wanted to. While divorce in the late 1970s still held a stigma for women, I was too euphoric to notice it. I didn't realize the weight bearing down on me in the marriage until I was out of it. I had enormous energy and enthusiasm for my life as it opened before me, even as I worried about proper care for the children and adequate financial resources.

Shortly after Jack moved out I took the children on a holiday trip up the Mendocino coast. On the way home they were hungry, so I stopped at a coffee shop in the small town of Guerneville, along the Russian River. I didn't have enough money for all of us to eat, so I fed them. Joshua noticed. "You mean you're feeding us and not eating yourself?" he asked, astonished.

"Yes," I said. "It's fine. I'll eat something when we get home."

Joshua's eyes widened. Then he cut his hamburger in half. I was so moved that I had a hard time getting the food past the lump in my throat. For the first time since college, I was short of money, but now I also had the children to think about.

Jack was conscientious about paying child support, and he kept the children on his medical insurance policy. I was still working only part-time, however, and with the divorce my income plummeted. Also, I discovered that I had no credit. All of our credit cards, the telephone, sanitation, water, gas, and electricity were in Jack's name. I applied to get a credit card from our bank and they refused to issue one because I had no credit history. When I threatened a sex discrimination lawsuit against them, they issued me a (very limited) Visa account. These experiences gave me new understandings of the ways society structured women's economic subordination to men.

I told Jack to take the car and whatever furniture and household appliances and utensils he liked. I wanted to be free of all the material possessions that symbolized my marriage. He emptied the living room and a portion of the bedroom, and of course he took his books, records, the stereo, and his desk. But I didn't care. I got used to doing things for myself, and set about ordering my life. The kids and I played baseball in the now-vacated and very large living room, using a Nerf ball and a plastic bat. Our new way of living drove my mother crazy. My parents were now living two streets away from me, and Mom visited often. "You have to get decent furniture," she said. She didn't understand that I didn't care about the furniture. A huge weight had been lifted from me. In the year before our separation I had suffered chest and heart pain. Mary had said it was stress. In retrospect I'm sure it was a combination of stress and pressure from an insistent internal voice that grew louder with each passing year, a voice that I could no longer ignore. I had to begin to live true to myself—my lesbian identity, my interests in a new teaching career, and my dedication to immersing myself in a feminist life. Once Jack left, I wanted to change everything about my routines, my appearance, and my ideas. It was an enormous relief to be alone. I didn't want Jack to be in the house at all, as if his very presence violated my space.

My anger at Jack, though, was misdirected. He was in many ways the least responsible for my pain. During our marriage we had argued about the things most couples do, like money, for example. But many of my conflicts stemmed from my need for the freedom to come into my own life. Jack represented, both symbolically and in fact, the old life, the safe structure, the party discipline, the defined routine, the rigid, confining limitations that I could no longer abide. It was not so much what Jack did to me as what he could not do to radically change our lives. The tensions both of us carried in our daily lives tore us apart, both individually and as a couple. About three years after our divorce we met together alone in a restaurant over a glass of wine. It was immensely pleasant, visiting an old and dear friend, and I again felt a well of gratitude that we were no longer married.

Without a car, I rode my bicycle everywhere; Jenny rode in a child's seat on the back of my bike, and Joshua rode his own bicycle for our daily outings. I changed my diet radically, eating fresh vegetables and fruits and no red meat. I began jogging and working out in a fitness center, and I lost more than thirty pounds. I was a new woman with a new body, entering a new life.

In the year and a half following the divorce, my mother was, surprisingly, a bedrock of support. When I told her I was leaving Jack she told me about her first marriage and how she felt about her divorce. For her, all the way back in the 1930s, it had been the right thing to do. She had real empathy for me. Living now in San Jose, so close by, she saw the children often and was very attached to them. Since my time with her after her mastectomy and her time with me during my pregnancy with Jenny, our relationship had improved greatly. I still feared her temper and her judgments, but we were easier with each other. She kissed me on each cheek after I told her about the divorce and said, "Good luck to you always, darling, in whatever you do." A few weeks later she gave me a check for $2,000. When I protested that I didn't need it she said, "Then put it in the bank. It'll do as well in your account as mine. And then when you need it you don't have to worry about asking for it." She bought me a stereo and season tickets to the symphony. She treated me to dinners in restaurants, "the fancier the better," she said. For several years she took the children shopping in the fall before school started and told them to pick out whatever clothes they needed. She accomplished these things in a matter-of-fact, casual manner, as if it were nothing more than going for a walk on a sunny day. I was stunned by the clarity of her understanding and the generosity of her actions.

When Mary was going through her last round with breast cancer her oldest daughter, Ellen, had returned from the East Coast, where she had been teaching, to take primary responsibility for her mother's care. This was how we met. Ellen and I became best friends when she arrived in California. We were able to support each other through the tough times we were both going through. Whenever I became overwhelmed with all the errands and tasks I had to do on top of working and taking care of the kids, Ellen, ever practical and calm, would say, "Let's make a list." We made budget lists, legal lists, moving lists, shopping lists, graduate school application lists.

I had decided soon after my divorce that I wanted to resign as chair of the party in Santa Clara County and extricate myself from as many party committees as I could. It was part of my breakout from old structures and my desire to have more time to build my own life. Nothing dramatic had happened in my relationship to the party; it just no longer seemed relevant to the new directions I was going in, especially in the women's and lesbian rights movements. But as soon as I contemplated these resignations I was overwhelmed by panic. So Ellen made a "Party List": I explained each committee I was on and she wrote it down. Then we placed them in order of priority and I began to withdraw from my party responsibilities, the first being my role as chair.

In her mid-twenties, Ellen had begun a career in theater, teaching, performing, working in small, experimental theaters in stage design, costume, and lighting. She seemed to me a free spirit who cared deeply for those around her. Together we went through the adolescence I never had. Ellen and I climbed the hills in Palo Alto, camped on the beaches of the Northern California coast, went to jazz concerts, and read widely, always talking about what we read and passing books back and forth. We both became enthusiastic runners, doing 220s and 440s at the track to increase our long-distance times. I began running every day and competed in 6.2-mile races. Once we successfully completed a ten-mile mountain run in Big Basin between the Santa Cruz Mountains and the coast. We lifted weights and played baseball. We threw each other long-distance fly balls as hard and as far as we could and watched each other go for a spectacular catch or a diving crash. For my birthday one year Ellen took me to a sporting goods store and told me to pick out any baseball mitt I wanted. I joined a women's softball team in the city leagues in San Jose and fulfilled a childhood dream when we played at night under the lights in the municipal stadium. Ellen, Joshua, and Jenny, in a little baseball cap, were there cheering. When I came up to bat the announcer called my name over the loudspeaker like they do in the big leagues: "Batting next, for the Title IXers, the right fielder, Bettina Aptheker. . ." That was our team's name—the Title IXers— after the affirmative action section of the civil rights legislation. As my name was announced, my son leaned over the railing in the box seats next to home plate and yelled, "Go get 'em, Mom," and blew me a kiss. As his childhood collided with mine, I was profoundly moved. This year, 1978, was a time of unbridled freedom.

The changes I had made in my life filled me with energy. They also reawakened the sexual feelings I had for some of the women around me. I moved myself out of the master bedroom in our home and turned it into a playroom for the children. I established myself in the attic, which I outfitted with a new double bed. I awaited lovers. However much Ellen and I were bonded, however passionate our friendship, and however much I yearned for a sexual connection, Ellen's liaisons were with men. But she said to me with absolute certainty, "You will fall in love with the perfect woman."

Spurred on by the women's movement and especially by my experiences in teaching women's studies at San Jose State University, Ellen and I continued to read feminist literature: Shulamith Firestone's *The Dialectic of Sex*; Robin Morgan's *Sisterhood Is Powerful*; Juliet Mitchell's *Women: The Longest Revolution*; Kate Millett's *Sexual Politics*; Dorothy Dinnerstein's *The Mermaid and the Minotaur*; Virginia Woolf's *A Room of One's Own*; and Adrienne Rich's *The Dream of a Common Language*. We had long discussions about sexism in language, about how women were oppressed as a group, about how violence affected women's lives, and about race and class as part of interconnected systems of domination. Once I began teaching the course on sex and power at San Jose State on my own, Ellen and I revised my whole syllabus in light of our studies. Departing from a single, traditional textbook that emphasized a sociological approach to women in society, I introduced poetry and stories into the syllabus, as well as greater racial diversity, especially using the literature of black women writers like Alice Walker and

Sonia Sanchez, Nikki Giovanni and Ntozake Shange. We read Audre Lorde and Adrienne Rich. I allowed students to talk about their personal experiences, and how these related to the books and stories, poems and plays we were reading.

During spring quarter of 1978 I taught my first class in women's studies at the University of California at Santa Cruz. It was the course on black women in American history that I had been teaching at San Jose State. I interviewed for the job with May Diaz, a professor of anthropology, and with students in the women's studies collective. Compared to my experience at UC Berkeley and as an instructor at San Jose State, this process was striking in the way that it put collective and nonhierarchical politics into practice. I was elated when I was hired. I was moving out of the old environs of my life, physically and intellectually, and could feel myself launching into a new world. Though I was only hired to teach one class, and for only one quarter, I sensed new possibilities in my life.

The Santa Cruz campus was set in a redwood forest in the hills overlooking Monterey Bay, and on a clear day you could see the forty miles across the bay to Monterey, Pacific Grove, and Carmel. The campus had lush meadows, and deer, raccoon, fox, bobcat, and coyote in abundance. Red-tailed hawks circled in leisurely spirals. The campus had been open for only thirteen years and it had fewer than five thousand students. They were clustered in colleges, and each college provided students with a singular academic focus. Kresge College, for example, where I was to teach, housed the literature department, women's studies, and American studies, along with a graduate program mysteriously called History of Consciousness. All were under the broad rubric of the humanities, and the college's required core course introduced students to these fields with a heavy emphasis in American literature. Except for the library, which was centrally located, the colleges were dispersed throughout the forest, and the architecture was a blend of cement buildings with narrow slits for windows—like a medieval castle— and split-level asymmetry. When it opened in 1965, Santa Cruz was designed to be the UC campus for the offbeat '60s students who wanted small classes, an unconventional curriculum, and an equally unconventional grading method that used pass/fail instead of the typical letter grades. It was rumored that the scattered placement of the colleges and their bunkerlike design were intended to thwart student protests by affording no central locus for the natural flow of pedestrian traffic.

Soon after I arrived at Santa Cruz that spring, I began discussing with Ellen the possibility of getting my PhD, something I had always dreamt of doing. When I asked Billie Jensen, the faculty mentor with whom I was closest at San Jose State, if she thought I should do it, she agreed heartily. And when, still doubting my intellectual abilities, I asked her if she thought I *could* do it, she just rolled her eyes. Then she asked maybe the more important question, "Can you support your children now?" At that moment it became clear; I shook my head no. "Go get your PhD," she said, "so you'll be able to."

So, with a course set for pursuing my dream while also managing to support my children, I applied for admission to Stanford University's education department and to the History of Consciousness program at UC Santa Cruz. HistCon, as it was popularly called, was an experimental, interdisciplinary program with an emphasis in twentieth-century radical and Marxist philosophies suited to the diverse interests of the faculty. I was clear that I did not want to be enrolled in a traditional history department, although it was the discipline with which I had the greatest affinity. I was bored by traditional approaches to historical problems, and I was not interested in learning one more time what I saw as the patriarchal lineage of American historians, many of whom I had already read, in some cases from a precociously young age because I felt so much pressure to master the field. In my required statement of purpose to each of these programs, I said I wanted to "t/ease the juxtaposition of Marxism and feminism into a unified theory of liberation," owing much to my current reading and to my youthful arrogance. After being accepted into both programs, I met with faculty on both campuses, all of whom were extremely cordial. Both programs made very generous financial offers for scholarships and employment.

I chose Santa Cruz for two reasons. Though I could have commuted to Stanford easily, I was determined to move out of our house in San Jose. It was a driving emotional need. Palo Alto itself was prohibitively expensive, so I had no realistic hope of moving there with the children. Equally important, I was struggling to come out as a lesbian, and Santa Cruz had a large and identifiable gay and lesbian community. I thought that if I had hope of being out anywhere it was in Santa Cruz.

Three years before I started graduate work in Santa Cruz, Lou Diskin, the head of International Publishers, called and asked to see me while I was in New York for one of my regular party meetings. My book on Angela's trial had been published the previous spring, and Lou said that it was their best seller. He wanted to know if I would consider writing another book for International, "on women." At our meeting Lou was still vague but, he said, given their paucity of titles—joking, he brought up August Bebel's nineteenth-century treatise on "the woman question" as an example—he was confident that a book by me would be worthwhile and sell very well. I was both flattered and excited. I told Lou that I had amassed a great deal of material on the history of African American and radical European American women that was well beyond the scope of my thesis, and that I thought I could probably do a book of essays with some additional research. I went home to think about it, and two months later I sent Lou an outline for a book I called *Woman's Legacy: The Anti-Racist and Working Class Tradition.* Within a few weeks I had an enthusiastic letter from Lou and I began work, reading more widely and digging into archives. I worked in the research as best I could between teaching, chairing the party in Santa Clara, and taking care of my children. Lou continued to press for a manuscript, and I continued to send him reports of my progress. In mid-May 1979, a year after Jack and I had separated, Lou sent me a contract. By the time I entered UC Santa Cruz in the fall I had relinquished most of my party responsibilities and had completed a first draft of six of the seven proposed essays.

Immersed in my first quarter of graduate school that fall of 1979, I sent Lou what I had and promised to come up with the final essay and an introduction as soon as I could, and then proceed with revisions and a second draft. When I saw Lou that November he was reading what I had sent and said he was thrilled. He said he'd had no idea of the "scope of women's oppression." He told me we'd have to get party approval, and I suggested that he ask an African American comrade to read it. She had been in my first party club in Brooklyn when I was seventeen. She was now head of the party's national women's commission and doing a lot of organizing with Women for Racial and Economic Equality (WREE). I still bristled at the idea of party approval, and I told Lou there would be a controversy over my chapter on domestic labor because of the way it discussed women's unpaid labor in the home. He said not to worry about it, that party approval in this case was just a formality. But having been burned before, I knew differently.

In writing *Woman's Legacy* I was, in fact, seeking to put Marxism and feminism into a unified theory of oppression and liberation— just as, in my graduate school applications, I'd said I hoped to do. By now I had changed the subtitle to "Essays on Race, Sex, and Class in American History," and I no longer saw class as the principal or only instrument of oppression upon which all others rested. I was working out ideas about how systems of domination based on race, sex, and class were interdependent and interlocking, and showing how women's subordination to men predated capitalism by hundreds of years. The chapter on domestic labor was where these ideas were most evident. It was precisely here that one could see most vividly the connections because black women, embodying the collision of race, sex, and class, had been employed as domestic servants in such overwhelming numbers, especially between the 1930s and the 1960s. Insights into the plight of domestic workers came, as well, from my own childhood experiences, and my unease with the way my parents employed and, I felt, exploited black women's labor.

As I examined black women's working conditions, their struggles to organize, the sexual harassment they endured, and their stories and writings, I argued that it was precisely their historical subjugation under slavery as the property of their masters that now aggravated and tainted their conditions of domestic employment. They were paid more or less at the whim of their employers, had no recognized hours, no right to organize into unions, and were frequently subjected to sexual harassment and assault by the white men who employed them. By extension, I suggested, all women, regardless of their class or social status, had experienced themselves as the property of their fathers and/or their husbands, and this ownership, while no longer literal, was at the heart of their "domestication," sexual exploitation, and subjugation. The ownership of women (and their children) was the result of patriarchal (not capitalist) social relations, the one coming well before the other. Now, I suggested, the two systems, combined with racial oppression, were intertwined. For example, at the time I was writing, married women could not be legally raped by their husbands because sexual access was part of the marriage contract. Likewise, women dealing with domestic violence could get almost no legal relief because the law protected men in marriage, and counseled women to make their marriages "work." It reinforced and privileged a nuclear family with a male head of household.

In writing this chapter it was perfectly apparent to me that I could not hold on to the orthodox formulations of Marxism and still see women as the co-equals of men in the making of history. Marx and Engels were as theoretically (and personally) sexist as the historical times in which they lived, although Engels, at least, acknowledged what he called "the world historical defeat of the female sex" in his book *The Origin of the Family, Private Property, and the State,* a hotly contested text among Marxist feminists. In orthodox Marxist theory the only people who were exploited under capitalism were workers *at the point of production.* Some women, of course, were employed in industries like auto and steel, but they were very few. However, a very large number of women, certainly the overwhelming majority, worked in the home caring for children, the sick, the elderly. All of this household labor was unpaid. Were women exploited or was this merely a "labor of love," with trivial economic meaning? Those of us working to bring Marxism and feminism together in theory argued that this free household labor may have had a loving aspect, but it also made possible the *re*-production of the working class upon which the whole economic system of capitalism depended. This constituted, we argued, a *co-equal* form of exploitation.

Breaking out of the party's orthodoxy as I worked out these ideas about domestic labor, I was exhilarated, but I knew that party approval would not be "just a formality." At the same time that I was so theoretically alive with these new ideas, reading everything I could find by the new wave of Marxist feminist scholars and activists, I was also personally engaged in the struggle to acknowledge and claim my lesbian self. I was alternately terrified and ecstatic.

Shortly after I separated from Jack, I found a Xeroxed copy of a small chapbook by Adrienne Rich called "Twenty-One Love Poems" in the women's studies office at San Jose State. By then I had read more of Rich's work since my first encounter with Mary Timothy's copy of *Of Woman Born*. I read a few lines from the poetry. My heart fluttered. Quietly I let myself into the small room that contained our copier. I made myself a Xerox of the Xerox. I cycled home at top speed with what I thought was an underground pamphlet tucked securely in my backpack. Later that night, with the kids safely asleep, I pulled the poems from my pack, propped myself up in bed, and began to read. I read most of the night, savoring words and lines again and again. Nothing had ever spoken so directly to my lesbian experience: to the energy, the aching to be with a woman, to the beauty of the sexual encounter. "The Floating Poem" took my breath away. It began:

> Whatever happens with us, your body
> will haunt mine—tender, delicate
> your lovemaking, like the half-curled frond
> of the fiddlehead fern in forests
> just washed by sun. . . .

That summer of 1978 I attended the Fourth Berkshire Conference on the History of Women, where I heard Audre Lorde read her essay "Uses of the Erotic: The Erotic as Power." This experience was one of the most pivotal of my life and forever changed the way I thought about sex, lesbian desire, and my own destiny. The conference was held at Mount Holyoke College. Little did I know then about Mary Woolley and Jeannette Marks and the lesbian goings-on at Mount Holyoke at the beginning of the century. Mary Woolley was president of Mt. Holyoke from 1901 to 1937, and Jeanette Marks was a professor of English literature and drama. They were lovers for fifty-two years. As I was still alternately euphoric and insecure about my lesbian identity, I was both fascinated and reassured to discover this history. My mother gave me the money to make the trip, and Jack took care of the children for the week I was gone. I felt lucky to have their support.

A biannual event, the Berks, as it was called, brought together over a thousand women (and some men) engaged in research on women's history. Audre Lorde was part of the panel "Power and Politics: A Lesbian Perspective." It was held in the largest auditorium on campus. When I arrived for the panel, nearly every seat was taken and people were crowded down the aisles and standing along the sides and in the back. Audre Lorde was perhaps the most visible among a group of black lesbian feminists in the 1970s. Her poetry and essays influenced several generations of feminist activists and scholars.

At the Berks that summer Lorde proposed that women's erotic experience, whether lesbian or heterosexual, could be a source of knowledge, a way for women to find their own sense of authenticity. Because sex was such a powerful physical and emotional experience, it could also be deeply clarifying if we paid attention to the feelings of happiness and satisfaction. It could become a lens through which to measure the feeling of our daily lives, the pleasure (or absence of pleasure) in our work, the satisfaction (or lack of it) in achievements. Ideas about the degradations of racism and the exploitations of capitalism, so familiar to me, were now incorporated by Lorde into an erotic landscape that spoke to my deepest feelings and experiences with both lesbian and heterosexual relations. What heartened me and spoke to my reality was the way she drew on her own reservoir of personal experience as a way to understand the world more broadly. All of the panelists, in fact, collapsed what I had always understood to be a necessary opposition between personal experiences and objective scholarly research. What were so new to me were the ways that each presenter had an outward focus on power and politics while also placing personal experience at its analytical core, blending personal testimony and critical analysis. This was the birth of a new kind of scholarship for me. What I saw was that I could do serious scholarship in which politics were intimately intertwined with personal experiences.

In the discussion period following the formal presentations, I had my first opportunity to prove to myself that I identified as a lesbian, though I was still too fearful to do so publicly. After the panel ended a woman stood up in the front of the auditorium to make a statement. She said that the program committee responsible for decisions regarding panels and presentations had objected to the word "lesbian" in the title for this panel, and had ordered that the word be deleted from the official printed program. In addition, the panel had been scheduled in one of the smallest rooms on the campus. For these reasons, she explained, a group of women, including herself, had printed a special leaflet announcing this panel, placed the word "lesbian" back into the title, and scheduled it for this large hall. "Obviously we were correct in our understanding of your interest in this panel," she said, sweeping her arms out over the audience. Then she said she would appreciate it if all the lesbians in the room would stand, just for a moment. My heart pounded furiously in my chest, but I remained glued to my seat. Three-fourths of the women in the audience stood. I was stunned, and then I realized that everyone was standing because they wanted to make a political statement to the program committee. *Most of them were not, could not, be lesbians,* I thought as my eyes swept over the audience, knowing for a fact that some of the women I saw standing were married to men. In fact, I flashed on the idea that probably those of us still clutching at our seats were the true lesbians, all of us in the closet. But I understood political statements, and these women were making one, saying that they would not allow themselves to be divided, that they would stand in solidarity, and that if everyone stood you couldn't single out, ostracize, and punish the "real" lesbians. I had not summoned the courage to stand; I was still not out to the academic community. But I had gotten the political message.

A woman spoke up and said that though she loved women, she was not a lesbian. She resented the last speaker's request, which forced her, she felt, to either assume an identity that was not her own or feel that she was betraying women whom she loved. Audre Lorde replied, "The first thing a minority must do is make itself visible to itself."

This response was life changing for me. Every experience I'd ever had confirmed the wisdom of Lorde's words and the demonstration of solidarity I had just witnessed, but I had never applied it to surviving as a lesbian. I knew that this pride had been central to the assertion of the intrinsic beauty of black people during the civil rights movement, and that Lorde, in this way, was speaking again directly out of her own experience. Although I knew there was still debate about whether it had actually happened, the story about the Jews in Denmark during World War II was an important one to me. It had been the apparent willingness of everyone in the population, led by the King, to wear the Star of David that had made it much harder for the Nazis to persecute the real Jews during the Occupation. For the first time I could see a strategy for my survival as a lesbian. I was not alone, I was not a freak. I could be part of a civil rights movement for lesbians and gays. Above all else, it was the strength of all those women standing around me that brought me to tears. I had been closeted for so long and had thought of myself as perverted and evil for so long that this came as an indescribable relief and joy. These women could not all be lesbians; but neither could they believe that lesbians were perverts.

The following summer, in 1979, Josh, Jenny, and I prepared to leave San Jose for Santa Cruz. Though only forty-five minutes apart, they couldn't have been more different. Santa Cruz then was a relatively small town on the Monterey Bay that swelled with tourists in the summer and with students the rest of the year. A lot of retired folks lived in the area, and just to the south was Watsonville, a major agricultural center with a large Latino community, most of them working in the fields or the food canneries. That year in Santa Cruz was my first experience living in a small town. Between Santa Cruz and Watsonville were the villages of Capitola, Soquel, and Aptos, with large ranches and a country feel. All of this was to change in the next twenty years, as Silicon Valley folks moved into the coastal communities, the cost of housing skyrocketed, and development became a speculative boom.

I finally gave in and bought a car with my parents' help. I had resisted my mother's generous offer for a while because I loved my newfound freedom, savoring every day on my bicycle. But once I planned to move to Santa Cruz I knew she was right. I was still working at San Jose State, and if I wanted to see her I would need to commute. I pored over the classified ads in the local paper and eventually purchased a yellow 1972 VW Super Beetle for $1,900. The kids and I named her "Cory" for reasons I no longer remember. Sometimes we pretended Cory was the USS *Enterprise* from *Star Trek* and put her into warp drive. We had to make the necessary sound effects to make up for her actual very slow speed.

After a frantic but ultimately successful search I found the perfect house for us in Santa Cruz, on King Street near campus. Before the summer I had resigned as chair of the party in Santa Clara County, but I remained for a time on the district committee and on the Northern California women's commission. Kendra Alexander, with whom I had worked so closely on Angela's case, headed the commission and was also gradually assuming the position as district party chair, and her friendship made things more palatable for me in the party. I joined the club in Santa Cruz, which provided a refreshing change from my experiences in San Jose. Named the William L. Patterson Club after the black Communist and civil rights lawyer, the club comprised about a dozen comrades, all in their thirties. They were creative and energetic; I was relieved to find myself in such a congenial group after the more conservative style of politics in Santa Clara. There was also an excellent middle school for Josh and daycare for Jenny near our new home. It was feeling like a good move.

The one terrible loss in this otherwise happy transition to Santa Cruz was the death of our dog, Igor. Very shortly after we moved, Igor, who was ten years old, became lethargic and ate almost nothing, no matter what I offered. I bought him fresh hamburger meat and cooked it for him. He could hardly be enticed even to drink a little water. I took him to a vet, who after a careful examination gently and remorsefully told me that Igor was riddled with tumors. He didn't think there was any way to save him, and he recommended that I put him to sleep to minimize his suffering. It was September 2, my birthday, but it didn't occur to me that I could have waited a day or two, or that I could have pursued other options. I just didn't want Igor to be in pain. The vet, seeing how attached I was to Igor, left us alone. I sank onto the floor of the examining room and cradled Igor in my arms, weeping uncontrollably. He licked my face and nuzzled up close to me, weak as he was. It was almost as if he understood. After a while the vet came back in and led Igor away. My last sight of him was walking feebly but obediently beside the vet, who had promised me that death would be swift and painless. I paid the bill at the front desk, feeling vaguely that there was something surreal—and incredibly painful—about paying to have your dog put to death. I went to my car and began driving home. I could not stop crying and when I stopped for gas, the young station attendant asked me what was wrong. "I'm okay," I said. "I just lost my dog." For months afterward I imagined seeing Igor on the street while I was jogging, or in the park, or on the beach. My heart would skip a beat, and I would rush forward, only to discover it wasn't Igor.

Having successfully completed the move to Santa Cruz, I made a pilgrimage to the hills above Palo Alto, to the oak tree where we had scattered Mary's ashes. At the top the earth was flat and parched from the summer heat. In the forest below, the ground was soft and wet and the exposed roots of the trees were caked with moss. The oak spread its limbs into a vast canopy. I had come to give thanks—for the move, for the new turn my life had taken, for my children.

When I moved into our new house in Santa Cruz, Josh and Jenny each had their own bedroom. I took a corner of the living room for myself. I furnished it with a bed, which doubled as a couch. Naturally, having abandoned privacy and a double bed, three months later I began what many of our friends have since laughingly called the love affair of the century. We met at a Holly Near concert in Santa Cruz on the occasion of Josh's twelfth birthday.

Kate Miller and I had met before, in 1974. We had known each other in San Jose. She had been a student in classes I had taught, both on campus and in the community. She had also worked as a volunteer at the Communist Party's local bookstore, Bread and Roses. And I'd received a letter from her in June 1976, just after both of us had graduated with our master's degrees, hers in women's studies and mine in communication studies. She was forwarding a letter from a mutual friend, and told me she had gotten a job teaching U.S. women's history at Monterey Peninsula College. Though she asked me to give her a call to talk about my research on black women, I wrote her a letter instead. It was my way of putting people off when I felt weighed down by too many meetings and not enough time to myself.

The children and I found our seats in Santa Cruz's civic auditorium, along with two thousand others buzzing in anticipation of Holly Near's performance. Holly wrote much of the music she sang, stirring my feelings for social justice and the beauty of lesbian love. Her music spoke to every social issue that was important to me. She was class conscious, antiracist, antinuke, and prolesbian. I could not have felt more at home.

We had been seated only a few minutes when the woman sitting next to me tapped me on the shoulder. I turned. "Are you from Brooklyn?" she asked. "The accent, you know; you sound like you're from Brooklyn." I nodded and she said, "Are you Bettina?" and identified herself. It turned out that we had gone to the same elementary school. Her mother was in the Communist Party, and I even remembered her grandmother. She lived in Big Sur now, and had brought her husband to the concert to celebrate his birthday.

A hand touched my arm from the other direction, and I saw that a woman had come to our seats. I turned and she hugged me, once and then again. She drew back and pressed my arm. "Do you remember me?" I looked into her face. "Kathy," I said. "You're Kathy Miller." "Yes, that's right, but I call myself Kate now, and this is my daughter, Lisa." My eyes fell upon an adolescent girl who smiled, looked at me, and then looked down and blushed at her mother's introduction. By this time my Brooklyn acquaintance was also hugging Kate. It turned out they were best friends. Kate had spotted her in the crowd, and then seen her talking to me. "I just knew," Kate claimed later. "I knew the minute I saw you. I knew that we would be together. It was like I recognized you." Kate and I exchanged addresses and telephone numbers, and promised we would call each other.

Kate wrote to me a few days later, and this time I called her back in response. The husband of one of our mutual acquaintances was celebrating his fiftieth birthday, and I invited Kate to come with me to his party in Palo Alto. Kate agreed and suggested that she bring Lisa to my home to stay with Josh and Jenny. Lisa was thirteen, and she thought they'd be fine together while we went to the party. As the evening approached, I was in a speculative dither: Was she or wasn't she a lesbian?

At the party our hostess asked Kate how long she had been "out." Kate whispered the same question to me as we sat on a gigantic pillow amidst the swirling crowd, and I realized then that most of the crowd we knew from San Jose State had known I was a lesbian—

even as I was trying hard to conceal it. After an evening of intense conversation and connection, we got back to my house at three in the morning and Kate woke Lisa for the trek home. She stood, still half asleep, clutching blankets and pillows, while Kate and I stood at the front door, an inch from each other, supposedly to say goodbye. Actually, we were poised to kiss. Lisa said, "Hey, you guys, are we going home, or should I go back to sleep?" I inched back and Kate smiled. She gathered Lisa to her and they left. As Kate turned the ignition on her car I controlled an impulse to run out into the driveway. But in an instant she was gone. Then all I could think to say to myself was, *You're an idiot!* and, for variety, *What an idiot you are!*

I lay awake, my mind racing. Fear surged in and out and around the fierce desire to be with a woman. I would see Kate's face, hear her laugh, feel her warm energy, but then I would feel a surge of fear, adrenaline shooting through me. It sounds crazy looking back on it, but because of my experiences with the FBI and in prison, I felt the familiar paranoia creep back in: *Suppose it's a trap? Suppose I'm caught? Suppose she's a government agent?* I tossed and turned, unable to stop thinking of her. Finally, at eleven the next morning, I called her. After exchanging messages we were able to connect, and I asked her to dinner. Our date was set for Wednesday, November 7, the anniversary of the Bolshevik Revolution.

I cooked an elaborate feast and set a candlelit table. I put Chopin's nocturnes on the stereo. The smooth, casual aura I had so carefully orchestrated went awry early in the evening, however, when I spilled the grease from the roast chicken all over the bottom of the oven. In what was supposed to be our relaxed before-dinner ambiance, Kate and I mopped up the mess.

With our dinner over and my children long since asleep, we sat next to each other on the living room floor. Finally, heart pounding furiously, I said, "May I kiss you?" These were the last words either of us spoke for a long, long time. At five in the morning, Kate leapt from the bed, grabbed her clothes, dressed, kissed me long and passionately, and dashed out the door. She and Lisa had made a deal: Kate could spend the night with me as long as she was home by six the next morning when Lisa got up to go to school. Driving time between Santa Cruz and Kate's home in Pacific Grove, a small town near Monterey, was one hour. Kate put her key in the door at six each morning as Lisa waited inside, listening for the click of the lock.

For the first months we were together, we celebrated weekly anniversaries. We'd send each other cards and buy each other flowers or chocolates. Kate had the softest brown eyes I'd ever seen, always alight with a kind of mischief just waiting to bubble over. Once, Kate showed me an album of family pictures. There she was as a toddler with a serious expression, dressed in a 1940s frilly dress, her hair all curly, her legs crossed just so. As a young adult, she was the perfect, stylish 1960s girl, even wearing her hair in the beehive tease of the times. Then she was Mom, with Lisa, a blue-eyed, blond-haired toddler, Kate wearing large gold hoop earrings. Then the master's degree graduate with cap and gown and serious smile. Kate had all these personas over the years, but always the eyes were the same, unmistakable, shining, with the hint of laughter.

By Christmas, I was in love with Kate. I was in awe of her, too. I'd never met anybody who held so many jobs at one time to make ends meet. When I met her, she was teaching women's studies at two colleges and working at the county jail in San Jose, where she reviewed arrests and negotiated for prisoners to be released on their own recognizance. When Proposition 13 passed in the June 1978 California elections, Kate lost all of her jobs and the possibility of a full-time teaching job because the position was cancelled. This proposition authorized a huge reduction in property taxes, which had provided the fiscal base for public education and for most of the state-run social programs. Within a few months, however, Kate landed a job as the advisor for undergraduate education at Antioch West, located in Pacific Grove. It was one of the small branch facilities created by Antioch College in Yellow Springs, Ohio. In addition, Kate was still teaching at Monterey Peninsula College. Her ability to spring back after a crisis was inspiring to me.

Kate was born in Devils Lake, North Dakota. She was raised in New Rockford and later in Grand Forks. She is of German heritage, was raised Lutheran, and her parents were Republicans. She can still repeat the psalms and liturgies of her church-instructed childhood and quote whole sections of the Old and New Testaments. At eighteen she had an affair with a young, Utah-born man who was then in the Air Force. She became pregnant and was forced to marry him. "Abortion," Kate explained, was a word she had never heard. The marriage lasted, on and off, for six years and through settlements in Minnesota, Utah, Louisiana, South Carolina, and California. She felt trapped, finding marriage untenable because of the subservient role it forced upon her. Ironically, it was her mother-in-law who provided Kate with emotional support, and who first suggested the possibility of divorce. Our backgrounds could not have been more different.

This difficult early marriage and a car accident in which she and Lisa narrowly escaped death were life changing for her. Every day, she said, was a precious gift. During the years right after her divorce she lived in Los Angeles, a single mother struggling with little or no child support. She loved the city's cosmopolitan atmosphere, its multiracial neighborhoods, and its culinary delights. However, salaries in factories and offices were small, hours long, and benefits few. At times she went hungry to feed her daughter. She and Lisa lived in Compton, a poor African American community. For a time, they also lived in a rundown apartment under the San Diego freeway. Everywhere they lived, neighbors offered soup for dinner, secondhand clothes, books to share. These times were some of the most difficult she could imagine, Kate explained, but she also gained confidence in herself, in the goodness of people, and in her capacity to survive. In my largely middle-class existence I had never experienced anything even remotely like this.

Once, Kate said, she received a $1,200 check for child support from her former husband. She was so stunned she called him up to find out what had happened. He said his girlfriend found out he hadn't been paying child support and she refused to sleep with him until he paid up. "Bless that woman," Kate said.

After a long-term relationship with a man ended amicably, Kate decided to leave Los Angeles. The relationship may have ended, but it provided her with a new sense of herself and of her worth as a human being. It was 1972 when she and Lisa moved to San Jose and Kate decided to go back to school. It was the same year as Angela's trial, and Kate told me that while in L.A., she was very aware of the case. When she heard the news that Angela had been arrested, she threw a shoe at the television set. Her spiked heel shattered it. She never bothered to get another TV.

In San Jose, Kate worked as a drug counselor in a teen program. She often worked the streets, and they were not always safe. Kate could survive on the streets both in L.A. and San Jose in ways completely outside of my protected, middle-class, largely academic experience. And yet, through all of this, she maintained her compassion for people; she did not fear them. She became more and more involved in the women's movement, which spoke so directly to many of her experiences and feelings. In fact, almost all of her friendships were with women, many of them lesbians. She told me she lamented the fact that she seemed to have no sexual feelings for women, so she dated men and formed a wide circle of lesbian friendships.

It was as a graduate student at San Jose State, doing research for a paper on the Communist labor heroine Elizabeth Gurley Flynn, that she first connected with people in the party. She attended Marxist classes the party offered, including one I taught, and frequently visited the party's local bookstore, Bread and Roses. Her master's thesis, which she wrote in 1975 and 1976, was an oral history with a Chicana neighbor in San Jose who had been born and raised in a small mining town in Arizona. Kate's oral history of Maria Garcia was one of the first ever done in the new wave of feminist scholarship. The heavily used, dog-eared copy of her thesis is still available in the library at San Jose State.

Kate has educated me in a dozen fields, from Asian art to Islamic culture and religion to African peoples to Native American life to Eastern philosophy and Buddhism to all varieties of fiction, from French and English classics to American potboilers. And she's had some wonderful reading adventures. While living near Ogden, Utah, during her first marriage, Kate once asked at the public library for a copy of *The Communist Manifesto*. The librarian was surprised, but she acquired the book for Kate through interlibrary loan. In Ogden, Utah. I gaped. No Communist would ever have done such a thing. One summer, Kate told me, to keep her sanity she read all of Shakespeare's plays because she could lose herself in the beauty of his language, and the wit and sparkle of his comedy.

One of the first things Kate told me after we met was that she was a recovering alcoholic. She explained to me that alcoholism was a progressive disease, that it was an addiction that took over your life. She described the awful tension she so frequently felt in her gut, the emotional pain in her life, and the way alcohol relieved it. "It's a drug," she explained, "just like any other. I could drink and drink sitting on my bar stool, sounding perfectly coherent, and have no memory of it the next day."

When we first took up together, Kate had not drunk any alcohol for six years. She stopped, she explained to me, while she was working in the county jail. Kate worked nights, and a lot of the people she saw were alcoholics, arrested for driving under the influence. She said she could see herself in them, and she resolved to stop drinking before it was too late.

At first, her talk of her alcoholism didn't make sense to me because Kate didn't fit my stereotype of an alcoholic. I didn't fully grasp that this was truly a problem for Kate, and thought nothing of offering her a drink. And so she and I would sometimes drink wine at dinner, and I still would have an occasional brandy or a Jack Daniel's on the rocks. One night, however, about a year into our relationship, we had friends over to dinner and stayed up late talking with them. As the conversation flowed, so did the wine. I stopped drinking after two glasses, which was my limit if I wanted to stay awake, and the others also stopped. But Kate kept drinking until the gallon jug was gone. She was her usual talkative self and I detected nothing unusual, but when I saw the empty bottle the next morning I started to finally understand what she meant when she said she was an alcoholic; it meant that sometimes she couldn't stop. She decided that morning that she would no longer drink. That was in the fall of 1980 and she has been sober since. Occasionally she'll attend an AA meeting with a friend to be supportive, but she quit drinking by her own sheer will. Kate had also smoked cigarettes very heavily before I met her, upwards of three packs a day. She said quitting smoking was worse than giving up alcohol. Nicotine is much more addictive, she explained. She quit smoking cold turkey, too. I'd never met anyone with a will even remotely comparable to Kate's, except maybe Angela.

This is only a brief accounting of Kate's life, the main lines of the story. But it marks the beginning of an understanding. The fuller substance of a life takes longer. It is harder to cull. There is the subtlety of will, the strains of a stubborn core, the lines of integrity worked into a face, into hands, into the arch of a foot. There is the way toes curl with pleasure, and fingers wrap themselves around a pen, the flex of a muscle, the intensity of light in the eye, the burst of laughter, the way tears come. There is an essence that is at once familiar, as when one turns in the morning to see the same happy face on the pillow next to your own, and also elusive. There is the memory of her face, flung open in a smile, as radiant as the sun. A love such as this I had never known.

Two days after Kate and I first slept together, I flew to New York. I was scheduled to give a paper at the First National Scholarly Research Conference on Black Women, which was to be held in Washington, D.C. I stopped over in New York primarily to see Lou Diskin, who was busy editing my book. He told me that the comrade from the party's women's commission didn't have time to read the manuscript, and he was trying to arrange for someone else in the party to do it. I said that was fine. I wasn't paying attention. I was much too excited by the start of my new relationship with Kate.

While in New York I stayed at the home of Renate Bridenthal. I'd met Renate at a conference at Stanford a few months earlier; she was a professor of European history at Brooklyn College. A little older than I, she was deeply involved in the developing field of Marxist-feminist studies and we spent hours in animated conversation about our work. She introduced me to two other women deeply engaged in this emerging project, Joan Kelly, also a professor of European history, and Blanche Wiesen Cook, a U.S. history professor. Blanche was then working on a study of lesbian support networks among early-twentieth-century peace activists and social reformers, including Jane Addams and Crystal Eastman. Jane Addams had won the Nobel Peace Prize in 1931, and Eastman was a radical feminist and social reformer. Blanche's partner, Clare Coss, was a playwright, and Renate took me to see her play, *Electra Speaks,* at a small, off-Broadway theater. It was my first experience with burgeoning feminist theater. Clare had reenvisioned the Greek tragedy from a women-centered perspective. A huge piece of butcher paper hung in the theater lobby, and we were invited to comment on the performance as co-participants in the making of feminist theater. At the time I could scarcely formulate a coherent thought because I was so excited. However, the play eventually was to occasion the opening for my introduction to *Woman's Legacy.*

The next morning, Renate and her husband, Hobey, took me to Central Park. It was a sunny November morning, and the park was overrun with thousands of people in every manner of costume and sport, and hundreds of dogs. The three of us began jogging, running the periphery of the park. I was so involved in thoughts, sights, and sounds, and so full of energy, that I missed my exit. I had long since passed Renate and Hobey, and the park is designed so you can get to the street only at designated exits. I ended up jogging more than ten miles. I knew I would be muscle-bound and sore the next day, so when I got back to the apartment I took a long, very hot bath, hoping to ameliorate the effects of my run. That evening I flew to Washington, D.C., for my conference. The next morning I could hardly move. Although I was in pain I thought it was hysterically funny. I hobbled around the conference and barely negotiated my way up the three or four steps to the stage where I was to give my paper. I leaned heavily on the podium and commenced reading.

The paper I read at the conference, excerpted from my forthcoming book, was on Ida B. Wells-Barnett's anti-lynching campaign. In it, I argued that the crusade against lynching was also a movement against the rape of black women. The main justification for lynching was that black men raped white women, and that rape was such a horrendous crime it caused white men to rise to the defense of "their" women by lynching the culprits, as though lynching was an unfortunate but justified response to such depravity. Ida B. Wells-Barnett showed that the vast majority of lynch victims were never even accused of rape. She demonstrated in case after case that black men (and some women) were lynched either as a response to their civil rights activism or as an act of random terror. Likewise, I argued, these same white lynchers, and white people in general, stereotyped black women as being wanton and promiscuous. This stereotype was used to justify the rape of black women by white men that happened so often. My paper argued that these two stereotypes—the one of the black man as rapist and the other of the black woman as Jezebel—mirrored each other and were used to justify white violence. I showed that black women like Ida B. Wells-Barnett understood this connection; the defense of black men against lynching was also a movement against the rape of women. By breaking one stereotype they shattered the foundation of the other.

While in Washington, I lodged at the home of a community activist. As we discussed my work on Ida B. Wells-Barnett, she said, "Would you like to talk with her daughter?" I was flabbergasted, but I managed to keep my head. I thought my host was going to give me her name and address. Instead, she picked up the telephone and dialed a number. My jaw slackened. "Her name is Mrs. Duster," she said to me over the receiver, "Mrs. Alfreda M. Duster. She lives in Chicago." And then into the telephone, "Alfreda! Good morning . . ." And the next thing I knew I was talking to Mrs. Duster! I was astonished and discombobulated. I don't know how much sense I made, but my host beamed at me in encouragement and Mrs. Duster told me to be sure and come to Chicago to see her. Then she gave me her address and telephone number.

Less than a month after Kate and I started seeing each other, I received a letter addressed to me in care of the graduate division at Santa Cruz. The postmark was Illinois. Even before I opened the envelope I knew it was from Martha, my lover from a decade earlier. It had been eleven years, almost to the day, since I had seen her. Martha had seen a poster announcing that I was to keynote a graduate student conference the following month at Purdue University, near where she lived. Would I like to see her?

As soon as I got home that evening, I got her number from the information operator in the small town where Martha lived. A child answered the phone and said Martha wasn't home, but she would be shortly. When I called again, Martha answered the phone herself.

"I knew it was you callin' as soon as he said the call was from California!" she exclaimed. She sounded exactly the same, with her southern Illinois twang. It was wonderful to hear.

"Can you come to Purdue? Is it very far?" I asked.

"About seven hours. Sure I can come," she said. It was as though no time had elapsed, as though we were picking up a conversation begun only the day before. I gave her the address where I would be staying in West Lafayette and she said she would find me. And she did, on a rural road in the middle of nowhere, in December, driving a Volkswagen van. We had twenty hours to spend together.

Before I left for Indiana I told Kate the whole story of my relationship with Martha. I told her about the FBI, the pornographic photos I had found in my suitcase in Washington, D.C., my terror at being outed as a lesbian. I told her about Martha's visit to San Jose when Joshua was a year old. I explained how much I wanted to apologize to Martha for my behavior in leaving her in the way that I did, and to make amends.

Kate said, "Of course you should see her." Then she was silent for a few minutes. Finally she said, "If you want to make love with her, you should." Then Kate talked to me about how lovers are not possessions. Kate and I were in a committed relationship, and yet she didn't feel that she owned my sexuality. I think she also knew that my relationship with Martha was over, that this was a journey to heal an old wound, and she didn't want me to feel any guilt about whatever happened.

Martha had been living with a woman for several years. Her partner was a professor in a small college town, and Martha was in school getting her master's in sociology. They were raising four children from her partner's marriage. However much hurt and anger Martha had experienced a decade ago, she told me now only of her disappointment when our affair had ended. She said she had assumed I had chosen between the love I had for my husband and for her. I told her that I was trying to fit into a life that felt wrong and had felt pressured to do so. I had behaved, I said, very badly. I related as much of the truth as I could get out then, enough so that she understood the extent to which I had been driven by fear.

We spent a wonderful day together, as carefree as we had been years earlier, then stayed the night at a friend's house who was gone for the weekend. Our loving that night was healing, quiet, and caressed by memory. In the morning we sat at a table in the front room, sipping coffee. Sunlight streamed in through the windows. She looked beautiful, and I told her so. She laughed. "You too," she said. "There's nothing in the world like the first love." It was, I thought, not often that one gets an opportunity to make an apology such as this.

While at Purdue I also had a brief fling with a male graduate student, a charming Irishman with whom I was staying. Though I had felt free in seeing Martha because Kate and I were open about it, I felt tremendous guilt about this spontaneous ill-advised adventure. I knew I was somehow going to have to tell Kate about it. One thing about Kate was clear to me: Lying, even by omission, was not okay. I sent her a telegram: "I had a safe crossing," I wrote, referring to my time with Martha, which I thought Kate would understand. "Home tomorrow. I love you."

Back in my house on King Street I told Kate everything. When I got to the part about my Irish rogue, my heart was pounding and I had a hard time speaking. When I finished my story Kate was absolutely still. After a while, though, she started laughing. She said, "Now that you are free you have so much sexual energy," explaining to both of us my uncharacteristic behavior. Then she grew serious. "Maybe we shouldn't commit ourselves to a monogamous relationship," she said. "Maybe you need time to . . ." I think she said "rove" or "experiment." No, no, no, I shook my head vigorously, feeling like a kid who promised he'd never make another mess. It hadn't even occurred to me that Kate could also, and might want to, have flings. No, no, no, I promised. No more.

The History of Consciousness program at Santa Cruz was a marvel to me. Historian Hayden White and anthropologist Jim Clifford were its mainstays, Hayden having been recruited recently to save the program from being cut. I soon learned that HistCon had been through several incarnations and was regularly in need of saving. It attracted philosophers and theorists who didn't quite fit into the traditional disciplines from which they emerged, and also students who were nontraditional, even by Santa Cruz standards.

All of us entering HistCon were required to take a yearlong seminar as an introduction to the program, the content of which could be described as twentieth-century European political theory and philosophy, the readings depending upon the instructors' whims. That year we read Louis Althusser, E. P. Thompson, Jacques Derrida, Michel Foucault, who had recently published the first volume of his *History of Sexuality*, Sartre on existential psychoanalysis, and the poststructuralist anthropologists Claude Levi-Strauss and Clifford Geertz. They were all white men, of course, which I noticed right away.

The non-Communist Marxist writers were fascinating to me because I had only read the party's polemics against them. Now I had an opportunity to judge their ideas for myself. I was one of only two or three students in our seminar who had actually read Marx, and I became a sort of expert-in-residence. Everyone, even Hayden and Jim, seemed either to find Marx indecipherable or to reduce his work to purely economic terms—that is, that Marxism could explain the exploitation of the workers in basic industry and how profits were made, but not much else. I spoke about Marx's historical and dialectical methods, and how these might be applied to many different problems in society. Marx now seemed transparent to me. It occurred to me how emotionally invested I had been in Marx from a very young age; mastering him had been not simply an intellectual enterprise, but a matter of survival.

The most important work I read that year, however, was not for the seminar. Rather, it was Adrienne Rich's collection of essays *On Lies, Secrets, and Silence*, published in 1979. It was the first time I had read a sustained feminist analysis from a place of feminist awareness in myself, and this standpoint dramatically shifted my perspective. It was like looking into a kaleidoscope and seeing the world with the same pieces in it but completely rearranged.

In my first two years of graduate school my feminist readings were complemented by graduate seminars taught from a variety of perspectives. I was lucky enough to study with sociologist Nancy Chodorow; with an emphasis on psychoanalytic theory, she coined the phrase "the reproduction of mothering" to describe how women collaborated with men in reproducing patriarchy. I was equally enriched by a seminar with Helene Moglen and Tillie Shaw on gender and literature in which I was introduced to feminist literary criticism. I was often overwhelmed by the number of novels we were expected to read for this course. I remember, for example, that I had managed to finish only about half of Henry James's *Portrait of a Lady*. Kate had read the novel, and she skimmed it again the night before my seminar. Our discussion prepared me very well for the next afternoon. Donna Haraway, who was soon to join the History of Consciousness faculty, taught a seminar in feminist theory that introduced me to more materialistic and scientific approaches to feminist scholarship. Nancy Hartsock, whom Donna had known when she taught at Johns Hopkins University, sent me the manuscript of her essay arguing for a feminist materialism. Reading Nancy's work revolutionized my thinking. I had been inserting feminist theory into Marx; she reversed the process.

In my second year at Santa Cruz the dean of the humanities division, who at that time was my literature professor, Helene Moglen, authorized a search for a senior hire in HistCon and designated that it be in feminist theory. Hayden asked if I would be the graduate student representative to the search committee. We interviewed the historian Joan Kelly, whom I had met in New York, Evelyn Fox Keller, a preeminent scholar in psychoanalysis, who had begun her academic career in physics, and Donna Haraway, who trained as a molecular biologist but was rapidly turning toward a feminist re-visioning of the history of Western science.

Both Donna and Joan had strong theoretical interests in and political commitments to socialist feminism. Evelyn was also immensely attractive to me because of my fascination with the more philosophical aspects of physics. In the end the committee offered the position to Donna Haraway. She accepted it and was to become an extraordinary mentor to me and to scores of graduate students, not only in HistCon but across the campus and beyond.

Following the interviews that winter, however, I continued corresponding with Joan Kelly. Her essay on the methodological implications of women's history, published in *Signs*, a new theoretical journal in feminist studies, radically changed the way I saw history itself and the way the discipline was informed by male assumptions about progress, historical periods, and the invisibility of women's labors. For example, she explained that if women were truly co-equals with men, we had to know what they were doing in every historical period, and we couldn't focus on just a few famous women. Likewise, she pointed out that we had to rethink the meaning of progress. For example, between the thirteenth and seventeenth centuries, millions of women in Europe were burned at the stake as witches; it was not simply a period of enlightenment, reason, and the advent of modern science as history so often portrayed it. Joan and I became good friends, and our intellectual affinity accelerated my confidence in my own scholarship. When I sent her an essay I had written on women's alienation, using works by the young Marx but shifting their male center, from men's labor to women's labor, especially domestic labor, Joan wrote: "I could tell from your article, except I already knew, that we're grappling with the same problems, pushing toward the same breakthrough." Joan and I stayed in touch until she died from cancer while still in her fifties.

Even in the joy of our first months together Kate and I faced immediate decisions, many of which revolved around the problem of coming out: to the children, to our respective parents, friends, colleagues. How and when and what to say occupied hours of discussion and speculation. After all, it was only 1979. Our instincts could not have been more different. I had been closeted for twenty years. I was cautious, apprehensive, sometimes truly terrified of the consequences of my actions, and stunned by my daring to do what I had previously only imagined. Kate, on the other hand, was much more open. She had many lesbian friends and all of her primary emotional and intellectual bonds were with women. Having assumed her lesbian identity in this context, and against the backdrop of a large and supportive women's movement, she congratulated herself on having sexual feelings that were congruent with her political choices. She had been celibate for more than three years when we met, having resolved to engage in no further power struggles with men.

Kate's initial response to our relationship was to call all of her friends on the telephone. "Guess what?" she'd exclaim to the astonished person on the other end of the line, "I'm a lesbian," followed by a cheerful, five-minute conversation about how free she felt, and how happy. Her friends had varying responses, as might be imagined given that she was calling friends in places like North Dakota, South Carolina, and Utah. "If we have no ambivalence about what we are doing, neither will others," she said. That was her strategy; it often worked, and when it didn't Kate was sturdy enough to let the disapproval slide off her. For me, Kate's calm courage, her clarity, and the joy I experienced in our love were deeply healing. I felt very fortunate to have fallen in love with a woman who did not harbor the same terrors that had held me hostage to fear for so long.

We didn't hide anything from the children. That is, whether we were in Pacific Grove at Kate's house, or at my house in Santa Cruz, the kids knew we slept together and weren't shy about climbing into bed with us. Lisa was thirteen, Josh was twelve, and Jenny was four.

When Kate told Lisa that she was a lesbian, Lisa said, "I know that! I was wondering how long it would take you to figure it out!" This initial adolescent bravado gave way some months later to grief as it became apparent that our relationship intruded upon their prior unassailable mother-daughter bond. Outwitting Kate's male lovers for attention and intimacy had been a relatively easy and fun-filled pastime for Lisa, but Kate's connection with me was altogether different. In a sense, the timing of our relationship was very good because it coincided with their inevitable separation as Lisa grew into adulthood.

In those years Lisa and I developed an enduring bond. My first impulse in parenting is to do physical caretaking, and the first weekend I was in Pacific Grove I went into Lisa's room on Saturday morning and asked her what she would like for breakfast, something I did often with my own kids. She looked at me as though I had landed from Mars because her mother had never done such a thing. When I actually prepared what she had requested, Lisa decided that even if I was different I was still basically okay. As I grew to know her better I was amazed by how similar in temperament we are: We both love routines and schedules, a fixed order, a comforting repetition in the ways of eating and dressing and doing the mundane, everyday tasks of living. We were also both prone to drama, wailing out of all proportion to events. These things drove Kate crazy. She would shout, "Two of them, I've got two of them in my life now!" But she was laughing and we were too, and soon Lisa and I forged an easy and playful alliance.

The first attempt I made to talk to my son about my relationship with Kate ended after only a few moments. He grunted his acknowledgment and fell silent. I let it go. Two weeks later I approached him again, on one of our drives back to Santa Cruz after a weekend with Kate. Yes, he knew. No, he didn't think it was any big deal. He asked if his father knew. I said yes. When I told him that his dad would never seek custody of him and Jenny because I was a lesbian, he looked visibly relieved. It turned out a custody battle was what he had feared the most. Then there was a flood of words from him about Kate. Though he adored her and had a considerable crush on Lisa, he was understandably concerned about what his friends might think. I told him I could see how he would feel that way, and I wasn't planning to post a sign announcing, "This is a lesbian household," on our front lawn. "You're not?" he asked, uncertain as to whether I was kidding. "No," I said. "You have to decide how and when you want to share this information with your friends." By now we were in front of his school and he was just barely on time, so he grabbed his book bag, gave me a quick kiss on the cheek, and charged off into the rest of his day.

Jenny was four when Kate and I began our relationship, but she proved to be a far more complex family strategist than either of us had anticipated. She couldn't have cared less about the sleeping arrangements, of course, but she did care about parental authority: She was not about to have another mother. By the time she was five she had a set of well-oiled tactics for making me think that Kate was a cruel stepmother foisting unreasonable demands and discipline upon her. She would turn her face just so, or cast her eyes down, or cringe her shoulders in movements as subtle and sure as those of a cat shimmering before a leap onto its prey. I fell for it every time, rushing to her defense or picking a fight with Kate five hours later, usually about something entirely different. Kate saw this dynamic for more than a year before I did, but no matter what she said I wouldn't believe her, and any criticism of Jenny just made it worse.

Jenny was a little dynamo, full of energy and wit, twinkling with mischief and intrigue. Unlike Josh, who was good natured and even tempered, Jenny always wanted things her own way. She was brilliant, quick, and determined. I loved these qualities in her and encouraged her spirit because I saw in her the adventure and the fearless, dogged independence that had been so squelched in me as a child. Jenny was beautiful, with thick, curly brown hair, brownish hazel eyes, and a dimpled smile that lit my world. The trauma of her birth stayed with me for years, and I bent over backward to meet her every need and placate her every wish. These were not the best parenting skills, especially for a child as willful as she was. Kate had none of my emotionality, so she saw Jenny's behavior with us in a much clearer light. She wasn't trying to dampen or destroy Jenny's spirit; she was trying to channel it. But I didn't understand that at the time.

Kate decided that the best thing to do under these circumstances was to stop parenting Jenny. She assumed the role of a friendly adult. Kate apologized to Jenny for presuming to be her parent, and in a comforting and supportive way expressed her kindness and respect. Not too long after this Jenny was trying to get me to do something, I no longer remember what, and when I resisted I saw a look on her face that finally gave her game away to me. Once she saw that I had caught on she abandoned her tactics of doleful defeat.

Although I feared how my parents would respond to my lifestyle, I was also proud of Kate and wanted them to meet her. I was not prepared to directly acknowledge our relationship, but I wanted my mother to see us together. I was fairly sure she would figure it out without my having to say it in so many words. With these ambivalent feelings I called her at home in San Jose and said I had a friend I wanted her to meet. It was about a month after Kate and I started seeing each other.

The evening was extraordinary. My mother, then approaching her seventy-fifth birthday, had not cooked an elaborate dinner in a long time. But when we entered the house it smelled of her special dishes, especially her baked cauliflower, which I recalled from childhood. The table was covered with her finest cloth and set with her best dishes and silver. She was wearing an elegant, colorful dress swept with silk. I had brought her roses and she arranged these in a vase, which she set on the grand piano. Although her eyesight was beginning to fail, she still played the piano regularly. If my father understood anything of the importance of the evening to me, he gave no hint of it. He just seemed himself, absorbed in his own world, as he so often was. As we sat down to dinner my mother filled our wine glasses and made a toast. She welcomed Kate into the family. Soon after, my mother invited us to spend the night, as we were driving farther north in the morning to visit Kate's parents. We accepted her offer, sharing the sofa bed in the living room, and giggling like a couple of teenagers for half the night. In the morning my father made breakfast for all of us in his typically methodical way, asking each of us individually if we wanted juice, raisins and/or bananas in our cereal, milk and/or sugar or saccharin in our coffee. While I showered my father regaled Kate with stories from my childhood, the ones he told over and over again, about our playing baseball together, and our visits to the botanical gardens in Brooklyn.

My parents had adjusted well to their move from Brooklyn to San Jose, and my mother in particular loved being near me and the children. The women's movement helped me to rethink many aspects of her life and the choices she had made. I was much more tolerant and tried to make up for the way I had sided with my father in childhood. I also knew that whatever conclusions she drew about my relationship with Kate, she would be welcoming to her.

I don't know what my father understood of my relationship with Kate because we never talked about it directly. He was, however, very homophobic toward gay men. I remember one occasion, for example, at a concert in San Jose when he loudly and rudely commented to me about a young man's long hair and gay appearance. The man was sitting a few rows in front of us and must have overheard his comments. I was very embarrassed and sharply rebuked my father's intolerance. I silenced him, but I don't think I changed his attitude.

Kate's parents, Millie and Art Krieg, lived in a mobile home park for seniors in the Napa Valley, one of the most beautiful regions in California and renowned for its vineyards. Retired and in his late sixties, Art had worked in the agricultural industry all of his life, operating a grain elevator or otherwise employed in the sale of wheat. He was a bulk of a man, with rough-hewn hands and a gruff manner. He had a deadpan sense of humor and would crack a very thin, appreciative smile if you got his joke. He also teased a lot, and in my gullibility I took all of his statements literally, until in some confusion I realized the joke. Millie often intervened to be sure that my feelings weren't hurt, and admonished her husband. Art, however, was incorrigible, especially, I think, because I was such a perfect foil.

Art liked one highball before dinner, and in the first years I knew him we had one drink together every evening of our visit. He'd say, "I'm ready for that drink now," and make highballs for the two of us. I drank mine even though I didn't like scotch because that's what you did when Art told you to do something. Kate said Art had this ritual for us because I was like his "son-in-law." That was the category he had for me, and that's what you did with a son-in-law you liked. He did not approve of my relationship with Kate, but I think he couldn't help bantering in the friendly manner he had. Despite everything, we liked each other.

Kate's mother was gregarious and friendly. A petite woman in her early sixties, with short gray hair and sharp features, she walked with rapid, purposeful steps and spoke in a short, almost abrupt manner. Raised during the Depression, the youngest of five sisters in rural Minnesota, she never fully recovered from the acute poverty of her childhood and still fretted about money and the cost of things. She was passionate about her children—Kate and her younger brother—and gardening. Both Art and Millie were very active in their branch of the Lutheran Church in Napa, as they had been in North Dakota, and they volunteered their time at the nearby veterans' home and at other community service organizations. In times of natural disaster or famine anywhere in the world, Millie always wrote a check immediately and sent it to the International Red Cross. Her generosity made an impression on me. My parents never made such charitable contributions, nor did they volunteer their time. They said the government should provide the relief and employ enough people, and once we had socialism that's how it would be. The longer I was with Kate the more I realized what different childhoods we had had.

The first time Millie saw me and Kate together, she knew we were lovers. We weren't holding hands; we didn't even have our arms around each other. We were just walking down the street together. She saw us talking and she knew. On Kate's next visit to Napa, Millie expressed her disapproval, asking Kate, "How can you do this to me?" Hours later, at one in the morning, Millie was still upset, but said to Kate, "Well, at least you can't do anything worse," to which Kate answered, "Oh, I'll think of something. Give me six months." There was a pause, and Kate reported that she just started laughing because the whole conversation suddenly seemed ludicrous. And her mother seemed to relax about it, just a bit.

Kate made it clear to her parents that if they wanted to continue to see her it was going to be with me, and they would have to be at least civil. Art and I had our highball; for Millie it was more difficult because her connection with Kate was more intense. Often her hostility was palpable. If we spent the night with them in Napa we would sleep on their sofa bed in the living room. When Millie got up at the crack of dawn to make tea, she would come stomping through the living room en route to the kitchen. Kate and I were both awake, of course, huddled under the covers. Millie would "accidentally" and invariably give the sofa bed a good, solid kick, and I would just as invariably get a nosebleed because of the tension I felt. It would have been funny had it also not been so hard for me to be around anyone whose approval I could not win.

We persevered because we felt it was important to sustain the relationship with her parents, as we did with mine. I cut Art and Millie a lot of slack when Kate explained to me that as devout Lutherans they both sincerely believed that an unrepentant homosexual would literally burn in hell. This was surely a fate they could not fathom for their daughter, whom they truly loved. I was most amazed, however, by their family interaction. The content may have been conservative, but at least everything was out in the open. In my family everything was communicated by innuendo and undercurrent, and we kept so many secrets from each other, lying by omission, by denial, by erasure.

Some twenty years into my relationship with Kate, Millie introduced us to one of her friends. She said, "This is my daughter, Kate." And then she turned toward me. "And this," she hesitated for a moment, "is my other daughter, Bettina." We had long grown comfortable together as a family, and I felt a strong and growing affection for Millie. Still, to be introduced as her daughter seemed to me a remarkable transformation.

My parents were invited to Berlin in the winter of 1980 as guests of the German Democratic Republic. My father was to lecture at Humboldt University in Berlin for the term, and they were given an apartment in a building reserved for government dignitaries in a fashionable section of the city, a few blocks from the Brandenburg Gate. My mother was to turn seventy-five at the end of February, and I toyed with the harebrained scheme of flying to Berlin to surprise her for her birthday. I decided I could commandeer some of the money my mother had given to me to pay her bills while they were away for such a good cause as a trip to Berlin. When Kate offered to stay with Josh and Jenny in Santa Cruz I had both the means and the opportunity. I planned with my father and arranged to fly directly into West Berlin from San Francisco. With the machinations of the Cold War, flights into East Berlin from the West did not exist. I would have to fly into another socialist city, for example, Prague or Warsaw, and then fly back to East Berlin. Such a route was prohibitively expensive. Once in West Berlin, I thought, I could take a taxi from the airport to Checkpoint Charlie in the American sector of the divided city and cross the border from West to East Berlin. This is, in fact, what I did, but once my father informed the East German comrades of my plan, they insisted that my parents meet me at the West Berlin airport with one of them in tow to facilitate the crossing back into East Berlin. This turned out to be a very good idea. In any event, my mother had to be in on the surprise before her actual birthday. But it was worth it.

Once in Berlin I got in line at the immigration counter. The officer took my passport, looked at the name, and looked at me as if to verify the photograph. Then he picked up the telephone on his desk and made a call. I understood enough German to know that he had called the police. He then motioned for me to step aside, presumably so that the line of incoming passengers could proceed. My heart thudded in my ears. I contemplated the historical irony of being shot by Berlin police, another Jewish Communist killed. Then I heard my mother's laugh, which was surreal indeed. She was on the other side of the barriers, of course, and we could not see each other, but she had a distinctive soaring musical laughter that I would have known anywhere. Absurdly, I thought, *My mother is here. She'll protect me.* The phone rang on the immigration officer's desk. He picked it up. I heard him say my name and then a string of sentences I couldn't understand. He hung up, motioned me forward, stamped my passport, and sent me on to the baggage claim. As I stepped out into the rotunda I saw my parents on the other side of the turnstile, along with their East German comrade. The next thing I knew I had my suitcase in hand, I was through customs, and Mom was hugging me. My parents introduced me to Horst Idhe, their German companion, a professor at the university where Dad was teaching.

When I asked Horst about all the soldiers and police and described what had happened at immigration, he said security was tight because the trial of a prominent leader of a left-wing anarchist group was beginning that day in West Berlin. At Checkpoint Charlie we cleared the U.S. border guards easily, and then confronted the East German authorities. Horst explained who we were and we showed them our passports. The officers were intensely concerned about all the books and magazines in my luggage, which they searched thoroughly. They seemed particularly concerned about Rita Mae Brown's lesbian novel, *Six of One*. It was at least an hour before Horst succeeded in negotiating a twenty-four-hour visitor's visa for me, which, we were sternly warned, needed to be taken to the East Berlin police to be extended.

By now it was dark and well into evening. The four of us entered East Berlin and walked down Fredrichstrasse to Unter der Linden, and then to the apartment complex where my parents were living. The comrades had arranged for me to have my own apartment, for which I was grateful. I was exhausted and hauled myself off to bed.

The next morning Horst arrived very early to take me to the police station to have my visa extended. He kept up an amiable chatter, and as we exited the metro that morning he pointed out various sights to me, especially the needlelike radio tower that reached high into the sky, by far the tallest structure in East Berlin. He was, I thought, inordinately proud of it. I noticed the construction in progress everywhere I looked, how clean the streets were, and how few cars there were. "Socialism under construction," he said happily in a singsong. As we approached Alexanderplatz, Horst noted that the police headquarters had existed in the same location under the Nazis, and during the Weimar Republic before that.

Horst approached the window of the appropriate official; it had iron bars like the old bank teller windows in Western cowboy movies. He spoke in German and gave the official my passport and the one-day visa. The officer said in German, "This visa is no longer valid." Horst said, "It was good for twenty-four hours!" translating for me. "Comrade Aptheker arrived late last night." The officer just shook his head. It was not good for twenty-four hours, but only for the day on which it was issued. We should have come in last night to have it extended. Horst, exasperated by this bureaucracy after our long delay at the border, spoke angrily in German and produced a card showing his membership in the Socialist Unity Party, the GDR's Communist Party. The officer looked at his party card, took my passport and visa, and disappeared behind another door. Horst was agitated. In English he said, "He can make big trouble for us." "Like what?" I asked stupidly, innocent in my faith in socialism. The officer returned. I did not understand his words but it was clear from his tone that he was reprimanding Horst. Nevertheless, somewhere someone in authority had cleared something, and the officer issued my one-week visa with a stern warning that I leave the country on the required day.

Horst had known my friend Ursula, although not well, he said. I was anxious to know how she was in the last months of her life, and I asked Horst about her suicide. Even after five years I was still shaken and distraught over her suicide, but hearing an account from someone who'd known her was helpful to me. I had wanted to visit her grave, but the Thuringian district where she was buried was, Horst said, quite far from Berlin and I had only a few days altogether, so I didn't go. But I thought about her often during my time there.

My mother's seventy-fifth birthday was lovely. The best part came when the German comrades sang "Happy Birthday" in heavily accented English. They were so off key Mother couldn't stand it, and she joined in with her still resonant if somewhat husky soprano.

My father walked me to the border the day after my mother's birthday. Before dawn, with the sky showing the beginnings of a pale light, we stood in front of the Berlin Wall on Fredrichstrasse with its barbed wire atop the brick fortifications, guard stations, and heavily armed soldiers patrolling on foot. I hugged my father and picked up my suitcase. As I cleared the East German sector and entered the no man's land between East and West, I looked back and waved and he waved back. He looked very small and distant in the shadows of the wall. It was the first time I had ever seen him in this way. He no longer loomed larger than life. I crossed into the American sector, where a very bored and very young U.S. soldier glanced at my passport before sending me on through.

Three months after we became lovers I decided I wanted to live with Kate. One Sunday early in February—before my trip to Berlin—we were hiking the Old Coast Road near Big Sur, in the mountains alongside the winding coastal Highway 1. We were above the Bixby Bridge, about twenty miles south of Monterey. As we stood looking at a breathtaking view of the ocean I said, "Let's live together." Kate's face froze in what looked like some combination of shock and alarm. *Whoops,* I thought, *faux pas;* I stayed very quiet.

I had been driving up and down Highway 1 between Santa Cruz and Monterey every weekend and half the nights of the week, piling the kids into the car. Joshua was invariably late for school the next morning as I drove back to town at 8 AM, hastily scrawling him the same poor excuse for a note to his homeroom teacher: "Joshua is late due to circumstances beyond his control." He was so good natured about it. But the real reason I wanted to live with Kate was that I thought she would help me to control the paranoia, despair, and self-loathing that still overwhelmed me at times. Even as I began my life with Kate, these feelings periodically resurfaced, and the euphoria and optimism I felt would be hurled aside by the force of these negative emotions.

Finally, Kate spoke. She didn't know if living together was such a good idea because she worried that our passion would soon be swamped in domesticity, and she hated domestic life. She was also concerned that I had had such a brief time on my own, while she had had eleven years to satisfy needs of autonomy and independence. "Let me think about it for a while," she said. A couple of weeks later, together on a thoroughly domestic errand to the bank in Pacific Grove, she said she thought we could do very well living together, and she laughed joyously. But, she cautioned, we've got to watch all this domesticity!

We set June, the end of the school year, as the date for moving. With few roots in Santa Cruz and with all the years of moving Kate and Lisa had experienced, we thought it made the most sense for me to move in with her. I could commute to work, and her home was only an hour and a half from San Jose, still allowing the children to make weekend and holiday trips to visit their father. The only thing left to do was to talk to Jack. As a condition of our divorce, I could not move without his consent. Though, for the sake of the children, we had maintained a cordial relationship since our divorce, we both still harbored a lot of anger toward each other. He was opposed to my move to Pacific Grove because he feared being that much farther away from Josh and Jenny. I was locked in a state of fury that my actions could be limited by his authority. Kate feared that he would invoke the fact that we were lesbians and seek custody of the children. I was confident that he would keep his word on that, but I thought he might seek custody on other grounds. She said, "There are no other grounds." Still deadlocked in May, I proposed that the three of us go out to dinner and talk.

The minute we were seated and the waiter was out of earshot, Jack and I were at each other as though we were still married. Kate, distancing herself from the impasse that had occasioned our meeting, assumed the role of marriage counselor. Using her therapeutic skills, she began pointing out the false assumptions each of us was making about the other. For example, Jack thought I wanted to move to Pacific Grove to be farther away from him. And, discounting his feelings for the children, I thought he simply wanted to interfere in my life.

Startled by Kate's strategy as counselor, I felt my spine bolt straight. Hey, whose side was she on, anyhow? Calm, smiling warmly, with gracious ease, she continued. I felt something shift inside me. Our marital patterns, so deeply embedded, were crazy. We were like racehorses grooved into a track on a set course. Halfway through the dinner I read a shift in Jack's body language. I knew, long before Kate did, that it was going to work out. Finally he said, "We're very close to agreement; I just need time to think out some of the details and talk with you again later." After dinner the three of us embraced outside the restaurant, tears of relief welling from all directions. I felt terrific, but poor Kate had indigestion for three days.

I rented a five-ton U-Haul truck with one of those slogans painted on its side: "An adventure in moving." All five of us packed the house. Even Jenny boxed her own books, toys, and clothes. A friend of Kate's who owned a pickup truck and had lots of experience packing vans came to help us. She may have loaded the U-Haul but I was going to drive it. I found an appropriate cap to wear for the occasion, opened the door to the cab, and pulled myself up into the driver's seat. We stopped and started and jerked and bumped our way down Highway 1. Kate and Lisa's once-spacious home shrank as we jammed in a double-decker bed, dressers, books, desks, clothes, and my household paraphernalia.

Soon after we moved in together, Kate and I attended a women's studies party at San Jose State, celebrating the end of the school year. I had taught in the program through the fall 1979 semester, and Kate, too, had many friends in the program from her years in graduate school. Amidst the conviviality and laughter Billie Jensen, the senior professor who had been so important to me as mentor and friend and from whom Kate had also taken classes, took us by the hands and pulled us toward her. Standing between us and beaming, tears pooling in her eyes, she brought our hands up in front of her and told us how very, very happy she was for us. In this beautiful way she blessed our union, performing a small spontaneous ceremony honoring our love.

International Publishers sent out its spring 1980 catalog listing new books and, to my considerable excitement, announcing *Woman's Legacy* for publication in July. Then in May I received a completely unexpected letter from Lou Diskin. He informed me that two members of the national women's commission had both read the manuscript and had "lodged the most serious complaints. . . . We are back to square one. . . . We are eager for discussion, but cannot pay your fare. . . . Disappointment in the publishing house is very great." At the same time that Lou's letter arrived I received a two-and-a-half-page, typed, single-spaced letter from one of the women that began,

> It is clear that you have developed some basic differences with the Party, and I should add, with Marxist-Leninist theory, on the source and nature of women's oppression under capitalism. While I was aware that these differences have been developing for some time I was surprised at just how wide a gap had developed.

Her letter then quoted a long paragraph from Marx describing capitalist class relations (in which only the male pronoun appears) and concluded that my formulations of women's domestic labor were "the *opposite* of Marxism." Finally she stated, "I have recommended . . . that the manuscript not be published. . . . I do hope that when you speak publicly that you indicate that [these are] your own opinions only, and not those of the CPUSA." She did "look forward to discussing these differences in person, if at all possible." The fact that I had a contract with International to publish the book obviously meant nothing.

I was in complete turmoil over her letter. I had expected controversy over the chapter on domestic labor, but I had not expected a broadside like this, which dismissed all of the research I had done and decreed what constituted Marxism-Leninism. I roiled around for a few days before responding. Although I didn't acknowledge it to myself, my underlying anguish was about the viability of my continued membership in the party.

International's decision not to publish *Legacy* was compounded by another event that astounded me. I was scheduled to teach a "cadre training" class for the party in San Francisco early in

June. The class was called "The Struggle for Women's Equality," and I was to talk about women's oppression and the women's movement. Not long after I received the letter, my comrades in California informed me that I would not be permitted to teach this class because they had received word from New York that I was no longer ideologically fit to teach for the party. I knew the national leadership had issued this decree because my politics differed from the party's "line," since I acknowledged and talked about issues like domestic and sexual violence. I felt as though I'd been kicked in the gut, the more so because Kendra and Max and many others with whom I'd worked for years simply acquiesced to the edict from New York.

Kate was much less surprised than I about all these goings-on, having been more realistic in her assessment of the party. As an outsider she was much clearer about the politics and process of the party. Seeing how hurt and angry I was, she did everything she could to be supportive and encouraging. I decided to battle out my differences with the women's commission members who had reviewed my manuscript and Lou late in June, when I would be on the East Coast to lead a workshop at a Marxist retreat center in the Berkshires.

Kate and I flew to New York. Jack was happy, he said, to have the children for the two weeks we would be gone. Whatever his feelings about the divorce, Jack was outraged by the actions of the party's national leadership. Kate had never been to New York, where we planned to begin our trip, and this afforded us our first opportunity to travel together. I was enthusiastic about showing her the city and taking her to Brooklyn so she could see where I had grown up. Renate Bridenthal again extended an invitation for us to stay with her and Hobey; Blanche Cook and Clare Coss generously did likewise.

Although I knew Kate and I would have a great time, I wasn't looking forward to my dealings with the party leadership.

My father, who had read *Legacy,* encouraged me to struggle with International. Early chapters in the book drew upon some of his research, and he was insulted that the manuscript could be so easily dismissed. He disagreed with my discussion of domestic labor, but he felt my views were within the bounds of legitimate debate. I think also, in retrospect, although he didn't say so, that he could feel me pulling away from the party and the orthodoxy that he personally endorsed.

I entered the familiar offices of International Publishers on Park Avenue South. The receptionist, Madeline Bradshaw, whom I adored and hadn't seen since childhood, greeted me with a warm embrace. Ensconced in Lou's office with comrades from the women's commission, I learned that in fact only one of them had read the manuscript. I came prepared to discuss specific revisions, but none were proposed. I said I could not respond to general ideological statements; the comrades had to be specific. Privately I was seething at the whole process of interrogation and censorship.

We finally agreed that one of the comrades who had a more academic background would review the manuscript and make specific recommendations by page and section. Lou, who was going to be in California in late July, would review these with me. I felt cautiously optimistic; Kate was much less hopeful. I felt confident that once we got past the sweeping ideological pronouncements about what constituted Marxism-Leninism and got to specific proposals, I could deal with them. Kate was less optimistic because, she said, the party had no intention of allowing the book to be published because I was living as a lesbian; they were just going through the motions. I couldn't afford to believe that.

While in New York, Kate and I stayed with Blanche and Clare. They had been together for thirteen years, living in a large apartment in uptown Manhattan, each with her own workspace, and the whole place overflowing with the trappings of intellectual life. Huge posters of Angela Davis and of Cuban and Vietnamese women adorned their walls. Blanche was beginning the research for what was to become a definitive multi-volume biography of Eleanor Roosevelt, and Clare was working on a new play based on the life of Emma Goldman. It was so important to me to see them, a lesbian couple with a stable, loving relationship, each of them living a full and creative life. All that had seemed so terrifying and impossible to me just a few years before was now tangible and viable. One morning Blanche, her curly brown hair spotted with gray, emerged from their bedroom in her pajamas, rubbed the sleep from her eyes, walked across the room in her bare feet with a little bounce in her step, and roused us from our nest on the sofa bed. There was such a sweetness in her.

Both Blanche and Clare were outraged by the story of my party saga. Blanche expressed political distress for what, she said, this meant for the Left and for the women's movement. I'd been so self-absorbed I hadn't really thought about these things. Blanche believed that Marxist and feminist components were vital to all liberation movements, and the failure of the Communists to divest themselves of sectarian and doctrinaire habits was another unfortunate example of how male domination pervaded the Left.

Those of us raised in Brooklyn hold firm to the belief that it is *the* borough in the New York metropolitan area, and I was determined to prove this to Kate beyond all reasonable doubt. She was not that impressed at the end of our day's excursion, but we had a very good time and I forgave her for her tempered enthusiasm. We took the D train into Brooklyn and exited at Prospect Park. It was the line that had been the BMT when I was growing up, and the stops were all the same. I excitedly pointed out the sights of my childhood. The Flatbush section of Brooklyn had completely changed colors; that is, all the Jewish and Italian shopkeepers had been replaced by Jamaican and Haitian ones. But Erasmus Hall High School still sported its gray walls, draped with ivy and spotted with mold, and the statue of Desiderius Erasmus, green with age, was visible at the center of the campus, although a steel gate now barred the entrance. It was in the Brooklyn Botanic Garden that Kate really took to the advantages and character of Brooklyn, and we spent a long while lounging in the shade of a weeping willow inside the Japanese garden, its green branches skimming the waters of a small lake dappled with sunlight. In the midst of the frenzied city life around us, here was a place of complete tranquility and refuge.

The Berkshire Mountains are geologically much older than the Western mountain ranges to which I had become accustomed. The Berkshires are rounded with age and heavily wooded. In early summer they are a mass of rolling greens, still luxuriant from the spring rains. Our drive was restful and immensely pleasant once we got through the frenetic inner city rush.

Stopping in Great Barrington, Massachusetts, in the late afternoon en route to the Berkshire forum where I was to do my workshop, we walked up and down the main streets, looking for a town map or some sort of landmark or memorial to Dr. Du Bois, who had been born in Great Barrington. I knew that his family home had been demolished sometime in the 1950s, and a librarian from the public library directed us to the site. All that remained of it now were a few bricks from what must have been the fireplace, and an empty lot overrun with weeds. Still, I thought we must have to walk in a little ways, that there would be a statue or a marker. There was absolutely nothing, just as the librarian had told us. I was so disappointed and wondered why the town, or the state for that matter, could not come up with the funds to at least provide a marker.

When we arrived in Amherst I telephoned Leone Stein, the director of the University of Massachusetts Press and a friend of my father. Leone had overseen the publication of three volumes of Du Bois's correspondence, which my father had edited, and one small book by Du Bois that my father had likewise compiled and edited, called *Prayers for Dark People*. When Leone had gone to the National Endowment for the Humanities to seek funding for the Du Bois correspondence, she was taken to lunch by the head of the endowment and told in no uncertain terms that as long as my father was editor, there would be no funding. The endowment, he said, would not fund a Communist. Although this had happened more than a decade earlier, Leone was still stung by the rebuff.

I talked to Leone about my book and what was happening within the Communist Party. She asked me a few questions about the book, I think to establish some sense of my scholarship, and then offered to have a look. I told her I couldn't until and unless it was finally rejected by International. She said she understood, wished me luck, and said hoped she got the book.

Kate and I flew to Chicago a few days later. Mrs. Duster, the daughter of Ida B. Wells-Barnett, true to her word, had written and invited Kate and me to come to Chicago and stay with her and her sister,

Miss Ida Barnett. She offered to share with us her memories of her mother and as many of her mother's papers and memorabilia as were available. For all the difficulties I was facing in my struggle with the party, the trip had blossomed into an invigorating and extraordinary opportunity. With directions from Mrs. Duster we made our way from the airport on the train to Chicago's south side.

We were greeted by a diminutive elderly black woman with white hair and a radiant manner. This was Mrs. Duster, and she placed her hands on each of my shoulders and gave them a firm squeeze in a motherly greeting. I introduced Kate and we went inside. Miss Barnett, Mrs. Duster's sister, was there to greet us also. We sat in the kitchen drinking tea and were soon laughing and sharing stories. "I know your father, of course," Mrs. Duster said. "How is he?"

Mrs. Duster had been a social worker and a renowned activist in the Chicago community. Mr. Duster had died years before. She had never remarried, though she had lots of suitors. "I'd bring them home for dinner and introduce them to my children," she said. "'These are the five little Dusters,' I'd say, 'and they're all going to college.'" Miss Barnett had taught school and moved in with her sister after her husband passed, to help her raise the children. The two sisters had lived together, counting childhood, on and off for seventy-five years.

"Well now," Mrs. Duster said, "come on into my bedroom. I have things to show you!" As we passed through the living room again en route, I noticed the photographs of her mother and of her father, Ferdinand L. Barnett, who had been an attorney, and of many of the "five little Dusters." She had one of my favorite pictures of Ida B. Wells-Barnett, a formal portrait taken in 1931, white hair framing an earnest expression with the faint hint of a smile. Seeing our interest in the photographs, Mrs. Duster reviewed each of her children, now, of course, all having graduated from college and well launched into professional careers. I knew that her son, Troy Duster, was a professor of sociology at UC Berkeley. And then there were all the grandchildren, each one with a story. Once in the bedroom, Mrs. Duster went to her closet and from its uppermost shelves she pulled down boxes and folders and spread everything out on her bed. She told us to look at whatever we wished. I grabbed for my notebook.

Mrs. Duster had collected dozens of newspaper clippings, many of them related to her mother's life—for example, the story about a Chicago apartment complex named the Ida B. Wells Apartments. She had also kept reviews of her mother's posthumously published autobiography, which Mrs. Duster had edited. It wasn't published until 1970, although it was largely complete at the time of Wells-Barnett's death in 1931. "Forty years," Mrs. Duster said in exasperation, "and nobody wanted it!" She had also saved letters and memorabilia from her own life, awards she had received, and community efforts with children that she had initiated. Kate and I pored over the treasure trove for several hours.

Later, I asked Mrs. Duster if she had a copy of a pamphlet her mother had published along with Frederick Douglass in 1893, called *The Reason Why.* Mrs. Duster did, and she produced a small, hardbound booklet with a blue cover. Black people had been excluded from the World's Columbian Exposition held in Chicago in 1893, despite significant protests. To garner some sort of recognition of the discrimination, Ida B. Wells had written and published *The Reason Why the Colored American Is Not in the World's Columbian Exposition*, which included an introductory essay by Frederick Douglass. Widely distributed at the World's Fair, it explained segregation, documented lynchings and other racist atrocities, and gave evidence of the many contributions black people had made to the New World, including, for example, a long list of patented inventions. I had searched everywhere for this booklet and had finally located a copy of it in the basement of the British Museum in London. The museum had sent me a Xeroxed copy. To actually hold the original in my hands was thrilling. I saw, too, the small notice on the back cover that it could be ordered by mail at a cost of two cents, and a Chicago address was given.

The following morning Mrs. Duster gave Kate and me very careful instructions about which streets in her neighborhood were safe to walk and which were not. And, she said, walk purposefully in nice long strides. With this, she directed us to the Regenstein Library at the University of Chicago, where the papers of Ida B. Wells-Barnett were preserved. "There's not too much there," she warned us, explaining that a fire in the family home had destroyed much material. We set off and soon came upon the southern border of the university, which faced the ghetto. Entrance to the campus from this side was impossible, as it was bordered by a huge wrought-iron gate, with spikes on its upper extensions and a literal moat such as one might expect to see at a medieval castle. I was too stunned even to speak; the racist message of such a barricade was unbelievable. We walked north along the western perimeter of the campus and soon found ourselves amongst the shops and cafés marking a familiar university ambiance.

The library staff were expecting us; they had laid out boxes of materials on the wide, polished wooden desks typical of an archive. It was emotionally overwhelming for me to touch Ida B. Wells-Barnett's papers, to scroll through her Memphis diaries on microfilm, to read the letters home to her family in Chicago, to see the many family photographs, and to study the newspaper clippings recounting her years of struggle. The anguish and guilt she felt in being separated from her children while traveling was evident in the letters, and touched me in a very personal way. In the Memphis diaries Kate and I were particularly struck by her struggles with sexism and her worry over the innuendos about her morality as she broke conventional Victorian standards to travel unchaperoned and without the benefit of an older male relative or husband. As I sifted through these artifacts, Ida B. Wells-Barnett came alive to me, so that the icon of a crusader became also a human being with the imperfections and anxieties we all experience in our lives.

Upon my return home I anxiously awaited word about *Woman's Legacy*. It was well into August before I met one of the women who had reviewed it. As I knew it would, most of the contention centered on the chapter on domestic labor, and on a section of the introduction that critically assessed the failure of socialism to liberate women. Kate had warned me that the party would never agree to those paragraphs, and I had already decided that I was willing to let them go.

In Marxist theory and socialist practice it was assumed that once women were gainfully employed outside the home and no longer economically dependent on a male provider, they would be liberated. Socialism provided for medical care and education up to and including university and professional training, including for women. And yet domestic and sexual violence remained serious problems in the socialist countries, and many patriarchal assumptions of male dominance in the family remained unchallenged. In a few short paragraphs I had addressed these issues. I thought I could remove them from the book because it was primarily a history and very much located in the United States. The commentary on socialism was really part of a different project.

Immediately after the reviewer left, I wrote to Lou Diskin and sent him a four-point proposal for revision. I said that if these proposals were acceptable I would proceed at once with the revisions. Two weeks later Lou telephoned me to say that my four-point proposal had been accepted, but that the reviewer would like to do one final review of the manuscript before production was resumed. I saw no problem with this, made the revisions, and sent them off. Three and a half weeks passed with no word from Lou. So I telephoned Lou. It was now the beginning of October; he said he had just gotten the revised sections of the manuscript to our comrade. A week later I telephoned Lou again and was informed that he was now in Moscow and would be gone for two weeks. That same day, October 10, a package arrived from International Publishers. It had been sent first class. It was the original manuscript, unrevised, copyedited, many pages with blue tags for queries to the author. There was no letter.

Upset and angry, I telephoned the comrade from the women's commission, and after several attempts I reached her at her office in New York. She knew nothing about a four-point proposal to revise the manuscript; she had not seen or been told about any revisions. Through all my battles and struggles in the party I had never been lied to like this. I asked her if she would read the revisions I had made now. She said she would. I sent everything directly to her, but to no avail. Whatever she read of the new material she reiterated, in a final letter sent less than two weeks later, her original view that *Legacy* could not be published. I believed at the time (and still do) that someone very high in the party leadership had ordered that this book not be published under any circumstances. I believed that I had been lied to, and that Lou Diskin was the hapless and ineffectual go-between. I also believed that apart from any issues with the manuscript, it was the increasingly public affirmation of my lesbian identity that sealed *Legacy*'s fate with the party. It was 1981, and the party was not to deal seriously with issues of sexuality and gay and lesbian rights for another decade, and even then it never really analyzed or affirmed the importance of these struggles. My father, however, remained firm in his support of me and in fact wrote a letter to Lou Diskin condemning the decision and my treatment. He also said that he would no longer publish any new work with International Publishers, an extraordinary gesture.

I was in the worst psychological state I'd been in since my nervous breakdown at twenty-three. I was thirty-seven years old, and felt a sense of overwhelming betrayal by the party. The difference now, and it was huge, was that I had Kate. Outside the party and the madness of its ideological strife she provided a calm and reasoned counterbalance to the wildness of my feelings, and I knew I had her unconditional love. Good to her word, Leone Stein reviewed the manuscript and then sent it out for the required peer review. Meeting with academic approval, *Woman's Legacy* was published in 1982 by the University of Massachusetts Press. It was widely and favorably reviewed in the feminist, black, and scholarly presses. Gerda Lerner, who was a professor of history at the University of Wisconsin in Madison and was shortly to become president of the Organization of American Historians, endorsed the book, as did Adrienne Rich, who pronounced it "feminist to the core." Gerda's work in women's history had influenced me a great deal; she had been part of the Communist Left in the early 1950s, and my book was in many ways a legacy of work she and other Communist women, like Eleanor Flexner, Eve Merriam, and Claudia Jones, had begun thirty years before.

In the end, despite all of my pain, the party's refusal to publish *Legacy* turned out to be a gift. The final coup de grâce to the original debacle was the response of Hayden White, who was on my dissertation committee. Hayden had read portions of the book, as I had submitted a few précis as papers in my graduate seminars with him. He read the book as soon as it was published. Late in the summer I ran into him while retrieving my mail at the university. In an offhand manner that is his trademark, he said, "I just finished your book." Before I could gather my wits he continued, "It's very good." He was leafing through his mail; only half of his attention was on me. "I think it should be your dissertation."

"My dissertation?" I said, not understanding his point. I had passed my qualifying exams a year before, and was working on a new book that I thought was going to be my dissertation. I was still working out the contradictions between Marxism and feminism, and my qualifying essay had been a theoretical exploration of "women's alienation," using Marx's 1844 *Economic and Philosophical Manuscripts* and works by contemporary feminists like Nancy Hartsock, Joan Kelly, Sandra Harding, and Zillah Eisenstein. It was this essay-in-progress I had shared with Joan Kelly before her death.

"Yes," Hayden said. "A dissertation is just an exercise to prove your ability to do scholarly work. The book establishes that." I officially graduated with my doctorate in March 1983, and I walked through the graduate ceremonies in June with my whole family in attendance—Kate, Josh, Jenny, Lisa, and my parents. Donna Haraway, who had been my dissertation advisor, "hooded" me, placing the blue and gold garment ceremoniously over my head and draping it down the back of my black academic robe. It was a wonderful and gratifying moment.

In the time that had elapsed since I had taught my first course at UC Santa Cruz, on black women's history, the situation in the women's studies program had changed radically. The student-run collective had been dismantled, and faculty were now in charge of the program. Barbara Epstein, a professor of history, had assumed the role of coordinator. I had known Barbara fifteen years earlier in Berkeley. A few years older than I, Barbara had come to Berkeley as a graduate student fresh from the New Left trenches at Radcliffe. A Marxist with ties to both the Old Left and New Left, Barbara had worked in the antiwar movement. The changes in women's studies at Santa Cruz had been wrought by Helene Moglen when she became the dean of humanities in 1978. Helene was a feminist literary scholar and deeply committed to women's studies. She believed that the program would survive in a changing and more conservative political climate only if tenured faculty committed themselves to running it. In spite of my status as a graduate student, Barbara convinced Helene to appoint me as an adjunct lecturer. Specifically, Barbara wanted me to teach her course, Introduction to Women's Studies. Helene agreed. This course was to become foundational in building the program, and a defining experience for me as a teacher, activist, and scholar.

I redesigned Barbara's curriculum and retitled it "Introduction to Feminism," making it more overtly political, and taught the class in the context of the women's movement. Most of the thirty-seven students that first winter were activists themselves, and knew at least as much as I did about the movement. We had animated discussions on rape, domestic violence, abortion, and lesbian identity. I taught them a feminist reworking of Marx's "Value, Price, and Profit," with women at the center of the exploitative process, and incorporated material on women's history focused on the activism of black and white women in the abolition, suffrage, and trade union movements. My main texts were Adrienne Rich's *On Lies, Secrets, and Silence,* Audre Lorde's *Sister Outsider,* and an assortment of essays, poems, and stories that I compiled into a class reader. What I wanted to convey to them more than anything else was that we could change our lives not only as individuals, but as part of a global movement for liberation from all systems of domination.

With its comparatively small size its commitment to undergraduate teaching, and its encouragement of experimental courses and innovations, Santa Cruz was an ideal setting for me. I loved teaching and felt blessed to be there. I also taught evening classes at Gavilan Community College, in a nearby farming community, to supplement my income. Teaching became a form of political activism for me, replacing the years of dogged meetings and intrepid organizing with the immediacy of a liberatory practice and lively, open theoretical debate. Every day brought thrilling discoveries.

I resigned from the Communist Party on October 12, 1981, one year almost to the day after the party's rejection of *Woman's Legacy*. I agonized about it for weeks because I didn't want my resignation encumbered by international events so that it could be construed that I had left because of one or another Soviet action. I wanted my resignation to stand on its own merit, as a consequence of my assessment of and relationship with the U.S. Communist Party. I knew I had to tell my parents of my decision before I announced it publicly. In the days leading up to my visit with them I became more and more nervous. Being the "perfect" daughter had been my way of coping with our family pattern, and I was about to break that mold cast over thirty years. I was in a state of such agitation I could not eat; it was hard for me even to stay calm. My decision had been a long time coming. The party had in many ways been my family; I had been to meetings since I was a child. Marxism had been the centerpiece of my scholarship. It had been the center of my life for as long as I could remember. But since the late 1970s I had been systematically dismantling my old structures, which had once felt so safe but were now suffocating me. In resigning from the party I was removing a huge chunk of my former life.

Unable to imagine myself speaking the words, I wrote a formal letter of resignation that I typed and signed. It was addressed to Gus Hall, general secretary, and Henry Winston, national chair, with copies to Max, who was still the chair of the Northern California district, and to Kendra, who would soon take over Max's position. I took this letter with me to my parents' house in San Jose early in October. I handed them each a copy and sat in silence as they read it.

My father said, "You must not send this."

"Why not?" I asked.

He said, "What if *The New York Times* got hold of it and printed it?"

I was completely nonplussed. I gathered my wits. "All right," I said. "I won't send that letter, but I am resigning from the party."

My mother spoke. She said, "Why don't you just stop attending meetings? Why do you have to resign like this?"

This was something Mother had done for years. That is, she'd get angry with someone or disgusted with some situation and stop going to her club meetings. Then, when she felt better, she'd go back.

I spoke very softly, explaining. "Mom, I've been a public spokesman for the party for years. I've been very public about my membership. I can't do it that way."

Then my father started shouting. He had never yelled at me before, and I don't remember what he said. I shouted back. My mother stopped it. She said, "Herbert! That's enough!" Then she turned to me. "Darling, if that's what you need to do, then you should do it."

My father said, in a more normal voice, hoarse with regret, "The Soviet comrades will never understand it. Never!"

That was so far from anything I had even imagined he might say. It sounded crazy. Why would the Soviet comrades care about what I did? But I repeated in a steady voice and with finality, "I will not send this specific letter, but I will resign."

My mother repeated her words of support. My father rose and returned from the kitchen with a bottle of red wine and three glasses. He almost never drank. I watched while he poured each of us a glass of wine. He set the bottle down and picked up his glass. Mother and I did likewise. He said, "To the family," and raised his glass in a toast. I thought my father was telling me that whatever I did, wherever I went, I would always be his daughter, we would always be a family. This, too, was very far from what I had expected, given his feelings about others who had left the party. He had always presented this to me as the ultimate betrayal, from which there was no redemption. But now, in the face of my resolve, he was not prepared to renounce me; he was not prepared to lose me.

That was it. In all the years after, my parents never once mentioned my resignation from the party. Gradually they stopped talking about the party in my presence, except to tell me about the death of one or another comrade.

Instead of the formal typewritten letter I had intended to send and that I dutifully destroyed, I handwrote a three-page personal letter to Max and Kendra. When I showed it to Kate she blinked at me. "You must have been raised Catholic," she said, referring to the split hair between formal and handwritten letters. She also said my handwritten version was more revealing. After referring to my experience trying to publish *Woman's Legacy* I wrote:

The last Club meeting which I attended was an open one—with non-Party people present. They were being invited to join. I listened attentively. It was a good meeting in organization and spirit. I realized as it progressed that it would be very appropriate for me to say a few words to encourage people to join the Party. And, what became obvious to me as well was that I had nothing to say. This silence filled me finally with a profound sense of loss and grief. The feelings I have had for the Party, the internal sense in myself of a willingness to fight for it even when my work and activities were severely criticized—was gone. . . .

I ended my letter by affirming that:

I do not wish to discuss or argue about my decision, but I would like to effect it in a way which is least disruptive for the Party and to myself. I have a great deal of love and affection for many individual comrades and no desire to stimulate a turmoil of activity. . . .

Despite my action here, I do remain
with love and respect

The first response I had was ten days later from Evelyn Martin. It was a handwritten note sent while she and Max were on vacation: "Just a note to tell you that I love you and feel very sad about the decision you finally felt you had to make. . . . The struggle for truly comradely relations is hard, hard, hard." Max wrote four days after Evelyn:

I am unalterably opposed to accepting your resignation from the Party and intend to fight it very firmly. You are too valuable a Comrade for me to agree to any such status. It is also very unfortunate that it comes when the working class in this country is in the beginning stage of a new powerful upsurge that is going to alter the class struggle in our country. To leave the Party at this time is unthinkable. . . . I send you my love Bettina, and intend to fight for your membership.

I was very distressed by Max's letter, and furious with him. "He can fight for my membership all he wants," I sputtered, slamming around the house. "Who the hell does he think he is telling me he doesn't accept my resignation?" And "What 'upsurge in the working class'? The working class just elected Ronald Reagan, for Chrissake!" I found his arrogance unconscionable, especially given his sexually exploitative relationship with me and his failure to defend me when International wouldn't publish my book. After I finished banging around the house I sat down and wrote him a letter:

> I understand your desire to fight for my membership in the Party . . . but I am not willing to engage in such a struggle. I am very clear that it will not be easy for you (or any of the comrades) to accept my decision, but I am not willing to meet to discuss it. I consider that I have resigned from the Party, effective the date of my letter.

I did sign my letter "with love," ever in denial of the complexity of my feelings. I was trying to create a space in which I could leave the party without becoming a renegade or an enemy. This was almost impossible because the party was such an insulated and embattled entity, but I was going to try.

Yet another letter, dated November 22, came from Max, still wanting to meet:

> I have talked this over with Kendra and we still want to meet with you to discuss your relations with the Party, and how to handle your resignation. In addition, I will want to have some discussions with you on the differences which you

feel have developed between yourself and the Party, this on
a personal level and separate from the above meeting.

I wrote back immediately, proposing dates for us to meet. Max
never responded. We saw each other only rarely after that exchange
of letters. He and Evelyn came to Joshua's high school graduation,
and to a seventy-fifth birthday party for my father in San Jose. Some
years after, Evelyn called to tell me that Max had been diagnosed
with lung cancer. Kate and I drove up to Oakland to see him. He was
still looking okay, but told us that he got "completely exhausted"
very easily. We never mentioned my resignation from the party,
and he made no attempt to apologize to me for his sexual advances.
When he died in the summer of 1989, Kate and I were away on a
holiday. I sent condolences to Evelyn and her family, but I did not
attend his memorial.

When Kate and I began our relationship, we often marveled at
our compatibility. We joked with friends. "I'm six weeks older
than Kate," I would announce in mock superiority. "Yes, but I'm
five inches taller, and thank the goddess for that!" would be Kate's
prompt rejoinder. Beneath the jest was another reality.

I assumed many class and gender privileges in our
relationship, privileges that came from my experiences growing
up in the middle class and in the elite circle of a revolutionary
intelligentsia. Privileged in so many ways, I saw myself "above" the
everyday humdrum of most women's lives, engaged in a struggle
of "world historical forces." That's how I had learned to think in
the Communist Party. I may have left the party, but I had not yet
recognized all of the ways I had internalized both its sexism and
its homophobia.

The passion Kate and I had for each other carried us a long way—until, in fact, the beginning of our third summer. Until then Kate had done all of the emotional work in the relationship, dragging feelings out of me, working through them, using her repertoire of skills to keep the garbage from accumulating between us. I remember one day, in exasperation, she shouted at me, "Enough! Who ever heard of dragging someone into therapy! This is ridiculous!" As one adept at concealing emotion, a strategy I had perfected over many years, I did not reveal many of my actual feelings. Kate guessed them and her accuracy was uncanny. I focused inward, observing the smallest change in her as evidence of some wrongdoing on my part—as though her life revolved around perfecting me. Of course, I was enacting the only way I knew how to do intimacy, in the distorted shadow of childhood sexual abuse. I projected onto Kate much of my ambivalence about work, daily priorities, child rearing, parents, and so on, and then got furious with her for placing these constraints on me. For the most part, also, the relationship revolved around my needs in schedule, priority, and conversation. Kate announced unilateral changes that September. The relationship would not last, she said, if this pattern was allowed to continue.

We struggled with this for a year. I clung to my privilege; she matched my will in strength and endurance. We were locked in a power struggle every bit as wrenching as any each of us had known with men, except that we did not lash out at each other, and we did not go for the emotional jugulars we knew so well in one another. Sometimes, though, I would be stopped short, hearing words from Kate I myself had spoken to my husband, and hearing myself make his reply. This juxtaposition of roles allowed me to see that for all my apparent privileges, I was increasingly dependent on Kate for approval and repair. She was, I realized, the autonomous person.

Perhaps it was vanity that provoked this insight, perhaps it was something else, but my tenacious hold snapped. I said, "I understand. You love me, but if this doesn't change you are going to leave me, no matter how much you still love me."

"Yes," she said. "That's right." And that's when I realized that I had to change. Our relationship meant everything to me.

Even in battle, the love Kate and I shared sank its roots deep into each of us. Often we wished to be with no one else but each other. Our lovemaking seemed to fit the subtle shifting sands of mood and spirit. Sometimes it was like feeling a gently rolling breeze, and at other times like the rush of water cascading over a fall, always beautiful and tender. We also shared times of total comedy, when one or the other of us just couldn't get it together. Any mention of these incidents in the future would set us off into renewed sprays of laughter. On mornings once a week for months we rose before dawn, bundled in our warmest clothing, and walked the few blocks from our house to the ocean. The surf would have quieted, but the beach would be littered with the debris of its nighttime thrashing. In the solitude of this normally public space, calmed by the steady pounding of the waves, we held hands, or sat on the rocks, our arms around each other. If there was dense fog, as was usual, the sun rose into the mist, surrounding us in a thin, cold veil of orange and pink.

To escape the domestic drudgery that sometimes threatened to engulf us, we went away for weekends when we could afford it. Actually, we often didn't leave town. We rented a small cabin, equipped with a kitchenette, at a motel a few blocks from the house. We'd load the car for our big trip, the kids snorting with laughter on the front porch. We'd be at the motel in three minutes, unload the car, and snuggle in. Eventually we decided to share office space, and we rented a small cottage that housed our libraries and provided for our coveted retreats. After we rented the cottage my son said, "I get it. You guys are moving out and leaving us the house!" "You got it!" Kate said cheerfully.

One evening, Kate and I were invited to dinner at the home of another lesbian couple. There I met a woman who had also grown up in Brooklyn. We immediately broke into our thickest New York accents. She said, "You remember the Bond Baker on Empire Boulevard?"

"Yeah! Sure I remember the Bond Baker," I answered.

"Well, my father baked bread there," she announced, triumphant.

"He did?" I said, truly impressed. "No kidding!" We must have said "no kidding" at least thirty-five times in ten minutes.

"And the clock on the bakery tower, remember the clock?" she yelled.

"Yeah! Sure! I remember the clock on the tower," I yelled back.

"And the smell," she continued, "remember that wonderful smell of the bread as it came from the ovens? It would fill the whole neighborhood!"

"Yeah! Sure I remember the smell! It was great!" I bellowed.

We went on like that for half an hour at least, through Ebbets Field, home of the Brooklyn Dodgers, and our passion for baseball, to public schools and high schools and movie theaters. We were sitting a foot from each other at the dinner table, shouting the way you do when you ride the BMT into Manhattan. Linda and I had three very important things in common: We were both from Brooklyn, we were both dykes, and we were both "out."

After several such conversations at similar dinners and events, I began to understand that I was part of the lesbian community on the Monterey Peninsula. This connection to community represented a big shift in my identity. I had always seen myself as singular, shunning associations with lesbians, whom I saw as Other, definitely not me. How wonderful it was to shed this isolation.

The women's community also sported a softball team, and I enthusiastically joined. We called ourselves Demeter, the earth goddess, our name embossed in white lettering on our black T-shirts. We played in the Monterey County league. The men's teams always had the best fields and more access to practice times. Monterey had not yet caught up with Title IX, but this seemed to me a minor inconvenience compared to the sheer joy of playing. When she wasn't coaching softball, our coach, Kate Elvin, was an artist; several of her murals are still evident on buildings in Pacific Grove. A short, powerfully built woman in her late thirties, Kate was a skilled trainer. Our twice-weekly practices were serious workouts, and we usually played on alternating weekends from late spring through the end of summer. I started out pitching, but I no longer had the eye or the speed necessary, and Kate moved me around, from right field, to third base, to shortstop, and finally to catcher. I had never played catcher before and I liked the position a lot. There was constant action, and I could see the whole field. I also liked all the padding I got to wear and loved flipping off my mask when I went after a pop fly.

Our friend Teramota was at the hub of our lesbian community. A nurse, she was from a large Italian family in New Jersey. Her self-adopted name meant "earth-mover." When she went to Nicaragua to help in the rural communities after the Sandinistas came to power, her name caused a considerable stir lest she bring on an earthquake. Teramota kept her fingers on the pulse of our community; she knew where everyone was when they traveled or left the area, and she organized many events to provide a relaxed and nonalcoholic space where women could meet each other. When *Woman's Legacy* was published, Teramota organized a public celebration and book signing. Given the history of *Legacy*'s publication, this celebration marked a particular kind of homecoming for me into my new life. I felt so at home, in a way I had never experienced before.

A year earlier, in 1981, as part of this effort to build a safe and nonalcoholic environment for the lesbian community, Kate began a storytelling circle on the first Friday of every month. That first year she rented a space at the Pacific Grove Art Center; later she moved the storytelling event to a building recently purchased by the local YWCA. Sponsored by the Lesbian Alliance, a completely nonpartisan group, the storytelling circles were open to all women. I was very judgmental about Kate's initiative in the first year because I didn't understand the need. But as an alcoholic Kate understood what it meant to have a social space that was not a bar scene. I also didn't yet understand the power of storytelling. Kate did because she had studied Native Americans and knew how oral tradition had helped to keep the cultures alive despite the genocidal assaults to which they were (and continue to be) subjected. Kate proceeded, and eventually I started coming along. Hers was a truly wonderful innovation in community organizing.

The storytelling events were free, but Kate solicited donations. Once the rent for the room was paid, Kate gave the remaining money to the women's shelter run by the Y on the Monterey Peninsula. Over the years hundreds of women came to Kate's storytelling circles, and after a few years she began to encourage the women to share their own stories. She raised thousands of dollars for the shelter. Kate's stories deeply influenced me and became a source of healing, a gentle salve to the misogynist poisons all around us. Storytelling also became such an institution that it profoundly influenced the political fabric of our community. Kate had helped to establish an ethos of respect for political, religious, racial, and cultural difference. As a result, the lesbian community on the peninsula never splintered into the kind of factions that wracked the hearts of so many lesbian communities in the 1980s and 1990s.

When she was nine years old, Jenny asked Kate if she would be her mother again. I was thrilled, but Kate shot me a warning glance lest my enthusiasm affect Jenny's own emotionality. Given our history, Kate questioned Jenny briefly but carefully about her feelings. Then she said she would be honored and happy to be Jenny's mom, but if she did so she would begin parenting her again and exercising discipline. Most important, Kate said, if she became her mom now she would not withdraw again. She urged Jenny to think about it for a few days to be sure of her feelings. Three days later Jenny asked her again. Jenny became our daughter in the truest sense, that is, by her own choice. Afterward, if you saw the three of us together it was impossible to tell whether Kate or I was the biological mother.

On the day of our fifth anniversary, November 7, 1984, Kate and I came home from work and were just getting settled in to make dinner when Jenny, bursting with excitement, insisted that we come with her to the rock garden. At first we didn't see anything, and then we noticed a cloth covering something in the corner. Jenny unveiled it, wishing us a happy anniversary. It was a traditional Japanese lantern made of stone. It fit perfectly into the garden. Jenny was glowing.

How did you do it? we asked. How did you get it here? How did you pay for it? After all, she was only nine years old, and it must have weighed twenty pounds.

Jenny told us that she'd gone up to the outdoor garden shop about a mile and a half from our house. She had seen the lantern and determined to buy it. She had a little red wagon. She walked up to the store with $40 worth of pennies in the wagon. She bought the lantern; the shopkeeper loaded it into the wagon for her, wrapped it in cloth to protect it, and she walked home. She got Josh to help her unload it and place it in the garden.

Later we learned that one of our friends, Deb Busman, had driven by in her truck and seen Jenny and her red wagon. She'd offered her a ride home. No, Jenny had said, thank you, but she preferred to walk.

After the first few months of our joint residence, the two older children relaxed into our relationship. Lisa decided to tell her high school friends that we were a lesbian couple about a year after Kate and I started living together. She girded herself for the announcement one afternoon as she walked home from school with her best friend, Betty, and a few other girls. "Oh, yeah," they said, "we know," and they went on talking about whatever it was that had their attention. It was no big deal. Josh was more cautious, but eventually he also chose a few close friends to tell. Their response was the same. They already had figured it out, and it was no big deal. Later, Josh told us about an incident in one of his high school classes. His history teacher had made a particularly stupid and, Josh thought, stereotypic comment about gays and lesbians. Josh stood up in class and challenged the teacher by saying he knew gay and lesbian people and they were nothing like what he had described. He felt so good about his statement in class. Many of Josh's classmates came from very conservative Pacific Grove families, and speaking up had not been an easy thing for him to do.

Kate's parenting mode, so different from my caretaking, provided me with another model that eventually allowed me some relief from consuming functions like chauffeuring the kids and racing home every evening to eat dinner with them. I learned, instead, the importance of doing emotional work, of spending nondomestic hours visiting with each of them while we walked, or sat in a park, or visited an art gallery.

Kate and I were also to learn that sibling rivalry was not a biological but a social phenomenon. After initially liking each other, Josh and Lisa began a sort of guerrilla war, in bouts of teasing and the confiscation of treasured possessions. We tried to intervene with family councils and quiet individual talks with our respective halves of the sibling war; then we gave it up. In their own time they worked it out, and things calmed down considerably. They began referring to each other as "brother" and "sister," although in their adult lives they have not retained this connection. At the time the presence of our children also greatly facilitated larger family gatherings and dinners with a variety of friends. Indeed, the three of them became so adept at putting on a performance of familial bliss and positive adjustment before all our company that Kate and I were sometimes left dumbstruck at the apparent transformation: They became courteous to each other, remembered their manners, cheerfully completed their chores, cleaned their rooms, and presented themselves scrubbed and shining.

Thanksgiving 1981, a watershed date. It was the first time our parents met. Millie and Art drove in their RV from Napa, and my parents came from San Jose for the day. Our joint effort might have been described as a move toward détente: German, Republican North Dakotans meet Jewish, Communist New Yorkers. However, my mother almost blew our plan. Outraged by Ronald Reagan's presidential onslaught against everything she had fought for in the 1930s New Deal, she raised her glass for a toast saying, "And may Ronald Reagan dis— . . ." Our glasses upraised and poised to drink, there was an ominous silence, and a suddenly motionless family tableau. She had intended to say "disappear." Lisa was the first to recover. Downing her juice, she replaced her glass on the table and said cheerfully, "Grandma, would you pass the turkey, please?" Josh and Jenny quickly followed suit and, through their collaborative charm, saved the day. In fact, since our parents were all of the same generation, they actually ended up doing very well together, as long as they stayed away from politics.

Ever since I had spent Christmas with Mary Timothy and her family, I wanted to reproduce the feelings I associated with it. I loved the search for the perfect tree, the ritual of ornaments, the festivity of lights. This to me had nothing to do with Judaism or Christianity, but with celebration and giving thanks for what we all had. I reveled in the excitement of holiday presents, searching for those parts of childhood I had never had. Christmas mornings with Kate seemed to me like a fairytale, the kids appearing very early in their pajamas, still tousled from sleep.

Some weeks before our third Christmas together, Kate bought me a menorah. Knowing my internalized anti-Semitism and my profound ambivalence about being Jewish, she proposed a more ecumenical holiday season, combining the daily lighting of menorah candles to celebrate Chanukah with the Christian traditions. I was thrilled; I felt the first tinges of pride in my Jewish heritage.

Around the same time, Judith Roth, an activist in the women's movement in our community and a member of the YWCA board of directors, asked me to participate in a panel discussion on Jewish women. Nervous and exhilarated all at the same time, I agreed. The other panel participants were Judith and Ricky Sherover-Marcuse, the scholar-activist who had created the "unlearning racism" workshops that were later to become a national movement. Ricky believed that people could never transform their political consciousness if they didn't simultaneously heal the wounds caused by racism, whether they were white or of color. The wounds, she said, were like an abscessed tooth, festering and debilitating a person's psyche with unresolved pain and suffering.

I had met Ricky during the long struggle for Angela's freedom. While a student of Herbert Marcuse's at UC San Diego, Ricky had become good friends with Angela. After Herbert's wife, Inge, died from cancer in the early 1970s, Ricky and Herbert developed a closer relationship. Despite the thirty-five-year difference in their ages, they were married in 1976, and Ricky cared for Herbert in the last years of his life. His death in July 1979 had been a grievous loss. Ricky moved from San Diego to Oakland to be nearer her sister. It's there that she had launched her workshops.

Ricky's version of unlearning racism included unlearning anti-Semitism. Attending one of Ricky's workshops was an extraordinary experience for me. She was a splendid therapist, intuitive, caring, compassionate. And she combined this compassion with an acute political analysis of racism and anti-Semitism, which she codified in pithy handouts that we could take with us. I used mine in classes for years.

On one of the turns around the circle in the workshop I attended, I gave a brief summary of my Communist heritage and my father's work in black history. "I have always felt black people were superior," I said, "because of the way my father represented their history as a kind of superhuman struggle for freedom." A couple of the black people in the workshop laughed at the idea of black superiority, and I realized, of course, that they knew their community intimately, from the interior rooms, in a way that my father never could. I saw how emotionally embedded this idea was and how foolish and condescending it was without meaning to be. In those moments I also saw that my father had substituted black people for Jews in his work. That is, he made black people larger than life by erasing their foibles and failures. He accurately *reported* betrayals in his writings, for example, in slave revolts, but in lectures he *represented* the history as one of undaunted heroism. This was to compensate for his deep shame about the way, he believed, the Jews had acted during the Holocaust. I remembered his words at the Ravensbrück concentration camp, about how only the party could be counted on in the resistance. It was there in Ricky's workshop that I began to understand that the Jews in Europe were just trying to live their lives like everyone else. They were trying to survive. Only a few Jews had collaborated with the Nazis, sometimes under very complicated circumstances. These instances of collaboration seemed to be the entirety of my father's focus, the place of his guilt and rage. But I also knew that many Jews had fled. Still others had tried to take care of their families, and some had joined different groups in the resistance as Zionists, Communists, trade unionists, and social democrats.

Identifying Jews as an oppressed people, Ricky showed us the centuries-long history of anti-Semitism in Europe and the Jewish resistance to it. She also pointed out the complications of naming Jewish culture and tradition in the context of the Diaspora. She wanted us to savor Jewish cultures, honor our many traditions. Ricky was a Marxist, and I identified with her antiracist and anti-imperialist politics. I trusted her judgment, the righteousness of her purpose. Her workshop was the beginning of my new understanding of myself as a Jew.

Participating in the panel Judith had organized and rekindling my friendship with Ricky were touchstones in reconciling with my Jewish heritage. In my presentation at the panel I gave a history of the uprising of twenty thousand garment workers in New York City from 1909 to 1910. The revolt was led by Jewish women, and in the course of my research for the presentation I discovered the story of Clara Lemlich, one of the heroines of the strike. I had known Clara in my childhood; she was then an elderly Brooklyn woman who devotedly delivered weekly stacks of the *Worker* to our house so that Mother could take them to comrades who did not want their names on a subscriber's list. "Little Clara," my mother called her, to distinguish her from Clara Licht, who was also elderly but very tall and lived on Eastern Parkway.

The next year Judith organized a community Seder for more than a hundred women at our town's community center. Using the Jewish liberation from Egyptian slavery as a centerpiece, Judith's Seder celebrated all peoples' struggles for freedom in stories, poems, and songs. This event was a marvel to me. The few family Seders I had attended in childhood were riddled with strife and political dissension. Here, the Jewish heritage became an occasion for unity and a celebration of freedom. When I learned that Judith's parents were Holocaust survivors, I better understood the profound ways that Judith was healing herself, and that healing extended to so many of us. In later years Kate and I replicated Judith's idea, holding Seders in our home. Moving all of the furniture out of our living room and renting long tables, we could seat upwards of twenty people. We didn't know all of the prayers and songs, but we had a Haggadah from a women's group in San Diego that helped us to sustain the feelings of freedom and renewal.

When my father's oldest sister died, I attended her funeral. Minna Artson had lived in San Francisco for more than twenty-five years, having moved from Brooklyn in the early 1960s to be nearer to her children and grandchildren. A tall woman with reddish blond hair that she dyed and styled regularly, she looked remarkably like her mother in the photographs I had seen of my grandmother. I had not known Minna well, but I felt good about supporting her family in their loss. I drove my parents to the funeral. It was held at Temple Emanu-El, where Minna had been an active congregant and president of Hadassah, the women's Zionist organization.

After the funeral my cousin drove my parents home to San Jose and I drove myself home to Pacific Grove, taking Highway 1 along the coast. As I crested a hill I was treated to a spectacular view of the ocean and waves gently lapping a beach. I thought about Minna's life, and then about each of our lives as a grain of sand, minuscule in the overall scheme of the universe, alive for only a fraction of a second in geologic time. In that moment it seemed to me ridiculous that the only time I was in a synagogue was to attend a funeral or, very rarely, a wedding. I resolved to locate a synagogue in Monterey and attend services. I knew almost nothing about Jewish ritual, except that services began on Friday night and continued on Saturday morning, the Jewish Sabbath. When I looked up "Synagogue" in the yellow pages, the telephone directory referred me to "Churches." Under "Churches" I found a listing for Congregation Beth Israel. I telephoned and secured the time for the services that weekend. I went at ten o'clock on Saturday morning. The temple building turned out to be an old elementary school that was no longer in use. The congregation leased it from the city and had converted one room into a sanctuary. Former classrooms served as offices.

The rabbi was out of town that day, and an elderly white-haired man of solid build and resonant voice named Joseph Vessel conducted the services in English and Hebrew. I followed the prayers as best I could and was surprised at how familiar the Hebrew sounded to me, and how I felt almost that I knew the music. Joseph gave a brief sermon in which he talked about how grateful he was to the family who had sponsored his immigration to the United States from Yugoslavia at the end of World War II. He was a Holocaust survivor. Six electric candles—one for each million Jews killed in Europe—burned continuously on the wall of the schoolhouse-temple, eternal flames of remembrance.

I began attending services regularly, and when *Kaddish* was read at the end, I stood to honor Aunt Minna. The rabbi, Mark Gross, it turned out, was a civil rights activist from the 1960s, and he and many in the congregation extended a warm welcome to me. I attended Yom Ha-Shoah services that spring, commemorating the Holocaust, and sat in the back of the sanctuary weeping. I joined the temple and began studying Hebrew with Rabbi Mark so that I could at least read the liturgy.

Kate was a little startled by the fervor with which I embraced Judaism and teased me, saying that I was in my "nationalist phase." It felt like a wondrous new world had opened before me, and yet it was also oddly familiar, as though it were in my bones. When Rabbi Mark sang the prayers with his beautiful tenor voice, it felt as though my whole body dissolved and my mind soared to the rafters of the old schoolhouse. Kate attended high holy day services with me for Rosh Hashanah and Yom Kippur. She brought a more critical eye to my glossy film, pointing out, for example, the obvious sexism in the prayers. From her extensive knowledge of Judeo-Christian liturgy learned in childhood, she taught me Jewish history alert to a more feminist reading.

Meanwhile, I studiously hid the fact that I was going to temple from my parents. I knew that my mother was too embittered to listen to anything I might say to assuage her feelings, and I thought that my father, while less venomous, was of a generally like mind about any kind of religious practice. However, one day when my parents were visiting us in Pacific Grove the truth came out because my father spotted my Hebrew grammar book on our bookshelf. "Who's studying Hebrew?" he asked in surprise.

"I am," I said. And to my utter astonishment my father began to speak in Hebrew, the prayers he had learned in childhood, which I recognized from the services I was attending.

"We studied very hard," he said. "I was bar mitzvahed with the rabbi's son, on the same day, and it was a big deal." I was speechless. "That's very good," he continued. "When I die you can say Kaddish for me." A few years later I learned from my cousin Sunny, Minna's daughter, that our grandfather Benjamin had been the principal founder of one of the oldest synagogues in Brooklyn.

Lisa graduated from Monterey High School in June 1983, and two years later Josh graduated from Pacific Grove High School. We experienced remarkably easy teenage years. Kate ran a tight ship, and we were both emotionally available to them. Each did very well academically, and both went out for sports. When Lisa graduated from high school, Kate and I threw her a huge party at our home. I suggested that it was easier to handle complicated family relationships in a crowd. I called Kate "Big Mama" for the day. Lisa had taken to calling me "Mama B." We rented tables and dozens of chairs and set them up on our front lawn. We served piles of food, and champagne, but no other alcohol. Kate circulated with it, one bottle at a time. Russ, Lisa's dad, came from Utah, my first time meeting him. He was skinny with an angular jaw and an easy drawl, dressed in Levi's and boots. He drove a beat-up Ford pickup all the way from southern Utah using only back roads. He said freeways and interstate highways were built for the semi trucks, which he occasionally drove to earn a living.

Lisa's grandma, Ann, Russ's mother, also came, along with Art and Millie, of course, and my parents. Kate invited a former male lover whom she hadn't seen in years but to whom Lisa had been attached, and old friends from her years in Utah, Los Angeles, and San Jose, some of whom I was meeting for the first time. I invited Jack. And into this mix of grandparents, ex-husbands, and former lovers came our lesbian friends, effortlessly gliding through the crowd while our children charmed and the grandmamas beamed.

When Joshua graduated two years later, in June 1985, we repeated the offering. Russ returned from Utah. Jack, of course, could hardly contain the pride he felt for his son. Rose and Sam flew in from New York, and my parents came, along with a large contingent of my cousins who lived in the San Francisco Bay Area. Some of the old party crowd showed up, including Evelyn and Max, and Dobby Walker, the attorney who had seen Jack and me through the divorce. Our lesbian contingent did a second shift. I wore black pants, a magenta silk blouse, and a black tie. Josh had to fix the tie for me. Kate and I strolled across the high school football field toward the bleachers for the graduation ceremony with our arms linked, Kate in a long flowered dress. A friend took a photo of us at that moment. As it happened, my parents were also caught in the frame. "The couples," Kate chortled when she saw the picture.

The couples, I thought, amazed. I had transformed my life.

six

AN OPENING OF THE HEART

KATE AND I went camping at Florence Lake for the first time in 1981. It is in the High Sierra, the smallest of a series of lakes created by man-made dams, south of Yosemite. Fresno is the nearest large city. Kate had been introduced to the lake the previous summer by her best friend, Barbara, the woman who had occasioned our meeting at the Holly Near concert a year and a half before. Kate said I would love it. I was a reluctant camper. Anxiously, I questioned her about this place, how we would get there, and how we would cross the lake to get to our camp. She drew me a map using black ink on a small piece of white paper to show me the lake, the boat landing, and our destination, marking it with a little X. "It's nothing." she said, "and you'll love it. It's so beautiful." I was still doubtful. Kate packed food and books, and borrowed a tent and camping equipment while I labored excessively over writing the narrative evaluations required for each of my students. Exasperated, Kate finally insisted that I help her pack.

The day of our departure arrived. I had hardly slept; I was both apprehensive and excited. We had loaded Kate's 1971 blue Datsun station wagon the night before, and we left Pacific Grove at three in the morning. Kate explained that it was a nine-hour drive to Florence Lake and we would need to arrive early enough to cross the lake and set up our camp before dark.

We breakfasted with the early-rising farmers at a diner in Los Baños. They were wearing denims and work boots like uniforms, faded bandanas hanging from back pockets, wide-brimmed hats on the counter beside them, chugging coffee and smoking, hunched over eggs and steak. As we resumed our journey, dawn broke over the central valley and my spirits lifted. We continued on into the foothills of the Sierra Nevada Mountains, the hills spread golden before us. As we ascended the mountain the smell of pitch from the pine trees filled the air and the first of the three lakes, of which Florence was the highest, came into view.

Shaver Lake was huge. Small pleasure boats were moored at one end and resorts, cabins, and boathouses ringed its shores. It was still early and few people were up; the blue water shimmered in the morning sunlight, reflecting mirror images of the shoreline. I thrilled to the sight and began babbling gratitude to Kate. After we passed Huntington Lake, Kate explained that our next twenty miles would be along a narrow switchback road that would climb to over nine thousand feet at Kaiser Pass and then drop a thousand feet to Florence Lake. This road, built in the 1930s, had been used for mule packs during the construction of the dam at Florence. It was paved now, but it was only one lane.

Kate drove, pulling over with judicious alacrity to allow approaching motorists the right of way. Granite cliffs rose off one side of the road; off the other was a sheer drop thousands of feet to the valley below. Every time a car or truck approached, which thank goodness was not very often, my foot automatically slammed on my nonexistent brakes while Kate calmly pulled over. "You have nerves of steel," I announced.

Snowcapped peaks came into view and vanished again as we climbed and curved. At Kaiser Pass it was very cold and snow was still evident along the sides of the road and in the rocky cliffs. We were now near the tree line, and alpine meadows spread around us, deeply green and soggy. Although still given to nervous spasms, I was completely swept up in the beauty of the mountains.

We arrived in Florence at about noon and made arrangements to rent a small motorboat. We were to motor across the lake with all our gear and leave the boat moored on a beach, where the store manager would retrieve it the following morning. We could rent a boat for the return trip as well. Meanwhile, Kate explained, there was a trail above our campsite; we could hike out to the store anytime we wished. It was about three miles, she said, along an easy, well-marked trail. Oh yes, and the nearest telephone, we learned at the store in response to my inquiries, was twenty miles away at Huntington Lake.

We drove down to the boat landing to unload our gear and then back up to a makeshift dirt parking lot, where we left the Datsun. We walked back to the boat and loaded it up. Neither of us had ever piloted a motorboat before, so the store manager gave us a three-minute lesson. A muscled, short, olive-skinned fellow with curly black hair, he was highly amused at our ignorance, but he kept a straight face and remained solicitous. Piloting an outboard motor was as routine for him as driving a car. He said as much while each of us grasped what we could of the boating lesson. Kate sat at the rear to pilot. I sat in front facing her, apparently, she instructed, to guide us. Kate pulled the choke out rapidly, as he had shown, and the engine coughed to life. *Slow and easy,* we thought. *Piece of cake.*

Kate knew our landing site; our problem was a directional one. I would shout to Kate, "Right! Right! Turn right!" meaning to turn the rudder to her right. But she was facing me and dyslexic, so she turned to my right, which was her left, and I would frantically shout above the clatter of the engine. She would slow down to figure out what she was supposed to do, and stall the engine. Then we would drift toward the dam, pulled by an inexorable current. Panicked that we would soon find ourselves at the dam and over it (which upon later and careful inspection we realized was impossible), Kate pulled the choke and fired the engine, shooting us forward and away from that fateful plunge. In this manner, and with as much dignity as we could muster for any passing boat enthusiasts, we made our way to our destination, the little X on Kate's map.

Kate and I began a tradition in the summer of 1981 that would last for twelve years. It marked the beginning of a time during which I became much more attuned to the rhythms of the earth and my place on the planet; it marked the beginning of my spiritual growth. That first year we stayed at Florence Lake for only ten days; in the succeeding twelve years we returned every summer, leaving as early in June as we could and staying for progressively longer periods of time. As the years passed, this annual summer trip marked for us the importance of time away from our academic lives and commitments, a time when we could renew ourselves in the silent vastness and beauty of the mountains. We also had just plain fun, and startling encounters with coyotes, bears, a bobcat, and a resident yellowbelly marmot.

Kate and I did, in fact, become seasoned campers, handling torrential rains and the unexpected late spring snowfalls. Kate woke one June morning, for example, and said, "What's all this funny white stuff on the ground?" I said, "It looks like snow, honey." Hailing from North Dakota, Kate found snow in California in June to be too much of an anomaly. We learned to store our food in a separate tent away from where we slept, since there were frequent bear sightings.

We learned a new (for us) technology of cooking with wood on an open fire. We discovered that different woods, like manzanita, cedar, and pine, burn at different rates and temperatures, so we could determine which would be best to use for what we were cooking. Eventually, Kate hauled enough rocks to our site to build a beautiful small ovenlike fire pit where we did all of our cooking. She got the idea for it after seeing a film about the Hopi called *Songs of the Fourth World,* in which the women use small wood-burning stoves to cook a special, very thin bread called *piki,* made from blue corn. Kate thought the fire pit would help us conserve wood. We also learned from rueful experience to gather dry wood immediately upon arriving and *before* it stormed.

We hauled water up from the lake and boiled it for drinking. We learned to make tortillas and the Indian flat bread called *naan,* and one summer, experimenting with a lidded pan, I figured out how to bake bread using Bisquick. Of course we made pancakes, and I experimented with making jams from dried fruits. Cooking became a wonderful challenge as I figured out wood temperatures, the available ingredients, and what I could substitute for what.

Having lived in cities all of my life, I was amazed to see how very distinct wilderness landmarks can be, and I came to recognize a particular rock marking a path or a tree marking a turn. I soon felt like I knew every rock and tree and bush in a radius extending out from our camp. About a quarter mile south from us, for example, there was an aspen grove, a deciduous oasis among the pines and cedars. The aspen leaves rustled in the breeze and shimmered in the sunlight like silver coins.

Every year at Florence brought new experiences, taught us new lessons. One year there was an earthquake. We were awakened by its roar at about seven in the morning. It sounded like a train speeding through a tunnel. Then we felt the earth start to quiver. Still in our sleeping bags, lying on the ground, we felt the earth roll under us in successive waves, first in one direction, and then a few minutes later, it rolled back again the other way. Our tent poles rattled. About an hour later we heard a tree crash. For hours afterward, the birds, chipmunks, and squirrels hid away, silent. We learned later that the epicenter was near the town of Bishop, about forty miles east of us (as the crow flies), and that the quake was 7.1 on the Richter scale. Because there was only sparse population, nobody was hurt and there was little damage.

The night sky at Florence was unlike anything either of us could remember seeing. On a clear and moonless night, without the interfering lights from a city, the sky was a breathtaking panorama of stars, the Milky Way a mammoth stream of light. We would sit by our campfire for hours, heads tilted skyward. Sometimes we laid our sleeping bags out on the rocks and fell asleep watching the night sky. "Look!" one of us would call out. "A shooting star!" "And another!" "And another!" We tried to remember the names of the few constellations we knew. Dwarfed by the universe, we were as two dots on a rock in a mountain by a lake.

Florence took on a persona for us. We'd say, "When we're at Florence . . ." or "I can't wait to see Florence . . ." or "I wonder if Florence will be full this year," which depended, of course, on the snowfall of the previous winter. The level of the lake affected the ease with which we could get to our campsite, and how long we could stay.

The summer of 1982 was Kate's third year at Florence and my second. Already the place was changing us, and that summer marked a turning point. Kate began a meditation practice, and I read Alice Walker's novel *The Color Purple*. Slowly, inexorably, we were being pulled from the orbit of our culture, establishing priorities and making decisions that many in our families and among our friends and colleagues could not understand. For example, I declined invitations to speak at scholarly conferences in women's studies typically held in June because we wanted to get to the mountains as soon as we could. The land had begun to heal me, providing me with a space to read and write, to sit quietly, and to feel a connection to the earth I had not thought possible, or even understood.

In January of that year one of Kate's closest friends, Polly Parker, the owner of the Open Book bookstore in Pacific Grove, had been diagnosed with lung cancer. She was in her mid-fifties. I remember being at her home with Kate shortly before the diagnosis was confirmed. Polly was standing in her living room with her hands stuffed into the back pockets of her jeans, her face a gray pallor, saying, "I guess it's really serious." By April the cancer had spread to the brain, and early in June she died. Polly had been a dear friend of ours and a guiding light of the women's community on the Monterey Peninsula. She was warm, bright, and fun-loving, with a fantastic imagination, and we felt a great loss at her death.

Polly had been in hospice only a short while when early one morning Kate woke up suddenly. She knew Polly's death was imminent. She dressed quickly and drove to the hospice facility. She arrived just as Polly was taking her last breaths. Kate told me that even after Polly's last exhalation her spirit lingered in the room, a palpable presence, something that Kate had never experienced before. She felt in Polly's lingering presence a parting gift from her. She felt there was a spiritual dimension, another level of reality that our minds could touch apart from the corporeal one in which we lived.

Kate had been searching for months for a way to give focus and greater meaning to her life. She loved the teaching that she did at both the community college and Antioch, but it was not enough. Sitting in a café one afternoon over a cup of tea, and before Polly's death, Kate said to me, "Maybe I should become a cellist."

"Or," I said, "study physics," which reflected my fascination with its more philosophical dimensions.

"Yeah," she looked at me with a faraway expression, "or an obscure language."

What made sense to Kate after Polly's death, and in the many moments of peace and deep introspection in Florence, was to begin a spiritual practice. She turned to the Buddhist tradition because it offered what she thought was the best guidance for meditation. She brought *Zen Mind, Beginner's Mind,* by the Japanese Zen master Suzuki Roshi, to Florence with her that summer. When I saw the author's photograph on the back cover of the book, I pretty much went berserk. I had left the Communist Party only a year before, and without that political mooring I had known all my life, I felt myself buffeted on the high seas. Kate was discovering a new mooring, and I panicked at the spiritual sighting. Where was she going?

Communist rhetoric about New Age, nonproductive "drug seekers" and "parasites" living off the labors of the working class, who couldn't afford the luxury of "time off" to "find themselves," was about the sum total of my spiritual knowledge. The party supported Native American rights, but gave indigenous struggles scant attention and had absolutely no concept of spirituality as a way of life, much less as central to Native American culture. In the nine months since I had resigned from the party, I had been searching for a space in which to exist politically, one where I did not become hostile to the Communist Party, the "renegade" of my father's venom. I was still a revolutionary, a good person. I had left a corrupt party. This is what I told myself. Still, images of Max and my father danced in my mind, while venomous snakes, fangs bared, chased me across ferned forests steaming in mist in my dreams. I shivered and sweated and whimpered, and Kate put her arms around me, told me lots of people had dreams about snakes, and explained that we internalize self-hatred and it comes out in our dreams. I *was* a good person, she said. I was making a huge transition in my life, undoing old structures with great rapidity, doing those things that had once seemed forbidden.

The first years at Florence I was overwhelmed with guilt. I didn't deserve so much time off. I didn't deserve such happiness. I should call my parents; I should call my father on his birthday at the end of July. This meant hiking out to the store and driving twenty miles down Florence Lake Road. I never did go out and call, but I worried about it, felt bad about not doing it, gnawed at myself.

So I looked at Suzuki Roshi's picture and I yelled at Kate about spiritual "crap" and "dead ends" that didn't lead to any kind of social change. I don't know how much Kate understood about my emotional state and the source of my panic in that moment, but she stayed patient and never once raised her voice in anger.

"I am not you," she said. "And you are not me." I didn't know what the hell she was talking about. I didn't understand anything about boundaries yet. I didn't even know there was such a thing or why it might be a problem. I had no understanding of why I had merged with my father, or even that I had. Now that I had broken from the party and was breaking from him, I needed another person with whom to merge, but I could not have begun to explain that in 1982. I didn't even know merging was a process. A few years later I developed a more sophisticated understanding of how intimate couples can confuse their boundaries and one part of a couple can lose herself in the other.

While Kate studied Suzuki Roshi I picked up Alice Walker's newly published novel, *The Color Purple*. I loved Walker's work, all of her poems and especially an essay she'd written in the mid-1970s called "In Search of Our Mothers' Gardens." I began the novel in the evening even though Kate, who had already read it, warned me that I shouldn't because its first pages were so hard. She was right. "Dear God," Celie wrote. Incest. Rape, Mr. _____. I stopped reading. Went to bed. Awoke the next morning and sat on a rock overlooking the lake and read it straight through.

In the sweltering heat and poverty and racism of the rural South we find Celie, a girl of perhaps twelve or thirteen, repeatedly raped by her stepfather. She bears two children. She is just a child herself, and the infants are taken away from her at birth. I got to the moment when Shug Avery kisses a grown Celie, when it was clear they were going to be lovers, and I started to cry. I cried all the way through to the end. Love, unconditional, all-encompassing love, was the surefire healer. That Shug—that sassy, brazen, sexually outrageous, dancing, clucked-about, and cast-out woman—should be the instrument of Celie's healing is as brilliant a casting as one is apt to find in any work. Here was Christian love turned on its head, the acts of the fathers truly named and reckoned, and above all, women cherished.

I finished the book and sat in a trance, eyes looking out over the lake. I was brought to attention by the tree directly in front of me, a young, scrawny-looking pine pushing its way up through the granite. As I looked at it, a thought suddenly came to me, unbidden: *You don't have to produce.* I stared at the tree and the thought came again. *You don't have to drive yourself to produce.* The moment held, and then it was gone. And it changed everything.

I was so excited. I staggered to my feet, raced down off the rock to find Kate. "I don't have to produce!" I shouted.

"Yes," she said, a little startled by my exuberance. "Yes, that's true, darling."

I had never felt more sane or more whole. This realization was an awakening, an opening of the heart born out of love for Kate, for the wonders of the magical place where we were camped, for the vista of the new life I was making.

I didn't have to produce. I didn't have to be driven the way my father was. I didn't have to write a book a year. I didn't have to be famous. I didn't have to publish and attend conferences and give scholarly papers for the sake of getting tenure. I didn't have to get tenure at the university. I could just teach and write about what I wanted, when I wanted, because I loved teaching, and I loved writing, and I could just be myself. By the end of the summer I saw, too, that I didn't have to be so afraid of Suzuki Roshi, or of Kate's spiritual path.

Kate began her meditation practice that summer, perched on a makeshift cushion on a granite slab out of which grew an old cedar. It was a beautiful, rugged, weathered tree, split in half at its top by lightning. Facing the mountains to the east, with a view of the lake, she sat in a half-lotus position at the base of the cedar. She followed her breath and watched her mind, following basic Zen instructions.

When we returned to Pacific Grove that August in time for Kate to begin her classes at the community college, she decided she needed to find a place where she could learn more about Buddhist practice. She looked up "Buddhist Churches" in the yellow pages and found a listing for a Sambosa Korean Buddhist Temple, called Sambosa, just off Carmel Valley Road. Kate telephoned and was told that they had prayers and meditation at six every morning and she was welcome; there was no charge. I was in awe of how Kate just decided on something like this, so radically different from anything either of us had known, and I could hardly wait for a report about what Sambosa was like.

The first morning, Kate left our house at five. She had no idea what to expect. When she got home, she reported that there were three people at the temple besides herself. There was a monk, Soen Sunim, Abbott Lee, and a younger man whom she did not personally meet. They chanted and prayed and performed full-body prostrations to the Buddha in rhythm with the chanting and the beating of a magnificent old gong. And then they sat in silent meditation for thirty minutes. Having no idea how many prostrations were to be done, Kate said, she began them and just kept going. There were 108! When she tried to stand up after the meditation her legs gave way under her; it was quite some time before she wobbled upright. She said that Abbott Lee watched her discreetly to be sure that she was all right, a small smile playing on his lips.

That academic year Kate went to Sambosa almost every morning. Eventually, of course, I went with her. I wanted to see what it was like. I loved the feeling of the predawn, the coolness of the air, the crow of the rooster that lived on land adjoining Sambosa. Carmel Valley Road extends east from the coastal town of Carmel into a green, lusciously fertile valley, with mountains of the Los Padres National Forest rising on its southern flank. The Carmel River cuts the valley as it continues its ancient path to the sea. The valley is a well-populated countryside with expansive private homes in the hills, and expensive restaurants and resorts off its main road. Sambosa was on Robinson Canyon Road, only a short distance from the intersection with Carmel Valley Road. We parked and walked toward the temple. To our right we saw a series of smaller buildings, which, we learned, were for housing visitors. On our left was a very large old cast-iron bell, which had been brought from Korea at enormous expense.

We climbed a few steps to the temple entrance. The temple itself was one very large room with a sliding glass door, polished wood floors, and an elaborate altar directly in front of us, spreading almost the full width of the room. There was a large enthroned golden Buddha, and two smaller statues of bodhisattvas—beings of great compassion—on either side of him. Colorful, finely woven silk cloths in bright reds and yellows covered the altar, which was laden with offering bowls of fruit and rice and water. Brilliantly colored fresh flowers completed the arrangement. To our left was an enormous cast-iron gong suspended within a sturdy frame with elaborately carved inlay. I had never seen a room such as this, and felt overwhelmed by its beauty and the loving care with which it was attended. Then I noticed a loft running on three sides of the temple's interior, stacked with boxes and cloths and meditation cushions. I was alarmed to see repeated images of the swastika. I motioned toward them and whispered inquiries to Kate. A very ancient symbol in India, she whispered back, which the Nazis appropriated and reversed. *That's right,* I thought, remembering a Rudyard Kipling book I'd read in childhood that had the symbol running the margins of each page. Asia has its own history, much older than and quite apart from Europe's.

That first morning I went to Sambosa, I sat on a meditation cushion in a half-lotus and listened to the prayers and the chants as they were sung in Chinese, knowing how very old they were and understanding nothing. The men's voices undulated, with hardly a pause for breath. Having been forewarned, I did only a few of the prostrations, and then sat down again on my cushion. Formal meditation began. I closed my eyes. Almost at once I was flooded with a clear, blazing, incandescent light. I'd never seen anything like it. I opened my eyes, thinking that the sun must have risen. But the sky had the purple-gray cast of dawn. I closed my eyes again and the light returned. For thirty minutes I was in a state of sheer joy, and when the bell sounded at the end of it I felt as though only an instant had passed. I didn't want to come back into the world. Kate touched me lightly on the shoulder; I opened my eyes and looked up at her, smiling.

After a couple of weeks, with Kate showing up every day, Soen Sunim, the monk she had met on her first morning at the temple, invited her to stay after the service and have breakfast with him. Over breakfast Soen began to teach Kate the rudiments of Buddhist practice. He also asked for Kate's assistance on a major project. Soen was translating the *Surangama Sutra* from Chinese to English. He would give Kate a few pages at a time, asking her to improve the fluency of the English. She came home with these pages of sutra, studied Soen's translations, edited them, and returned them to him for further work. She then retyped the corrected sections that he returned to her. "Sutra" refers to those texts recorded directly from the Buddha's oral teachings. In this way Soen introduced Kate to Buddhist practice. He did this with the firm belief that the female was inferior to the male, and that in assisting Kate he would help her to be reborn as a man and have a better chance for enlightenment in her next life! Meanwhile, Kate repeatedly edited out the sexist language in the sutra and changed all of the male pronouns. Soen, of course, persistently reinserted them. Through the many months of this "war" of pronouns, Soen sent Kate home with armloads of kale and Swiss chard from his garden in exchange for her labors. No doubt Soen won out, since it was his translation.

What I noticed about this project was how relaxed Soen was about it. When I worked I was always in a state of high tension, frantic to "get it out," a trademark of my father's drive. His was the only model I'd ever had. Soen worked methodically, little by little, a few pages at a time, carefully. He seemed to enjoy the work, and gradually the project grew, word by word, page by page. I was so impressed with this way of working because it was infinitely saner.

One of my breakfasts with Soen happened to take place after a particularly horrific incident in the Cold War between the United States and the Soviet Union, when a Soviet missile shot down a Korean Air passenger jet, Flight 007, September 1, 1983, sending fragments of plane and bodies plummeting into the Sea of Japan. There were no survivors. Soviet military spokesmen justified the decision to attack on grounds that the plane was flying over "highly sensitive" military sites on Soviet soil, having "strayed" from its approved flight plan. The Soviets claimed that repeated calls to the pilot failed to elicit a response. Whatever the truth of the matter, I felt that there could be absolutely no justification for the murder of the 269 men, women, and children aboard that flight. I was furious, too, as one more peg in my socialist construct was ripped out. Given my Communist history, and the fact that this was a Korean flight, I was embarrassed to sit next to Soen under his tree, on his small wooden platform, and drink his tea. I was out of the party, but an umbilical cord holds a strong pull.

On my next visit with my parents I violated our unspoken rule not to talk about politics. The tragedy of Flight 007 haunted me. My parents supported the Soviet military's action in bringing down the plane. My mother said the Soviet military would not have shot down the plane unless they had had to protect a vital military installation. I could not believe my parents would sanction such an act, that they could justify it. We had a huge argument. My father waved articles from the *Nation* and *The New York Times* showing "conclusively," he shouted, that Flight 007 was on a spying mission. I said I didn't care what it was doing, you don't commit mass murder. To which my parents responded that it was "impossible" to talk to me because I had become, in my mother's words, a "fanatical pacifist"! I was so angry I was beyond any capacity for speech. My whole body shook.

Soen, of course, had no idea who I was, or anything about my Communist past, and this lie by omission felt intolerable to me on that particular morning. So I told him. He had nothing but compassion for me. After all, he said, that was the family into which I had been born. Then he started talking about the Communists in Korea, speaking from personal experience. Flight 007 was just one more atrocity in a long history of unspeakable crimes, Soen said. He was becoming more and more agitated as he spoke. And then I saw him do an amazing thing. He stopped himself mid-sentence. He sat very still and closed his eyes. I watched as he deliberately, consciously shifted his mental state.

When Soen reopened his eyes he was no longer angry. I had never seen anyone let go of his anger like this before. He just let it go. It was as though he had vacuumed his mind. His anger was not useful, he explained to me when I asked what he had done to release it. It produced only suffering for him. There was nothing he could do directly to stop the suffering of those grieving for their loved ones on that flight, or for the atrocities already committed. What he could do was not add to the anger that fed the violence within him; he could practice peace.

I wanted to know how he had let go of his anger, especially now when I knew my own capacity for rage. I was still fearful about this new journey upon which Kate had embarked, but I was curious. I knew then from my experiences in meditation, from conversations with Soen, and from Kate's earnest exhilaration that there was some magic or mystery yet to be known. As Kate raced into her new interests I trotted along beside her, or just behind her, a little breathless, trying to keep up.

The most accessible text Kate found on Buddhist practice from my point of view was by Kathleen McDonald, and it had the very straightforward title *How to Meditate*. This I could understand, and in the summer of 1983 at Florence Lake I sat every day on the rock shelf next to my thin, scrawny pine. Now I had a truer experience of meditation practice because the light came only occasionally. More likely my mind would sink and I would start to fall asleep, or it would scatter with a dozen thoughts a second, boomeranging off the rocks around me. What I saw, though, through this experience, was that thoughts just came and went. If I "saw" my thoughts as though they were floating along a stream, I could just watch them as they floated by. The trick, I realized, was not to get snagged by a thought and drift along with it unawares for ten minutes. If you got snagged you brought your mind gently back to the breath and let the thought go, and if it cycled back you did the same thing again; you always came back to the breath. With repeated effort the mind

could grow quite still. It was amazing. When my mind was still I
became more relaxed than I had ever thought possible. When my
meditation was over, my mind often felt very sharp and clear. For
a while each day my usual mental clutter was cleared away; by
focusing on each moment I was precise and efficient. Of course, it
didn't last.

Meanwhile, over the next months and years Kate assembled
her own eclectic combination of prayers, drawn largely from the
Tibetan tradition, but from many other lineages as well, all mixed up
together. Most were in English. A few were in Sanskrit or in Tibetan.
She used Kathleen McDonald's helpful guide to order the saying of
the prayers. If a prayer sounded "right" to Kate, she incorporated it
into her liturgy. She began to memorize them, one after another, bit
by bit.

The purpose of prayer, McDonald explained, was to remind
yourself of all the elements of compassion and wisdom in your
practice. The prayers helped you to set up your meditation, freeing
the mind from all the junk and chatter that accumulated in a day,
the small hurts and jealousies, the numerous, sometimes disturbing
encounters, and the concerns about work, money, and relationships.
All that could be put aside. This in turn helped you to set up your
day, reminding you to be generous and loving, open and supportive
and peaceful, "to be of benefit to all living beings."

Kate assembled prayers, and at Florence she and I sat under her
cedar tree every morning and said them. And when we returned home
we continued doing them. We woke up at four in the morning, drank
cups of tea, and visited with each other. Then we sat for an hour doing
our prayers and meditation as the sun rose and a new day began.

Kate's assemblage of prayers included this one from the Chinese
Zen tradition:

Green fog, red clouds
Miles of bamboo
To a place where quiet lasts
Just let go and worries end
Stop to think and they're back
An unpolished mirror holds millions of images
A bell doesn't ring until it's rung

Your real nature is the true Buddha
Not form or space
Nothing Old or New.

From the seventh Dalai Lama came this first stanza of a much longer poem that we recited in full:

An image of a sun enthroned in the heavens,
Radiating one thousand beams of light:
Were one to shower bright rays of love upon all beings
How excellent.

From Shantideva's *Bodhisattva Way of Life:*

In the spiritual energy that relieves
The anguish of beings in misery and
Places depressed beings in eternal joy
I lift up my heart and rejoice!

In the goodness producing illumination
I lift up my heart and rejoice!

From Tibet came this prayer, which incorporates the Buddha's Four Immeasurable Thoughts about suffering and how to end it:

May all living beings have happiness and the causes of happiness

May all living beings be freed from suffering and the causes
of suffering
May all living beings never be separated from the happiness
which knows no suffering
May all living beings dwell in equanimity
Free from attachment and aversion which
Holds some close and others distant.

From the Tibetan sage Tilopa came "Song to Naropa," one of his
disciples:

As space is always freshly appearing
and never filled,
so the mind is without limits
and ever aware.
Gazing with sheer awareness
into sheer awareness,
habitual, abstract structures melt
into the fruitful springtime of Buddhahood.

And later in the same song:

Transcend boundaries of kinship
by embracing all living beings
as one family of consciousness.

I loved, absolutely loved, the prayers. I loved saying them; I
loved how they made me feel, all open and warm and content. They
filled me with hope. Eventually Kate and I came to understand that
"enlightenment" was not an event, it was not a moment when you
dropped into clear light and stayed there. Rather, it was an ongoing
process toward greater clarity, increasing calm, and an internal sense
of utter well-being. How different this was from the chaos of my
twenties and early thirties.

Even as her practice grew and became the focal point of her life, Kate was always clear about one thing. "Although I am so grateful to my teachers, I am not a Buddhist," she would say. When she first told me this I was completely surprised. "But . . ." I started to object, thinking about her altar and her *mala* (the Buddhist equivalent of a rosary) and her beautiful bronze statue of Tara, the Tibetan goddess of compassion, believed to be the mother of all the Buddhas. She explained. The Buddhists, with their sects and lineages and monasteries, were riddled with sexism; men had overriding privileges and such a deep sense of entitlement they didn't even notice it. She also observed that the Buddhist institutions and lineages were often the sites of terrible power struggles and rivalries, even violence. "There's lots of money involved," she explained to me, "and power." Kate didn't want to get caught up in any of that, so she separated her practice of the Dharma from its institutions. There was a way in which this was a great source of relief to me. After my Communist Party experiences, I was afraid of formal affiliation anywhere. With Kate's sensible approach she steered us away from institutional commitments. We sought and appreciated the gifts of many teachers, but aligned ourselves with none.

It was of the most astonishing benefit to me that I should have fallen in love with a woman such as Kate. Of course, I didn't always know it was a benefit, and I fussed a good deal along the way. The unconventionality of our lifestyle sometimes made me insecure, and I fell back into worrying what everyone thought. I mean, wasn't it a little crazy to camp at the top of a mountain for six or seven weeks every summer? Being a lesbian was surely enough of an outside curve. I had periodic bouts of my old paranoia. Then I worried that Kate was going to leave me in order to enter a convent. This because I took literally the Buddha's instruction "to leave home" and to renounce worldly concerns. It was a while before I turned a feminist lens on leaving home and realized it was mostly the men who got to do it, leaving their wives and children. Later, too, I came to understand that the renunciation of worldly concerns was a mental attitude about the self, not a renunciation of the world's suffering. Then, in a related way, I worried a lot about how to reconcile my political activism and commitments with what I perceived then to be the Buddhist "indifference" to the state of the world. It was a profound misunderstanding, but I didn't know it at the time.

One Saturday as Kate and I were leaving Sambosa I said in amazement, "I used to spend my Saturdays at district committee meetings of the Communist Party." And she said, "This is not so different." I thought about that reply for a long time. It was the first sense I had that a meditation practice and political concerns might be related to each other. It also gave me a glimmer of the idea that I could find my own path, one that would help me to satisfy all the parts of myself.

Meanwhile, my experiences at Florence Lake were transforming my life. Whenever I thought of Florence my heart surged with happiness. It's hard to explain this, because living outside in a tent for weeks—going without indoor plumbing, cooking over a wood fire, dealing with flies and mosquitoes, rain and snow, sleeping on the ground—doesn't sound like fun. It was certainly uncomfortable, and yet it was glorious.

The majesty of the mountains, the night sky, the solitude (oh, how I craved the aloneness, freed from roles and expectations), the intimate connections with what the Lakota people call "all our relations" among the trees, the rocks, the birds, the animals—all these were wondrous things. I'd never really watched animals and birds before. Now I would sit absolutely still and study the tree squirrel with its brown belly and black button eyes and twitching nose, industriously storing its winter food supply. Occasionally it would stand on its hindquarters and carefully hold a delicate stalk of wheatlike grass in its paws, chewing hastily. All the while, its eyes and ears were alert for predators. I noticed that it never ate the whole stalk; it left enough so it could grow back. Then I saw that the deer did the same thing. Once, a hawk swooped out of the sky and seized a chipmunk in its talons. The hawk was airborne again in seconds, and the dying chipmunk issued a pathetic squeak as its life ebbed in the hawk's grip.

Sitting on a rock under a waterfall. Filling a bucket with water and dumping it over my head, the water so cold that it burned and my ears hummed. Eyes feasting on a carpet of tiny, delicate purple flowers. Coming upon a deer, both of us frozen in the sighting. Sinking to the ground ever so slowly so as not to frighten. Clicking my tongue to make a sound like a raven's mating call in response to his, waiting in the silence for the returning *click-click.* Nothing. Laughing because the raven knows it's me. Listening to the sound of wind as it surfs the pines and cedars.

My heart opened at Florence. It was a physical thing, a weight lifted. Like a morning glory opening to the light.

Having received my doctorate in 1983, I was now free to write without the academic constraints usually imposed by doctoral committees. I wanted to write in a way that made my work accessible to my undergraduate students, to their mothers, grandmothers, aunts, and neighbors. I wanted to write my next book for women, to see how much strength we had, how intelligent we were, how much we knew from our experiences, how well we could nurture, how we sustained life. I was infused with the spirit of the women's movement of the 1970s and '80s, and drenched in the novels and poetry, art and music that poured from it.

It took me four years to complete what would become *Tapestries of Life: Women's Work, Women's Consciousness, and the Meaning of Daily Experience.* Every summer I brought one carton with me to Florence. It was my work box. In it I packed two oversized black notebooks that were actually artist's sketchbooks, ballpoint pens, and the books I wanted to read, or had already read and would look to for material and inspiration.

My main theoretical argument in *Tapestries* was that women had a consciousness (or standpoint) distinct from men's, and that from this consciousness women produced specifically female cultures. These cultures were visible in the expressive arts, and also in particular settings where women congregated or worked. These were the subcultures in which women talked, strategized, resisted, and comforted. I claimed that this female consciousness had arisen because of two conditions. First, in all cultures there was a sexual division of labor: Women performed labors different from those of men—often involving raising children and caring for the sick and the elderly. Women also took part in specific arts and specific forms of paid employment. I wanted to show that women's work, choices, and decisions could be made visible and appreciated on their own terms. As an example, I used a short story by Tillie Olsen called "I Stand Here Ironing," which told the story of a working-class mother. Her child was not doing well in school, and a teacher was going to come to talk to her. The mother's love for her daughter was apparent, and so too were her conflicting emotions of guilt and defiance as she juggled paid employment, domestic chores, and poverty. The child's father had deserted his family. In *Tapestries* I recounted this story and others like it that showed the reality of women's daily lives and their personal struggles to survive.

My second point was that in virtually all cultures women were subordinated to men. I knew that there had been traditional indigenous cultures in North America and elsewhere in which such subordination did not exist, but those cultures were no longer intact. Indeed, it occurred to me that the furious European assaults on Native Americans were driven, at least in part, precisely because women were powerful and equal participants in those cultures, a model that the patriarchal imperatives of European colonialists could not permit. Most important, however, the existence of these indigenous cultures showed us that women's subordination to men was not the "natural" order of things, but a particular social arrangement. Here I tried to show that patriarchy was transitory, and that we, as women, could change the conditions of our lives.

In sum, then, I argued that it was these "material" conditions of women's labors and subordination that produced a distinctly female consciousness, which in turn gave rise to explicitly female cultures that could be explored, mapped, and honored. My use of the word "consciousness" did not refer to individuals per se, or to their psychological issues. I was using the word in its Marxist incarnation, referring to a collective social and political consciousness.

I also offered two cautionary injunctions. First, I argued that women were not "essentially" any particular way. For example, women were not "naturally" closer to nature than men, or "naturally" more nurturing. I asserted that these characteristics, insofar as they might be true, were orchestrated by social conditions and expectations.

My second cautionary note was that women were not all the same; just because we were women did not mean we all had the same consciousness. Conditions of race, economics, religion, geography, historical circumstances, and so on also shaped women's standpoints. But, I maintained, the women of any particular group had ways of thinking and acting that were different from the men of that group. By respecting these differences, and "pivoting our center" of attention, we could also make connections between women.

This was my way of working out the relationship between the Marxist (social conditions) and the feminist (women's consciousness and cultures) that I had worked on for so long. I wanted women to see that we had historical independence from men, that in ordinary women's daily lives we created meaning, beauty, art, literature, poetry, stories, and strategies for survival and resistance. I wanted us to stop blaming ourselves for the violence in our lives, the alcoholism and drugs that crippled us and our children, the narcissism and indulgence that sapped our strength. For example, I argued that women were made into sexual objects for men's gratification. This happened to virtually all of us regardless of our behavior or our appearance. It was simply a consequence of being female in a patriarchal world. If some women internalized this sense of themselves by excessively focusing on their appearance in order to attract more men, we then blamed them for being narcissistic. I wanted us to distinguish between individual failings and weaknesses (for which we can certainly be held personally accountable) and the social conditions of patriarchy, racism, poverty, and cultural genocide that produced them.

Then there was what I called or thought of as a lesbian sensibility. It was not primarily about sex, but rather about extending our love for women into an unconditional embrace, a harbor of safety and refuge, understanding and compassion. I believed this was especially important in countering the effects of male violence against women.

Rape, domestic violence in its myriad forms, and incest were all forms of "sexual terrorisms," as Susan Griffin once put it, and they held patriarchy in place.

In the wide expanse of the Sonoran Desert on the Colorado Plateau lies the Navajo Nation. Its tribal headquarters are in Window Rock, Arizona. This name describes a literal rock formation, a large red sandstone arch through which you can gaze out and up into a clear, very blue sky. The arch frames the sky and so you notice it, see its details instead of taking it for granted. Writing *Tapestries* was like that. It was like I was standing in one place and seeing an expanse of sky for the first time. It had always been there, but I had not seen it before. Writing the book provided me with a frame to see what was already there. Women's lives had always been there, but I had not noticed them before, or understood their meaning.

My father read the first two chapters of *Tapestries* while they were still in draft form. We were in my office in downtown Pacific Grove. I had been nervous about his reading it because I had moved a long way from the old Communist formulations of things. He said, "You don't believe in Marxism anymore." It was a statement, not a question, and he spoke in a sad, almost melancholy way. All the fight had gone out of him. I noticed that he was getting old.

"No," I said, "I don't."

He said, "You should read . . ." and he rattled off the name of some Soviet theoretician. "I have found him very helpful." I had no intention of reading whoever it was, and he knew it. I was through with trying to conform my thinking to orthodox Marxism. I felt relief that my thinking was no longer a secret from him, and then I felt a kind of grief. It took me back to that moment, after Mother's seventy-fifth birthday, when I had walked through the no man's land at the

Berlin Wall and into the American sector. I had walked away from my father that morning, waving goodbye to a solitary and shrinking figure in the predawn light.

When I was hired in 1980 to teach the introductory women's studies course at UC Santa Cruz, my title was "adjunct lecturer." I was employed only part-time, but I was in fact functioning as regular faculty; I just enjoyed none of the amenities. For example, I did not have office space for the first three years that I taught at the university, and I was not eligible to accumulate sabbatical credits. My salary was prorated somewhere between 51 percent and 75 percent time, which allowed me to receive medical benefits, but I was only paid per course. My senior colleague, Helene Moglen, partially remedied this situation when she invented an administrative category so that my hours of student advising could be counted as a course "equivalency."

These work conditions were not personal to me. Rather, they reflected the low priority given to women's studies by most of the administrators I encountered in the 1980s. Moreover, most adjunct lecturers were treated in similar ways, and a majority of them were women. From the administration's perspective at the time, women's studies was a bastard intellectual child with no paternal lineage of founding fathers typical in every other discipline. Indeed, we were offering substantial critiques of the "fathered" disciplines. But I felt no resentment. I was so happy to be teaching women's studies, and to be paid for such a wonderful opportunity.

I commuted from Pacific Grove to Santa Cruz two or three days a week, putting in ten- and twelve-hour days there, and working long hours in a rented office space in downtown Pacific Grove. My office was in a second-story loft on Lighthouse Avenue, above an antique shop and across the street from the post office. I treasured this space. After my summers at Florence I spent weeks there before school began, editing, typing, and reediting manuscripts composed at the lake.

Finally, I was assigned office space at Kresge College, where women's studies was located on the Santa Cruz campus. For a few years, though, my office was outside the faculty office building, adjacent to the college Laundromat. Given what I was teaching, I thought it was hysterically funny. Before I had this office I carried a box of files around with me and met my students in various coffee shops on the campus.

After the initial quarter in which I taught Introduction to Feminism in the winter of 1980, it was offered every fall, and students lined up outside my door to see me during office hours. The third year I taught the course the enrollment soared to just over two hundred, more than double the previous year. Word of the course was apparently spreading among students on the campus. I was assigned one graduate student teaching assistant. She was Ruth Frankenberg from the HistCon program, who was to emerge in the 1990s as a leading scholar in race and gender studies. Arriving in the program from England, Ruth was part of my graduate student cohort, and we went through several graduate seminars together. She was a brilliant scholar, and we shared a vintage 1970s socialist-feminist politics, meaning that we were as much against capitalism and racism as we were committed to women's liberation from all forms of oppression and exploitation. Though at first we weren't sure how we would teach such a large class, we agreed to let the overenrollment stand. We divided the students' papers in half, each of us reading a hundred for each of the three assigned essays, followed by a term paper. It was grueling, but rewarding too. At the end of the quarter, I told Ruth that

I would write all of the narrative evaluations myself; I couldn't see encumbering her, immersed as she was in her graduate studies. It took me until June to finish them.

The following fall I was able to secure two graduate student teaching assistants, which was still far below the number needed for a class of that size, and I recruited undergraduate juniors and seniors who had completed the course to assist us. I could not pay the undergraduates, but I could give them course credit. All of the undergraduate assistants conducted weekly discussion sections, and read and graded the papers of the students in their sections. The undergraduates were, of course, inexperienced so I met with them informally to discuss their work. Within a year or two of this ad hoc arrangement, I instituted mandatory sections for the course and began regular meetings with the assistants. It took a few more years until I could get administrative approval for what was, in fact, becoming a seminar, so I taught it as a group independent study for which I was not paid. The introductory course continued to increase in enrollment, and I was forced to abandon the relative comfort of a small lecture hall. Intro to Fem, as it became known, was relocated to the largest lecture hall on our campus, with a seating capacity of just under five hundred. And in 1986 I got administrative approval to teach my seminar as a regular course called "Feminist Methods of Teaching."

The problem that I found with the large lecture format, especially for a course such as this, was the potential loss of intimacy and trust that the subject required. Teaching from a multiracial perspective, I began with an overview of women's history and work, but then we very quickly moved on to subjects like anger, racism, sexuality, sexual harassment, economic justice, violence against women, and reproductive rights. I sought to model the class after the feminist process I had learned in the 1970s, in which personal experiences were used as a way of mapping political consciousness. For example, if many, many girls and women experienced sexual assault and we put those experiences together, it became apparent that such devastating violence was not the result of individual "luck" or bad judgment. We could show patterns of power that propelled men toward those acts of violence as part of a patriarchal definition of manhood. And we could help women to stop blaming themselves and to learn how to change or successfully confront those patterns. Feminism forced us to redefine what was personal and what was political because of the extent to which the lived experiences of women's oppression were often located in women's most personal relationships with men.

Likewise, we could see that political issues like racism were often experienced in deeply personal ways. I defined issues of race, class, gender, and sexuality from a theoretical perspective and worked to show how they were connected and how each reinforced the other. I reached for a balance between subjective and objective ways of knowing—that is, knowing from experience, and knowing because of empirical, statistical, or historical evidence. Healing was my motivating force. I hoped that in providing students with a *political* analysis, they could free themselves from the devastating effects of violence and subordination, build their self-esteem, see the strength of their mothers, grandmothers, and sisters, and bring themselves into a greater wholeness.

I created a teaching style that established boundaries of trust and respect no matter what the size of the class. I think this was possible because of the feeling of unconditional love that welled up in me as each class began. It was a learning from the heart; learning by invention. Whether or not students agreed with me on any particular subject didn't matter. What mattered was offering them a space in which to unleash their creative talents, their passionate intelligence, their ability to think critically and come to their own conclusions. What mattered was that they learned to love themselves "regardless," as Alice Walker put it. I also understood that our intimacy was a fragile thing. It could never be assumed, and it must never be abused.

Over the years I added new topics to the course. For example, I developed more detailed material on anorexia and bulimia as they reached epidemic proportions among young women. I did the same as the AIDS pandemic escalated, along with the homophobic and racist discourse around it. I added material on women and immigration, on the global economy, on the prison-industrial complex. I invited guest speakers, organized panel discussions; sometimes, outside of class, my assistants showed films related to lecture materials. But mostly, I think, I tried to teach students to see what was already there and to know from that which they had already experienced. It was about reframing experience through a feminist lens.

Race, and its impact on women's lives, was a central component of the course. It was not always a comfortable space. For example, I had African American students who objected to my teaching black women's history, culture, and politics because I was white. This forced me to rethink what a multiracial approach to teaching might mean. So I developed a lecture called "Racism and the Meaning of White Superiority." It was intended to define racism as an institutional and persistent system of white power and privilege, with a particular history rooted in conquest and slavery. Then I tried to show how racism existed in our everyday lives, from police violence and racial profiling to its subtler forms. For example, many white students on campus thought that students of color had been admitted to the university solely because they were classified as "minorities," and never because of their own merit. I heard white students scapegoating students of color, blaming them if their white friends had not been admitted to the university. I used this as an example, named it as a form of racism. This lecture brought the white students up short and validated the experiences of my students of color. Only then, I saw, when we were out of denial about how pervasive racism is, could I teach the history and begin a fruitful dialogue. White students chafed at and sometimes openly opposed my support of affirmative action. Once, I overheard two white students talking about the class. One said to the other, "Bettina's right about a lot of things, but she's wrong about affirmative action."

That was when it occurred to me that my students understood affirmative action exclusively as a "race issue." After all, I realized, these were the Reagan years. My students were raised on TV media news. The civil rights movement might as well have been in the 1860s as the 1960s for most white students. Students sat bolt upright when I explained that affirmative action was intended to correct both racial and gender discrimination. "Gender discrimination?" they said in disbelief, arguing with me until I produced the texts of Title VII of the 1964 Civil Rights Act and Title IX of the 1972 Education Amendments, and gave them employment statistics that showed that white women had benefited the most from affirmative action programs. I watched them begin to understand the way race had affected all of our lives. Of course, this didn't mean they all now agreed with affirmative action. Racism runs deep.

It was in these classes on race that I began to think of teaching as a process of rolling up our collective sleeves and getting down to work. And sometimes I got scared. I worried about what students, especially students of color, thought of me. And I worried about having the right answer on every issue. After all, I had been trained in a Communist regiment. Gradually, I saw how useless and counterproductive this attitude was to the understanding we all needed. I saw that I needed some compassion for myself.

Over the years it was my students who taught me to be more and more inclusive. It was my students who guided me toward my own healing. For example, in the early 1980s I screened a slideshow I had put together on women in U.S. history. The women I represented were European American and African American. The slides showed a couple of token Chicanas, Native Americans, and Asian Americans. Unlike the other slides, however, these women were anonymous, rather than famous and accomplished.

One day a Chicana student, Blanca Tavera, confronted me after class. She told me what I could do with my one or two Chicana slides. She was furious and I saw right away it was, because her feelings had been hurt. She, and her history, had not been reflected in my presentation. Of course my immediate impulse was to be defensive, but I didn't respond that way. I said, "You're right." And then, "Will you come to my office hours so we can talk?"

Blanca was stunned when I agreed with her, and most of her anger dissolved. She took a chance on me and came to see me. Eventually she assisted in teaching the class. I learned a great deal from Blanca. She helped me to locate early writings by Chicana feminists, and more important, she taught me the contours of a Chicana standpoint. Blanca was from Watsonville, an agricultural center just south of Santa Cruz with a large Mexican and Chicano/a population. Blanca was a reentry student in her early thirties, a single mom with three young children. She graduated with a degree in women's studies, and went on to get a master's degree in social work at San Jose State University. With other Chicana feminists Blanca helped to organize, and became the founding executive director of, Defensa de Mujeres, the first domestic violence agency for Chicanas and Latinas in the Watsonville and Santa Cruz communities.

On another occasion a group of Jewish students came to my office hours. They appreciated my lectures on racism, they said; when was I going to do one on anti-Semitism? Having just begun the excursion into my identity, I was still very much a reluctant Jew. But I knew that these young women were right, and they were forcing me to confront my own internalized junk. I was ashamed of Israel's foreign policy, its furious violence against the Palestinians, its investments in South Africa's apartheid regime, its complicity with the Chilean fascists led by Pinochet. I had to think about how to honor Zionism as the national liberation movement of the Jewish people (as Congresswoman Bella Abzug had so forthrightly put it), honor the progressive and radical traditions and struggles of the Jewish people, while dissenting from the particular policies of the Israeli government. "Just like you dissent from U.S. government policies," Kate explained. "You don't demand the annihilation of the United States!" she went on. "You protest, but you don't question the right of the United States to exist. Israel is a nation among nations!" I knew she was right. But still, I felt so ashamed that Jewish people, who had been the victims of genocide, could themselves become the perpetrators of such unspeakable violence.

I studied hard and fast and added to what I already knew, and before the end of that quarter I put together a lecture called "Anti-Semitism and the Legacy of Jewish Women." I drew upon my own experiences, of course, as I had done with every subject. I taught about the horrors of anti-Semitic violence, primarily in Europe, extending through the centuries and culminating in the Nazi Holocaust. I balanced this with stories about Jewish women, illustrating their courage, wisdom, and humor. I talked about Israel, and shame, and how we internalize our oppression, believing ourselves to be "less than," believing the stereotypes about ourselves as being obsessed with money or inherently evil.

I was not comfortable with this material yet, and I was nervous before class. One of my undergraduate assistants that quarter was Maria Zamora, a Puerto Rican reentry student. Maria had the fiery temperament of a warrior; she was a fervent supporter of Puerto Rican independence. Before class Maria said, "I know about internalized oppression!" and punched me gently on the arm. She sat front and center that day and made continual eye contact with me. Her confidence and warmth, her nods of encouragement and broad smiles, brought me through my first lecture on Jewish women.

Afterward, I incorporated this material into the course. I discovered that most of my non-Jewish students, including most of my students of color, knew virtually nothing about anti-Semitism. Many of the non-Jewish students had simply accepted the stereotypes they heard about Jews. During one lecture a young (white) man shouted out that the Jewish American Princess was not a stereotype; it was how Jewish girls were. In another class a young woman seethed, "How dare you talk about the German people that way! My mother and grandmother suffered horribly during the war! It was all the fault of the Jews!" And then there were the Jewish students. One, who said, "My grandmother jumped from a second-story window in Paris holding my father while the Nazis rushed through the door into the apartment!" And another, who telephoned her mother the evening after the class. "Mom, are we Jewish?" The question elicited the phenomenal story of her mother's survival in the camps, orphaned, rescued by an uncle, brought to Vienna at the end of the war, and hiding, hiding, hiding her Jewish identity until her daughter asked the question.

Everywhere, students spoke of things about which they had before been silent: about the internment of their Japanese American mothers and grandmothers in the United States during World War II; about incest, rape, domestic violence, illegal abortions; about feeling the shame in being forced to ride on a segregated bus in the South *after* the civil rights movement. A Chicana student told us of standing in an imaginary "no man's land" on the elementary school playground, caught in terror between her African American schoolmates on one side and her white schoolmates on the other, not knowing where to go until she was rescued by her sister and brought out of the schoolyard altogether. A young woman talked about being raped. "He was without mercy," she said in a clear, strong voice. "He showed no mercy." A young man described years of childhood sexual abuse at the hands of his stepfather, his mother refusing to listen, refusing to protect him. He spoke his words as though to his mother, the odor of fear radiating from his body until the class, riveted and silent, held his pain. Then he moved into a calm space, blue eyes focused and clear. He finished his story and fell weeping into my arms.

These classes were like miracles to me.

As problematic as my Jewish identity was to me, the other site of internalized oppression was my lesbian identity. For the first years that I taught Intro to Fem, I did a couple of lectures on lesbian-feminist politics, always near the end of the quarter. I felt that by then most of the students would approve of me enough not to be overtly hostile. One year in the early 1980s, during the first of these lectures, a young man in the class interrupted me with a question. This in itself was nothing unusual; students often interrupted with questions. He wanted to know the outcome of a story I had told; depending on how I answered his question, the class would or wouldn't know I was a lesbian. I flubbed the question deliberately and went back to my lecture notes. Later that night I felt terrible about it.

The young man was Chicano, and I knew he was gay because I knew his sister. He had asked the question because it really mattered to him to see people "out," to feel the strength in our numbers and visibility. At the next class I began my second lecture on lesbian-feminist politics, and then, all of a sudden, impulsively, I threw the notes aside. I told the students that I was just going to talk to them about being a lesbian. I told them stories from my life, explained how homophobia could be internalized until it became such a corrosive force that it destroyed you. I talked about falling in love with Kate. I talked about how fortunate I was to be in Santa Cruz, with its large lesbian and feminist communities, and on this campus, with its commitment to nontraditional education.

I was filled with an indescribable happiness as I finished the class. I was gathering myself together, looking down at my papers and my backpack, when I heard the roar of the students. I looked up. They were standing, whistling and applauding. They filled the room with so much love that it felt as though the bunkerlike cement walls of that old chemistry building would surely dissolve by an alchemy older than the natural sciences. I started laughing and applauding with them and to them in gratitude. From that fall of 1983 onward I was "out," and in succeeding years I came out to my students earlier and earlier each quarter, until it was finally happening on day one. I also moved the "lesbian lecture" to early in the quarter, alongside race and class, where it was, at last, an integral part of the theoretical coherence of the course.

As much as I loved teaching, I also wanted to build women's studies into a viable academic department, one that would be treated with respect, as an equal among others. I did not yet understand the contradictions this struggle for recognition would bring, although Kate tried to warn me. Trying to institutionalize women's studies would propel us toward an increasingly academic feminism, in contrast to the activist feminist scholarship I assumed would always drive us. Instead of acknowledging this contradiction, however, I thought about how the women's movement would ebb and flow the way all social movements did. If we could hold on, if we could dig in for the long haul, maybe we could create an institutional space for future generations. Adrienne Rich had once written, "The feminist politics of the past has been turned back again and again because we had no way of handing on a collective female vision." Oh, how I wanted to change that!

Through the 1980s women's studies at UC Santa Cruz was what was called a "program," rather than a department (or board of studies, in Santa Cruz's specialized language). As a program we could not hire our own faculty in tenure-track or tenured positions. At the time only tenured faculty were permanently employed. Full-time lecturers, or those over half-time like me, were automatically fired at the end of six years. (This would change in the late 1980s, when lecturers succeeded in organizing a union and gaining what was called "security of employment.") All of this meant that women's studies was funded with "soft money," allocated or not each year at the whim of the dean. We could hire only temporary lecturers, and we ran our office and staff on a shoestring budget.

An executive committee, composed of feminist faculty from other (regular) departments like literature or sociology, made the policy decisions for the program. These women received no compensation and no reduction in their teaching load for serving on the executive committee. Some were among our founding mothers, and others were younger and more recently hired. The younger faculty especially took a serious risk in working with us, often experiencing the disdain of male colleagues in their home departments. In addition to those who served on the executive committee, there were faculty affiliated with women's studies who taught a range of feminist courses in their own departments, which our students could take to fulfill their requirements for the major. Many of these faculty faced departmental struggles to convince their reluctant colleagues to allow them to teach (and fund, of course) feminist courses. In these ways women's studies was sustained.

Helene Moglen, whose home department was literature, served continuously on the executive committee and chaired women's studies for many years. Donna Haraway, who was establishing herself as one of the leading feminist scholars in the history of science, joined us and worked selflessly for women's studies, teaching in the program and occasionally relieving Helene as chair. Marge Frantz, a lecturer in American studies and later in women's studies, had been a mainstay of the program from its inception. I knew Marge from Berkeley; she was a former member of the Communist Party, and one of Decca Treuhaft's oldest and closest friends. Marge had gotten her doctorate in 1976 in HistCon after returning to school in her forties. Her life partner was Eleanor Engstrand, a retired librarian from UC Berkeley. Their relationship, although not publicly known until the 1990s, was a source of great comfort to me.

Helene, Donna, Marge, and I shared a feminist vision that was overtly political, with a decidedly socialist bent. We saw ourselves as scholars and activists. Helene was probably the most academically traditional member of our quartet, and by far the most savvy about campus politics. She also had extensive administrative experience and the most senior faculty position. We took an ecumenical approach to building the women's studies program. We welcomed feminist faculty onto the executive committee and as affiliates, regardless of their particular disciplinary, theoretical, or political persuasions. We didn't exactly "decide" this ecumenical style in a meeting, but it worked well, even if we did bump along when strong differences erupted. In the larger feminist and lesbian communities women were fighting all kinds of "wars" as the movement splintered under the pressures of the Reagan White House, but we didn't splinter. I felt strong personal affection for all of my colleagues, and given what I'd been through in the Communist Party, I wasn't about to reenact a sectarian politics. I grieved the factions that had developed within the women's movement.

I did, however, make at least one grievous mistake with a colleague, which I resolved never to repeat. He was a professor of politics, openly gay, and affiliated with women's studies. He taught a course on gay and lesbian politics, which was, I think, the only such class offered anywhere on the campus. It was, of course, listed as part of our extended women's studies curriculum. When some of our students complained to me that there was almost no lesbian content, I called him and asked for a meeting.

When we met I explained my concerns, pointing to this or that absence or flaw in his syllabus. He was defensive and I kept saying, "You're not hearing me," until he got really angry. Then I got angry, and our meeting ended on a rancorous note.

Later that evening as I ranted to Kate about my encounter I called this professor a "fag." "Whoa!" she said, and insisted that I apologize to Lisa for the use of such language. Lisa was still a teenager, and well within hearing range. The apology did me good. I was embarrassed by my "high and mighty" attitude, and I could see how I had rankled my colleague. I had no business criticizing his syllabus, and certainly not with the arrogance I had displayed. I was also ashamed by my use of such a terrible and violent epithet. I could see all of my internalized homophobia gathered into that word.

A few days later, referring to the professor with whom I'd argued, Helene remarked to me mildly, "You know, you and he really should be allies." Of course she was right. I apologized to him, but he remained wary of me, as well he might. However, the following year he added more lesbian content to the course, and he invited the outstanding lesbian-feminist historian Lillian Faderman to give a guest lecture, from which we all benefited.

Whatever the outcome, I regretted my behavior with him very much. I also saw in myself all of the sectarian and dogmatic arrogance I most abhorred in others. There I was, sounding just like the reviewer of my manuscript in her letter to me about *Woman's Legacy*. I saw how attachment to ideas could lead to such rigidity, and even rupture relationships. The experience confirmed my belief that the only way to build women's studies was to welcome any and all of our colleagues and students who defined themselves as feminists.

From its inception, women's studies had been allocated funding for one staff assistant to run the program office. In 1985, under Helene's guidance, we secured a full-time assistant, Nicolette Czarrunchick. She had been working on the campus for several years in the sciences and I had met her the previous fall when she had audited Introduction to Feminism. Nicolette was about as quick, efficient, and organized a program manager as we could have hoped to secure. She was also a strong feminist, an astute film critic, and a political activist who had been part of the ferment of the 1960s and 1970s. She shared our political vision of women's studies.

Nicolette loved our students, and within a couple of years she was renowned among them as the person to whom to turn if you needed help with anything. As is true generally in programs serving underrepresented groups, whether by race, gender, sexuality, politics, or some combination of these, students came to the women's studies office with myriad personal and academic problems and political initiatives. Nicolette handled these with efficiency and compassion.

In the day-to-day operation of the women's studies program then, there were three of us, Helene, Nicolette, and me, our feet firmly planted in the proverbial door. We had 114 students majoring in the program, which was a considerable number on our small campus; we also enjoyed something of a national reputation as a center for feminist activism and scholarship. Articles in *Ms.* magazine and *The New York Times* cited the strength of women's studies at UC Santa Cruz. Yet our own administrators, and some among the tenured faculty, were overtly hostile to us, and others just thought that women's studies was a joke. It was, we felt, irresponsible to have this many majors and no full-time faculty.

In an effort to change this situation, Helene arranged for us to meet with UC Santa Cruz's executive vice chancellor, Kivie Moldave. The purpose of the meeting was to discuss how women's studies could become a department and begin to hire its own faculty. And this was the highest-ranking campus administrator, apart from the chancellor, who could set this in motion. In preparation for our meeting we had sent him a report that included an overview of feminist scholarship, our curriculum development, a list of our affiliated faculty, and our projected faculty appointments. It was a modest and temperate proposal.

In advance of the meeting we were informed that Moldave had called in a battery of his administrative cohorts to attend it. He seemed afraid to meet with us alone. "Here come the Amazons," Helene quipped. Given the opposing cohort, we asked Marge and Donna to come to the meeting, and then summoned additional senior faculty.

The meeting was scheduled in a small conference room in the vice chancellor's offices. There was not enough room for everyone, but Moldave refused to move us to a larger, more accommodating space. Chivalry prevailed as the invited men sat on the floor or stood, leaning against the wall. Helene began the meeting by explaining our purpose and referring to the report we had prepared. It quickly became apparent that the vice chancellor had not read the report and had no intention of engaging in a substantive discussion. He blustered his way through the meeting and managed as well to personally insult Helene. The meeting ended abruptly when Moldave got up and left the room. I was used to university combat and took none of his bombast personally, but when I turned to Helene I saw that she was shaken. While she had expected administrative resistance, Helene had assumed that normal courtesies of colleagueship would prevail. Not so with women's studies.

We needed a new strategy. Within a few months we had mounted a public campaign for women's studies to be granted departmental status. Two thousand students signed a petition to that effect addressed to the chancellor, and sixty women faculty (which included virtually every woman then teaching at UC Santa Cruz, whether tenured or not) signed a letter to the chancellor requesting the same. Students organized a march through the campus culminating in a steady, upbeat chanting in front of the chancellor's office. All of this had an effect.

One thing I was learning in my years at the university was that administrators came and went, and while they were almost all white and male, some were more progressive and farsighted than others. Moldave was soon gone, and the chancellor, Robert Sinsheimer, a tall, distinguished-looking biophysicist, sent a letter to Helene as chair of women's studies, informing us that he had authorized women's studies to become a "committee" instead of a "program." "A what?" I said in exasperation. Who'd ever heard of a committee? Helene explained: It was an intermediate form; we were advancing from a program, but we were not yet a department. However, as a committee we could hire our own tenure-track faculty.

And so, in the 1986–87 academic year women's studies conducted its first-ever search for an assistant professor. My colleagues wrote a job description fitted to me, advertised it, constituted a search committee, and read and ranked the applications. I thought about it long and hard before applying for the position, and I consulted with quite a few people. I was not sure I wanted a tenure-track position at the university with all that that implied about serving on faculty committees, publishing under pressure, and attending scholarly conferences.

Helene just looked at me with a piteous expression, smiled, and in a concerned, motherly sort of way told me to get on with it. Donna said, "This is your job. Take it!" Marge said, "It's your revolutionary duty!" My friend and colleague Candace West, one of our affiliated faculty in the sociology department, said, "Do you want a sabbatical?" The new dean of humanities, Michael Cowan, took me out to lunch at a student hangout just off campus. Michael took my fears seriously and answered each of my questions with patience and kindness. He said, don't let yourself be pushed around. You decide your priorities. Don't serve on committees for a while if you don't want to. But, he said, you deserve to be a tenured member of the faculty.

And Kate? What about Kate? She wasn't concerned about whether or not I was tenured. She didn't want to see me hurt yet one more time. Always you want to be on the inside, she said. Like you were in the party. But for you to be on the inside you have to believe that whatever it is you are joining is pure and good. Remember that a university is run by a corporate-dominated board of regents; you can build a niche but you cannot change the institution.

I applied for the job and was selected and interviewed by the search committee, along with two other excellent candidates, both of whom certainly knew that I was favored for the job. My appointment was forwarded to the dean of humanities. Helene wrote the letter for my proposed appointment and asked that I be hired with tenure because I had already written two books and edited two others, and had been teaching for eight years. Dean Cowan approved it, but an assistant to the chancellor in charge of monitoring affirmative action objected because, she said, such an appointment would violate the search protocol by propelling it outside its advertised ranking. I liked and respected Julia Armstrong, an African American woman who fought a lonely battle of principle in a generally hostile environment. I understood the politics of her ruling, even as I was personally disappointed.

On July 1, 1987, the start of the next fiscal year, I became an assistant professor, appointed at the highest step, and in the following academic year, with *Tapestries* in production, I was awarded tenure. Helene threw a huge party for me at her home to celebrate. In addition to our many friends and colleagues, I invited my parents and, because of the supreme irony of the moment, Mario Savio and his wife, Lynne Hollander. True to form, Mario and Lynne arrived bearing a mock newspaper headline garnered at one of the many booths on the Santa Cruz boardwalk. It read, "Bettina Awarded Tenure! Will Former FSMer Be True to the Cause?"

It was done in jest, of course, and Mario and Lynne were grinning. But my father spoiled the joke. Under his breath he said, "How 'true' remains to be seen." I doubt that anyone else registered the comment, except perhaps my mother. I felt a surge of cold fury at the base of my neck.

It was another decade before women's studies became a full-fledged department. Three administrators in key positions stubbornly resisted the change, but it was finally approved by a courageous chancellor named Karl Pister. He had been part of the engineering faculty at UC Berkeley during the Free Speech Movement and joked playfully with me about my role in it. Karl also believed in affirmative action.

One of Karl's last acts as chancellor was to authorize the establishment of women's studies as a department. A one-paragraph letter in June 1996, a signature, and it was done. In November we received official notification of our departmental status from the UC Office of the President.

As Kate continued her meditation practice I followed in her wake. She was by now on many mailing lists, and in the spring of 1989 she announced excitedly that His Holiness the Dalai Lama was scheduled to give a teaching in San Jose in the fall. "We should go," she said. "Okay," I said, feeling less sure of it than I sounded. "It's a weekend teaching," she explained, "on Padmasambhava." And when I looked at her blankly, she said, "He was the Indian master who brought Buddhism to Tibet. He is revered." She went on, "Many Tibetans thought Mahatma Gandhi was his incarnation." "Oh," I said. I loved Mahatma Gandhi. "Okay," I said, feeling better.

I had one clear memory of the Dalai Lama. It was 1959, I was fourteen, and my parents had just moved us to the house on Ludlam Place. I was watching the evening news on television. There was a film clip of the Dalai Lama. He looked to be barely more than a boy, walking briskly, wearing robes. I couldn't see the bright colors of his robes because we didn't yet have color television. The newscaster said something like, "The Dalai Lama, spiritual leader of Tibet, crossed over into India today, in a harrowing escape from the Chinese Communists who have occupied his country." My father happened to walk into the living room at that moment. He saw the screen and hissed, "The bastard."

I didn't say anything, of course. China's socialist revolution was revered in our home in 1959. This was before China's split with the Soviet Union, when the U.S. Communist Party's allegiance shifted. I figured that the Dalai Lama, whoever he was, must not only be a religious leader (which would be bad enough), but some kind of anti-Communist to deserve the vehemence of my father's condemnation. Still, I never forgot that clear image of him in his robes, a little fuzz of hair, wearing dark, large-framed glasses, walking purposefully into India.

Kate's enthusiasm for the Dalai Lama worried me, but I was too emotionally dependent on her to communicate clearly. I was also embarrassed. Here I was, forty-five years old, and I was still afraid of my parents. I was alternately raging at them and acquiescing to their politics and social etiquette. I seemed to have no middle ground. For example, my mother was forever throwing parties at which she "required" my attendance. I was often loath to attend them because they reminded me of how I felt when I was a child, always on display. Yet invariably I went to placate her; then I raged afterward.

We bought our tickets for the Dalai Lama's teaching, and as the September date approached I said, "We won't tell my parents." "Okay," Kate said. It was ridiculous, of course, since the teaching venue on the San Jose State campus was only eight blocks from their house, and we needed to stay overnight in San Jose because the commute back and forth to Monterey was too far. We took a motel room for the two nights we were there. The day we drove up I picked a fight with Kate. It had nothing to do with anything except my anxiety. Going to hear the Dalai Lama was "bad," and I was six years old, throwing the childhood tantrum I never had been allowed.

A crowd of several thousand stood quietly on line at entrances to the San Jose State sports stadium. I think the quiet was what I noticed first. There was an expectant buzz amongst us, but people were extraordinarily respectful of each other. Then I spotted two people I knew from the Communist Party club in San Jose a decade earlier. I felt as though their presence gave me some kind of permission to be there. I was giddy with relief. I put my arm through Kate's. "This is amazing," I said, my eyes wide open.

Slowly we were admitted into the stadium as volunteers from the group sponsoring the event, polite and apologetic, searched our bags, primarily for cameras and tape recorders, which were not permitted. Once inside, our eyes adjusting from the bright sunlight, I could see that the stadium had been transformed. We were in the bleachers, about midway down, stage left. Below us hundreds of people sat in folding chairs on what was usually the playing court. A stage had been erected, and on it were dozens of robed monks and nuns on their meditation cushions. They were from many Buddhist traditions, evidenced by their different colored robes, from the bright maroons and yellows of the Tibetans to the grays of the Zen folks and the browns of the Therivadans. I noticed several very elderly Tibetans. Stage center was a throne draped in gold and maroon silk, and behind the stage was an elaborate altar with deities and offering bowls such as I had seen at Sambosa. Above the altar a half-dozen *thangkas* were hung. These, I knew, were Tibetan religious paintings done on large silk screens. I recognized the Buddha, of course, and Tara. "That's a portrait of Padmasambhava," Kate whispered, referring to an unfamiliar figure. Mostly what I noticed were his thinly curved eyebrows, his razor-thin mustache, and the pink and white lotus flowers surrounding him.

The Dalai Lama came onto the stage and the audience immediately rose, in silence. He was accompanied by two or three young attendant monks and the translator, a Western man dressed in a suit and tie. The Dalai Lama's hands were joined in the universal gesture of prayer, and he was bent over to make himself lower than everyone else on stage; he was bowing and smiling. Then he turned his back to the audience in order to face the image of the Buddha above his throne, and he did three full-body prostrations, touching his head to the floor each time. Then he walked to the throne, slipped off his shoes, climbed a couple of steps up, folded his legs under himself, and sat down in a lotus position. He settled his robes, took his watch off and set it on a small table to his right, unwrapped his *mala* from his wrist, and immediately began rotating the beads, presumably to a mantra. Many people around me and all of those on the stage were doing prostrations. Kate said, "It's a traditional Tibetan gesture of respect to affirm that you want the teachings." I nodded, put my hands together, bowed my head once, and sat down. Then all the rustling of robes and papers stopped. The huge stadium was completely quiet.

The Dalai Lama began speaking in English, in a clear voice, suggesting a range somewhere between a tenor and a baritone. "Brothers and sisters," he began his welcome. Then he informed us that only a day or so before he had been notified that he had received the Nobel Peace Prize. The audience broke into prolonged applause. Then he chuckled and said, "I think it involves a lot of money." It was more a question than a statement, and there was much laughter.

His greetings completed, the Dalai Lama apologized for his "broken English," to which the audience objected, calling out encouraging words. For the teachings, he said, he would be more comfortable in Tibetan, more accurate. And so he began. He would speak for a few minutes, then stop for the translator, who spoke very fluently, pausing only occasionally in search of the appropriate English word. The Dalai Lama stopped the morning session promptly at noon for the lunch break. As a monastic this was his last meal of the day. Later in the afternoon he responded to audience questions that were submitted in writing, read aloud in English by the translator, and then quietly translated into Tibetan for the Dalai Lama.

Kate, writing in shorthand on her stenographic pad, took copious notes of the teachings. I, on the other hand, understood very little of the teaching. I did not have enough foundation or the meditation experience to follow the relatively esoteric points of doctrine. Occasionally the Dalai Lama told a story, and these I enjoyed. For example, prior to his death, Padmasambhava left written teachings hidden in the rugged mountains and caves of Tibet. They were called "*termas*," and there were stories about how they were found, and by whom. I knew the details of the stories probably held much cultural and spiritual significance, but I was not sophisticated enough to understand them at this level.

Somehow none of this really mattered to me. The sincerity and kindness of the man were transparent. And what I did understand was very useful to me. The Dalai Lama made continual allusions to what he called "inner peace" as the basis for world peace. Though I had been a peace activist all of my life, I had never before heard anyone refer to my inner peace or their own. In fact, I thought, how ironic it was that the peace movement was riddled with anger, split into factions. I could see, although I was reluctant to admit it, that our public declarations often replicated the self-righteous rhetoric of those who waged war. *Huh!* I thought. This was definitely something to chew on.

On the last day of the teaching, the Dalai Lama was to give an "empowerment." This meant that he was to transform himself into Padmasambhava and transmit to us the practices that we needed in order to focus on him as an object of our meditation. When we returned from lunch, we were told that His Holiness was on the stage, already doing the preliminary practices for the empowerment. We were invited to take our seats but asked to remain silent. As we entered the stadium each of us was given a spoonful of saffron-colored water and asked to rinse our mouth as a purification prior to the ceremony. Kate and I did as requested, and walked in. There were five thousand of us, and the only sound was the swish of shoes on the cement floors. As Kate and I passed a stone pillar on the way to our seats the stage came into view. I was almost knocked off my feet by the power of the energy that the Dalai Lama was generating. In fact, he was no longer the Dalai Lama or anyone; he was just an energy field. I looked over at Kate in time to see her stagger a step or two before regaining her balance. We were both crying.

I don't remember very much of the empowerment itself. The Dalai Lama, through his translator, gave rapid instructions to us to visualize this color at the crown of our heads, and that color at the throat, and another at the heart ("The chakras," Kate whispered). And then, he said, you visualize . . . and I was lost and no longer tracking. There were a lot of prayers and chants in Tibetan, and the Dalai Lama formed *mudras* with his hands and picked up a small metal object called a *vajra* ("Symbolizes lightning," Kate whispered again, "to cut through illusions") and rang a bell at repeated intervals. His attendants, a portion of their robes held in their teeth to cover their mouths (I presumed to shield the sacred from impurities), moved swiftly back and forth between the Dalai Lama and the altar behind him carrying religious objects. Then we were taught the accompanying mantra: "*Om ah hum vajra Guru pema siddhi hum,*" which was to be repeated very quickly, rotating a bead on the *mala* for each completion of the mantra.

When the empowerment ceremony ended, volunteer ushers moved along the aisles with red strings for each of us to take, and bowls of candy. Kate explained to me that Tibetans wore the red string as a "protection cord," until it disintegrated, which symbolized impermanence. Each of us was also given a postcard-sized picture of Padmasambhava for our visualization practice, with the words of the mantra on the reverse side.

We were given the words to a long-life prayer for the Dalai Lama, in a Tibetan alliteration with an English translation. We recited this prayer and then the closing dedication for the well-being and happiness of all sentient beings:

> For as long as space endures
> And for as long as sentient beings remain
> Until then may I too abide
> To dispel the misery of the world.

"This is the prayer for generating *bodhicitta*," Kate said. "This means you are generating the motivation for your life to be a vehicle to serve all living beings." I was so moved to hear the words of that prayer, to be included in such an aspiration. I thought I had a glimmer of understanding about what Kate had meant at Sambosa about my work in the Communist Party not being so different from this. She had meant my motivation or, at any rate, the best part of my motivation, and my desire "to dispel the misery of the world."

As the Dalai Lama rose so did the audience, now finally releasing itself into thunderous applause. He stepped down from the throne, slipped on his shoes, bowed, waved, and he was gone. The weekend had gone by so fast. I wanted to slow it down, to rewind the tape, so to speak. I wanted it to start all over again. I wasn't ready for him to go.

I may not have understood most of what the Dalai Lama had said on that weekend in San Jose, but I did know that energy field. It was compassion, unconditional compassion. And it was vast. There were no tricks, no special effects, no special lighting, nothing. Just one human being. With one-pointed concentration. And in those moments of deity generation he had had no self. I thought, *This is where Kate wants to go. Toward generating that kind of compassion.*

Sometime after attending the teachings of the Dalai Lama in San Jose, we learned that there was a Zen Center in the Monterey area. It was under the direction of a woman named Katherine Thanas. Every Tuesday evening at seven the Zen Center group held a meditation session, followed by tea, and then Katherine gave a teaching, or what was called a dharma talk. The group met at a place called the Cherry Foundation, a community art center and gallery in Carmel.

Meditation was open to all and free of charge, although donations were requested to help defray the costs of renting the space. Katherine Thanas was a Zen priest who had been affiliated with the well-known San Francisco Zen Center for many years. We resolved to sit with this group, and our first evening was to have been October 17, 1989; it was Kate's birthday, an auspicious occasion, we thought.

I left the Santa Cruz campus at about four thirty that day to insure that I would be home in plenty of time to pick up Kate so we could drive to Carmel together. We thought we'd go out for a birthday dinner afterward. It was rush hour, and traffic was heavy. I was on the freeway heading south, just past the exits for the village of Aptos, when the car jerked forcefully. I took my foot off the gas, but I didn't immediately apply the brake because I wasn't sure what was happening. I coasted for a few feet, and it felt as though I had four flat tires. Looking around I saw that everyone in both directions on the freeway had slowed down or pulled off to the shoulder. I looked up and saw thick-trunked eucalyptus trees swaying violently, and that's when I knew it was an earthquake, a massive earthquake. I thought, *If this doesn't stop, I am going to die.* The thought was very clear.

I came to a complete stop with cars around me turned every which way, but miraculously there had been no collisions. My window was completely rolled down, and I finally registered that the guy behind me was shouting, "Get off the bridge!" and frantically waving me forward. I saw that I was on an overpass that could buckle at any moment, and felt a well of gratitude for that anonymous motorist. I inched forward off the overpass and cut my engine. We had all cut our engines. There was a surreal suspension of time, and then finally the tremor stopped. For several minutes we just sat in our cars. Then we started our engines, began driving, slowly at first and then with increasing confidence as everything seemed to be okay. We waved to each other and gave the thumbs-up sign, suddenly connected to each other by this experience.

I almost had begun to relax when traffic slowed again, and then came to a halt. A man was running back and forth along the center divider, shouting that the bridge ahead of us had collapsed. The highway was impassable, he called, hands around his mouth to focus the sound. That's when I felt my first wave of panic. *Jenny!* I thought. *Kate!* I had no idea where the epicenter was or how strong the quake had registered on the Richter scale, but I knew now that it was very, very serious. I had to get home! I had no car radio and no way of getting reliable information.

I drove across the center divider, heedless of the motor vehicle code, and edged into the northbound lanes. I exited at the first opportunity, and was very soon in a massive traffic jam in downtown Watsonville. I turned off onto a side street and saw a telephone booth. I rushed from the car to the telephone. The glass had blown out of the booth, but the phone was still standing. I lifted the receiver and got a dial tone. I used my credit card and dialed home. I heard the familiar recording, "Thank you for using AT&T," and then Jenny's voice.

"Are you all right?" I shouted above the tumult around me.

"Yes, yes, Mom, we're fine." She had been riding her bicycle home and felt nothing. It was when she saw the windowpanes rattling on nearby homes that she knew there was an earthquake. "It was nothing down here, Mom."

"Where's Kate?" I asked. Jenny didn't know; she wasn't home yet. I knew she was in Pacific Grove, though, so she had to be all right. I told Jenny to go across the street to our neighbors' house and stay with them until Kate got home.

"Dad's okay," Jenny said. "He called. He told me to do the same thing." Jack was living in Berkeley, so that told me how far the quake had extended. That meant my parents were also affected. At least Josh was fine. He was in Portland. I explained to Jenny that a bridge on Highway 1 had collapsed. "I'm all right, sweetie," I said. "I am not hurt, and I have some food in the car, but I don't know if I can get home tonight. Don't worry about me." And then, "I love you."

Then I tried to call Lisa. She was by then a graduate student in chemistry at UC Santa Cruz. She lived in a cottage in the village of Capitola, just south of Santa Cruz. My Watsonville telephone still worked, but on Lisa's end all I got was a too-rapid busy signal. Her phone was down. I hoped that she was all right. (We found out later that Lisa was calmly going from house to house in her neighborhood, wrench in hand, making sure that everyone's gas was turned off to prevent fires.)

Walking in downtown Watsonville, I thought about what to do. Most in this community were from Mexico, first or second generation, and I did the best I could to communicate with them in my broken Spanish. Traffic on Main Street seemed almost in gridlock. Much of the downtown area was on fire. I had no map of the Watsonville area, and I was low on gas. I got back in the car. I drove around, trying to find a way out of town that would take me back to Highway 1 going south.

As darkness descended I decided to seek shelter for the night. I heard a civilian at a busy intersection shouting directions to drivers ahead of me to the high school gym (or was it a church?), where, he said, a temporary shelter had been set up. I followed his directions, thinking it was probably the most sensible thing to do.

On my way to the shelter I found myself behind a big semi truck, and it occurred to me that semis were equipped with CB radios. He was driving south and I thought, *He's been given directions on his radio; he's going to know a way onto the freeway.* I stayed close on his tail, and about twenty minutes later we curved onto the on-ramp for Highway 1 going south. We were just north of Moss Landing and well past where the bridge on Highway 1 had collapsed. I felt a surge of hope. Then I saw a road crew and my heart sank. But they waved us on, calling to us to go very slowly. The semi and I dropped to a crawl and approached the crew working on yet another damaged bridge, which had settled itself below the roadway. They said it was passable. We dropped down onto the bridge and inched our way across it, Elkhorn Slough to the left and the ocean surf to our right.

The PG&E power plant at Moss Landing was completely dark. The familiar blinking red lights on its towers were out, the towers themselves standing as blackened sentinels against the night sky. I drove cautiously, following the semi, watching my gas gauge move toward empty. I had about twenty miles to go. I told my little gas-conserving Honda that it could make it home. Except for the semi in front of me, there was nobody on the road.

I exited in Monterey as soon as I could, preferring to negotiate my way along the city streets. They were deserted. No traffic lights. No streetlights. I stopped at every corner. There was an eerie stillness, as though the world had stopped. I stuck my head out of the car window, feeling the coolness of the night air, and glanced up at the sky. The stars were still there.

I pulled up in front of our house in Pacific Grove at nine o'clock. Kate and Jenny were sitting at the kitchen table, with every candle we owned lit; they had even lit the menorah. It looked so beautiful to me. Our friend Jenny Birnbach was there too. She had come over to wait with Kate until I got home. "Have a good strong cup of tea, love," she said, offering the British balm for all perils. I did and it helped a lot. Our gas for cooking and heating the house had already been restored. It was several days, however, before we had electricity.

From the two Jennys and Kate, I began to understand what had happened. The quake struck at 5:04 PM, and lasted fifteen seconds. It registered 7.1 on the Richter scale. That was the same measure as the tremor Kate and I had experienced at Florence, but here we were in a densely populated area. The epicenter had been in the Santa Cruz Mountains, only a few miles east of where I had been on the freeway. No wonder Watsonville had been hit so hard. So had Santa Cruz. Most of the buildings on Pacific Avenue, the downtown shopping center, had collapsed. Many people were injured. Later I heard that one young woman had been killed. She had worked in a coffee shop and was yelling for everyone to get out when the building collapsed around her. In San Francisco, homes built on landfill in the Marina district were either destroyed or sliding off their foundations. Portions of the Bay Bridge connecting San Francisco to Berkeley and Oakland had collapsed. Many there were dead or injured, but we did not yet have reliable figures.

I was traumatized for days after the quake. I couldn't focus on anything. I couldn't even read. In any event, I didn't have to go back to work because the university was closed for a week. Miraculously, there were no injuries on the campus, but our offices were in shambles and an estimated fifty thousand books were in piles on the floor of the library, bookcases leaning every which way.

The Red Cross set up stations in Pacific Grove, and I donated food and clothing to help folks in Watsonville. Without electricity none of us could get gas because all the service station pumps required electricity. It was fine with me not to drive anywhere for a while. With their freezers out, the owners of the Grove Market in downtown Pacific Grove gave away all of their frozen foods and ice cream. Kids were in and out of the store, their faces streaked with ice cream. When telephone service was restored I called my parents. They were fine; the only damage was to their fireplace chimney, which had been dislocated. The grandfather clock, Mother said, had trembled but it did not fall.

In the days following the quake, I wanted to be in motion. I spent a lot of time walking along my favorite paths by the ocean. I was so grateful to be alive, uninjured, my family safe. After my experience I thought a lot about death. I realized why so many of the Buddhist teachings emphasized death. It was because it could happen at any moment. I thought, *At 5:03 PM I was fine; at 5:04 PM I could have been dead.* The Buddhist teachings emphasized death because human life was so extremely precious. Every moment of it should be used to benefit "all living beings." Buddhists taught the certainty of death to counter our continual denial of it. We were like children, I thought, always looking for the next distraction, the next amusement, the next bowl of ice cream. I had never before been in a natural disaster. I had never before had such a visceral understanding of the magnitude of human fear, of the absolute fragility of our lives, of how complicated it was, really complicated, to generate *bodhicitta*.

> For as long as space endures
> And for as long as sentient beings remain
> Until then may I too abide
> To dispel the misery of the world.

The Tuesday following the earthquake Kate and I finally attended our first meditation with the Zen group. In contrast to the colorful flamboyance of Tibetan Buddhism, the Zen practice was austere. The altar was set on a small stand, with a sculpted Buddha, one stick of incense, a small rounded stone, and one candle. We sat on our *zafus,* which were placed on top of larger flat cushions upon which our folded knees and crossed ankles could rest. Each person in the group faced the wall, looking at it and away from each other. Zen practice required a particular protocol for sitting down; I stumbled through it in the beginning, until I got all the bows going in the right direction and sequence. A bell was rung promptly at seven. Once seated, we were instructed not to move for the forty minutes of meditation, and simply to follow the breath. An erect posture, with the spine absolutely straight, was imperative. Our hands were to rest comfortably in each other at the navel, thumbs touching.

Forty minutes was a long time for me to sit without moving. I was amazed by how many distractions there could be. I itched here and then there, my hip hurt, my legs fell asleep, my mind rattled on like a runaway train. But we were in a group setting and I wasn't about to move. Following the sit we did a walking meditation for ten minutes. In addition to allowing the obvious relief of movement, walking meditation was designed to achieve mindfulness. We were to execute each step very slowly, and to pay full attention to each movement. When I first started doing this I thought I would scream with exasperation, but gradually I began to appreciate the practice. It forced the mind to focus, and what had been automatic, and in this sense "thoughtless," became deliberate and "thoughtful." It was a practice for how we should approach all of our interactions in the world every day.

Walking meditation completed, we stood in front of our cushions, facing each other, hands gently pressed together in prayer. To the rhythmic beating of a drum, Katherine led us in chanting the *Heart Sutra.* The Zen practitioners knew it in Japanese; for those of us who didn't the English alliteration had been printed on a sheet of paper. After we chanted the Japanese we said it in English. I had already memorized the English version because it was part of Kate's liturgy.

The *Heart Sutra* was the Buddha's teaching on "form and emptiness." It was what Allen Ginsberg had chanted at the antiwar protest all those years ago. The way I understood it was that all forms and all life arose in relationship to each other. We were all dependent on each other. And no form or life had an "inherent" or "essential" existence. In the personal sense, this was also true for us as individuals. That is, we each came into being as a result of an infinite arrangement of causes and conditions that made our particular lives possible. This was the ebb and flow of life in the world, but we were "empty" of an inherent existence. This was the idea of "co-dependent arising." It was somewhat familiar to me because these ideas were similar to those of traditional Native American cultures. For example, I had studied Leslie Marmon Silko's novel *Ceremony;* interdependence, harmony, and balance between human beings, all other life forms, and Mother Earth were at the heart of this work. These ideas were also similar to those of the deep ecology movement in the West. The difference lay in the Buddhist concept of "emptiness" but, I thought, the English word for it was not a very good translation because it was too static and "permanent." This was the problem with English-language nouns in general. "Form" and "emptiness" were in relationship to each other, in constant motion, the one arising from the other. It was not "either/or," as though one or the other were a permanent fixture.

It was also hard for most of us to include ourselves in this schema of co-dependent arising and noninherent existence. We each wanted to believe in the solidity, autonomy, and permanence of ourselves while everything around us (to which we were *not* attached) could be co-dependent and ephemeral. The *Heart Sutra* also showed why the practice of generating *bodhicitta,* that is, unconditional compassion, was in accord with our true nature. We were all literally self-less! Of course, it was one thing to have a sort of vague intellectual understanding of "form and emptiness," and quite another to accept it emotionally.

Katherine Thanas was a tall, lean, angular woman in her fifties with a sallow complexion and very short gray hair. She wore gray robes and a brown ceremonial *rakusu,* which hung around her neck and looked like a long bib. She had been an artist before devoting her life to Zen practice, and when she spoke she often used artistic metaphors. Katherine had a particular way of folding her hands in her lap as if she had somehow to contain their strength. And she often pursed her lips as though resisting an impulse to smile, which she nevertheless did often. Her smile lit up her whole face, illuminating her dark, chocolate-colored eyes. She taught us with sincerity and patience for about thirty minutes each week, focusing on one paragraph or another of spiritual text, often from a Japanese Zen master named Dogen.

Every Tuesday evening I drove into Carmel, parked, and raced through the doors of the Cherry Foundation with perhaps two minutes to spare in my commute from Santa Cruz. I gathered myself onto my cushion with as much composure and decorum as I could manage. Sitting in that quiet and darkened room with the flicker of the candlelight, facing the wall, the work of the day just fell away from me as if it were heaped in a pile around my cushion. I adopted a little prayer from the Vietnamese Zen master Thich Nhat Hahn, which I said in my mind to get me started:

> Breathing in, I calm the mind
> Breathing out, I smile
> Dwelling in the present moment
> The present moment is wonderful.

I actually formed my lips into a smile, and that was when the day fell away. On a really good evening it stayed away and my light came to me. And I was filled with happiness.

One evening Katherine performed a full moon ceremony with us to generate *bodhicitta*. Kate and I had just returned from Florence, and I was still in my mountain space. I could see the light of the harvest moon through the windows and doors of the building. As I stood there next to my cushion, Katherine's voice washing over me, I felt as though my body had dissolved and I was floating in the moonlight.

Kate and I celebrated our tenth anniversary on November 7, 1989. Since the date fell in the middle of our fall classes, we managed only a dinner and then a weekend away, surely insufficient, we agreed, for such a momentous occasion. After all, in our first months together we had celebrated weekly anniversaries. We decided to rent a house in Borrego Springs, California, during the Christmas break, and spill over into the new year. *Tapestries* had been published that summer, and I felt a sense of denouement, as though one period in my life had ended and a new one was about to begin.

It was during this trip that we watched the continued dismantling of the fall of the Berlin Wall on TV. We watched the live broadcast of young people atop the Berlin Wall, tearing it down, brick by brick, wooden beam by wooden beam, tangles of barbed wire at its base. People were cheering and crying and flags were flying from atop the Brandenburg Gate.

For days we watched the live broadcasts on a satellite TV from Berlin, Prague, Bucharest, Budapest, Moscow. We didn't need to understand the languages to know what was happening. We were witnessing the end of European socialism. Tens of thousands were in the streets, cheering wildly, waving flags, spreading bouquets of flowers. I was in a state of emotional chaos, a bag of bones, a limp rag, on adrenaline overload. I could scarcely catch my breath for the enormity of it. Apart from the tanks in Moscow, there were no soldiers; there was very little violence, the state infrastructures simply collapsed. Kate said, "People stopped believing in their governments." *They stopped believing,* I thought, processing that idea, *and it was over.* European socialism was over. It was a cataclysmic shift in the world's political fault line, like the earthquake we had just lived through. The Berlin Wall, where I had stood, right there on Frederichstrasse, was gone, just a pile of rubble.

The U.S. Communist Party held its twenty-fifth national convention in the grand ballroom of the Cleveland, Ohio, Sheraton Hotel in December 1991. The upheavals in the European socialist world were central to the agenda. My father attended it, as did my former husband, Jack. Later they described it to me. The comrades were in a state of the highest possible agitation. Security at the Sheraton was very tight, reflecting, I thought, the paranoia of the party's national leadership. Ironically, Jack said, still disbelieving it, the party had employed Cleveland police officers to check members' identification before they could enter the hall. "The police!" he railed.

General Secretary Gus Hall was highly critical of Soviet leader Mikhail Gorbachev for *glasnost* and *perestroika,* his policies of openness and democratization, which in Gus's opinion had led to the overthrow of the government. My father disagreed with Gus.

He hailed Gorbachev; he said to me proudly, "The party produced him!" as if this confirmed the courage of his vision. In his public dissension from Gus at the meeting, my father pounded his fist on the table at which he was sitting. In his frustration he pounded so hard that blood spurted from his arm. Blood vessels burst through his skin, soaking his sleeve and splattering the blouse of a woman nearby. He later said that Gus looked at him, and their eyes locked. Comrades rushed to his aid. They got him out of the hall and up to his room, which was not easy since he didn't want to go. Trying to calm him down, someone shouted at him, "Herbert! Your blood pressure! Calm down!" To which my father snarled, "Yeah! And what's your blood pressure?"

"Gus was laughing," my father said to me later, incredulous. "He was laughing at me! The son of a bitch!"

My father had a stroke the following spring, April 1, 1992. He lost much of his capacity for short-term memory, and his right leg was permanently impaired. He was in the hospital, and then a rehabilitation center, for weeks. His historical memory remained intact, however. Gradually he improved, but he never recovered his mental acuity, and his health deteriorated. Mother took care of him, increasingly fearful. Ten years his senior, she was still in much better health.

Meanwhile, the Communist Party split into two groups. There were those who, like Gus Hall, insisted that a Leninist (they meant Stalinist, I thought, but didn't dare say so) party should be reconstituted in the former Soviet Union and go underground until it could once again take power and reestablish the Soviet Union. They maintained control of the U.S. party. And there were those, like my father and Jack and Angela Davis, who were for the democratic reform of socialism that Gorbachev had attempted; they were assessing how and why socialism had failed. They were also committed to building a broad progressive coalition within the United States. They left the party and formed a loosely knit coalition called the Committees of Correspondence, named, at my father's suggestion, after those preceding the American Revolution. My father and my mother, and so many of my old friends from the party, invited me to join the Committees of Correspondence. It was amazing to me that I had no inclination to do so. For all my years in the party, I had wanted something like what they were proposing to do. But it was too late for me. I was through with Communist politics, uninterested in arguments about Marxist "formulations" and political "estimates" and "lines." I was bored by what I felt to be the utter irrelevance of their discussions over why socialism had collapsed, over this "error" and that "policy."

From my experience in East Germany and at the Berlin Wall, the failure of socialism seemed no great mystery to me. Socialism had failed because of the corruption of those who had led it, and those who had lived under it. It was not that they were bad people; on the contrary, many of the comrades I met were wonderful, caring people. But I no longer believed that you could legislate altruism, which is part of what the Communist governments had tried to do, according to their own formulas for social justice. Greed and jealousy, anger and hatred, power and revenge were all inherent to the human condition. Unless political action was combined with internal development to produce true compassion, it would always be seriously if not fatally compromised. Altruism had to come from within each of us, from our own understandings of selflessness. At the very least, people themselves had to want to be generous. Of course, generosity could be encouraged, but it could not be coerced. When this coercion had been combined with a privileged party hierarchy and the denial of basic freedoms, corruption was inevitable, and popular fear and resentment predominated.

President George H. W. Bush launched war against Iraq on January 17, 1991, under the pretext of freeing Kuwait from Iraqi military occupation. Kuwait was a small emirate under the rule of sheikhs. Historically it had been part of Iraq. President Bush also announced the U.S. intention to overthrow Iraqi president, Saddam Hussein, the dictator we had previously sanctioned and funded, since he was no longer doing the bidding of the United States. This was Desert Storm.

At the Zen Center, Katherine Thanas said, "We must accept totally the inevitability of war, and we must do everything in our power to stop it." When she said that, I saw again that the Buddhist community was not indifferent to political events and worldly concerns, but it put them in the context of a different understanding about the causes of human suffering. Jealousy, greed, the desire for power and wealth were part of the human condition because we believed we had separate and permanent selves. This illusion of separation was a basic cause of human suffering. Katherine, I think, was teaching us that this illusion was the reason we needed to accept "the inevitability of war." In Buddhism, with our different understanding of the causes of war, we might bear witness to the desire and need for peace. In doing so, we could perhaps help ourselves and others to break through their illusions.

I was on campus the day the war began. At news of the first U.S. air strikes on Baghdad I became terribly distraught. The only constructive thing I could think to do was to find a way to be alone with the trees. I found a big old redwood. I sank down to its base, and in its shade I put handfuls of its sweet, earthy-smelling duff up to my face. I sat in a half-lotus and followed my breath. I could be of no use to anyone in a state of agitation. With the tree to help me, I finally calmed down. Expecting the outbreak of war, the students had planned a protest in advance and within an hour after the bombing had started, thousands had assembled at a predetermined site. I was so heartened.

That evening the Zen Center, in collaboration with many community organizations, held a silent vigil on a busy street in downtown Monterey. We held up our signs for peace. One read NO BLOOD FOR OIL! Some people driving by beeped their horns in approval; others simply ignored us. One woman, however, a passenger in a car, pushed her torso out through her open window, raised up both arms, shook her fists, and shouted, "Blood for oil! Blood for oil!" I was staggered by the cruelty of her declaration. *Surely*, I thought, *she must not understand the horror of war.* I struggled not to be angry at her.

Protests continued on the Santa Cruz campus. The students had formed a remarkable coalition uniting Jewish students (who condemned anti-Arab racism), Arab students (who condemned anti-Semitism), and virtually every campus organization, whether social, religious, or political. Among faculty, too, we had gathered broad opposition to the war. As Israel came under missile attack from Iraq, the student coalition, with its Jewish and Arab core, teetered but ultimately held. For many of us it was unbelievable to see the press photos of Israelis huddled in bomb shelters wearing gas masks, the images a haunting reminder of the Holocaust. In contrast to the 1960s, however, the media, with the exception of public radio and public television, gave scant coverage to the widespread antiwar protests.

Students asked me to speak at one of their rallies preceding a protest march to the government buildings in downtown Santa Cruz.

I used the occasion to test a way to combine my feminist, Marxist, and spiritual ideas. I began by conjuring the image of George Bush and Saddam Hussein as two patriarchs gearing up for war, testing their manhood like medieval knights in full body armor, wielding their mighty lances, swinging mindlessly at each other. I said it would be funny if not for the thousands and thousands of women, children, and men who would die as a consequence. I talked in some detail about the oil companies, their corporate priorities and imperial interests. I said this was not a war about freedom and democracy; it was about power and greed, and the continuation of U.S. domination in the region. With the Soviet Union gone, the United States had no military opposition with which to reckon.

I called upon each of us to strive toward inner peace, and to develop a sense of limitless compassion for everyone involved on all sides of this conflict. All of us knew greed, I said, all of us had attachments, all of us could feel what it was like to crave power. I urged us to think of the suffering everywhere. And I urged us to model ourselves after the Buddha, who had explained compassion by saying that it was like a tree that gives shade even to the man wielding the ax to cut it down.

It felt different to talk about war in this way. I felt less self-righteous, less strident, less angry than I had during the war in Vietnam. Instead, I felt an awful anguish for all of the peoples in the region, and for our own soldiers. I thought about my children, my lover, about what it would mean to lose them; I didn't know how people bore such losses in war.

Just before the start of the war in Iraq, Kate had attended a ten-day retreat with a Tibetan Buddhist teacher, Venerable Khenchen Thrangu Rinpoche. He was from the Kagyu tradition, and had the reputation of being a superb teacher of a meditation practice known as *mahamudra*. Kate returned home bursting with enthusiasm. It is a practice that focuses directly on the nature of mind, finding its vastness and serenity. When a second ten-day retreat was announced for the following fall, Kate urged me to go with her. The ten days spanned the four-day Thanksgiving holiday to minimize the impact on our work schedules. With help from a colleague who took charge of the two days of classes I would miss, I was able to go. I had never before missed even one class in fifteen years of teaching, and it felt very odd to do so now.

During the ten-day retreat we kept a rigorous schedule, with the first meditation session beginning at 6:30 AM and the last ending at 9:30 PM. We also maintained "noble silence" until the last evening of the retreat, except during the question period. This eliminated all the chitchat of daily life, allowing the mind to settle. Rinpoche taught for two hours each morning, and again each afternoon. One of his assistants, a U.S.-born monk named Lama Tashi, led the meditation sessions. It turned out that Lama Tashi had been president of the National Student Association in the 1960s, and active in the antiwar movement. He greeted me with exceptional warmth, thrilled and surprised to find me in such a setting. "We should write a memoir together," he said, "and explain our path to the dharma."

Rinpoche was in his fifties, stocky with a round face, prominent teeth, and dark-framed glasses. His head was not shaved; he had instead the soft black fuzz of a crew cut. He wore maroon- and saffron-colored robes, and battered-looking brown loafers. He taught directly from the *mahamudra* text in a methodical, pedantic style. He had little charisma, but he exuded a cheerful and finally irresistible sincerity. He didn't speak English, so a highly skilled, U.S.-born man provided a careful, fluent English translation of the Tibetan.

A significant moment for me at this retreat came during one of the question periods. A fellow practitioner, who was a clinical psychologist, wanted to know what Rinpoche would recommend for treating patients who were survivors of trauma, especially in childhood. I sat bolt upright. The therapist explained how symptoms of physical suffering and depression persisted for years after the events. The translator began to interpret the questions for Rinpoche, and then he paused. He was stuck, he explained to us in English, because he didn't know the Tibetan for "trauma." The translator then conversed with Rinpoche, explaining the concept of trauma in search of the equivalent word in Tibetan. Finally, Rinpoche understood. He said the Tibetan word; it translated back into English as "holding on to anger." I was stunned, riveted. "One who holds on to anger!"

Language reflects a specific culture, geography, and philosophy, and in turn, it shapes cultures, perceptions, and understandings. For example, the German language lends itself to dualities and dialectics. It was the language of Hegel and Marx. The Diné language reflects the Navajo worldview, in which everything is in relationship to everything else. There can be no separation, no self-contained objects. For example, the Dine word for a car battery translates back into English as "heart of car." I knew that the Tibetan language was constructed around the dharma. And so we came to the word "trauma," the Tibetan word itself already containing the answer to the psychologist's question.

This revelation held such personal significance for me. Healing was about dissolving anger. I was always denying that I was angry. The process that would work to release anger was not denial and repression, but acknowledgment and dissolution. I had watched Soen Sunim dissolve his anger. I knew that it could be done. To dissolve my anger meant to forgive; to forgive meant to practice compassion. A weight lifted from my chest. I had my first glimmer of how it could be done.

As the end of the retreat approached, my mind was clear, and it was free of almost all of its regular chatter; it was sparkling like the lake water near the high mountain retreat center. That's how I felt. "How do I look?" I asked Kate, thinking I must be glowing. "Like hell," she said, laughing. I looked in the mirror. I was physically exhausted from the rigors of our retreat schedule; so was she. But in my mind, in my mind I was jubilant.

After thirteen years of continuous teaching at UC Santa Cruz, I finally took a sabbatical. Jenny graduated from high school in June 1993, and this left Kate and me free to "leave home." With the status of women's studies finally secured, I planned a two-year leave; I got paid two-thirds of my salary for the first year, and took a leave without pay for the second. Jenny went to live and work at Hidden Villa, the organic farm in the hills above Palo Alto where she and Josh had attended summer camp as kids. She enrolled in a nearby community college and made plans to transfer after two years to the University of Washington in Seattle.

Kate and I gave notice to vacate our rented house and we packed up. We gave away most everything and put our few remaining possessions into storage. For the two years we were away, we lived in a VW camper fondly known as "The Silver Turtle." I had trepidations about leaving the children (even though they had already left us), but I soon learned that home to them was wherever we were. Each of them separately, and once all of them together, flew into various cities to meet us: Edmonton, Denver, San Diego, Albuquerque. They camped with us for a while and then went back to their lives. With no rent to pay, our expenses were minimal. We did discover, however, that we had to have a "permanent address" in order to retain a driver's license and the car registration, and to rent a post office box for mail. Our friend Teramota in Pacific Grove, ever efficient and inventive, allowed us to use her home as a "base camp." Having missed the hippie life of the 1970s, we seemed to have reinvented it in the 1990s, or so we were laughingly told by our children and friends. Ultimately we were to drive from Alaska to Mexico and as far east as El Paso. We came to think of this time as our "turtle odyssey."

We began that summer of 1993 at Florence, and at the first hint of autumn we drove to Tucson in order to attend a teaching with His Holiness the Dalai Lama. This was how I thought of him now, His Holiness, or "H.H.," we said jokingly. He was giving a teaching on patience, one of the six perfections of a spiritual practice. He was teaching from the text of an Indian master whose name was Shantideva. The text was called *The Bodhisattva Way of Life.* The title struck me as ironic, since as a teenager I had studied a book produced by the Chinese Communist Party called *How to Be a Good Communist.*

I remembered reading in His Holiness's autobiography what he had written about Communism. He wrote that it was "one of the greatest human experiments of all time, and I do not deny that I myself was very impressed with the ideology at first." He went on to say that he had become critical of Communism because in practice he felt that there was a great lack of personal freedom. While Communists spoke of "the people," he said, they privileged only special elites. He was also critical of the West for its hostility to the socialist countries, which, he said, intensified their own paranoia and systems of state repression. He concluded:

However, in as much as I have any political allegiance, I suppose I am still half Marxist. . . . my religious beliefs dispose me far more towards Socialism and Internationalism, which are more in line with Buddhist principles [than Capitalism]. The other attractive thing about Marxism for me is its assertion that man [*sic*] is ultimately responsible for his own destiny. This reflects Buddhist thought exactly.

Reading these thoughts from His Holiness was very helpful to me as I reconciled the different parts of myself.

The teachings in Tucson lasted a week and were held in the grand ballroom of a Sheraton Hotel, located at the northwestern edge of Tucson and grandly named "El Conquistador," an ironic twist given His Holiness's message of peace and compassion. The hotel was pushed up against the Santa Catalina Mountains, and the giant saguaro cactus stood everywhere around us, its "arms" upraised like those of the Mother Goddess. Lavish lawns and flower gardens sucking up hundreds of gallons of water every day spanned the hotel grounds, an imperial absurdity in the desert environment. We drove to the hotel each morning along a bustling four-lane avenue lined with strip malls, Burger Kings, and Taco Bells. The hotel ballroom held between 1,500 and two thousand people, and made for a much more personal encounter with His Holiness than we'd had at the San Jose stadium. He made it a matter of practice to walk out amongst us at the end of each teaching, bowing, shaking hands, and chatting with folks in a very informal manner.

Unlike my experience in San Jose, I understood these teachings. I had been doing a modest meditation practice, had studied a little, and had memorized a small portion of Shantideva's text so that I was already familiar with its ideas. I was so excited to understand the Dalai Lama, at least on some level, in some small way. It was there in

Tucson with His Holiness that I first took bodhisattva vows. I wanted to do this in order to set my practice more firmly, and to remind myself of its compassionate purpose. A bodhisattva consistently tries to act in ways to benefit all living beings. The vows are based in part on the kind of spiritual commitments, or "precepts," common to most religious traditions, but tailored in this case to lay, rather than monastic, practitioners.

The first precept is to avoid killing, directly or indirectly, including even the smallest of insects. The second is to avoid stealing, which also means not taking that which has not been freely given. The third is to avoid sexual misconduct. Kate and I listened to the wording of this one very, very carefully. It was worded in such a way as to make no assumptions or exclusions based on sexual preferences or practices. It stressed being a reliable and loving partner. The fourth precept is to avoid telling lies through either commission or omission, that is, lying by silence or implication so that you deliberately lead a person to draw a false conclusion. The fifth is to avoid intoxicants like drugs and alcohol.

In addition to the precepts, bodhisattva vows include "the six perfections." Each is intended to strengthen your own mind stream in order to be of benefit to others. The first perfection is generosity, not only in the conventional sense of giving, but also in the sense of thinking of others' comforts, needs, and wishes before your own. The second perfection is discipline, which refers to the self-discipline needed to follow the precepts and practice. The third is patience, which is primarily about the avoidance of anger and/or its dissolution. The fourth is joyful perseverance in the practice, which is my favorite because I love the word "joyful." The fifth is concentration, which refers to meditation. And the sixth is *prajna*, which is the Sanskrit word for wisdom. This does not refer to worldly or academic knowledge, but to the wisdom of knowing the vastness of our own minds and our interconnections with others.

Taking vows gave me a feeling of exhilaration and wholesome purpose. It was as though the vows put my life on track. At the time, in my exuberance, I had little idea of how truly hard they would be to follow. Like the Hippocratic oath "to do no harm," it would seem that each precept and each perfection carried within it a complicated and expanding depth of meaning. What did it mean to do no harm? None of us could see widely enough to know. I finally realized that the oath, like the precepts and perfections, was not about having an objective standard by which to judge one's actions; rather, it was about having an internal standard for one's own motivations.

As is the tradition at all such events, His Holiness set aside time to respond to questions. We were asked to write them out. Little pieces of paper sat in a pile next to the translator, who picked them up at random. He read them aloud, first in English and then in Tibetan. During one of these question periods a Western nun, Thubten Chodron, asked His Holiness when he thought there could be the full ordination of nuns in the Tibetan tradition.

Without full ordination, nuns were excluded from certain practices; they had more strict precepts to follow, and they could receive but not give empowerments, which limited their work as teachers. In short, no matter how skilled, dedicated, devoted, or accomplished they were, nuns in the Tibetan traditions were less than their male counterparts simply because they were female. The discrimination was also visible in other ways. For example, all of His Holiness's ritual attendants were male, and in any entourage nuns came last, following even the youngest of monks.

For several years Western feminist practitioners had been pressuring for reforms of the sexism that marked the Asian cultures in which Buddhism was most widely practiced. Thubten Chodron referred specifically to a recent conference she had attended at which His Holiness had spoken. She noted that his presence at the conference had been deeply appreciated.

His Holiness responded. He, too, referred to the conference, and he commented on the power and eloquence of Thubten Chodron's speech at it. She had moved him greatly, he said. There was discrimination against the nuns, he acknowledged. They didn't have adequate facilities, teachers, texts. This was true. He was working to correct this. All the monastic facilities in the Tibetan refugee communities were poor, but it was true that the nuns suffered the worst conditions. This was wrong. It was being addressed.

As for the full ordination of nuns on an equal basis with the monks, he couldn't do anything about that by himself. Lineages had to be established, or the rules had to be changed, but he was only one person. He alone could not order the changes, he pleaded. I groaned in frustration. Kate whispered to me, "He should announce that the next incarnation of the Dalai Lama will be a woman! That would take care of it!" Meanwhile, I thought how wise Kate had been to keep us on the periphery of all of these institutional limitations and struggles. And I thought how profoundly grateful I was for the teachings themselves.

One afternoon near the end of our week in Tucson, a huge thunderstorm rolled in. It rained in torrents as it can only in the desert with its flash floods; the earth was perfumed with the pungent odor of wet creosote. At sunset the storm clouds folded back and a double rainbow illumined the sky. I stepped outside and took a deep breath. I lifted up my arms as if to meet the arc of the rainbow. It was the first time in my life I could ever remember feeling completely at ease.

seven

ENDINGS

MY MOTHER TURNED ninety on February 28, 1995. We celebrated at the Victorian Garden, her favorite restaurant in downtown San Jose. For her ninetieth birthday party, Mother wore a black dress with gold brocade, gold shoes, and she carried a small gold handbag. She ate with gusto and relished the birthday cake that had been specially prepared for her. In her earlier years Mom had been reluctant to disclose her age. Now she trumpeted it. She loved it when people gasped in astonishment at how good she looked. "My God, George," one woman shouted across a crowded restaurant three years later, "she is ninety-three!" Mother quivered with pleasure. In the last years of her life she was a model of energetic old age. Whatever her ailments, she rose up over them all the way to the very end.

Though Mom gradually lost most of her vision due to macular degeneration, a gradual deterioration of a part of the retina, she was still able to read the newspaper and do her crossword puzzle every morning with a magnifying glass and a powerful reading lamp. She gave up walking in the neighborhood because her depth perception was unreliable and she had already taken a few falls; luckily, she had not broken any bones. So instead she exercised indoors, walking a route from the kitchen through the living room and around what she called the music room, which housed her piano and an ancient stereo system, and back into the kitchen—around and around for at least forty minutes each day. Her hearing was unimpaired, her mind as sharp as ever. She dazzled visitors. When students or journalists came to interview my father, she sat nearby and didn't hesitate to interrupt with corrections or elaborations: "No, Herbert, it wasn't that way at all!" He almost always deferred to her memory.

One afternoon, I decided to see to it that my parents had at least one working flashlight. Mom always wanted one in case of a power failure. She had a kitchen drawer filled with gadgets, screws, batteries, scissors, string, and flashlights, that assortment of junk we all stuff into one or another place. I had been looking for something on a previous visit and came upon the mess. Her batteries were so old they had all long since expired. None of her flashlights worked.

I arrived with C, D, and AA batteries, retrieved her flashlights from the drawer, and set everything on the kitchen table. Mother could hardly see; nevertheless, she was determined to help me. She had always been the mechanical one in the family, and prided herself on that fact. "*Your* father," she used to say, accented in such a way as to sound as though it were my fault he was my father and not her husband, "can't even screw in a lightbulb!"

For a couple of hours, we sat together at the kitchen table, our heads bent over our work, kibitzing—talking about this and that, nothing that I can remember now, just the comforting feeling of a gentle bantering. I had taken apart all of the flashlights at the same time—a big mistake since we got all their parts mixed up. We giggled a lot. Mom would pick up one part or another and say, "Try it this way," directing my efforts. Her directions were always right. At long last we salvaged three flashlights, and got rid of the fourth (although Mom was reluctant to throw anything out). I was sorry we were done. It was the best fun we'd had together in years. Although I remained wary of her criticisms and flaring temper, in the last years of her life she had been very supportive of me and Kate and of the children. Of course, I still hid things from her in an effort to head off confrontation, such as the reclamation of my Jewish heritage or my new affinity for Buddhist ideas. She had no idea that Kate and I did prayers every morning. I was her daughter, the successful professor, with a modicum of fame, and that was sufficient to calm the waters.

By her nineties, Mom could no longer plan the parties she loved so much, but she could certainly still attend them and entertain her guests. When Joshua was married, Kate and I wanted to have a reception for him and his wife for our West Coast family and friends. Mom enthusiastically suggested that we hold it at her house. "We have the garden," she said. "It will be lovely."

Joshua had been living in Japan since he graduated from college. He taught English as a second language. What had begun with sporadic jobs had developed into a successful teaching career. He had lived in Kobe for several years, but after the devastating earthquake in 1995 he moved to Kyoto. Josh loved Japan and he loved his work. He met his wife, Eka Japaridze, at a neurolinguistics conference in Bali. Eka was from the Republic of Georgia in the former Soviet Union, and her parents, both chemists, lived in Tbilisi. Josh and Eka's marriage was a prolonged international event. They were legally married in Kyoto. Then there was a celebration in Tbilisi with Eka's family and friends, and another very large affair in New York with the Kurzweil family. The third celebration was to be in my parents' garden.

I had ordered food from a Middle Eastern restaurant in Santa Cruz, and it was delivered in boxes to my parents' home in San Jose early on the morning of the party. Jenny, who was an experienced caterer, took charge. Mom seated herself on a chair in the middle of the kitchen, and Kate and I swirled around her, following Jenny's every command. We had brought our CD player, and we put on a recording by the Argentinean folksinger Mercedes Sosa. Mom had never heard her before. She loved the rich contralto of Sosa's voice, and took up the Latin beat still sitting in her chair, her feet dancing, her hands clapping, her whole body swaying to the music, and laughing and laughing.

All the things Mother did that drove me crazy also somehow provided me with the best memories of her in her last years. My acute terrors from childhood had fallen away as I matured; I could keep them at bay as long as I could stay in my adult mind. But she could still wield a mighty, guilt-producing, anger-inducing influence. I never talked to her about the incest. I never trusted her enough. I still doubted that she would believe me, and I was certain she would defend my father at all costs, including a family rupture. I didn't want to risk that. But a year and a half before she died, we had one of those frustrating half-tone conversations characteristic of my family in which nothing is explicit and yet much is implied.

I had called my mother one day when my father wasn't home. It was unusual to reach her at home alone, but he happened to have had a doctor's appointment. Because he wasn't there, my mother felt she could talk to me more freely. She said he was driving the nurses and doctor crazy with complaints about his vision. After his major stroke he seemed to be experiencing a series of lesser ones, like the aftershocks from an earthquake, affecting one or another part of his body. This time it was his right eye. It drooped and hadn't recovered. There was nothing the doctors could do. They said it would heal after a while.

Mother asked if I had a few minutes to talk and I said, "Sure." "When you and I talk on the phone," she began, "we're just natural with each other, we just talk. But when you speak with Herbert it's very stiff." I agreed. She went on, "When he reads books, stories about children, he weeps for them." I knew that my father was reading Jonathan Kozol's *Amazing Grace: The Lives of Children and the Conscience of a Nation* because he had told me something about it. The book had deeply affected him. Mother said, "You know, he's very naive, Bettina. It's very hard for him and he tries. He tries so hard. You have to forgive him." I didn't say anything in response; my heart pounded and I wondered what it was she meant I had to forgive him for.

Later, when I told Kate about this exchange, she said that I should have pursued it further, that I should have questioned her. "Over the phone?" I asked. *I'm such a coward,* I thought to myself in frustration, *and our conversations are so indirect.* Kate thought my father was weeping for his own sublimated sorrow about whatever had happened to him in his childhood. If you asked him, he always gave the same formulaic response I myself had once adopted. "I had a perfect childhood," he would say.

I knew that my father had had an older brother named Alvin. He and my father had been very close and they had shared a room together as boys. Alvin had committed suicide. My father wrote to me about it once in a letter dated April 4, 1968, the same day Martin Luther King, Jr., was assassinated. He wrote: "There is something you never knew because we didn't tell you—but you should know—my brother, Alvin, committed suicide. He was 28 and I 20; we had been quite close. One of my scars." "A perfect childhood?" I wanted to shriek. "You had a perfect childhood?" I don't know why he wrote to me when he did, because we never discussed it, but it was in the midst of my nervous breakdown. He may have sensed or feared something about the shape I was in, although I kept up a façade of normality with my parents through it all.

About a year after the telephone conversation with my mother, a neighbor called to tell me Mother had collapsed. It was a warm June day.

When Kate and I arrived at San Jose Medical Center, my father was already there. The ER physician told us that Mother had sepsis, a full-body infection. The source of it was not yet clear. They had started her on antibiotics and a drug to bring up her blood pressure. The prognosis was not good, especially in a woman of Mom's age. She said they had not put Mom on life support—the doctor called it intubation—pending consultation with us. One thing was clear: Mom was in critical condition. I realized then that this doctor was warning us about the dangers of putting Mom on life support, that in her estimate she could not be saved. My father and I went in to see Mother. He said, "You're going to be fine, baby. The prognosis is very good." I could not believe what I was hearing. Dad was always in denial, but I could not let this lie stand.

"No, it's not!" I snapped, outraged. "That's not what the doctor said." Dad looked startled, but he did not contradict me. I thought my mother needed to know she was dying. I believe that a person has the right to know that. I spoke to Mom more softly. I gave her the diagnosis. I said, "You are critically ill. Your condition is very critical." I explained what sepsis is, and that they didn't yet know the cause. I said she would be taken up to intensive care, where the doctors would try to get a more complete diagnosis. She said, "Bettina, I'm so nauseous. See if they can give me something for the nausea."

"Okay, Mom," I said. "One more thing. I love you." When I said that her pupils dilated, and I think she understood she was dying.

Mom was moved to the intensive care unit. I rode up in the elevator with her, holding her hand. "It's awful, Bettina," she said. "It's just awful." She gave a heavy New York accent to the word "awful" so the vowels were exaggerated and it sounded like "aaauwful." "I'm so sorry, Mom," I said softly. "I'm so sorry." In lieu of water—the doctors didn't want her to take in anything at all—a nurse produced a stick with a small green sponge on the end of it. I wet the sponge and rubbed Mom's lips with it.

I stood in the hall for a few minutes, consulting with an ICU nurse. She gave me the prognosis again, explaining that it was virtually impossible for my mother to recover from sepsis. She spoke more bluntly than the doctor had. I understood that Mom could not recover, and both the doctors and nurses were encouraging me not to put her on life support. "I don't want you to think I'm cold or uncaring," the nurse said. "No, no," I said. "I understand." A few more minutes and the diagnosis was completed. Mom had sepsis caused by gallstones. They were completely blocking the digestive tract to the liver. The surgeon proposed intubation, sedation, and surgery, first to drain the poison from the gall bladder; then later, if she regained sufficient strength, they could remove the gall bladder.

Now I faced two completely opposite strategies, one from the ER physician and nurses, who had made it clear that death was both imminent and inevitable, and another from the surgeon, who proposed an aggressive strategy to try to save her, which I understood to be impossible. My father, of course, wanted them to try to save her. I wavered, and went back in to talk to Mom. I explained to her that the acute nausea came from the blockage and told her she was in extremely critical condition. I asked her if she wanted life support, explaining that they would sedate her and put a tube down her throat. She understood. She said, "Yes." I asked her again, adding, "You understand, Mom, that once they put you on life support it will be very hard to take you off it." "Yes," she said. She understood. I realized then that despite all of her early protestations to me about not wanting her life prolonged by heroic measures, she was so uncomfortable that relief from the nausea was her only consideration.

My father was sitting outside her room. I explained everything to him, slowly and carefully, repeating myself to be sure he understood. I felt we had no choice now but to go with life support—because that's what my mother said she wanted. When I was sure my father understood, I signed the hospital's permission forms authorizing intubation and surgery to remove the gallstones and drain the poison from her system. I stood by the bed, holding Mom's hand, talking to her softly, saying how sorry I was she was so uncomfortable.

My father came in. He took Mom's other hand. He said, "You're going to be okay, baby. They don't know your courage." His voice cracked and he left the room. I stayed with her until the anesthesiologist arrived. I squeezed her hand. I thought it was the last time we would see each other, the last time we would speak. I had a lump in my throat the size of the near-century she had lived. "We'll be right out here waiting," I managed to say. "I love you." She nodded.

My mother never regained consciousness. Friday. Saturday. Sunday. Each day Kate and I drove to the hospital. We watched the urine output, the blood pressure, the respiration. There was almost no urine. They were hydrating her, and she was becoming more and more bloated because her kidneys were shutting down. Her blood pressure was wildly erratic. All of her breaths were assisted. Meanwhile, the surgeons proceeded according to their game plan to move on to the next surgery and remove her gall bladder.

Sunday night an anesthesiologist arrived to prepare the necessary paperwork for surgery the following morning. My father was sitting in the chair next to my mother's bed, his head bowed, hands clasped in his lap. Kate was nearby reading. I was standing by the bed holding Mom's hand. The anesthesiologist looked at Mom, read her chart, and exclaimed loudly enough for even my father to hear, "They're going to do surgery on her?" His tone made it clear that he was appalled at the prospect. The nurse caught his eye as if to say, "Don't go there."

"No," he said with obvious relief, in response to our queries, he was off tomorrow morning and would not be in surgery. Someone else would be in the OR. My father got up now, alert to possible new information. Although reluctant to counter his colleagues' opinions, this doctor made it clear enough that he thought surgery was unwise.

We took my father home a while later. Sitting at the kitchen table we talked to him about letting my mother go. "But the surgeons are experts," he said. "Who are we to counter their opinion?"

Kate said, "Surgery is all they know. They mean well, but their minds are very narrow because they are trained to think only in one way. They don't see anything else." My father said he would think about it carefully. One thing was sure: He didn't want my mother to suffer.

The next morning Mom's condition remained unchanged. The surgeons recommended waiting one more day before attempting to remove her gall bladder. I asked the chief surgeon if I could talk with him alone. I repeated to him a conversation I had had with my own doctor that morning. I had called her office to cancel a routine appointment for myself, and when she learned that my mother was in critical condition, she came to the telephone. My doctor said, "There's a big difference between 'improvement in her condition' and 'recovery.' Even a much younger person would have a hard time recovering." Two sentences and she had cut through the murk.

"Please help me," I said now to the surgeon in the hallway outside Mother's room. "I'm trying to cut through my father's denial. Help me." At that moment my father joined us. He asked the surgeon, "After you do the surgery can she come home with me? Can it be like it was?" With eyes full of grief and understanding, the doctor said, "Expect the worst, but hope for the best." Then he left. They were going to wait on surgery for another day.

My father and I went into the waiting room to talk. He said, "I remembered a conversation Mom and I had." He was agitated and spoke rapidly. "She didn't want this. We were joking, you know, but we said to each other not to do this, with all the tubes and the respirator. We agreed. We wouldn't do this."

A lump rose in my throat, but I managed to speak. Hearing my father say this was a great relief. A huge weight had been lifted off my shoulders. I knew now that my parents had had such a conversation. And I felt that he was ready to carry out what my mother had wanted. Even though he didn't want to let her go, he was prepared to have the life support removed. "That's terrific, Dad! That's right! I'm so proud of you." We had agreed. We went back into Mom's room. I took her hand. I said, "Mom, if you need to go, it's all right. Dad agrees. We love you, and if you need to go, we understand."

All day I urged Dad to talk to Mom himself, to tell her that it was all right for her to go, but he said he couldn't do it. "She'll hear me weeping," he said. He tried once. He took her hand, but he couldn't bring himself to speak. "That's all right," I said.

I talked to her all day. I sang to her, an old Yiddish melody she liked, "Tumba la la, tumba la la, tumba la la . . ." As always, I sang off key, but she couldn't tell me.

Tuesday, June 15. My mother's doctor of twenty years, the hospital surgeon, Kate and I, and my father were gathered in her room. Kate whispered to me, "They're talking about taking her off life support." "Good," I said. I went to my father. He was sitting down. I put my arm around him and pressed his frail, bony shoulder into my belly. The surgeon gave a more balanced and honest appraisal of my mother's condition, giving us the real statistics on her chances of surviving the gall bladder surgery in her condition. All of this while my mother lay in the bed, the respirator pumping air into her, the steady swish of its motor. I wondered if she could hear us.

My mother's doctor was wavering. He had known my mother for so long, and he was extremely fond of her. I said to him, "My mother really trusted you, and she liked you enormously." I noticed that I was already using the past tense. He brushed aside my words. I repeated them and our eyes met, and I knew he had heard me. Mom's doctor nodded slowly, the grief drawn on his face. He said, "Rick," speaking to the surgeon, "what do you think?"

Rick said, without hesitation, "Let's do it." They had agreed to take her off the life support. A well of gratitude to him swelled in my heart.

My father sat very still. Both doctors and the nurses were weeping. I forced my own tears back. We had decided to take my mother off life support—most important, in accord with what we felt her wishes to have been. It had been one of the hardest decisions I ever had to make. A nurse said to me, "Let us know when you're ready." My parents had been together for sixty-two years. How could they ever be ready? Another nurse, very young, knelt in front of my father and took his hands in hers. Through her tears she said, "Thank you for restoring my faith in people. This is why I wanted to be a nurse. To help . . ." Her voice broke.

I took my mother's hand. I had been doing a meditation for her for days, and I continued it now. In the meditation I visualized a radiant light above Mom that rained down upon her. I went over to my father. "You have to say goodbye to her," I said. "You'll regret it terribly if you don't." I forced him up and moved him gently to the bed. "Take her hand," I gently urged him. "Talk to her. It's very important."

"Will she hear me?" he asked.

"Yes," I said. "She's unconscious, but she's here and she will hear you." Of course, I didn't know this, but there is medical evidence that even in a coma a person can still hear.

He reached awkwardly under the sheets for her hand. He said, "Schnootzy?" his term of endearment. She gave no sign. He said to me, desperately, "She's not responding to me." And then, as if in recognition of the reality, more calmly, "She can't respond to me."

"That's right," I encouraged. "But go ahead."

"Schnootzy," he began again, "you're the lucky one. You get to go first. You were always the lucky one. . . ." In the stillness, with just the regular *swish*ing sound of the respirator, he said goodbye to her. Then he sat down in his chair.

Kate stood by the side of Mom's bed, anchoring the grief. I nodded to the nurse. She went to call the respiratory therapist to disconnect the life support.

I sat down on a little stool in a corner of the room near the bed and went into a meditation. I sensed my mother's presence and knew she was going toward death. She was off the life support. I stood up and went to the bed. I held her hand. Kate was on the other side. I closed my eyes, trying to sense her presence, but she was gone. She had taken only four widely spaced spasmodic breaths on her own. Kate and I continued to stand on either side of the bed. My father stood and walked slowly out of the room.

A few minutes later a doctor came in. He officially pronounced her dead, and a nurse clicked off the monitor.

I woke in the middle of the night. It was 1:26 AM. I thought, *My mother has been dead for fourteen hours.* A seismic shift. The loss of my mother felt exactly like a seismic shift in the earth's core, the core reality of my life.

July 2, 1999. It was seventeen days after my mother's death. I had been with my father almost every day, and when not actually in San Jose I had telephoned him. He and I had been running errands, mostly to the banks to put his finances in order. It was becoming apparent that he could not continue to live in the house by himself. He wasn't eating properly, and he couldn't take care of the house. In fact, he had already set fire to the stove when he mistook a plastic container for a glass one. Luckily he had been able to put it out.

My father hated to change anything about his life even in the best of times, and these were the worst. He resisted even the simplest of adjustments for his own safety. Meanwhile, I was insisting that he move into a secure senior residence where he would have regular meals, housekeeping and laundry services, and help available should he need it.

He would agree to move one day, and then refuse the next. Using my mother's influence—she had wanted to move into such a place a few years earlier—I finally got him to agree to be put on a waiting list for an apartment where one of his and Mother's oldest friends was already living.

With all of his resistance and reluctance, I found myself yelling at him in the car on several occasions as we drove from one errand to another. I knew even as I was doing it that I wasn't yelling primarily about these decisions. Underneath it all was my fury at the incest, which I had remembered five years earlier, but I didn't think I ever would confront him about it.

So when Kate and I went to San Jose on this particular day, July 2, seventeen days after my mother's death, I was determined to control my anger and simply attend to the myriad details before us. All went well, and in the evening we took my father out to one of our favorite vegetarian Vietnamese restaurants, called the White Lotus. It was a welcome relief from the coffee shop my parents had frequented. Dad ate well, chatting amicably, sharing a few stories about Mom and Paul Robeson that we hadn't heard before. We were on our way home when out of the blue he said to me, "Did I ever hurt you when you were a child?" I was sitting in the back seat, Kate was driving, and he was in the front passenger seat. I searched frantically for Kate's eyes in the rearview mirror. Our eyes met, and she nodded almost imperceptibly. I said, "Yes."

He asked, "What did I do?" I paused for a long time, uncertain what to say. He said hastily, "It's okay if you don't want to tell me. Never mind."

Finally I said, "You were inappropriate with me." In that moment, unrehearsed and unprepared, I couldn't think of what else to say.

Growing agitated, he said, "What do you mean?"

"You were inappropriate with me for my age," I replied.

He said, "What do you mean inappropriate? What are you talking about?"

As I felt the adrenaline course through my body, I looked again in the rearview mirror, where I saw Kate mouth to me, "It's up to you." It was so unexpected, so unplanned, and so surreal. I had never imagined having this conversation with my father, despite all my pent-up anger. I had had dreams, though. In one, two years before, I had said to him, "I remember everything about my childhood!" He just looked at me. I started screaming and raging at him. We were walking on the street and people were looking at us and I really didn't give a damn. I was yelling and tearing his jacket off. It was like a windbreaker, and it fell into something red like raspberry juice on the sidewalk. He picked up the jacket and put it back on. He zipped it up even though it was all stained in front. He didn't say anything and I was still yelling at him. Then I asked him if he understood why I had so much rage at him. He shook his head.

In the dream I said, "You always say you had a perfect childhood. Well, you didn't! I teach this stuff! I know! You abused me because you were abused as a child! Your brother Alvin killed himself!" I shrieked.

In the dream he spoke. He said, "I was always so careful with you," as if to differentiate himself from the abusers in his own family.

"Oh, yes!" I snarled. "You were careful, all right!" And then the dream petered out and the scene shifted, as so often happens in dreams.

Now, here in the car, in reality, I said, "You were sexually inappropriate with me."

He said, "Sexually inappropriate? What did I do to you?" He was visibly upset and his voice had risen.

I repeated the phrase because it was the only thing I could think to say.

By this time we had arrived at the house. Kate parked the car and cut the engine. He said, "When we were playing together?"

I said, "Yes."

He said, "Did I arouse myself?"

I said, "Yes."

He said, "Did I ejaculate?"

I said, "Yes."

He said, "Did I penetrate you?" crying out the word "penetrate."

I said, "No. You were always very careful not to hurt me physically."

He said, "Are you sure?"

I said, "I am certain."

He said, "I have no memory of this." And I thought to myself that for no memory, at least no conscious memory, his questions were precise enough. He went on. "This is unbelievable. I don't mean that I don't believe you. If you say this happened, it must have happened. But it's unbelievable to me. I have no memory of this."

I said, "I did not think you would remember. It was too painful for you to remember, and it would be in contradiction to how you see yourself."

He said, "Yes. Yes. I have no memory. This is unbelievable. I don't mean I don't believe you. How can I apologize to you? There are no words that are adequate. What can I say? How can you forgive me?"

I said, "I have already forgiven you." And it was true. In those few minutes his anguish had been so palpable that all of my anger had dissolved. Because, of course, I loved him. What arose for me in that moment in the car was a compassion so vast, so limitless that it embraced not only my father, but every being in the world. And just as suddenly this feeling of limitless compassion was gone.

He said, "Thank God Fay didn't know about this. She didn't know, did she?"

I said, "No, Dad, she didn't know. I never told her. I was so afraid of her when I was little. I never told her."

He said, "Thank God Mother didn't know. I don't know what she would have done." He paused, and then he said, "She would've killed me, that's what she would have done. And I would've deserved it."

I told him about how confused I was as a child, how I had held him in such esteem, worshipped him, been in awe of him, and how I thought there was something wrong with me, that I was evil. I said, "I felt these things about myself for many years."

He listened attentively. He said he could understand that.

I said, "It almost killed me. I attempted suicide when I was in my twenties."

He said, "Because of this?"

I said, "Yes, because of this."

I explained how I felt that I had no one I could talk to, that I was paranoid, afraid that if I talked to a therapist he might turn out to be an FBI or police agent.

Kate said, "She protected you." I was startled to hear her voice. I had been leaning forward from the back seat, and my father was facing straight ahead, his hands spread on his knees. Sometimes his left hand folded around his cane and he banged the cane on the floor of the car. The conversation was so intense, my attention so riveted on my father, I had forgotten Kate was there.

He said, "I can't live with this."

I said, "I have lived with this, and you can too." I talked to him about my experience as a professor, teaching students about the prevalence of sexual abuse, hearing their own stories over the years. I told him about the many books I had read and experts who said this often happened in families. Then I asked him if something like this happened to him when he was a child. He didn't respond to the question. He repeated that he couldn't understand how he could have done these things.

"You knew about this?" he asked Kate.

"Yes," she said.

"And you tried to help her?" he asked.

"Yes," Kate said. "I hope I was able to help her."

My father said, "I noticed that you avoided me. And I thought there must be something wrong with me. There was."

"I do have one memory," he volunteered suddenly. "But you were an adult, maybe eighteen, and you were home from college. You were dressing in your room, and I passed your door. It was open. You were naked. And you showed yourself to me. It was as though you were challenging me."

I said, "I don't remember that incident, but it's consistent with my experience, with my suppressed fury."

He said, "I registered it. And I thought it was very strange."

Later, I thought about it more. First, I got angry that with all the trauma, what he remembered was me as the seducer! Then I remembered something like what he had described, but I was twenty-three and pregnant with Joshua. I was already showing at four months, my belly rounding out. I was home with Dad to help while Mom was recovering from the mastectomy. The door to my room was open. I thought Dad was in the kitchen making breakfast. I was dressing. I was startled to see him standing there. We didn't speak. I gently eased the door closed and finished getting dressed. I remember the scene as though I were on the ceiling watching it.

After a while it was quiet. Then he said, "Let's go inside, shall we?" And with that the conversation was over. He had stayed with it for more than an hour. I was drenched in sweat, exhausted. I was in shock that we had actually just had this conversation.

After getting my father settled, Kate and I drove home. I did not sleep much during the night. I was worried about my father. I was afraid the pressure was going to cause another stroke. The next morning I checked messages on our voicemail. He had called the previous night after we had left to come home. Voicemail recorded the time as 11:16 PM.

"Bettina!" his voice was sharp, and he was short of breath. "I can't sleep! I can't live with this! This is worse than Fay dying! I have no memory of it! You must have dreamed it, or read about it somewhere! I cannot live with this. Therefore, I deny it!"

He repeated, more frantically, "I deny it! You tell your friend, I can't remember her name, tell her I deny it! Tell Kay I deny it!" He was always forgetting Kate's name or calling her Kay.

I called him. He was still terribly agitated. He repeated what he had said in his message the night before.

"I understand you, Dad," I said.

He shouted, "You don't understand how I feel! I cannot live with this. Therefore it did not happen! I deny it!"

I said, as calmly as I could, "I am certain, Dad. It happened."

"For how long?" he asked.

"For years," I told him.

"Schnootzy, please," he said. "I could not have done what you say. There has to be some other explanation. I cannot have done such a horror!"

He was becoming hysterical. I said, "We'll come over to see you today."

"What good will that do?" he wondered.

I said, "We'll help you with this."

"What time?" he asked.

"About four o'clock," I said. "We'll take you to dinner."

He said, "Okay, but I want to eat at the Good Earth."

"That's fine, Dad. We'll take you to the Good Earth." That was his favorite restaurant, and he didn't want any more of our foreign or vegetarian food. He wasn't going to accommodate us.

We didn't arrive in San Jose until five o'clock. Dad opened the door for us the way he always had. I took his hand and kissed him on the cheek the way I had always done. Kate did too. It felt strange to just go on doing these ritual things as if nothing had changed, as if everything was just the same, as if we weren't in the midst of this upheaval.

We got into the car to drive to the Good Earth. I was driving this time, and my father was in the passenger seat next to me. Kate was in the back seat. I put the key in the ignition and he said, "Just a minute. I want to say something first." I waited.

He said, "I searched my memory last night very carefully." His voice was authoritative, professorial. "What you say happened did not happen. I have no memory of it. I feel confident. I searched my mind very carefully."

I said, "It happened, Dad. Everything I said happened just as I said it did. I am certain."

He said, "It cannot be. I have no memory of it."

I said, "When an event is too painful, we erase the memory of it."

He said, "All right. I'll tell you what we are going to do. You will · have your reality, and I will have mine. Can we go on now?"

"Yes," I said. "I have forgiven you. And I love you. And we can go on now."

"All right," he said. "As far as I'm concerned, that is the end of it."

I said, "Okay, Dad."

He said, "Let's go eat."

It was surreal. My father's system of denial, refashioned to account for my reality.

We made conversation as we sat on the outside patio at the Good Earth. Dad said he couldn't understand why everyone didn't sit outside. Then he kidded with the waitress, whom he knew. "She's a wonderful person," he said of her, searching for conversation. I told him about animals we had seen when we were camping. Kate told him about an historical novel she was reading. Called *A Free Man of Color,* it was set in New Orleans in the 1830s. "Yes," Dad agreed, as she described the conditions to him. "That's accurate. That's how it was." Then he talked about the case of Angelo Herndon, a black Communist charged with insurrection in 1932 in Georgia after organizing poor people, black and white, in a protest, and how the party had campaigned successfully to free him.

As we left his house after dinner, he said heartily, "Well, it's been quite a day, hasn't it? Quite a day!"

A week later he said, "The two of you have made it possible for me to live." Then he said, "You're as good as your mother." I took this to mean that I was as good at taking care of him as my mother had been. I was taking care of him to make it easier for both of us.

Through much of July, Kate and I went together to San Jose. She did not yet want me to be alone with Dad. She wanted to be sure I could handle being with him. We went in part to be sure that Dad was not alone too much of the time, and in part to empty the house of Mom's things, which he had given us permission to do.

Toward the end of July, I was alone with Dad for the first time since our conversation about the incest. I took him out to lunch. We went to an Italian restaurant in downtown San Jose. Tables were set with linen cloths, signaling at least higher prices and I hoped a better quality of food than he usually ate. It was very busy with the lunch crowd from the surrounding banks and title companies. "Oh, yes," Dad said as we were seated, "I've eaten here before." He seemed pleased with my choice. We studied the menus, ordered sandwiches. Dad commented on how pretty the waitress was. She was maybe twenty; her eyes sparkled.

"I don't know if I can make it," Dad said.

"I understand, Dad," I said. His eyes were flooded with tears.

"I'm trying. But I don't know if I can make it," he said again.

"You should try," I said. "Take one day at a time. Enjoy the pleasantness of each day." I paused for a moment, and then I said, "I love you."

He responded by breaking the rule he had established about "being finished" with our conversation about the incest. He said, "What you told me about what I did to you—you believe it's true?"

My heart thumped. I said, "Yes, Dad. It's true." I knew it was true; the memories were detailed and clear. I had lived this in my body. This had come unbidden, spontaneously, in alternating waves. There would be vaginal pressure, a sore throat. My breasts hurt. There was pressure on my chest. My teeth ached. In the months following the first clear memories five years earlier, there were days I was in so much pain, my head pounding, that I couldn't get up. I felt as though my brain were encased in gauze, all my senses dulled. Kate stayed with me, sitting beside the bed for hours, saying prayers, mantras we had learned, doing whatever else she could think of to bring me comfort. I didn't tell my father how this had affected me.

He said, voice rising, "I can't believe it. I just can't believe it." I understood that too. I understood his erasure. He had lived a whole lifetime avoiding memories of the unpleasant, the untenable. It was how he had coped—with Stalin, with the war, with the party, with his family. He lived much of the time in a fantasy world of his own making. It was my mother who insisted on bringing him back into some semblance of reality. I remembered my dream, his jacket, the windbreaker, how he put it back on even though it was all stained with juice, because this was what he had always done. He always just forgot whatever terrible or hurtful thing was done to him, and he put his jacket back on and trudged on. I had a thousand images of him from my childhood, his shoulders hunched against the cold, hands in the pockets of his jacket, bareheaded even in the snow, ears pink with frost.

I said, "It's true, Dad, and it happened a long time ago."

He said again, very agitated, working his jaw to garner some modicum of control, "I can't believe it."

I put my hand on his in an effort to calm him. He was crying.

Suddenly he said, "You know a great moment in history?"

I nodded, knowing what would come, even if not the specifics of what it would be.

He said, "Nat Turner was in his cell. One arm chained to the wall, being questioned. This was written down. He was asked, 'Why did you do it?' Turner got up off the cot, his arm chained to the wall. He replied, 'Was not Christ crucified?'" Dad's eyes flooded with tears. He was chewing, and swallowed a bit of his sandwich.

I nodded. I'd known this story all of my life.

"They recorded it," Dad told me, "just as he said it. So we have his words."

Dad paused. He was silent, chewing and swallowing. Then he said, "Another great moment in history: Vesey's Rebellion, 1822. The men were being tortured for names. One of them began to speak intelligibly. Prosser raised himself up out of the blood and shouted, 'Ming! Die in silence as I will do!'"

I nodded. I'd heard this story all of my life, except Dad mixed up the name of Vesey's co-conspirator, Peter Poyas, with a particularly brutal slave owner, Thomas H. Prosser. But it didn't matter. Overwhelmed with a living reality, Dad could always turn to the shadowed agony of history. How often he had done this.

We finished our sandwiches. The waitress returned. Dad ordered decaf coffee and asked for the dessert menu. He ordered caramel custard and ate it contentedly. Waiting for the bill, I said, "Kate and I are flying to Indiana for a few days in August."

"Oh?" he said.

I wanted him to know we'd be out of town, and how to reach us.

I said, "There's a conference for world peace with the Dalai Lama and we're going." Telling him the truth was a test, my childhood memory of his response to the Dalai Lama still fresh.

Dad said, "That's wonderful!" with real pleasure. I felt a wave of relief.

It was actually a Kalachakra initiation with His Holiness, but I didn't know how to explain what an initiation was, and the event had been promoted as a teaching for world peace. It was as close to the truth as I could get with him.

Outside the restaurant, walking back to the car very slowly, unsteady even with his cane and my hand to hold, Dad said, "I've been thinking about ending my life."

This did not surprise me. And it made me very sad. I said, "I thought maybe you were."

He said, "Mother would not approve."

I said, "No. Mother would want you to live to the fullest extent possible. I think she would understand, but she would not want you to do it."

He nodded.

I said, "I understand why you are thinking this way. But it is best not to do it."

He repeated, "Mother would not approve." He was quiet for a few moments. Then he said, "She was all I had; she was all I ever wanted. I had no social life. She was all I had. She helped me . . ." and his voice broke.

Early on a December morning six months after Mother's death, I experienced an extraordinary feeling that she was present with me. Driving to the university, I was on the western perimeter of the campus. To my left was a meadow, spread like an apron. Beyond the meadow the ocean was clearly visible, extending all the way to the horizon. A thin veil of mist hung in the air. The mist was illumined by the sun as it rose over the eastern slopes of the Santa Cruz Mountains, and it glowed in soft pinks and pastel orange. A Vivaldi violin concerto pulsed with precision on the car radio.

Suddenly, I felt my mother's presence strongly, so much so that I had a clear picture of her. In my mind's eye, she was smiling and radiant, her long braid crowning her head. I told Dad the next time I saw him because I thought it would make him happy. I said, "I saw Mom."

He looked up sharply. I described the image I had of her as I was driving. "How old was she?" he wanted to know.

Startled by his question, I thought for a minute. "She was in her seventies. The way she looked when we were in Berlin."

He nodded, smiled.

"Do you dream about her?" I asked him.

"I miss her at night," he said. "I wake up feeling for her in the bed. She's not there, and then I remember."

In the years following Mother's death, my father's health gradually declined. He had more and more difficulty walking and fell frequently. He developed the same macular degeneration Mother had had, and the vision in his right eye was significantly impaired. Nevertheless, he kept reading, and he wrote a column called "Books and Ideas" for a Marxist journal that published sporadically. He worked at the library of the Martin Luther King, Jr., Papers Project at Stanford once a week for as long as he could. Tenisha Armstrong, one of my former students, was the executive assistant, and she often drove Dad home to his apartment at the senior residence at the end of the day. He was working with project director Clayborne Carson on an eighth volume of Dad's *Documentary History of the Negro People in the United States*. They were bringing it up to the end of the twentieth century. The work helped to keep Dad alive. The staff at the King Papers Project fell in love with Dad. His suffering was so palpable.

Sometimes Dad begged me to help him to die. "I can't do that, Dad," I would say.

"Why not?" he would plead. "Just bring me something I can take."

"I can't do that, Dad," I would repeat. "I don't believe in it." He was also ambivalent about suicide. Discussing it with me was only a measure of his grief and despair in the moment.

I telephoned him every few days. "Hello, Dad," I would say, always beginning the conversation in the same way. "How are you today?" He liked the predictability.

"Oh," he would laugh. And I would smile too, his laughter contagious. When I visited him, especially if I'd been away on a trip, he was thrilled to see me. I was always ambivalent, happy that he was happy, and riven with grief that he would always live inside his systems of denial.

Every visit, I started out from home with the same childish optimism. Today would be different. Today he would see me for who I was, not as an extension of his ambition, not as heir to his throne, not as an instrument for his needs. He would see me, and I would talk to him without censoring myself. But it never happened. He loved me, but never beyond the parameters of his fantasy of who I was, and the enormity of his self-absorption, things that were more acute now in old age, but had been true for his entire life.

For months he wouldn't say anything about the incest, and I thought he'd forgotten about it, and then all of a sudden he would bring it up again, as he had in the restaurant shortly after my mother's death.

He would say, "What you told me about what I did to you—you believe it's true?"

Then I would say something like, "It's true, Dad, and it happened a long time ago."

In the summer of 2002, three years after my mother's death, my father developed pneumonia, and then he suffered a heart attack. He lost the ability to write, but he kept on reading. After his heart attack, still in the hospital, he said, "You've forgiven me." It wasn't a question. It was a statement. I said, "Yes, I have forgiven you." He made the statement repeatedly in the months following, reassuring himself. That was how I came to realize that he had his own knowledge of the incest. It was always present in his consciousness, just under the surface, as it had been in mine.

My son, Josh, and his wife, Eka, visited with Dad twice, about a month before he died. Josh said they were able to share something of their lives with him. Eka was six months pregnant and, Josh reported, my father was excited about his coming great-grandchild.

Dad died on March 17, 2003, at a private residence in Mountain View, California, where I had arranged for his care, twenty-four hours a day. It was a beautiful sunny Monday, St. Patrick's Day, four days before the spring equinox. The window in his room faced out onto a garden, and from his bed you could see the blossoms on a fruit tree. On top of a bookshelf, facing toward him, we had placed a picture of my mother, and another of Dr. Du Bois.

Dad was in a hospital bed, with an oxygen tube inserted gently into his nose. The oxygen pump made a rhythmic popping sound like when you pedal the bellows of an organ without playing any notes. I was sitting in a chair next to the bed, holding his hand. He opened his eyes and looked at me. His eyes were clouded with the dullness of near death. I said, "You've been terrific, Dad."

He had been. In those last few days he had helped us in every way he could. The night before, he had kissed Senya's hand, the nurse who was his primary caregiver. "Thank you," he had said. Now, in the morning, he did not speak. I said, "It's almost over." Dad looked at me for another moment. Then he closed his eyes, and he stopped breathing.

I felt a small wave of panic, and then it washed away. I called to Kate. We could still see a pulse in the carotid artery. It continued for another few seconds, and then it was gone. I shut off the oxygen. The room was perfectly still. A little while later Jenny arrived, with her partner, Andrea, and their son, Jacob, who was two months old. Only a few days before, Dad had held the baby, his first great-grandson.

We didn't call the mortuary until the evening. With help from the hospice staff we bathed the body and dressed Dad in his best blue suit. After all, Kate said, he was going to meet my mother. Jenny went out and came back with flowers and candles and food. She arranged her grandfather's room just so, and put food out for our friends.

Elvi Cardona, a nurse at the San Jose Medical Center, where Dad had been taken following his heart attack, had been in charge of his ongoing care. Senya Butamay, Dad's primary caretaker, was Elvi's sister. Both were extraordinary. Senya, Elvi, and two more of their sisters arrived and prepared a traditional Filipino meal. "Eat, eat," Elvi encouraged us and our visitors, "we're all family." I telephoned family and friends who lived nearby, and they came in a steady stream all afternoon to say goodbye.

Kate and I stayed with Dad, doing prayers and saying mantras. Little Jacob sat on Kate's lap for almost two hours, fully awake but uttering not a sound, watching the body and the lights from the candles. We said Kaddish for Dad, as he had requested I do many years before. We read an English alliteration of the Hebrew words, the text faxed to me from a nearby synagogue:

Yit-ga-dal ve-yit-ka-dash she-mei ra-ba.

Be-al-ma di-ve-ra chi-re-u-tei . . .

O-seh sha-lom bi-me-ro-mav, hu ya-a-seh sha-lom a-lei-nu ve-al kol Yis-ra-eil. Ve-i-me-ru: A-mein.

May the Maker of peace bring peace to the bereaved and to all those who mourn.

Amen.

epilogue

LOOKING FORWARD

DRIVING ACROSS THE southwestern United States, there is a point in Colorado where you reach the Continental Divide. It runs along the crest of the Rockies, and when you cross it there's a sign on the highway that tells you so. Rivers east of the Divide ultimately flow into the Atlantic Ocean, and those west of the Divide end in the Pacific. I love this moment in our drive, and always announce it to Kate as we whip by. To me there's something so refreshing, so thrilling about a change in the directional flow of water.

I don't think that I ever would have moved out of the perceived safety in which I had enclosed myself by the mid-1970s had it not been for the fact that I was a lesbian. My strong desire to live my own life—as a lesbian and as a feminist activist-scholar—overrode fear, parental pressures, and Communist imperatives. Mary Timothy's death catapulted me into action by showing me that my life was finite. When I met Kate I had already begun a radical shift in my choices and priorities. But even if we had never met, still I would have continued across the divide. It would have taken me longer and been a much rougher road.

This process of crossing the divide is, I think, what the poet Audre Lorde meant when she talked about using our knowledge of "the erotic" as "a lens through which to scrutinize the quality of our lives." In her context "the erotic" referred to those things that give us the greatest sense of achievement and inner satisfaction. For Lorde it was writing poetry. For me, I think, it is teaching. But no passion can be fully and successfully engaged if an essential part of us is shut down, or denied, or, in some cases, as in my own, repressed and despised. Many women and men feel a passion such as Lorde's drive to write, or mine to teach; they have a feeling of some deeper sense of purpose. However, fear of change, of rejection, of loss, of the unknown holds most of us in check for a lifetime, or for a very long time. I was fortunate. I was only thirty-three years old when I started to break free.

There is also a tremendous irony in the road I traveled. From the outside, in the meetings I attended and in the speeches I gave, in the press reports about me and in those two-minute sound bites on the local news, I appeared certain, in charge, a no-nonsense, out-about-my-business woman. On the inside I was a basket case, even for a while suicidal. The outer bravado was a camouflage for the inner turmoil. Those of us who are survivors of abuse in one form or another—and this abuse may be gender-based, or sexual, or racial, for example—perfect this sort of crazy-making double life. Friendships and intimate relationships are very hard to sustain because we are badly fractured.

To begin to heal there has to be some place of complete trust, some person to whom we can tell the whole truth, and then that person must extend to us a sense of unconditional love. In my life,

Mary Timothy was that first person. It was an incalculable gift. I think others would have been willing to do this for me. For example, my friend Gerri Jacobs would have been. But I was not ready. So the timing also has to be right. A really good therapist will do this also, but of course, until I was much older I was unwilling to go to one because my level of paranoia was too great. When some level of trust is established somewhere with someone, the split between outer and inner realities begins to narrow. Once this happened for me, I was willing to take another small risk, and then another, and in this incremental way I grew stronger. Eventually my inner reality and outer appearance were more congruent with each other. I was able to live openly as a lesbian. I was able to leave the Communist Party. However, I was never able to talk to my mother about the incest. I could not bring myself to a point of sufficient trust in her and sufficient strength in myself. I was very fortunate that my father initiated a conversation with me, and stayed with it as long as he did, and never doubted my word, even though, as he said, he couldn't live with the reality.

As I have grown stronger I have begun to help others. But again, the timing also has to be right for them. The only thing I can do is make a space, and if someone wants to they can walk into it. Then I do the best I can to help: no judgment, no fear, loving kindness, compassion, and above all else, safety.

From these experiences, primarily in teaching, I have sought to combine the intellectual, the political, the personal, and the spiritual.

In Shantideva's beautiful text *The Bodhisattva Way of Life,* there appears this line: "In the spiritual energy that relieves the anguish of beings in misery I lift up my heart and rejoice!" I love these words. I often say them to myself just as I begin a meditation session to set my motivation more clearly in my own mind.

I have learned that all the experiences I have had in meditation—
the incandescent light, the sense of bliss, and so on—have very
little meaning. What matters is the ability to quiet the mind so that
it is concentrated and its incessant chatter stops. Then what you
experience in the few seconds of quiet *between* thoughts, before
another one actually arises and forms, is that the mind, in your
awareness of its silence, is as vast as space.

In March 2005, I was invited to speak at Wellesley College. My talk
came out of writing this book, of the retrieval of memory, of staying
as honest as possible, of being careful to write only from my direct
experience and not from hearsay, to refrain from telling others'
stories except as they affected my own, and to believe that I was a
reliable witness to my own life. The day before my talk there was
yet another huge snowstorm in Boston in a winter that had seen
many. My colleagues were through with snow for the season, but
to my erstwhile Brooklyn sensibilities and my California central
coast realities, I thought the snow was wonderful. Behind the hotel
where I was staying is Lake Waban, and surrounding it, a forest.
The lake was only partially frozen, and everything was covered
in unblemished snow. Ice crystals hung from the trees. My talk
went well and generated an invigorating discussion about feminist
autobiography. That night, I dreamt a poem. I woke up very early in
the morning and wrote it down:

Snow glistens in my
mind
a clean arc

acknowledgments

THIS MEMOIR WAS many years in the making, and without the continuing support and critical judgment of family and friends it would never have been completed. It has been the most difficult project on which I have ever worked. With gratitude then to:

Irene Klepflisz, for the Yiddish translations; Akasha Hull, for her early and later critical readings of the manuscript, and her assistance in locating the poem by Sonia Sanchez; Jack Kurzweil, for allowing me to give my version of our marriage, and for his continuing friendship; Angela Davis, for her extensive reading of the manuscript, her permission to use excerpts from her letters to me from prison, and her many thoughtful suggestions; Aida Hurtado, for her friendship and colleagueship over so many years, and for her exceptionally detailed and critical reading of the manuscript; Veronica Selver, for her leap of faith in providing me with a page-by-page critique of the manuscript; Ann Jealous, for her healing, her love, and her consistent belief in me and in this book.

I thank additional colleagues at the University of California, Santa Cruz, for their readings of portions of the manuscript in various stages of completion and their helpful comments: Helene Moglen, Emily Honig, Carla Freccero, Donna Haraway, Chris Connery, Gail Hershatter, and Candace West. Likewise, I thank readers Deb Busman, Paula Marcus, Phyllis Peet, Estelle Freedman, and Barrie Thorne, who gave of their time and helpful judgment. And I thank members of our lesbian community in Pacific Grove, California, including especially Raindance and Teramota for their abiding love and faith in me and for their memories of events I have described here.

I wish to thank my agent, Charlotte Cecil Raymond, for her extraordinary persistence, professional expertise, and friendship, and my editor at Seal Press, Jill Rothenberg, for her patience, perseverance, and brilliant editorial work. I thank Betsy Wootten for typing this manuscript through repeated incarnations with extraordinary professional skill, and for the gift of her friendship.

My family has provided me with a bedrock of emotional and critical support through this project. Thank you to Andrea Roth for her steadfast encouragement and loving support, and for being my number-one baseball buddy, where all important thoughts can be contemplated! Thank you to my adopted daughter, Lisa Miller, especially for permission to relate stories from her childhood. Thank you to my son, Joshua Kurzweil, whose early reading of the manuscript was a wonderful and healing experience for both of us. Thank you to my daughter, Jenny Kurzweil, for her repeated readings of various sections of the manuscript, over the years as she was coming into adulthood and then motherhood, and her excellent editorial judgment. Thank you to all three of my beautiful children for their friendship and love.

Finally, none of this would have been even remotely possible without my partner, Kate Miller, who read every draft of this book with a brilliant and compassionate critical eye. She has been with me through emotional storm and calming waters; she taught me to love myself unconditionally as she has loved me; she introduced me to the dharma and taught me the meaning of hope.

Bettina Aptheker
Santa Cruz, California
March 2006

The dedication includes an excerpt from Marcia Falk's "Listen," from *The Book of Blessings*, Harper/San Francisco. Reprinted with permission of the author.

In the Prologue, the article by Israeli novelist David Grossman is reprinted with permission from the July 11, 2005, issue of *The Nation*. For subscription information, call 1-800-333-8536. Portions of each week's *Nation* magazine can be accessed at www.thenation.com.

In the Prologue, the lines from the poem by Muriel Rukeyser are from "Kathe Kollwitz" and may be found in the book *In Her Own Image: Women Working in the Arts*, ed. Elaine Hedges and Ingrid Wendt (Old Westbury, New York: Feminist Press, 1980), p. 266.

In the Prologue, the lines from "Transcendental Etude" and "(The Floating Poem, Unnumbered)" of "Twenty-One Love Poems" from THE DREAM OF A COMON LANGUAGE: Poems 1974–1977 by Adrienne Rich. Copyright © 1978 by W.W. Norton & Company, Inc. Used by permission of the author and W. W. Norton & Company, Inc.

In the chapter "A Childhood in Two World," the poem about Shirley Graham Du Bois is by Sonia Sanchez, "Kwa mama zetu waliotuzaa" (For Our Mothers Who Give Us Birth) in Sonia Sanchez, *I've Been A Woman: New & Selected Poems* (Chicago: Third World Press, 1985), pp. 100-101.

notes ON sources

The following archival collections have been consulted for this work:

Bettina Aptheker Archive, Special Collections, McHenry Library, University of California, Santa Cruz.

Herbert Aptheker Archive, Green Library, Stanford University.

Free Speech Movement Archive, Bancroft Library, University of California, Berkeley. Also see the website www.fsm-a.org.

Angela Davis Case Collection (including the trial transcript and related documents), Meiklejohn Civil Liberties Institute, Berkeley, California.

Angela Davis, "Opening Defense Statement Presented by Angela Y. Davis in Santa Clara County Superior Court, March 29, 1972," in Joy James, ed., *The Angela Y. Davis Reader* (Malden, MA: Blackwell Publishers, 1998), 329–46.

———

Insofar as is possible, I have checked factual and historical information about people and events in texts, with individuals, and on Internet sites. Any remaining errors are mine.

Bettina Aptheker
Santa Cruz, California

about the author

Bettina F. Aptheker is a professor of feminist studies at the University of California, Santa Cruz, where she has taught one of the country's largest and most influential introductory women's studies courses for twenty-four years. She is the author of *The Morning Breaks: The Trial of Angela Davis* (Cornell University Press, 1999) and *Tapestries of Life: Women's Work, Women's Consciousness, and the Meaning of Daily Experience* (University of Massachusetts Press, 1989). She lives in Santa Cruz, California, with her longtime partner, Kate Miller.

selected titles FROM seal press

For more than thirty years, Seal Press has published groundbreaking books. By women. For women. Visit our website at www.sealpress.com.

The F-Word: Feminism in Jeopardy by Kristin Rowe-Finkbeiner. $14.95. 1-58005-114-6. An astonishing look at the tenuous state of women's rights and issues in America, and a call to action for the young women who have the power to change their situation.

Voices of Resistance: Muslim Women on War, Faith, and Sexuality edited by Sarah Husain. $16.95. 1-58005-181-2. A collection of essays and poetry on war, faith, suicide bombing, and sexuality, this book reveals the anger, pride, and pain of Muslim women.

Above Us Only Sky: A Woman Looks Back, Ahead, and into the Mirror by Marion Winik. $14.95. 1-58005-144-8. A witty and engaging book from NPR commentator Marion Winik about facing midlife without getting tangled up in the past or hung up on the future.

Pissed Off: On Women and Anger by Spike Gillespie. $14.95. 1-58005-162-6. An amped up and personal self-help book that encourages women to go ahead and use that middle finger without being closed off to the notion of forgiveness.

Waking Up American: Coming of Age Biculturally edited by Angela Jane Fountas. $15.95. 1-58005-136-7. Twenty-two original essays by first-generation women caught between two worlds. Countries of origin include the Philippines, Germany, India, Mexico, China, Iran, Nicaragua, Japan, Russia, and Panama.

Reckless: The Outrageous Lives of Nine Kick-Ass Women by Gloria Mattioni. $14.95. 1-58005-148-0. An entertaining collection of profiles that explores the lives of nine women who took unconventional life paths to achieve extraordinary results.

Without a Net: The Female Experience of Growing Up Working Class by Michelle Tea. $14.95. 1-58005-103-0. A collection of essays "so raw, so fresh, and so riveting, that I read them compulsively, with one hand alternately covering my mouth, my heart, and my stomach, while the other hand turned the page. *Without a Net* is an important book for any woman who's grown up—or is growing up—in America." —Vendela Vida, *And Now You Can Go*